❧ OUR LIFE TOGETHER ❧

JEAN VANIER

OUR LIFE TOGETHER

A MEMOIR IN LETTERS

DARTON · LONGMAN + TODD

Published in 2008 by
Darton, Longman and Todd Ltd
1 Spencer Court
140–142 Wandsworth High Street
London SW18 4JJ

First published in 2007 in Canada by
HarperCollins Publishers Ltd
2 Bloor Street East, 20th Floor,
Toronto, Ontario, Canada
M4W 1A8

ISBN-10: 0-232-52740-7
ISBN-13: 978-0-232-52740-7

A catalogue record for this book is available
from the British Library.

Printed and bound in Great Britain by
Athenaeum Press Ltd, Gateshead, Tyne & Wear

This book is for Barbara, as it was of Barbara. She typed all of the letters written after 1967, when she became my secretary, my memory and my assistant. She also translated all of the letters that were written in French into English, and in many she added or removed little things, which she called "her five cents worth." She was looking forward to this book and had ideas about it, but she died before it came out.

I have often been in the sun, visible; she has always been in the shade, invisible, humbly hidden. In her room, six feet by six feet, where she prayed, slept, worked, met people and sometimes ate, she was in some ways at the heart of L'Arche. She was a tender and gentle presence, a listening presence for so many. Her light and her life revealed the presence of God.

"Come and live with the weak and rejected,
and we will find peace."
JEAN VANIER

CONTENTS

Author's Note   XI

My Thanks   XIII

INTRODUCTION
A SEED IS SOWN   I

PART 1: 1964–1969
BEGINNINGS AT TROSLY:
A GOOD EARTH   9

PART 2: 1970–1973
ROOTS OF COMMUNITY:
BEGINNING IN CANADA, INDIA AND THE UNITED STATES   59

PART 3: 1974–1988
FAITH AND LIGHT AND L'ARCHE:
BLOSSOMING IN COUNTRIES STRICKEN WITH POVERTY AND PAIN   137

PART 4: 1989–2001
A TIME OF TRANSFORMATION:
MATURING AND FINDING NEW WAYS OF BELONGING
IN EASTERN EUROPE AND THE MIDDLE EAST   337

PART 5: 2001–2007
ONE DAY IN SEPTEMBER:
AN URGENT CALL TO NURTURE PEACE   489

CONCLUSION
LIFE FLOWS ON: GROWING INTO THE FUTURE   545

Index   555

CONTENTS

AUTHOR'S NOTE

Over the years my hopes, fears, vision, language, as well as my role in L'Arche have changed and I hope deepened. You will notice that in the early years I refer to the core members of our communities, the people with intellectual disabilities, as the "boys" and the "girls." It was the language of the time, and I would never employ it today.

Respectful terminology to describe the people who are at the heart of L'Arche and for whom L'Arche was founded varies from one country to another, from one era to another. I invite you to grow with me, and to substitute the terms used in these letters with those that you use and accept in your own home.

Forty years of writing makes for a lot of letters! I've selected the letters and the passages I think best illustrate the incredible journey L'Arche and I have taken together. To help with context—either within L'Arche or in the world—I've written a few introductory essays and footnotes. I've kept place names as they were at the time; so, for example, I refer to Madras in the earlier letter and Chennai in the later letters. The names have changed, but the places have not. I've also left quotations as I used them in the original letters—most of the time I was paraphrasing! Similarly, any translations are preserved here as I sent them in the letters; many are informal translations done by me or by other members of the L'Arche family. Quotations from the Bible are generally from the

Revised Standard Edition or are my translations from the Greek. It's been an amazing life together, and I have many people to thank and celebrate along the way. Every day is a good day.

MY THANKS

To Claire de Miribel, who read and checked through most of these letters before they were sent. To John Sumarah, who collected and edited in three volumes the letters from 1964 to 1994. To Christine McGrievy, who gave me great encouragement to work on this volume. To Joe Egan, Beth Porter, Martha Bala, Brenda Aburto-Avila and Nicole Langlois, for all of their help with bringing this book together. To my wonderful editors, Kate Cassaday and Adrienne Leahey, who, with their efficiency and competence, made of this collection of letters a more readable book.

OUR LIFE TOGETHER

INTRODUCTION ❧ A SEED IS SOWN

People have described L'Arche as a radical movement. It was born in the mid-1960s when many young people, including myself, were looking for something different, searching for something to follow other than the ladder of material success and individual accomplishment. Choosing community life and a life among the poor may have seemed strange or radical, but to my mind it was radical only in the sense of the word that means "touching the roots," the roots of our humanity.

L'Arche is rooted in love. We live in community with those with intellectual disabilities because as human beings we seek naturally to love and be loved: each of us wants relationships where our value as a person—with our frailties and poverty—is recognized, affirmed and celebrated. Each person, whatever his or her abilities or disabilities, strengths or weaknesses, is important and sacred. This idea is not unique to L'Arche, and it's not new or revolutionary! It is the Gospel message. It is the essence of what it means to be human and to be Christian. We discover how we can be healed by those who are the most vulnerable. It's not a question of going out and doing good to them; rather, receiving the gift of their presence transforms us.

I've never really considered myself a radical. I'm trying to live the Gospel message as best as I can, and I hope always to be touching the roots. One of the strengths of L'Arche is that on the whole we are loved by many people. We are seen as being with the poor and the downtrodden. We are seen as a place of mutual trust. In L'Arche we trust each other: people with disabilities feel trusted and allowed to be and to grow, and feel that they can do things and work things out; and assistants, those who come to L'Arche to live with the disabled, learn to accept and to trust themselves in all that they are. Trust is founded on the belief that you are important, that you are precious.

My father offered me an example of this kind of trust when I was very young. In 1939, he was named Canadian ambassador to France, and when war was declared in September my mother, my sister, Thérèse, my brothers, Georges and Bernard, and I took refuge in a chateau south of Paris, in the village of Baillou. When the Germans invaded Belgium and northern France in May 1940, we fled farther south to Bordeaux. A Royal Navy destroyer picked us up at the Bordeaux port and then transferred us to a merchant ship, the *Nariva,* carrying meat from Argentina to Britain. We landed in Wales. From London we took the Polish ship *Batory* back to Canada, and at dinner one night as we crossed the North Atlantic, we heard the Nazi English-language radio announce that our ship had been sunk! I don't think I felt any fear during those days; it all seemed part of a great adventure for an eleven-year-old boy!

So when, two years later, still in the midst of the war, I told my father that I wanted to cross the U-boat-filled ocean again to join the Royal Navy College in blitzed southern England, his answer to me was, "I trust you. If that is what you want to do, you must do it." My father's trust in me confirmed my trust in myself. When he said, "I trust you," he gave me life; he gave me permission to trust my intuitions and to just do what seemed right. I knew that if he trusted me, I could trust myself and others to do what was right.

Much of that trust was rooted in faith. I had grown up in a deeply religious Catholic family. My parents, even with all their busyness and social position, shared a deep faith and spent half an hour each day together in silent prayer. My father's spiritual life was the source of his success in public matters, and he was in many ways a living example of the "just man," the man of duty: duty to his family, duty to his country, duty to his God. His motto might well have been "I seek but to serve." My mother's faith was perhaps a bit more "at the roots," perhaps a bit less traditional. My grandmother, a very holy little lady, had introduced my mother to a priest by the name of Père Pichon, who guided her to trust in God's mercy and forgiveness and to surrender to God's love. As children, my sister, two brothers and I attended Mass regularly, and I went as often as I could while in the Navy. While I was overseas my eldest brother, Georges, joined a Cistercian monastery and took the name Benedict. Perhaps as result of the lessons and examples I had been given within my family I yearned for something other or more than the Navy.

When I left the Navy in 1950 my deepest desire was to be a disciple of Jesus and live the Gospel message—I didn't know whether it would be through the priesthood or another way, but I knew that I would know as time went on. I told my mother that I was contemplating joining the priesthood, and she introduced me to the man who changed my life forever, Père Thomas Philippe.

My first meeting with Père Thomas was deeply moving. I suppose that because of my innocence or freshness I needed a master, a teacher, a spiritual father. Listening to him, simply being with him, I felt transformed and I felt a presence of God. He was an authentic man. I learned from him that to pray is not just to say prayers but to be prayerful, to remain quietly in the presence of God, to simply be in communion with Jesus. Père Thomas was a French Dominican priest who had founded a small community called L'Eau Vive (Living Water) on the outskirts of Paris. Like Père Pichon he was considered a little radical by the Church and had known periods of rejection and exile.

When I resigned from the Navy I went to L'Eau Vive. L'Eau Vive was an international study and retreat centre for lay people who wanted to know something of the spirituality of the Church. They would afterwards take that knowledge back to their countries and use it to help shape and spur development projects. For me it was a place of great peace and grace, where I did some manual work, studied and prepared for the future.

In 1952, when Père Thomas was called to Rome, he asked me to take over the directorship of L'Eau Vive. I did this for four years, but without Père Thomas, L'Eau Vive could not live out his vision and it eventually closed. I still felt bonded to Père Thomas, however, and sensed that my future was to remain united to him, for he was truly a man of God. He had steered me to the writings of Aristotle, and I started studying for my doctorate in philosophy and theology. In 1962 I completed my doctorate on Aristotle's *Ethics* at the Institut Catholique de Paris. My thesis attracted the attention of the dean of philosophy at St. Michael's College at the University of Toronto, and in January 1964 I went back to Canada to teach.

This was the first time I had ever taught. I was supposed to teach ethics, but I found my students weren't terribly interested in justice, so instead I started talking about the meaning of friendship and about sexuality. And all of a sudden the classroom wasn't big enough to hold all the students who wanted to listen! As with the retreats I gave in later years (from which the retreat group Faith and Sharing eventually sprang), I discovered that I had a gift for announcing Jesus. God seemed to be at work in and through my words and the passion and joy that sustained them. I loved teaching at St. Michael's and loved the students, but I felt it was not my vocation, the final goal of my life. I was still searching for a way to live closer to "the roots."

During this time in Canada, I was able to spend time with my parents at Rideau Hall, as my father had been appointed governor general, the first French Canadian to be made head of state and the queen's representative. He was profoundly humbled by the role and often said to me, "I never could have imagined ending up in this position." He was convinced that he was but a messenger of God and that God had led him to the role. And from that came his trust in me: he had encouraged and trusted me when I joined the Navy, he trusted me when I left the Navy and he trusted me as I continued to search for my life's commitment.

Also while I was in Canada, Père Thomas moved to Trosly-Breuil, a small village about an hour north of Paris, to become chaplain of a small institution called Le Val Fleuri that welcomed thirty men with intellectual disabilities. After my first semester of teaching, I visited him at Le Val and was touched by the men who lived there, many of whom had been locked up in psychiatric hospitals or hidden by their families. Wanting to remain close to Père Thomas and to do something for these men, I began to visit institutions and psychiatric hospitals in order to see what society was doing for people with intellectual disabilities.

Soon after, with the help of my family and friends, I bought a small, rather dilapidated house in the same village, just down the road from Le Val. I called this home L'Arche, after the ark Noah built to save God's creatures from the Flood. I bought some furniture and moved in. On August 5, 1964, having resigned from St. Michael's, I welcomed into this first home Raphaël Simi and Philippe Seux, who had been locked up in a dismal institution when their parents had died. Today of course nobody would be allowed to start a home like L'Arche in such a haphazard way, but at the time the needs of the intellectually disabled were so great that local authorities did everything they could to encourage new initiatives. And it was evident to me from the beginning of my life in L'Arche that this was my call to a lifelong commitment; I had found what I was looking for.

When I welcomed Raphaël and Philippe there wasn't a specific or rational reason—it just seemed obvious. They were crying out for relationship, and I could provide it. Practically everything I did with L'Arche was intuitive, based on the sense that this is what should be done. There was a beauty in these disabled men that was being crushed at the large, dismal, violent institution in which they had been put. These men were persons and precious to God, and so it seemed right, even evident, for me to do something about their unjust situation. Though I could not do anything on a large scale, at least I could live with a few of them and help them to find a decent life and the freedom to be themselves. This search for justice flowed naturally from my faith in Jesus: my faith in the Gospel message revealed the value and beauty of men and women with severe disabilities. People often ask me the reasons for start-ing L'Arche, but I didn't have reasons, I just trusted and loved.

I remember being asked during a television interview what experience led me to L'Arche, what happened? And I said to the interviewer, "Are you married?" He was a bit taken aback. And I asked, "Well, why did you choose your wife? Was it because she's intelligent, was it because she was beautiful . . . or was it just because you thought it was right?" He said he thought it was the right thing at the right moment. And so for me L'Arche was just the right thing at the right moment. You do it because it's obvious; you just do it. There was a sense of urgency: let's just do it and follow the signs of the Spirit. I didn't rationalize my actions then, even though I may now.

And so it was for the first letters contained in this book. I had people I loved in Paris, in Canada and in my own family and since we were bonded together, it was obvious to keep them informed. It was intuitive. It was about relationships, not organizational cohe-sion; there was only one L'Arche home and no idea that there would be more! But sharing my experience in these letters was a sign that somehow I believed something important was happening. Welcoming Raphaël and Philippe was the beginning of something definite in my life. Whereas when I was in the Navy or teaching at

St. Michael's in Toronto, I knew that these were not forever. What was new or important in the early letters was the beginning of a permanent commitment.

The first letters were written with maybe forty people in mind, but as L'Arche grew I became conscious of writing to a wider audience and being given a wider perspective. It seemed obvious to share that too. And to rationalize it now, forty years later, I'd say that any real movement with real signification has to have universal meaning, to address our common humanity. It's the sharing of a world vision. We weren't just sharing life with Christians, we were sharing life with people who were suffering; and if you're talking generally about people who are suffering, then you're talking about people everywhere.

I don't know if the people who read my early letters understood that the situation, the isolation of the intellectually disabled in France, was not unique to France. It was all over the world. Little by little we were called to discover this universal pain. The letters in this book follow the story of the expansion of our communities. At first there wasn't much reflection or vision for the future, but instead a sense of risk, a lot of naïveté and, above all, a deep belief that Jesus was guiding and calling us to go forward into the pain and suffering of people in other countries.

Throughout the years, this intuition, where we feel or sense things but cannot always rationalize them, where the Spirit intervenes and inspires us to do things we had not planned, never left us. It guided us as we rooted ourselves in the radical message of love, and the universality of this message became manifest in the expansion of our communities.

PART ONE
1964 ❦ 1969

BEGINNINGS AT TROSLY:
A GOOD EARTH

I was deeply moved when I first went to an institution for the intellectually disabled, in the early 1960s, and heard the men there cry for friendship and relationship: "Do you love me? Will you be my friend? Will you come back and visit me?" I had little knowledge of people with disabilities and the causes of their handicaps, or even of an appropriate pedagogy. But I believed firmly that these men were important in the eyes and heart of God, and that they should be able to find their rightful place in life. And I realized instinctually that what they needed most was a family environment, a place of belonging where they could be themselves, grow in inner confidence and freedom, and enjoy life with others.

My trust in Jesus and my belief that God is close to those who are weak and vulnerable gave me the necessary energy to take this risk and begin this new adventure without any big, rational plan. In my heart I felt that God would provide and give me the necessary strength, wisdom and help for what I thought was his work. And I knew that God's call implied a lifelong commitment on my part: I realized that I could not take people with no immediate family out of an institution and then abandon them if things didn't work out.

There is a time for all things. There was a time for me to be in the Navy and a time to leave the Navy. There was a time for spiritual and intellectual formation and a time to seek my place in the

world, to find my "earth" and to put down roots, make a commitment to people and assume responsibilities. In 1964, this time had
come for me and there was no turning back.

Little did I know that I was on the road to an amazing discovery,
a gold mine of truth, where the weak and the strong, the rich and
the poor would be brought together in community and find peace,
where those who were rejected could heal and transform those
who had rejected them. We are not alone in this discovery—others
are sitting on the same gold mine—but I do feel that at L'Arche we
have been given something by God that is precious and vital and
yet so small and vulnerable that many can pass by without notic-
ing: we can be healed by those we reject. We can be transformed
by the weak and the poor, as long as we enter into an authentic
relationship with them and let ourselves be led by God and to God,
the God of unity, love and peace.

Over the years I've come to understand that there are five stages
of changing attitudes towards people with intellectual disabilities.
The first is to react to the disabled with fear of their "abnormal"
behaviour or disfiguration, to say they are a disorder, and as a
result to reject them and seek to get rid of them. This was Hitler's
reaction. The second is more widespread: the disabled are human
beings, but they are pitiful little fellows whom we should take
care of in big institutions. This was a common reaction in the late
nineteenth century. The third involves getting to know the disabled, understanding their needs and responding with competence.
This attitude seeks to help them to grow, recognizing that they are
not just pitiable but that they are human beings like us, who elicit
respect and compassion. You find this reaction a lot in places like
Canada, where we have integrated schools and so on. People with
disabilities can grow in maturity and autonomy if they are helped
and respected. The fourth stage is wonderment and thanksgiving:
we discover that, by becoming close to disabled people and entering an authentic relationship with them, they transform us. They

help us to move from the desire for personal success and power to a desire to be with those who are weak and help them to be just as they are, knowing that we receive as much or even more than we give. In the fifth stage, which is close to the fourth, we see the face of God within the disabled. Their presence is a sign of God, who has chosen "the foolish in order to confound the strong, the proud, and the so-called wise of our world." And so those we see as weak or marginalized are, in fact, the most worthy and powerful among us: they bring us closer to God. They turn our world upside down! And this stage is perhaps particularly related to L'Arche, where we seek not just to foster physical and emotional capacities but to nourish the spirit as well.

The first element in our relationships at L'Arche centres on the body—eating meals together, dressing, bathing, touching—just physically caring for people, being attentive to the body, attentive to medical care, revealing to them in a concrete way that they are loved. It's about compassion, about recognizing what is common among us—the body. And for some this relationship can be quite maternal, similar to the communion that takes place between mother and child early in life. The child is not an egotistical creature but a very fragile person who lives and calls forth a communion of love. This communion is at the origin of our lives when we're in our mother's womb: we live off her, are nourished by her blood and are one with her. As infants we are in her arms, nourished by her milk and one with her in another physical way. A mother reveals to her child "you are unique; you are precious; you are my joy." Through the experience of its mother's love, the child learns that it is lovable and worthy.

But not all children live the experience of love and communion at the beginning of their lives. Instead some are regarded as a nuisance and not wanted as they are. Their lives begin with a horrible sense of worthlessness and even guilt for existing. Père Thomas and I came to realize at L'Arche that the anguish and wounds of the disabled often came from a broken communion of hearts. To grow and develop harmoniously, they need first of all to have a relationship of communion. They need to know that they are loved and appreciated, not because they are able to do or say clever or witty things, but because they are a person, loved by God and created for love. It is their person who is important.

L'Arche was founded and grew at a time, in the 1960s, '70s and early '80s, when people were searching for better answers, for greater freedom for themselves and others, and when there was greater trust in ourselves and in the future. It was a time when peoples were fighting for liberation from decades of colonization or repression and when so many were standing up for issues of human dignity and equality. I think today people aren't searching in the same way for new paths to universal peace. Instead, people are distrustful and protective: protecting their country, protecting their jobs, protecting their need for security. There's been a real shift away from searching, from moving ahead, from relying on intuition and seeing where the Spirit of God can lead. And that's why the vision of L'Arche as a place of growth, communion and peace continues to be so important. It's timeless and universal.

August 22, 1964
Trosly-Breuil

Dear Friends,

With the increasing number of friends of L'Arche I am obliged to communicate with you by circular letter. I know that you will forgive me but I want to keep you informed about the developments of L'Arche. These circular letters will be sent to you from time to time and will become, I hope, visible signs uniting us all together.

L'Arche, as you know, wants to create a true spiritual family, a network of friendship and fraternity completely oriented towards the poor of our society, towards helping the physically and mentally handicapped. L'Arche is not the work of just a small group of people. If we have been able to settle so quickly in Trosly, it is due to the generosity of many friends. These mimeographed letters will keep you informed of the activities and progress of L'Arche. They will also help us to clarify our common ideal and to stimulate our love for the poor, who are, in a special way, the face of Jesus.

On the fourth of August our little community settled in Trosly-Breuil, and on the fifth of August (the feast day of Our Lady of the Snows) our first two "boys" arrived, driven by Mme Martin, from an institution. Dr. Preaut, Père Thomas, some friends and I were there to welcome them. We want to love one another as Christ taught us: gently, humbly and mercifully. Love is the distinctive feature of the message of the Gospels. During the next few weeks we are going to arrange the house and prepare things so that we can receive more boys. Indeed, there is still much to do but already we have cleared land for a garden and vegetables have been planted. We are waiting for the arrival of two ducks, two chickens and a rabbit!

Thanks to the understanding of the Social Welfare Office in Beauvais and the board of directors of Le Val Fleuri (a residence for thirty handicapped men in Trosly-Breuil founded by M. Prat in 1960), L'Arche can begin legally as an annex of Le Val Fleuri. This means that we are entitled to receive financial support. In a few months we will make our request for approval as a separate centre.

I am attaching to this letter a few pages which explain the main orientation and spirit of L'Arche. May God allow us to accomplish this ideal. In this first letter I want to thank all those who came to help us by giving us furniture or financial support. May our Lord and his Blessed Mother thank you by giving you the grace of inner peace.

Jean Vanier, the assistants and the boys of L'Arche

L'Arche

On the edge of the Compiègne forest, L'Arche has opened its first home for the mentally and physically handicapped. These family-like homes, each welcoming from four to nine boys, at least twenty years old, are lifelong homes. They are the first of a group of homes which will be linked together with workshops, a cultural centre, a chapel and the necessary medical help.

L'Arche is convinced that if the handicapped are unable to find their stability in modern society, which is becoming more and more complicated with its bureaucracy and techniques, they can find true human and spiritual growth in a family-like environment. L'Arche wants to create homes where life is focused on service to those who are the poorest of the poor in this twentieth century. L'Arche does not want to be a centre where those who have been rejected are simply kept or cared for; it wants to be a place where they can truly grow and develop according to their specific qualities and capacities.

L'Arche hopes also to open homes for the severely handicapped. By grouping those who are slightly handicapped with those who are more severely handicapped, the former can be of great help to the latter; they can grow and develop through their devotion to the less fortunate, and these latter will develop through the affection and attention they will receive.

L'Arche is a Catholic home. It believes that if those who are handicapped cannot be educated or work in the same way as others do, they are nevertheless open to spiritual values. Their very poverty is a predisposition to receive the graces of love that Jesus has promised them. L'Arche homes are open to all those who suffer, without any distinction of class, culture or religion; religious practice is entirely optional.

In L'Arche the poor are assisted by volunteers who wish to live the poverty of the Gospels, people with a heart who are willing to renounce certain human ambitions and who see in the poor a divine presence: "Whatever you do to one of these little ones, you do unto me." Together we want to create homes that radiate peace and joy in the spirit of the Beatitudes.

L'Arche is beginning in poverty. It wants to build these homes with those who have been rejected, but in order to do that, it needs all kinds of help. Besides gifts of money, it needs furniture, linen and help from people of goodwill who want to come and give their affection and assistance to the poor.

L'Arche
Trosly-Breuil

June 17, 1965
Trosly-Breuil

Dear Friends,

Several months have gone by since my last letter. So much has happened since then that it is difficult to tell you of all the events. First of all, we want to convey to you our friendship and our gratitude for your interest in L'Arche. We are here to serve handicapped people who are often rejected or pushed aside by society. You will never really know how much your friendship, your prayers, your visits, your letters, your gifts and your work help us. Without your prayerful thoughts and help we would never be able to bring to the handicapped the affection and the help they so urgently need.

What astonishes us more and more is the number of people who need permanent homes. The increasing number of requests from parents of handicapped children and from psychiatric hospitals makes us realize the role of our poor house and the responsibility it has. In our modern world, with all its demands for scholarship, with all its techniques and the priority it gives to production and efficiency, the integration of boys and girls who are slow or handicapped has become more and more difficult. Manual work has less and less value. Even in agriculture, technicians and mechanics are replacing the workmen who are not specialized. The handicapped, less caught up in ambitious desires and the seeking of honours, have pure, affectionate and simple hearts. Those who visit us are always surprised by the warm welcome they receive. The boys come and shake their hands and talk about their problems when asked, or are concerned about the problems and sufferings of others.

The Gospels have been the source of our inspiration leading us towards the "poor." It is this deep respect for each person that is at the centre of the message of Jesus. Whether deprived or rich in qualifications, we are all created by God in his image, saved by the blood of Christ and destined to an eternal life. L'Arche, while taking its inspiration directly from the Gospels, wants to make full use of psychiatry and medicine, and to work in collaboration with local authorities. To remain simple and open to Providence, to the inspirations of the Holy Spirit and to the teachings of Christ and, at the same time, to adapt to the methods of administration and professionals can often be difficult. It is our duty to find a healthy balance between the two.

Because the deepest inspiration of L'Arche comes from the Gospels, our doors are open to all those who need protection, whether they be Christian or not. We want them to feel free and at home. We want them to find the affection they need and that is rightfully theirs. Our hearts are open to all, for all are human beings.

In January, during my month-long visit to Canada and the United States, it was a joy to see the interest L'Arche has aroused. Little by little, people everywhere are trying to set up schools and to create sheltered workshops. Many are realizing the urgency of the problem of the future of those who are handicapped and the need for creating small permanent homes.

In March, I took on the responsibility of Le Val Fleuri following the resignation of the director. Founded in 1960 by M. Prat, Le Val Fleuri is a centre which welcomes thirty mentally handicapped boys. There are also workshops where the boys can work at their own rhythm. The joining of the two houses, Le Val Fleuri and L'Arche, has given a new impetus to our work. This unity could not have come about without the help of those at L'Arche who have taken on full responsibility for that house. This allows me to spend more time at Le Val Fleuri where I am assisted by M. and Mme Lepère.

Philippe and Pierrot are now working in one of the workshops at Le Val, where they prepare samples for Cerabati Ceramics. Jacques, Jean-Pierre and Lucien are wiring electric fixtures or boxing parlour games. Raphaël still prefers to work in the garden of L'Arche with

Christian. On Holy Thursday, Pierrot made his first Communion. It was a joyful occasion, a real family celebration with Pierrot at the centre, peaceful and happy.

We have much hope for the future. We confide our plans to you so that you can pray with us that they might become realities. The large property beside L'Arche is up for sale. The local governments of the Seine and of the Oise are very interested in our project and are presently studying ways of obtaining the necessary grants for the purchase of this property and for the construction of five new homes. A family-like home is the best place for the growth and development of any person, and especially for those who are handicapped. In small, family-like homes, they can find the affection they need as well as the stability that will allow them to develop according to their own abilities.

On the eleventh of July everyone from L'Arche and many from Le Val Fleuri will go on pilgrimage to Lourdes. Would you like to join us? The Cité Secours, which provides free food and lodging in Lourdes, has generously offered us their hospitality; the trip will cost ninety francs per pilgrim. May I ask those of you who can to help us defray expenses? Thank you.

Many of our thirty-seven boys have been so deprived of affection. For years they have been counted as "good-for-nothing" by those around them. Visits from friends or occasional invitations to homes of friends are a source of great joy for them. Also, they love to receive letters. You cannot imagine how eagerly they await the arrival of the postman each day. We know that you have little free time, but if you could invite them for a day or for an evening, it would be such a joy. As we have already told you, without you, your help, your compassion and your encouraging words, we would never be able to accomplish all that has to be done.

In closing, let me tell you about one of the most moving events of recent months. On May 21, after several months of illness, Marguerite Bilodeau, a Canadian, died in peace at the American

Hospital at Neuilly. She had come to work in Paris a year ago and used to visit us often. She loved L'Arche and we were all very attached to her. Her contagious laughter brought us great joy. We brought her body from Neuilly to our chapel in Trosly, where we were all there to welcome her. After the Mass we accompanied her to the local cemetery where she had asked to be buried. The funeral Mass was not celebrated in sadness. We did not feel so much that we were losing a friend but rather that we were gaining an intercessor for us in heaven.

May God bless you.
Jean Vanier, the assistants and the boys of L'Arche

November 5, 1965
Trosly-Breuil

Dear Friends,

Once again I am writing to give you news of our two communities, Le Val Fleuri and L'Arche. After four weeks of vacation, the year has begun well. Thanks to friends and to "adoptive parents" we closed the two houses for the month of August. These "adoptions" for the holidays and for weekends are a source of joy and well-being for those who are welcomed. All the boys benefited greatly from the change, and the assistants were able to get some necessary rest before beginning another year. We are grateful to those of you who welcomed some of our boys who have no family and who had no place to go.

During the last three days of the holidays, all the assistants met at the monastery in Ourscamp for a time of work, relaxation and prayer. In this beautiful setting, in the silence and prayer of the monastery, with Père André as our guide, we reviewed our Christian and human ideals and objectives. We tried to look at

our way of being with the disabled in order to discover our deficiencies so that we might do things better in the future. Above
all, we sensed our responsibility regarding them. Many have no
parents. Those who do were entrusted to us by their parents with
much confidence. We want to create a centre where our boys can
grow and develop according to their human and spiritual capacities, where they can be happy, work and receive the education that
corresponds to their needs, where they can be encouraged to use
their leisure hours in a beneficial way and be helped medically and
psychologically. Finally, they need to feel that they are at home,
"en famille," in the security that flows from love.

I think we all feel that our first role is to love the disabled, to
love them just as they are, in what is deepest in them. On the level
of reason they may be deficient, but often on the level of the heart,
they are very rich. Our role is to discover, respect and love each
person. We want to create a family rather than a school or a workshop where there are educators and those to be educated, those
who are superior and those who are inferior. We want to create a
family where there is peace, love and friendship.

We have all come back to Trosly full of life. The houses that
were empty for the month of August are once again full of joy and
the workshops back to normal. Some people were kind enough
to lend us a little house in Trosly where we opened a dining room
for six people from Le Val Fleuri. That makes the meals at Le Val
more peaceful.

Dr. Richet, our psychiatrist, and Mme Domenjoud, our psychologist, are now coming regularly each week. They are closely
following the boys on a medical level and they help us with their
presence, their experience and their advice.

The L'Arche family is growing. Benoît, who used to be at Le
Val, is now at L'Arche. Raphaël, Philippe, Jacques, Pierrot and
Lucien have urged him to come and live with them. Christian
has come back. Henri and Marie-Benoit are now helped by Mira

and Barbara (who teaches American folk dances at Le Val every Saturday morning). We are expecting Jean Claude from Canada. Raphaël is still busy lighting his pipe. Lucien is interested in birds. Pierrot, our nightingale, is preparing new songs. Philippe is still busy with his knitting and Jacques with his history books.

We will soon be saying goodbye to Louis. He has to return to Canada. His absence will leave a real emptiness in our hearts and in our house for he was here at the foundation of L'Arche. He always gave us good advice and watched over the house during my absence. Louis came for two weeks and stayed for more than a year! Many things in the house depended on him. With his departure a new era in L'Arche begins. The first months in L'Arche were lived in poverty and simplicity. Now that the foundations have been laid, we must build, organize and grow. We must create something solid that will last. We have welcomed our boys not just for a few months or a few years but, God willing, for the rest of their lives. Louis is leaving but the work he did remains and we remain united to him. We will never forget all he did for us. Our hearts cry out "merci."

Louis's plans for the house are now becoming a reality. The bathrooms are done and soon the attic will be remodelled with a new ceiling, windows and walls. All we have to do now is install the central heating, but that will not be ready for this winter. We will have to wait until the winter of 1968 for that!

Our plans to build and expand are not definite yet but we hope to develop them little by little. We receive many requests. There are so many parents in anguish over the future of their children and many boys who have no family, no place of welcome like L'Arche. At Le Val, I feel it is our duty to welcome young handicapped boys who have no parents or anyone to care for them. They need our help and support in a very special way.

I must tell you about two events that took place just before our holidays: our trip to Lourdes and our open house. On June 21 we invited our neighbours in Trosly and our friends from the surrounding area to come to our open house. Mr. Robillard, the representative of the local government, spoke about the importance of centres like ours. The mayor of Trosly emphasized how happy he was to participate in the growth of our centre, which welcomes boys coming from our local area. Dr. Preaut explained the role and purpose of our houses. M. Prat thanked the village people for the way they have welcomed our boys. We were happy to welcome so many of our friends into our houses. It was a magnificent day, lots of sun, lots of friendships, a real "open house." Some sixty students from a school for specialized educators were with us and helped make our celebration a success. There was also a group of four musicians from Trosly who played for us. It is so important to have good, friendly relationships with those around us, to be well integrated into the town so that the boys feel accepted and loved by the people around us. Our open house really contributed to that, I think, and was also a way for us to show our gratitude to our friends.

The pilgrimage that thirty of us made to Lourdes was wonderful. People at the Cité Secours, where we slept and ate, were so warm and welcoming. Those five days went by so fast! We were impressed to see so many sick people from all over the world come and pray to Our Lady at the Grotto. Some of the boys helped to push the wheelchairs of the sick from the sanctuary to the hospital. This contact with the sick was important for us all. How can we thank all those who helped to pay for this unforgettable pilgrimage? You can be assured that we prayed for you with much love and faith.

May I ask if any of you have any old birdcages or bicycles? Those of us who are most disabled could care for and watch the birds; others, accompanied by an assistant, could take bike rides in the forest.

As I end this letter, let me tell you once again how grateful we are for all you have done for us. Your interest in our communities and your help are a source of joy and encouragement for us. We remain deeply united in love.

Jean Vanier, the assistants and the boys of L'Arche

January 19, 1966
Trosly-Breuil

Dear Friends,

I write to you just before leaving for Canada. I know that you are very interested in what our boys have been doing and that you follow their activities with great concern. They appreciate so much all that you have done for them. I think that is one of their greatest qualities; they are deeply thankful and the smallest gesture is received as a sign of affection.

Our Christmas celebrations were very joyful. Most of the boys were able to go home; others were welcomed by friends. The rest, a small group of nine, celebrated Christmas here at L'Arche. After midnight Mass, we had a gathering with our friends from the village and with others who had come from farther away. All together there were forty of us.

On the feast of the Epiphany we had dinner by candlelight at Le Val Fleuri. Dr. Preaut came to preside at the feast. After the meal all seventy-three of us gathered together for an evening of song and music. Benoît was elected king and chose Mme Cagniard as his queen. We were happy to invite some of our friends from Trosly but were sorry that we did not have room for more.

I leave for Canada on February 18. During my three-week absence Mme Lepère will be responsible for Le Val Fleuri and Mira for L'Arche. I have been invited to give a series of talks at the University of Toronto and then in Vancouver, Edmonton and St. Boniface. I will also spend several days in Montreal. During these weeks I hope to be able to visit as many of our Canadian friends as possible. Alas, my time there will be short. I cannot leave our boys here at Le Val and L'Arche for very long, but I am happy to see friends of L'Arche and to be able to talk about our life here.

Soon after I come back we will be leaving for Italy. This should be quite a trip! The trip we made to Lourdes had a very profound influence on the boys. For many of them it was the first time they had ever travelled. This Jubilee year, with the end of the Vatican Council, seems to be the perfect time for us to journey to the centre of Catholicism. The boys have already seen the Holy Father on television and are anxious to see him in person. There will be about sixty of us—forty boys and about twenty assistants, travelling in individual cars. We are planning to pass through Lausanne, Milan, Florence, Assisi, Rome, San Giovanni Rotondo, Loretto, Bologna, Turin and Lyon.

With our limited resources, we are obliged to rely once again on the generosity of our friends. We estimate that the trip will cost about two hundred francs for each boy. The boys themselves will contribute something from their modest salaries to defray the costs of the trip. I have written to friends in some of the cities in Italy hoping to find free lodging. The dates for the trip have not yet been fixed but will be somewhere between the third and the seventeenth of April. We will know the exact dates once we know the date of our audience with the Holy Father. We would really appreciate it if some of our friends could join us with their cars.

With all our love and gratitude,
Jean Vanier, the assistants and the boys of L'Arche

April 18, 1966
Trosly-Breuil

Dear Friends,

I wanted to write to you right after our pilgrimage to Rome and to send you the text that the Holy Father read to us during our audience with him. It is a beautiful, sensitive text full of understanding. Anything I may say about it would probably complicate rather than clarify it. As we listened to him, we were amazed. The Holy Father understands so well that if one compares our boys with a modern worker on the basis of productivity and capacity for autonomy, they are indeed handicapped. However, if the comparison is made on the basis of the heart, of their ability to give themselves, to make sacrifices for others and to achieve holiness, then they are indeed far from being handicapped. It was beautiful to see the Holy Father asking for help from "the poor," saying that he was counting on them. In some way our group represented handicapped people throughout the world, and in speaking to us the Holy Father was speaking to them all.

The rest of the trip was entirely eclipsed by our visit with the Holy Father and the Easter vigil celebrated by the Pope in St. Peter's Basilica, where we were given special seats in the gallery. We were so moved by his radiant goodness and peace and by the weight of all he is carrying. After reading the text he had prepared, he greeted each one personally, permitted us to kiss his ring and gave each one of us a little souvenir. We were all quite moved when we realized that this Bishop, who carries the concerns not only of the Church and of all Christians but of the whole world, that this man who has freed himself from any ties to a particular country to be totally given to the work of Christ in all countries would give us, a very small and insignificant group, so much of his time, affection and encouragement.

One of the benefits of the trip, besides the meeting with Pope Paul VI, was the spirit of love which inspired the whole group. Sixty-five of us went in fifteen cars and we travelled in groups of two convoys. There was much joy every evening when we all met to recount the day's exploits. There was much mutual help during the minor breakdowns of our cars. The trip is over and daily life has begun again, and now we are living the fruits of our pilgrimage.

Several days before our departure our new Bishop of Beauvais, Monseigneur Desmazières, was kind enough to come and visit us. During the Mass he celebrated in our small chapel, he spoke to us about the meaning of our trip and later joined us for a meal. We were extremely happy to have him with us and were very touched by his words of encouragement.

In closing, we just want to express our gratitude to all of you who were united to us in heart and spirit during the pilgrimage, and to all who encouraged us and helped materially to make this trip possible.

Jean Vanier, the assistants and the boys of Le Val
and L'Arche

His Holiness Pope Paul VI's speech to pilgrims from Le Val Fleuri and L'Arche, Holy Wednesday, 1966

Dear Sons and Daughters of Le Val Fleuri and L'Arche,

It is a great joy for us to welcome you into our house. You have made a long trip and met with many difficulties and much fatigue in order to come here. With all our hearts we thank you and we are so happy to have you here, around us, like a privileged crown made of beloved sons.

As you travelled along the way, you saw beautiful country, big cities, pretty towns; that shows you what a beautiful world God has created, and also how men throughout the ages have contributed to make it beautiful through their talent. These sights, I am sure, have widened your minds and hearts and renewed your courage. You are happier and your prayer rises up with more love towards God who has created all things in such an amazing way.

Seeing you all together makes us realize that you are a small group united by love and an active will to help one another. You are a community in whose midst Jesus is happy to live. If some of you may think that you are not amongst those who have had the greatest luck in life, know that God loves you perhaps more than others. At any rate, we affirm that for us you are cherished sons whom we are very happy to receive.

God calls all of you, in spite of your difficulties, to be saints, and He reserves a special role for you in his Church. So continue to live with courage, doing the best you can, loving each other and being brothers for one another. Live united like one big family, knowing that each one gives and receives more than he thinks. Love your life in all its humility and poverty. Remember always the words of Jesus: "Whoever becomes like this little child . . ." (Matt. 18:4).

Now that you have come on pilgrimage to the tomb of St. Peter, and you have seen the Pope, his successor, and have felt the heartbeat of the visible Church, we can ask you, in exchange for the blessing that we are going to give you, for you, yourselves, your family and benefactors, to promise to offer your sacrifices and prayers for the Church. In this way you will have the joy in knowing that thanks to you the Church will make Jesus Christ better known to others, that it will be able to put into practice the decisions of the Council and obtain from God priests, religious brothers and sisters who are more numerous and more holy to serve God and mankind.

We count on you, dear Sons, and we bless you.

September 10, 1966
Trosly-Breuil

Dear Friends,

I am writing to you now as the new work year begins to give you news of our communities. The last letter told you about our magnificent pilgrimage to Rome and our audience with the Holy Father. Since then, during the month of July, we made another trip, this time by airplane! The Canadian air base at Montmédy, France, invited us to spend a weekend with them. They came to pick us up at the American Air Force base at Laon in three Dakota planes. Saturday afternoon there was an air show; two jet planes flew low over the runways, just over our heads. Sunday morning we went to Mass in the air base chapel, and after a tasty dinner and many warm adieus and thank yous, we flew back.

Trips like these are very important for our communities. They give us new hope and, for some, are the beginnings of a whole new way of life, a life of deeper peace, more open to the world, to society and to others. Most of our boys have no "worldly" hopes for the future. They cannot hope to advance in the professional world nor to found a family. Life could become monotonous if their hearts and spirits were not stimulated by holidays and trips, opening them up to the world around them. Obviously, these trips must be more than tourism. They must be oriented more and more to the world and to others, that is, to a universal love and to spiritual values.

But our life here is more than just trips! Our workshops are now in full swing again. Work from our shops brings in about four thousand francs a month, which is entirely shared by the workers. However, in accordance with the labour laws for sheltered workshops, the boys have to turn in half of their salary to the houses where they live to defray living expenses. Now that many of our workers have reached the minimum salary level necessary, we have been able to register them in the Social Security program. As a result, they have a right to be reimbursed for medicine and medical visits and are paid half their salary if they are sick. You should see how happy they are when their salary rights are explained to them and when they find out that they have a right to an old-age pension!

At this time we do not think it is good to tie ourselves down only to factory work. We want to start manufacturing our own products. This has many advantages on the educational level including the joy of creating and producing our own products. We are starting by making woollen cushions with very pretty designs and colours. Philippe is our principal craftsman. Michel is our specialized worker in decorative designs for mosaics. If you like, you can order the model of your choice. In a month we will open a small book-binding workshop. If you have books that need binding, would you like to send them to us? We are on the lookout for all sorts of second-hand materials to equip this new workshop.

Our communities here are growing. We have been accepting a number of day-workers from the surrounding areas: Compiègne, Creil, Carlepont, Croutoy and Jaux. They come to work in the morning and go back home at night.

In addition, at Carlepont, M. and Mme Fauquembergue have welcomed some of our boys into their family. Every morning they bring them to work here in our workshops and at night they drive them back home. And so more boys have found a new family where they can grow in joy and in fraternal love.

It is painful for us to receive so many urgent requests for help and not be able to respond. There is so much pain hidden away in our world, so many mothers courageously braving great difficulties, so many handicapped adolescents and adults who are persecuted, misunderstood and alienated from society. They need a place to live. Our society is hard on them and sometimes unjust. Those who have the greatest need for understanding and affection are the ones who receive the least. Everywhere there are cries for help! Despite our expansion we are still far from meeting the needs. The local government has given us the permission to place some boys in local families with, of course, proper remuneration. Can you help us? I cannot tell you how much good you could do in this way.

I want to take this opportunity to thank all those who have shown such affection for our boys, who have spent time with them or invited them for a meal. As our community expands we realize how limited our capacities are. I also want to thank those who, like Françoise, come regularly to our community to supervise the leisure-time activities.

In the next letter (this one is getting a little long) I hope to tell you of our future plans, renovations and construction. Right now I would like to ask you to help us in the renovation of a stone barn which we hope to use as a chapel. The one we are using now, so generously lent to us by Mlle Gsell, has become too small. It can no longer accommodate all of us, so we have to fix up a new chapel quite quickly. This, of course, involves new expenses.

We remain deeply united with you all.

Jean Vanier, the assistants and the boys of Le Val
Fleuri and L'Arche

March 26, 1967, Easter
Trosly-Breuil

Dear Friends,

I would like first of all to thank you for your expressions of sympathy at the time of my father's death. Even though I usually spend only about ten days a year in Canada, through the grace of God I was there in Ottawa when he died and was close to him during his last days. His death was peaceful and gentle, just an hour after he had received Communion. My father died just as he had lived, with great simplicity. In spite of the pain and suffering we, his family and friends, were feeling, his funeral was marked by a sense of joy. Instead of the traditional black funeral vestments, the concelebrating bishops, representing the ten Canadian provinces, wore white as a sign of our hope and certitude that my beloved father was already in the eternal love of God.*

I was still able to fulfill some of my commitments in Canada. Wherever I went I noticed a growing interest in L'Arche. Many people are becoming more conscious of the problems and the challenges men and women face who are neither efficient nor productive in a world that puts such emphasis on efficiency. It is encouraging to see this new wave of humanism, people trying to discover the more profound, personal value of those who are called handicapped. Many centres or residences are beginning where men and women who will never be completely autonomous can grow and develop according to their human and spiritual capacities.

During a talk I gave to some eighteen hundred students in Toronto, I was touched by the generosity of those young people. For many, ambition and the desire for personal gain have truly been replaced by a deep desire to give their lives to others and to make a commitment to a worthwhile cause. However, we need to create places where they can come and serve and give of themselves. L'Arche is trying to do that. At L'Arche we are called to create homes and workshops where assistants can live and give their lives to others in community. L'Arche is not just a place to welcome a few mentally deficient boys so that they can grow and develop. It is a sign of hope for many others throughout the world.

Since my last letter, the cleanup, "paint up," "fix up" team has been very active. The most important fruit of their labours is the

---

*After my father's death, I discovered some notes among his papers that showed he felt an intimate relationship with Jesus. They formed the basis of the book I published about my father's spiritual journey, called *In Weakness, Strength*.

new chapel. We opened it on December 21 for the first Mass of Philippe Gruson, a great friend of ours. Midnight Mass was celebrated there and was beautiful.

M. and Mme. Fauquembergue have now welcomed six of our boys into their home as family placements. Michel* was the first to go there followed by his brother Jean Claude, Abdallah, Roger, Jean-Pierre and, finally, Bernard in January. They are all happy in Carlepont where the family atmosphere is so wonderful. Each morning, three of them come to work in our workshops here in Trosly, while others have jobs elsewhere, except for Bernard who stays and works on the farm.

The new little family of Les Rameaux (The Branches) is made up of Bernard, Jean-Pierre and Jean-Marie, with Steve and Ann as heads of house.

Since November we have been trying to better organize our leisure activities in the community. Television can be a diversion sometimes, but in the long run there is the danger that it will stifle all creativity in our people. We have organized a number of clubs that meet regularly: stamp collecting, painting, photography, basket weaving, plasterwork and rope design. Some boys are also learning to play the guitar or the recorder. Saturday mornings are set aside for singing and folk dancing. There is also a bicycle club, and when the weather is good, some go fishing on Saturday afternoons. We cannot forget Roger Brechotteau and Bernard Penot who often come and show us excellent films.

In February each one of us had the choice of going either to the circus or to a concert. At the circus we laughed ourselves silly watching the clowns and the chimps, and we admired the acrobats and the elephants. At the concert Philippe said the Mozart symphony was "sensational!"

---

*A different Michel from our specialized worker in decorative designs for mosaics.

As I bring this letter to a close, I just want to thank all of you for your interest in L'Arche. You cannot imagine what a source of support and encouragement you are for us. We remain deeply united with you.

Jean Vanier, the assistants and the boys of L'Arche

October 1967
Trosly-Breuil

Dear Friends,

We all came back from our holidays on August 27 (except for the little group that had stayed in Trosly with Steve and Ann). Before telling you about our plans for the coming year, let me tell you about our summer activities.

The sunny weather encouraged many friends from near and far away to come to our open house. Mr. Turon from the local government came. He spoke from his heart directly to the boys and then to all our friends. His words were very encouraging for us. The mayor of Trosly also spoke and expressed his hope that places like L'Arche would grow and develop. Monseigneur Desmazières, the Bishop of Beauvais, was kind enough to come. Each workshop presented itself in a humorous way. The gardeners grew gigantic flowers in a few seconds' time! There was a parade of members of the book-binding workshop with a bottle of glue and scissors, the workers from the mosaic workshop, the "tramps" of the antenna workshop and the whole administration team (with Marius as M. Fauquembergue's donkey) calling for more pens! The highlight of it all was Steve and the maintenance team, who constructed a prefabricated house in three minutes' time (connecting the central heating into the neighbour's heater!), but the house fell apart a minute later! Young people from a home in Tracy-le-Mont came and danced, and there were clowns from a home in Carlepont. Our Pierrot was also a highlight, singing a solo, "Je suis à toi pour la vie" ("I am yours for life").

After the celebration, there was an exhibition of our work. Friends could see the beautiful mosaics made by Michel, Marcel, Benoît, Alain and Abdallah. They could also see Philip's cushions and samples of our book binding. Thanks to the presence of some students from the school of educators in Epinay, we had games that attracted young people from Trosly.

Two days after the open house, our first group of pilgrims left. Thirty-three boys equipped with their tents, courage and smiles set out for La Salette in four cars and a minibus. Gerard, Jean Claude and François learned a new song: "Jesus, je voudrais te chanter sur ma route," which became the theme song for our whole trip.* We arrived on the "holy mountain" of La Salette in the midst of thick fog. The next morning the sun was out, so Michel, an assistant, and Alain helped us put up our tents. But the nights were cold (we were at eighteen hundred metres), so only a few courageous ones slept outside! Those few days spent close to Our Lady of La Salette were wonderful. We remember so well our evening prayers and songs as well as our walks in the mountains with Michel and Lucien as our guides. We also remember Claude who went off all by himself. After many hours in search of him, we found him sleeping soundly in his tent!

From the "holy mountain" of La Salette we drove south to the city of Saintes-Maries-de-la-Mer. We put up our tents at a camping site. Our meals had a wonderful sand flavour to them. We enjoyed swimming in the Mediterranean and we had an unforgettable meeting with the Little Sisters of Jesus living in their caravan with the gypsies. Perhaps our greatest joy was to sense the deep love among us and to be able to share that with others.

*This hymn, "Lord Jesus of You I Will Sing," is identified with the Little Sisters of Jesus, but the song's translator, Father Stephen Sommerville, called it "The L'Arche Hymn" in English, and that's how it's known in English Canada.

Five days after our departure, a second group of twenty-six under the leadership of Mira left for Lourdes and Spain. At Lourdes the group stayed for five full days at the Cité Secours. Because of the crowd at Lourdes, the group separated during the day but came together each morning for the Eucharist and in the evening for prayer. Raphaël, faithful companion to Mira, watched over everyone like a benevolent, wise grandfather. The five days passed by quickly. They were tiring but prayerful and joyful.

From Lourdes the six cars left for Montserrat, where the Benedictine Fathers welcomed us and gave us a beautiful little house four kilometres from the monastery. During our stay Philippe really loved the Gregorian chant. René said quite correctly, "People pray here." We also took advantage of being so close to the Mediterranean and went to a beach near Barcelona. The pilgrims came back tired but happy.

The night before they returned home, another group set out for Fatima with Steve and Ann. Things started off badly as Mme Domenjoud's car broke down. However, everything got fixed and the whole group arrived safely in Portugal. We were in Portugal for the big annual pilgrimage, the twelfth and thirteenth of July. On the twelfth a number of different groups of pilgrims arrived, singing their beautiful songs. We stayed on the esplanade until midnight. Then on the thirteenth there was Mass in the pouring rain. We huddled together under our umbrellas. Roger said, "We are real pilgrims; we stayed until the end!"

We came back with our hearts full of joy after this pilgrimage to Our Lady of Peace in Fatima. In fact all three pilgrimages were under the sign of peace. We all went on pilgrimage to pray for peace: peace in our hearts, in our community and in the world.

A new year has begun, but a few faces are missing! Steve and Ann have left for Switzerland and then in April will go to Toronto. Bernard, Jean-Marie and Jean-Pierre, who lived with them in Les

Rameaux, were sad to see them go for they loved them very much. They have brought much to L'Arche.

You will be happy to know that thanks to a loan from a bank in Paris, we have bought the property next door to L'Arche. A grant we received has allowed us to fix up the house there. L'Ermitage will be our fourth house and will soon welcome six boys.

Everyone has come back from the holidays in very good health. We are ready for work! On Monday morning, August 28, the workshops were in full production! We have all made good resolutions! This letter is already too long. We still have much to tell you but it will have to wait until the next letter. For now, I send you our deep friendship.

Jean Vanier, the assistants and the boys of L'Arche and Le Val

April 1968
Trosly-Breuil

Dear Friends,

I have waited for a few weeks since my return from Canada before sending you another newsletter.

Thanks to a grant received from the municipal authorities of Paris, we were able to commence work in the autumn on L'Ermitage, our new home for six men. It is situated just behind L'Arche. By the time you receive this letter, Roger, Claude, Jean, André and the two Michels assisted by Henri, François, Thérèse and Marie Elisabeth will be installed in their new home.

For some time now we have been thinking of starting a home for girls. There are, in fact, few places which provide homes and work for women. We have observed the peaceful atmosphere in several workshops in France where there are men and women working together. Some of us have visited homes in England and in

Switzerland where boys and girls live in the same house. We decided that, with prudence, it would be good to follow their example. Thus, last November, we bought the former presbytery of Cuise-la-Motte. I do not think, however, that it will be open before next year. The total cost of repairs will be covered by a generous gift we received from Canada, plus a loan and various grants. Members of a local Rotary Club have helped us very kindly with a substantial gift and will furnish material at reduced rates. I must admit that I am always amazed by the deep understanding and help of government officials and individual people when we want to open a new home.

We have been concerned for a long time by the fact that a number of our boys (we shall soon have fifty-eight in our homes or in family placements, and eleven day-workers) have no place to go for summer holidays. Last January, thanks to numerous friends and a loan from M. Prat, we were able to acquire a very beautiful house in the southwest of France which we have called La Merci. It is rather old but in good condition. There are a number of adjoining smaller buildings and about five square kilometres of land. In July, Agnes and a few assistants and boys will go there to prepare for the arrival of the larger vacation group in August. Later on we hope that La Merci will become a sheltered workshop for the boys and girls of the region and then, God willing, a centre with residential homes. If you happen to be in that area this summer do not forget to visit us and let your friends know about our plans there. They might have things to spare in their attics. The new community will need furniture this summer.

All these new projects mean, of course, more work, but we are deeply aware of the pressing needs. There are so many handicapped persons who are waiting for a place to live, a place where they can grow and develop and find work. At the same time we realize that we must not grow too quickly and disperse our energies.

Here in Trosly there have been difficult moments, but all is well. Christmas and Epiphany were truly joyous celebrations for us all.

At midnight Mass, Père Thomas inaugurated the new extension to our chapel. Mlle Gsell graciously allowed us to make changes to her house. So now the new chapel, which is well heated, can hold about seventy people.

The community in Carlepont at M. and Mme. Fauquembergue's house progresses in many ways. The boys who have been placed there are so happy and have acquired an extraordinary autonomy thanks to the goodness and wisdom of their foster parents. René and Roger work with farmers in the area while Michel continues to work at the printing shop of M. Finet. Bernard, Abdallah, Jean Claude and Daniel come regularly to work with us.

I spent the month of February in Canada speaking at various places: Trois-Rivières, Quebec, Kingston and London, and at the universities of Montreal, Toronto and Ottawa. The general theme of the talks was "Love and the Conquest of Misery." The welcome I received moved me profoundly. I would like to thank all those who helped in one way or another. The trip and the contact with so many young people was very enriching. As in previous years, I sensed deeply how much people are interested in our work.

We are awaiting the arrival of many friends from Canada, Holland and elsewhere who will come to help us during the summer. It will be wonderful to have them with us. Father Bill Clarke, SJ, arrived a few days ago. He will be here until the middle of May. It is such a joy to have him with us.

Did you see in Canada on April 20 the TV program on L'Arche, a film of half an hour produced by Peter Flemington? I have not seen it yet but Peter sent it to us. I am sure it will be good for I know he put a lot of time and energy into it.

Last November we opened a small apartment in Paris, La Rose des Vents,* with Anne Marie and Colette at 15 rue de Mézières. We

---

*This means "compass rose" or "wind rose," a navigational figure that shows the four cardinal directions or winds. La Rose des Vents was a small apartment where friends of L'Arche could gather.

needed a place in Paris both for the boys and the assistants. Shortly after the opening, Anne Marie and Colette were joined by Marie-Annick. The permanent members of this little community, while being open to receiving friends, continue to study at the university. Every Thursday evening the friends of L'Arche meet at La Rose des Vents for a community Mass said by Father Gruson and share a meal. We are thankful to all those who have helped us to furnish this apartment.

I leave you with a reassurance of our great affection which binds us to all of you.

Jean Vanier, the assistants and the boys of Trosly

November 1968
Trosly-Breuil

Dear Friends,

So much has happened since our last letter: strikes,* trips, holidays and the return to our normal routine. Since the first of April, the new home, L'Ermitage, is in full swing directed by Marie Elisabeth and Henri with the assistance of Françoise. Dédé, one of the lucky members of this family, in reply to my query, "What is peace?" said, "Peace is to be here." This new home, decorated with such care by Marcel, is indeed a sign of peace and tranquility.

The events in Paris and throughout France last May were for us, as well as for many others, a source of both concern and of hope: concern because after several weeks of this paralyzing strike we wondered how we would be able to continue to function; hope,

---

*The strikes in the spring of 1968 started as student demonstrations against the conservative French establishment. By the end of May, ten million French people were on strike and calling for President de Gaulle to step down. In June, de Gaulle dissolved the National Assembly and called an election.

because the spirit of working together spread throughout France and could have been the start of a new dynamism in favour of those who suffer. Fearing food shortage during this crisis, Charles planted potatoes. But, alas, the crop was not up to our expectations. The potatoes were too small; we had planted them too late! Fortunately this crisis did not last too long.

Scarcely had the strike ended and the gas pumps reopened when our first pilgrims wended their way to Our Lady's shrine in La Salette in the French Alps under the guidance of Gilbert and Jacqueline. Patrick, driving the minibus, managed to climb six thousand feet without any accidents. The next day there was rain, fog, hail and snow, but our valiant campers stood the test in their tents. In this beautiful country where thirty-two thousand varieties of flowers grow, Jacqueline organized a game to see who could discover the rarest specimens. When I went to see them on the weekend I was received by smiling faces; there was not a single complaint. "It is wonderful here, it rains all the time," they told me. Everyone seemed to benefit from this prayerful and peaceful atmosphere close to the weeping Virgin.

The group from La Salette had barely returned home when the pilgrims for Lourdes took off under the guidance of Mira, Michel, Henri and Raymond. During their stay they loved the ceremonies and made good friends with some Spanish orphans. Then they set off once again in the direction of Zaragoza and Montserrat. There the Benedictine Fathers, like last year, gave us the use of the house Santa Cecilia.

On the eighth of July a third group left on pilgrimage for Fatima. During the trip we encountered all sorts of difficulties. The brakes of the minibus driven by Thérèse needed repairs. We stopped at Guarda and that gave us an unforgettable evening at the house of some new friends. Three windshields broke with a deafening sound on the Spanish roads. Marie Paule and Carole in the Deux Chevaux were the first victims; then there was Colleen and finally it was the Citroën D.S. with Dédé, who cried out, "How beautiful! How beautiful! It is just like crystal!" We spent two days in Bayonne with Anne Marie and Sister Monique, who came to our rescue. The oilcap on Alain's car disappeared and with it quite a lot of oil! Have you ever looked for an oilcap in Spain on a Saturday evening? These episodes were always accompanied by joy and by encounters with new friends. That is where I began to discover the importance of welcoming the unexpected with openness, trying to see the positive elements in these events.

During this unforgettable week we participated in the beautiful liturgies of Fatima, the torchlight procession amongst the immense crowd on the esplanade and morning Mass. Then there was the sea bathing at Nazare; the joy of Claude, Michel* and Jacques who swam like fish in the water.

In August for our summer holidays, thirty-five of us went to La Merci, our house near Cognac. A few days after we arrived, Agnes came to take on the responsibility of this little, joyful community. Adriano, of course, joined her very quickly! (They were married on the twenty-sixth of October.) It was a wonderful month, especially for those of us who have no family and who would not have had a vacation otherwise. Who can describe the joy of Raphaël with Lorraine, or of Marcel who went to work every day with a local farmer, M. Coisman, or of Michel at Mme Boutinet's while her daughter Helen stayed with us? Who can ever forget the joy of the celebrations in our little chapel where Father Clarke said Mass, or of our evening celebrations by candlelight, or of the visit of the local Bishop and the presence and kindness of so many friends who helped us in so many ways, giving us furniture and even the use of their showers and bathtubs!

During the month of August, M. Lamoilette, the administrative head of the Charente county, received M. Pracomtal and me with

*To avoid confusion, this is our mosaic specialist Michel.

much kindness and encouraged us to start a sheltered workshop for the mentally deficient in his district. I hope that by January 1970 this new centre for thirty handicapped men and women will be in operation under the responsibility of Agnes and Adriano. M. Convert, our architect, is busy with the plans. Now it is only a question of finding the necessary financial help to start the repair work and put in the necessary installations. Funny how money counts in life!

In early September we were all happy to be back home at L'Arche. It was so good to see each other again, to talk about summer holidays and to return to our work. We have just acquired the former café-hotel of Trosly, which will be our fifth home. The ground floor will be used for the day-workers; they need a place of their own for the noon meal. Danielle will be there evenings to organize all our recreational activities. The first floor will be a home for six people.

In the middle of October all the assistants spent five days at Ourscamp, where we reviewed our life together. We reflected on our fundamental goals in L'Arche and on the ways of reaching them. We tried to put in place new structures which correspond to new needs and growth as well as a desire in some assistants to assume greater responsibility in the community. We set up a Community Council composed of a few elected members along with those who have specific responsibilities in the houses. We also elected a committee to look at salaries and working conditions. Committees of finance, research, liturgy and pastoral activities and admissions were also set up. These meetings are important for us. They prevent isolation which can lead to discouragement and authoritarianism; they bring greater efficiency as each person becomes more deeply aware of his or her responsibilities for L'Arche. Thanks to Père André and Père Thomas, we were able to deepen our vision and to share our aspirations. Dr. Franko, our new psychiatrist, gave us much of his time and helped us to better understand our role on the psychological level.

I am certain that these meetings will bear much fruit and that we will become a more united community where each person can assume his or her specific responsibility. In this way each one of us will grow in his or her own personal vocation as well as in our vocation as a community.

Before leaving Ourscamp, Michel, the assistant, had organized a new work program with the director of the Sefara factory in Mouy. Instead of working in our own workshops, a group assisted by Gaby will go to work in the factory. We have a room apart and can work at our own rhythm. Every morning Gaby drives Marcel, Pierre, Jean-François, Claude and some others to Mouy in the Volkswagen minibus that we bought. You should see the joy as well as the seriousness with which they take their work! We must admit Gaby is a good captain!

On the thirteenth of October Louise and Thérèse set out for Cognac with a group of thirteen for grape-picking at Mme Boutinet's. It is hard work: up at 7:00, work from 8:30 to 12:00 and another four hours of work in the afternoon, and all this with a group of Spaniards and Portuguese. The first day was discouraging, rain and mud up to their knees! What an idea to go and pick grapes so far from Trosly! But the next day the sun came out and the long faces became round ones as spirits were revived. Michel and Philippe carried the grape-filled baskets and Daniel and François were excellent grape-pickers. Some came back to Trosly after ten days because of the fatigue. We had to send others to replace them.

The work on our home at Cuise-la-Motte is well underway. Martine will take on the responsibility for this home for ten girls. We hope the work will be finished by June 1. We look forward to the opening of this new house which we will call "Valinhos," Portuguese for "Little Valley." It will be a source of enrichment for us all.

On the first of November Françoise and Chantal will be responsible for La Rose des Vents in Paris. They replace Anne Marie who has passed her examinations at the Sorbonne and has come to work full time in Trosly as a psychologist. Marie-Annick has returned home to teach and to be closer to her sick mother. Soon Colette will pay us a visit from the United States. So when you come to 15 rue de Mézières, you will be greeted by two new friendly faces. Do not forget that every Thursday at 7:30 p.m. the apartment is open to welcome you.

Before ending this long letter, I would like to give you some news of Steve and Ann and their son, Jean Frederick. Steve and Ann are working in Toronto with the Canadian Association for Mental Retardation and preparing to begin a new L'Arche community there.

There is also some sad news to share. We had to send Gerard, Jean-Pierre and Marceau back to the psychiatric hospital at Clermont.* This is very painful and we ask you to pray for them. We hope that some day we will be able to welcome them back with us or else find another place for them where they will be happier.

I am sure that there are many things I have forgotten to tell you but now I must stop. I thank you for your presence with us in thought and in prayer. You do not know how much your friendship and your affection mean to us. Know that you have ours. We hope to see you soon.

Jean Vanier, the assistants and the boys of Trosly

*Unfortunately, these men just couldn't find their place in the community. They were quite violent and needed more contained surroundings. When we saw we couldn't help them, we had to take them back to the psychiatric hospital, about forty kilometres from Trosly.

May 1969
Trosly-Breuil

Dear Friends,

I want to bring you up to date with our new projects, hopes and activities. Last October, M. Buchez came to see me after closing his business in Venette, a suburb of Compiègne. Having had extensive experience with young people in various social activities, he wishes to devote the rest of his life to the service of the handicapped. After several meetings and long discussions, on January 1 we opened his house to accommodate eight of our boys. We hope that they will gradually find their place in society. Some of the boys are working in factories. We hope that their stay in this new house will be for a transition period between life here in Trosly and a more independent living situation and so we have named this home Le Tremplin, "The Springboard." The spirit that prevails there is slightly different from that of our houses in Trosly; it is that of young workers who are beginning to earn their own living. They are proud of this and so are we. We were concerned about a certain number of boys in Trosly who we felt were capable of greater autonomy. They need this "springboard."

In our last letter we spoke to you about the acquisition of the café-hotel of Trosly, which we have named La Source. Maryvette, Brigitte and Charles opened this home on April 8, with Georges, Claude, Marc, Ali, Jean-Pierre and Daniel. This little family seems to be off to a good start, but of course it will take a while for it to find its own character. It is most important that each home find its own identity, not imitating other homes but living in its own way according to the particular dynamism of those leading it. Le Tremplin is very different from the first L'Arche home, and just as L'Arche differs from L'Ermitage, La Source will be equally different.

Valinhos, our house in Cuise for young women, will open on July 1. Work on the house was delayed so we had to postpone its opening.

Fortunately, Bob and Dave arrived from Canada in December and have helped us tremendously. Every morning they go with Daniel, Jacques, Pierrot, and others to do the painting, etc. M. Rocher, our architect, estimates that the work will cost ten thousand francs. Martine is in the process of forming a team of assistants. Valinhos will also have a character of its own. The young women there will make dolls that will be sold. We got this idea from Botton Village in England, which both Martine and I have visited. It is interesting work in which people with diverse handicaps can participate. We feel it can be financially profitable as well.

We have recently bought another house at Cuise, next door to Valinhos. It will require very few alterations. Six young women can be welcomed there quite soon. Little by little, we are growing in Cuise.

Thanks to many friends in the Charente, we will be able to open La Merci in Courbillac on January 1, 1970. The local government authorities have granted us a subsidy and the bank has given us a loan. Repair work has begun. Agnes and Adriano will arrive in July and, with Gabrielle, will coordinate the holiday group. They will stay on afterwards to supervise the final repair work and to run the day workshops for thirty handicapped men and women of the area.

We had a wonderful Christmas holiday. As Christmas fell on a Wednesday this year, for the first time the whole community assisted at midnight Mass and the traditional Reveillon afterwards. On Christmas Day, most of us went home for a few days with our families. Those who have no family were received warmly by the Dominican Sisters at Flavigny and were thoroughly spoiled by them.

Every year in the month of February I go to Canada. This year I gave lectures on the theme of "Beauty in Love and in Life." I was mainly at St. Michael's College, University of Toronto, and at the University of Ottawa. I tried to show how, in our world today, we are losing a sense of beauty and of wonderment, a certain simplic-

My family on holiday in England. I'm on the far left with my Scottish nanny, Isabelle Thompson; my sister, Thérèse, is with Dad; Bernard is with Mum; and Georges (Benedict) is with Isabelle's niece Agnes.

The four eldest Vanier kids at the beach at Berwick-upon-Tweed. Our youngest brother, Michel, was not yet born.

Here I am at age seventeen in 1945 as a young naval cadet at the Royal Naval College, Dartmouth, England. In this naval formation, my mind and body became disciplined, and I lived in the world of competence, power and status.

*When I first met Père
Thomas in 1950, I
recognized almost
immediately that he was a
man of God and someone
I would be involved with
for my whole life. Here
he is at L'Eau Vive in
1952, in the habit of the
Dominican order.*

*I went to L'Eau Vive in
1950, seeking a place, as
many young people do,
where I could just be;
where I could find myself
and be born in prayer and
inner freedom. I stayed
there until 1956.*

*Le Val Fleuri was a
private home converted
into a residence for thirty
intellectually handicapped
men in 1960. It is the foyer
to which I am now most
closely attached, the one I
always come home to.*

*This is the very first
L'Arche house in 1964. I
invited two intellectually
disabled men to come live
there with me. The house
was named after the ark
Noah built as a refuge
against the Flood and as
a sign of his covenant
with God.*

In 1950 I visited the community Catherine Doherty had founded in New York's inner city. I met her later at Madonna House in Combermere, Ontario.

Père Thomas and I in 1964, as we start the great adventure that would become L'Arche.

Two years after we first moved in, the family at the L'Arche house had grown to include (from left) Henri, Pierrot, Mira, Barbara, Benoît, Lucien and me.

Playing together in the yard at the first L'Arche home in 1966.

Meeting Pope Paul VI on pilgrimage to Rome.

Ravi, Gopal and Srinivas at Asha Niketan–Bangalore in the early 1970s.

"Tall Uncle" and Mother Teresa talking with Bangladeshi refugees who we'd come to know through the children. We're standing on the wide sidewalk in front of St. John's Church, in the basement of which we had our workshop. Many refugees came from the crowded train station (in the background) and settled on the pavements of Calcutta. (Courtesy of Brian McDonough)

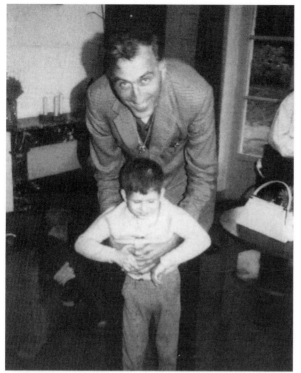

This is Loïc Proffit in 1970. His family's terrible experience on holiday at Lourdes led to the creation of Faith and Light, which was initially a pilgrimage and then became a federation of support groups for people with intellectual disabilities, their parents and friends.

Lourdes is a place of healing and consolation. The Faith and Light pilgrimage in 1971 showed parents that they weren't alone and put their children, so often rejected and pushed aside by society, at the centre of events.

Marie-Hélène Mathieu and I never imagined that one pilgrimage could turn into such a big international movement! (Courtesy of Faith and Light International)

Twelve thousand people came to the 1971 pilgrimage. Today, Faith and Light comprises 1,500 communities in 80 countries. (Courtesy of Faith and Light International)

The tenth anniversary of Faith and Light in 1981 showed that what we had created spontaneously and by instinct was in fact something that fulfilled a lasting need.

Our thirtieth-anniversary pilgrimage to Lourdes in 2001 was another tremendous gift. (Courtesy of Faith and Light International)

This retreat was held at an apartment in Moscow in 1989, just as the Soviet Union and its form of Communism were collapsing. There was a palpable desire among people for an authentic, lasting vision.

A Lebanese Faith and Light group meeting and sharing in the midst of their country's civil war.

Archbishop Hélder Câmara (in the middle) came to visit us at Trosly in the early 1990s. He spoke to us about the terrible pain in Latin America at the time. He had a wonderful gift for understanding the poor.

I first visited Slovenia in 1991, just as the region entered a period of so much war and anguish. Here I am in happier times with the Skupnost Barka L'Arche community in Ljubljana, Slovenia, in 2001. (Courtesy of Skupnost Barka)

Jing had been an assistant at L'Arche communities in England and India before founding Punla ("The Seed"), a L'Arche community in Manila. Here he is in 1988 with Keiko, Helen, Jordan and Roy.

Juanita sits to the left of Martine outside the first L'Arche in Mexico, 1986.

ity of heart which sees beauty in the present moment and is capable of being enraptured by it and of giving thanks for it. I must admit that I have personally learned much from our boys in this respect. They may not be able to work as much as others, but they have a greater capacity for contemplation. If their slowness seems to render them inefficient, it has the advantage of making them more sensitive to wonderment.

I saw Ann and Steve in Toronto. In Canada, we have now formed a corporation and are in the process of studying the conditions required for starting homes similar to those in Trosly. We hope they will start soon. Steve and Ann are marvellous in their hope and dynamism. You should see their little son, Jean Frederick!

When I was in Canada I had the opportunity to visit a certain number of hospitals for the physically handicapped and for people with cerebral palsy. I have returned with the firm conviction that we must create homes for people with all kinds of infirmities. How is it that our society, which often refers to its Christian origins and its democratic principles, permits such injustice against the weak and defenceless? It is absolutely necessary that people of goodwill come together to work effectively to set up homes for those who cannot fend for themselves.

We must also look beyond the sufferings and injustices of our own countries. Today more than ever before, the world is becoming more unified. We cannot ignore the suffering of our brothers and sisters far away. What is happening in Africa, Asia and Latin America is of capital importance for the future of humanity.

It is from this deep awareness that the desire was born to extend our community of L'Arche to include our brothers and sisters in other countries. We are thinking of founding a L'Arche in India, following signs which we see as quite providential. Gabrielle joined us at the end of February with a deep desire to leave for India with Mira. Gabrielle has been in contact with L'Arche ever since its foundation. She knew Louis well. For eight years Gabrielle directed Crossroads, an international student centre in Montreal, where she met Mira. She will spend some time in Trosly where she will be working on the preparations for the Indian project, which will be financed partly by a Canadian organization. We shall need help, however, and so I turn to you in all simplicity to ask if you can help us in this new foundation by sending us a contribution. We hope that after the first few years, this project will be able to find its own financial resources within the country itself. For the moment, we must help get it started. There are, of course, many unknown factors in regard to this project. It is difficult to foresee the identity of our homes there. What is certain is our desire to share our life with the poorest to whom God is calling us. We are confident that he will help us. We ask you to pray with us that he may bless this project and reveal to us, through the poor in India, new aspects of life and of the Gospel.

In Canada I had the opportunity to speak to many young people in different colleges and high schools. I am full of admiration when I see their maturity and their desire to do something worthwhile. If many young people no longer have a sense of law and of tradition as before, many of them do have a sense of the importance of each human person and above all of the weak and the poor. That is wonderful! It is so easy to crush people in the name of law! Our boys, and the poor in general, need people who know how to accept and respect them. I am convinced more than ever of the necessity of communities like ours which permit young people to discover that the supreme value of human beings is in their capacity for communion with others.

We are expecting a number of Canadians this summer and also next year. Those who were with us this year left in April. We are sorry to see Mary, Judy and Ron leave. Each one of them brought us all so much. They worked hard in a quiet way, always with a smile. We are very grateful and remain very deeply united to them.

While I was in North America I visited a centre for the mentally deficient at Mansfield, Connecticut. I admired their excellent work and the efficient workshops. Gerry had also visited the centre when she participated in a conducted tour organized by the Kennedy Foundation for directors of workshops. In Mansfield I was impressed by their concern for the reintegration of the mentally handicapped into society. I visited some homes for twelve handicapped workers as well as small apartments in which four men managed all alone. This visit made me reflect upon our boys' capacity for greater autonomy.

Shortly after I returned, M. and Mme. Fauquembergue, foster parents of eight of our boys, were struck by a terrible death in the family. Their daughter, Marie-Gabrielle, was killed in a car accident. We were shocked by this accident which brought us face to face with the stark realities of life and reminded us of the fragility of our own lives and of our own intrinsic poverty. Our pilgrimage on earth is short and we know neither the hour nor the place where it will end. At the same time, we have confidence in God. He is our Father. He watches over us and waits for us. The pains of life are slight compared to the plenitude which awaits those who learn to open their hearts to love on this earth. Our affection for M. and Mme. Fauquembergue and their other daughter, Marie-Flore, was deepened by this time of suffering.

Again this summer we are organizing three pilgrimages: to Lourdes, to Fatima and to La Salette. With the growing number of boys we shall need a greater number of cars and we hope that some of our friends in France will join us.

May I close for now by telling you once again of our gratitude and affection for you.

Jean Vanier, the assistants and the boys of Trosly

November 1969
Trosly-Breuil

Dear Friends,

I have not written for a long time and people are asking for news.

Perhaps the most important thing that has happened to us since we first opened our homes was the death of Claude Debailleaux. Claude came to Trosly on October 27, 1968. He lived at Le Val and was very happy there. He used to go home to his parents every weekend and tell them all about his friends, his work and the outings. He was looking forward to the trip to Fatima in July. He died in his bed during the night of May 18. His death has affected us all. We prayed fervently beside the body of our friend and everyone went to his funeral. We wept with his parents for we loved him very much. There was much peace, unity and silence in the house. We felt much serenity as we touched the fundamental reality of our lives. Friends who came to visit said that they were struck by the atmosphere of peace in the community when his death was announced. Claude's death brought us a deeper sense of our vocation: to create homes where those we welcome can live the rest of their lives. I was touched by the words of his mother when she gave me the hundred francs that she had set aside for his trip to Fatima—she asked me to give the money to another boy—"We are so grateful to you because Claude spent the best months of his life with you." In our evening gatherings, many still speak about Claude. He remains deeply engraved in our hearts and memories.

On June 7 we had our annual open house. Many came and spent a joyful afternoon with us. They appreciated the way each house was represented: L'Arche with Noah (Raphaël), surrounded by animals; the pirates of Le Val Fleuri who took possession of L'Arche with shouts of joy; the gentle meal with all the people of Les Rameaux; the different "hermits" from L'Ermitage who were transformed into an orchestra, the "Trosly-Birds"; the Bedouins of La Source; and finally the circus of Le Tremplin. After the mime, there was an exhibition of our work in the new workshops behind Le Val. Mlle Diesnesh, secretary of state in the ministry of health, was with us. She spoke of the efforts she was making to bring greater aid to the handicapped in France. We were touched by her presence as well as by the participation of M. Michel, M. Salmon and M. Robillard from the local government and M. Bauge, our mayor.

A few days after that celebration, the first group of pilgrims left for Saintes-Maries-de-la-Mer and Lourdes. We camped at Saintes-Maries and enjoyed long moments on the beach. June is a wonderful month in the Camargue; it is not too hot and there are not too many people. Philippe loved being in the water; in fact, we all did except for a few "grandfathers" who preferred to look at the store windows and enjoy soft drinks in the local cafés. The list of all those who welcomed us along the way is too long to mention. We received such warmth and kindness and we feel a new strength and courage. The trip from Aix en Provence to Lourdes was long, especially with all the breakdowns and flat tires. Each time we stopped at a garage, they sent us to another and we left singing "Alleluia," even though in our hearts we were quite worried. Water was the trademark of our three days in Lourdes—rainwater as well as grace! Once again we were graciously welcomed at Cité Secours, where we received free room and board.

No sooner had we come back, cleaned the minibus, changed the oil and checked the cars, when the second group left for Portugal, via Charente and Burgos. There were forty in the group, with Gabrielle as leader. Those were unforgettable days which climaxed on May 13, when we joined forty thousand other pilgrims for the celebration. The day was marked by Jean Claude's disappearance. Everyone thought we had lost him in the mountains. One whole night of anguish was spent with the police. We made numerous telephone calls, trying to explain the situation in Portuguese! The next morning was filled with joy when we found him on the main esplanade. From that moment on, we never let go of his hand.

On July 20, the group left for the Alps and La Salette. We put up our tents on the mountain. Thanks be to God, we had good weather this year. Maréchale Leclerc came with us and brought some of the pilgrims in her own car. She was full of energy and courage. Unfortunately she broke her arm on one of the walks. We had to send for Peter from Trosly to drive her car back!

When the last car from this final pilgrimage arrived safe and sound, I must admit I felt relieved. One hundred and ten of us had travelled thousands of kilometres without any accidents, only a few breakdowns. There was fatigue, especially for the drivers, but I think we calculated the distance between stopping points a bit better this year. And I believe we grew in greater love for one another. Living together more closely under the tents and in more difficult situations created a very lively spirit amongst us. These trips continue to be privileged moments each year for the whole community.

The trips would not be possible if friends, especially from Canada and the United States, did not come to be with us during the summer months. They replaced assistants in the workshop and houses. I cannot mention the names of each one but they have all left their mark in our hearts. I must, however, mention Tom who learned our particular method of manual work in Trosly. He pumped water from one hole to another hole, only to find that the water kept coming back to the first hole through an underground passage. His dream is to bring modern techniques to L'Arche. We are waiting for them!

There was also the pilgrimage in May, when those who work in the factory in Mouy were welcomed for a week by the Sisters in Flavigny. Gabrielle and Odile accompanied them. As there was no work for them for two weeks, they were able to get away.

This makes me think of Michel, who continues to find subcontract work for us with the local factories and to set up work for some of the boys in the factory. Today there are twenty-six boys working in local factories or with farmers and craftsmen in the region. We hope that this work will not only give them a certain professional autonomy but also greater autonomy in their own personal lives. I have already written to you about Le Tremplin, our house in Compiègne that serves as a link between the more protected life in Trosly and society. Perhaps next year we can add another link to the chain that will lead to total reinsertion into society—a little rented apartment where five or six of our boys can live all alone and learn how to "fly by their own wings." In the United States, I saw apartments like that and they seemed to help the handicapped workers integrate more easily into society.

We see more clearly that our community has two objectives. On the one hand, we want to set up homes and training so that men who have been wounded psychologically or physically may find new autonomy. We must remember that added to this primary wound are other, deeper wounds caused by the way people look at them, continually condemning the handicapped to remain in an inferior place. We can rarely do anything to help the primary wound, but we can and must work on the wound of rejection, by giving new confidence, encouragement and support to those who are weak and who live in a world that seems only for those who are strong. Our second objective is to create a community spirit for those who are living in our homes and who, for one reason or another, are not called to complete autonomy. They need a home and work where primacy is given to love over and above personal pleasure. Is this not, in fact, what we all need? The pedagogy of the heart must go beyond our personal egoism and open us up more and more to the sufferings of others.

The month of July was marked by the opening of Valinhos, our first home for women.

In August I went to Canada to give some talks. I saw Ann and Steve; their house opened on October 15. It is called Daybreak.* Our Lady's Missionaries have very generously given us the house, which is quite big (thirteen bedrooms) and completely furnished. There are just a few things that have to be done before they can move in. Believe it or not, to continue their links with France, the couple who are helping Steve and Ann come from Nice! M. Doré was born at Montmartre—a real Parisian!

Speaking to you about the birth of these new homes makes me think of Gabrielle and Mira, who left for India on October 30 on a reconnaissance mission. They will spend three months there to identify the needs of the handicapped and see if we can do something to answer these needs. They are in Bangalore, where there is a school for handicapped children. I will be joining them from the end of November to December 17. I will go to Madras and New Delhi and come back through Bombay. This will be my first trip to Asia. I am anxious to know the Indian culture better, a culture which is rooted in the oldest human values, and to learn about their spirituality and way of life. For me, going to India means assimilating a new culture and not just "taking care of" their handicapped people. That attitude would wound them, and we truly do not want to go there in that spirit. Mira and Gabrielle will probably come back at the end of January, and then we will decide for the future. Mira's absence, even for three months, leaves an emptiness. As you know, she has been with us since May 1965, and whenever I am absent she takes on the responsibility and maintains the unity of the whole community. Whether she remains in Trosly or not, she will always remain deeply bonded to us. If we want to be truly present to handicapped people in Trosly, we cannot be indifferent to the suffering of people elsewhere.

---

*Located in Richmond Hill, Ontario, Daybreak is now our biggest L'Arche community in Canada, with eight homes on its campus and in the surrounding area.

On Thursday, November 6, Group Captain Cheshire came and spent a day with us. He was one of the great English pilots during the Second World War. He left the work of war in order to work for peace. He has founded fifty homes for men and women who are physically handicapped, often called "incurable"; there are fourteen homes in India, one in Bangalore. You can understand how important his visit was for us. His courage, perseverance, prudence and accomplishments are an inspiration and a model. He is preparing a foundation in France and we will do everything we can to help him. There is now a deep friendship that binds us together.

With love from all of us.

Jean Vanier, the assistants and the boys of L'Arche

PART TWO
1970 ❧ 1973

ROOTS OF COMMUNITY:
BEGINNING IN CANADA, INDIA
AND THE UNITED STATES

On my journey towards the founding of L'Arche I encountered community movements that, like L'Arche, were both countercultural—not driven by success or ambition or competition—and yet very much of their time, of a time when people were searching, willing to see where the Spirit of God could lead and concerned with the pain of others.

One of the first groups I mention in the letters is the Little Sisters of Jesus. In Montreal in 1954 I was introduced to them and to their mission, based on the spirituality of Charles de Foucauld. This is why they are also known as the Little Sisters of Foucauld. Foucauld was born into wealth and privilege in France. He lost his faith and then regained it and decided to root his life in the ordinary life of the poor, like Jesus at Nazareth. Foucauld lived most of his life among the Tuareg people of North Africa, learning their way of life and being present among them. He didn't seek to convert them to Christianity; he simply wanted to create fellowship and relationship through his presence, to break down barriers through an abiding love. He was killed in 1916 during the First World War and was beatified in 2005.

Charles de Foucauld didn't have any followers, and in fact he wasn't especially well known during his lifetime, but Magdeleine Hutin, a French woman, became inspired by his life and at the age of thirty-eight she went to Algeria to follow in his footsteps. She wanted her life to somehow reach across the barriers that separate people from one another and to be a sign of love to those who were rejected by others. Everyone thought she was foolish! But when she returned to France during the Second World War she realized her message wasn't unique to North Africa: she began to travel and saw the plight of migrant farm workers, gypsies, travelling circuses and carnival workers. Others followed her and eventually founded the congregation of the Little Sisters of Jesus. She died in 1989 at the age of ninety-one. L'Arche has always been very close to the Little Sisters and Brothers: we both strive to recognize Jesus's presence in the poor and to live a simple life together with them.

Dorothy Day's Catholic Worker movement also made a big impression on me. She was an American journalist who co-founded the Catholic Worker movement in the 1930s to care for the impoverished and downtrodden street people. She was seen as a rebel and even an anarchist by many within the Church. Her "house of hospitality" in the slums of New York City spurred the creation of over 185 Catholic Worker communities around the world today. Day believed strongly in the dignity of every person and was committed to nonviolence, voluntary poverty and the Works of Mercy as a way of life. Her faithfulness to the Gospel and living the "preferential option for the poor"* showed that lay people, not just priests and nuns, are called to live the life of the Gospel. She died in 1980.

Another influential community founder for L'Arche was Catherine Doherty. She was born to an aristocratic and devout Orthodox family in Russia. She married Baron de Hueck at the age of fifteen, but after the Russian Revolution they fled as refugees

---

*The "preferential option for the poor" became a priority in the Catholic Church in the 1970s and 1980s. It expresses a special concern for the poor and the vulnerable, based on Jesus's call for us to advocate for the voiceless and the powerless. It's rooted in the Gospel vision of social justice and charity.

to Canada, experienced terrible poverty and eventually separated. She worked her way to prosperity again, only to give it all up to live among the poor in the slums of Toronto during the Depression. She also came to know Dorothy Day. Many young people followed Catherine's Gospel way of life. Together they called themselves Friendship House and they lived the spirituality of Francis of Assisi—community life, poverty, compassion, peacemaking and a reverence for God's creations. Later she moved to Harlem and started another house devoted primarily to the needs of the inner-city black community. This is where I first came to know the community in 1950.

At the time, I was reading Thomas Merton's *The Seven Storey Mountain,* and when my ship, the HMCS *Magnificent,* docked in New York, I followed his path to Friendship House and spent many days in the community. I even invited them all aboard the ship for Easter dinner! Eventually Catherine and her second husband, journalist Eddie Doherty, returned to Canada and founded Madonna House in Combermere, Ontario. Madonna House consists of men and women and priests who live a life of voluntary poverty, celibacy and obedience.

Often when I was travelling or when groups from L'Arche went on pilgrimage, we were welcomed by a Foyer de Charité. This was a group started by Marthe Robin, a French woman who suffered from Spanish flu when she was young and was confined to her bed for most of her life. She was a mystic and stigmatic who founded retreat houses for priests and lay people. She died in 1981, and by 2002 more than seventy Foyers had been established.

When I revisit these letters I see how many people—both famous and unknown—had an influence in my life and the life of L'Arche. And how interesting to see the crucial role of women in the founding of L'Arche abroad and its stability over time.

I was able to write these letters about our life together because so many people were becoming firmly rooted at the community in

Trosly. As I was travelling around the world living the excitement of the birth of new communities, others were living the day-to-day life of community with all its pain and conflicts, with all its celebrations and the joys of people being transformed. I could not have done all this travelling if others were not there living so faithfully and beautifully what I was preaching.

July 1970
Trosly-Breuil

Dear Friends,

I want to write to you about my trip to India last year. My four weeks in Bombay, Madras and Bangalore impressed me very much. I was really touched by this visit to India where, through the kindness of many friends, I was able to see many things in a very short time. I was, of course, mainly concerned about the possibility of opening a L'Arche in India. That is why I visited schools for mentally handicapped children, homes for the physically handicapped, psychiatric hospitals and homes for lepers: places where rejected men and women live. I wanted to know what possibilities exist for financing, administering and managing homes. I was able to detect very quickly a great need for homes and workshops for mentally deficient adults. In India, as in most countries, there are quite a number of schools for handicapped children but very few homes for adults. In India, as in France, many handicapped men and women need a place of welcome adapted to their age and needs.

The welcome which Gabrielle, Mira and I received from the government authorities touched us deeply. The first minister of the state of Mysore and the minister of health eagerly encouraged us in the project which is now under way, thanks to the goodness and understanding of Major Ramachandra and his friends of the Social Workers' Brotherhood. The staff of this association, inspired by the thought and life of Mahatma Gandhi, are in charge of a large school, Deena Seva Sangha, in a slum area of Bangalore. They have put at our disposal an ideal piece of property: four acres of land with a house and two wells (which so far have not dried up!). We have formed a registered society, that is, a nonprofit organization with a governing body composed of professional Indian men and women in the medico-social field, government and business administration. All of them are genuinely interested in our project and very competent in their fields.

Gabrielle and Mira stayed on for a few weeks to complete all the business to be done in this first stage. I left on December 20. Gabrielle will be returning to India in the next few weeks, for she has just received her long-term residence visa for India. I think our home will open its doors before the end of the year. We are going to create workshops and make immediate use of the land. We hope to make this first house financially independent as quickly as possible. To achieve this demands careful study and an important initial investment so that later on we can live off the products of our workshops and our land. Our homes in India will be called Asha Niketan, "Home of Hope," hope for those whose minds and psyches have been wounded and who are living without hope in psychiatric hospitals or who linger without work in their homes.

I was truly amazed by the way everything seemed to fall so quickly into place for this new foundation. I got the impression that we were nothing more than poor instruments of Providence for the creation of these homes of hope and love.

Many things impressed me in India: the wonderful people I met, the joy in getting to know the Indian culture, a people so profoundly human and religious, not motivated by an individual materialism which one so often finds in our Western culture. I became more aware of the importance and value of Gandhi in our society, and I was privileged to meet Mother Teresa, who has opened many homes for those who are suffering. If God so wishes, I shall return to Bangalore in October to share the responsibility of Asha Niketan with Gabrielle for several weeks. Everyone in Trosly has shared in this experience in India and sees it as a new openness to the world.

The daily life of each one of our houses in Trosly goes on with work, times of celebration as well as moments of suffering and anguish. Our community is expanding, but remains united, and, I believe, this year more united than ever. As you can imagine, the increased amount of work and the increased number of handicapped people welcomed means a more complex administration. Mlle Maurice, who has followed L'Arche from the beginning, has taken on this responsibility with the help of Mme Lepère and François. Things are in good hands!

We have recently purchased five acres of land behind La Source, where we hope to construct several buildings to house eighty severely retarded adults. Within a few years we would like to open our doors to these men and women who have been deeply wounded. We will tell you more about this project later.

In March, M. Bernard, his sister and his daughter asked me to come and look at some property at Ambleteuse, near Boulogne-sur-Mer. I spent a day with them and they offered L'Arche three fine pieces of land which belonged to a charitable organization that is no longer in operation. There are several houses, one of which served as a school, and a series of buildings that could be used as workshops. I was amazed that all this has simply been put into our hands, so that, in turn, we might be able to put it into the hands of those who have neither work nor home.

So, this summer, instead of going to La Merci, we will go to Ambleteuse. It would be difficult for La Merci to welcome a group of forty or fifty of us for the month of August and to find something for all our workers to do. At Ambleteuse, with the sea four hundred yards away and all those buildings unoccupied for some years, there will be work to be done and leisure to be enjoyed! Then, during the course of next year we hope to open permanent houses there.

During the month of April, General Laubman arranged for a number of us to visit the Canadian Air Force base at Lahr, Germany. Major Labbé, the protocol officer who arranged the whole program for the weekend, greeted us with much warmth at the French air base at Creil where two Dakotas were waiting to fly thirty-five of us to Germany. It was a wonderful experience, watching the jet fighter flying low (Jean-Pierre was really frightened!), eating Canadian-style food and meeting many new friends. Just before sending this letter to you I received a letter from Major Labbé saying that they are sending us a truck full of clothing, which will really be useful.

As you already know, we went to Rome at Pentecost. It was truly an expedition, prepared in advance by Jacqueline who had gone ahead to find lodging for our stops at Milan and Rome. There were 188 of us in a fleet of cars, minibuses and a rented bus. We prepared this voyage with much care and I believe we experienced the fruit of this preparation. We visited ancient, Christian and modern Rome. Our trip reached its climax at the general audience with Paul VI in the Basilica of St. Peter's on the eve of our departure. The Holy Father addressed words of welcome to the pilgrims of L'Arche and then came down to our group to shake many of the outstretched hands.

We returned to Trosly on Saturday, May 24, safe and sound, with neither a single accident on the road, nor any serious health problems. Each one of us had a heart full of memories and a joyous face, in spite of all the fatigue of three days on the road from Rome to Trosly. It was the first time that we had undertaken such an expedition, the first time that we had travelled such a distance with such a large number. It is evident that everyone benefited from the pilgrimage and all its varied experiences.

This summer there are about twenty new faces in Trosly, mainly Canadian, American and English, who bring added life and new ideas when at the end of the year there is a tendency to flag.

We remain deeply united to you,
Jean Vanier and your friends at L'Arche

October 16, 1970
On the train between Bombay and Bangalore, India

Dear Friends,

I am happy to be in the third-class section of this train from Bombay to Bangalore. The train has stopped for the moment. Ronald is sleeping in the berth just above me.* Vendors are shouting, trying to sell their merchandise, and poor people are begging. In our compartment there is a real community spirit as people talk to each other, children play and people share their food. They ask if I am a missionary.

Ronald and I arrived in Bombay last night after a good flight. We were met at the airport by Sister Maria Delores and Dilip, a mentally retarded boy she found in the train about a month ago. He was naked, hungry, lost and all alone. Now he seems happy, gentle and simple. He speaks Hindi and talks little during the day but chants prayers for hours in the evening. We are told that he must belong to a high-caste family because of his type of prayers. In the evening he ate with us on the floor. I think he could come to Asha Niketan. I will speak to Gabrielle about him and see what we can do. If we cannot welcome him, he will go back into the street. It would be good to start Asha Niketan with someone poor like him. (Every time the train stops I add a few lines because while it is running it is impossible to write.)

It felt good to be in Bombay even though it was hot and very humid. It was good to spend the night in the Cheshire Home with some fifty handicapped people. I was touched by their welcome and I was happy to see them again. They remembered me and my visit to their home a year ago. There is a young man there with cerebral palsy; he has such a twisted body but a wonderful smile; you can sense his deep spiritual life, full of abandonment, a surrender

* Ronald Pickersgill was one of the earliest assistants in Bangalore.

of love and an acceptance of pain. I feel so poor in front of him, so full of pride, so "big." There is such a strong presence of God in some of these people, such love, clarity and purity in their eyes. I feel so comfortable with them, meeting them, one after the other. After dinner, Ron (what a wonderful man!) and I walked to the centre of the city. There were crowds of people; many were sleeping in the street as it was too hot to sleep inside their little huts.

Being back in Bombay gives me deep peace. I have a strange feeling of being both at home and yet very much a stranger, rich and powerful. People here are so easily crushed by misery, hunger and powerlessness, under the yoke of a static society where the gap between the weak and the powerful is so evident.

Saturday morning we took the train from Bombay to Bangalore. We got up at 4:40 a.m. A Spanish Jesuit had kindly offered to give us the Eucharist before we left. The train departed at 7 a.m. The trip took thirty-six hours. Everything is so simple. People on the train share their food. There is a lot of conversation about vital questions like war and peace, violence and love. There are many families with children, happy, obedient children playing together without any toys. Ronald and I were not well prepared for this long ride. We didn't bring much food except some bread, grapes and La Vache Qui Rit (the name of a French cheese: "the laughing cow")! We were a bit embarrassed to offer La Vache Qui Rit in India! We bought some bananas, peanuts and soft drinks from the various food vendors and some people gave us an egg and some idli (rice cakes).

We lie down for the night on hard wooden benches. In the morning, everybody gets washed and the women do up their hair; there is a very friendly "family" atmosphere. Everyone seems so at ease. The trip was not tiring but relaxing. India is a deeply human, friendly country. We arrived in Bangalore at 6 p.m. Gabrielle was there to meet us. She looked so happy and relaxed. We went to Mass in the cathedral. It was a joyful Mass said in Tamil. We were a group of poor people, some seated on wooden benches, others on the ground.

Then we went to Asha Niketan in a car someone lent us. The young night watchman, or gurkha, equipped with dagger and sword, opened the door. He smiled and we exchanged a few words. He stays outside all night, guarding the house and chanting prayers.

Gabrielle has accomplished much work: the electricity, sanitary system and bedrooms are all ready. The house has been repainted. Radha, an Indian woman, will be back on Wednesday or Thursday. We ate together Indian style and then had prayer. Everything is ready to welcome the boys. We will probably open the house on Thursday when Joseph and another boy arrive. Dilip, from Bombay, will probably join us. There are so many unknown factors and different traditions here. We have many questions about our way of life.

Gabrielle, Ronald and I began the day with a time of prayer, a reading from the Gospel, a few songs and silence. We hope that Radha will feel free to join us. We are arranging a prayer room in the house. The Holy Spirit will have to show what he wants for that room. We truly want to respect the path of God for each one, and at the same time we want to be faithful to the true face of Jesus: Jesus poor, humble, gentle and discreet, Jesus who loves the poor and the little ones, Jesus who carries in his heart all the love of the Father.

This new project in India may seem like pure folly. Imagine beginning a home for mentally deficient people when we do not know the language, the traditions or anything! But perhaps God can act more fully in and through our ignorance and folly. If we do not remain anchored in Him, everything will fall apart. With Him and in Him, everything is possible. Alleluia!

You cannot imagine how fragile the community is in Bangalore. There is no prototype showing us how to live with handicapped people who are Hindu. How should we eat, sing and pray together? How do we create community with them? We just have to be poor enough and trust that we will be shown how to create this new kind of community.

Yesterday I met the doctor at the psychiatric hospital. We must start work with the contractors: renovate another seven bedrooms, the kitchen and the sanitary system. There is still a lot of work to be done! I am happy to be here, to be able to live poorly with the people here. Pray for us.

I remain deeply united in Jesus,
Jean Vanier

P.S. I want to share a poem with you that has touched me very much.

> On this solitary road of life
> as I plod along all alone
> I have often felt distressed and afflicted,
> distraught and exhausted,
> seeking my way.
>
> It is only the bright trace of your garment
> that urges me to walk in your footsteps.
> I do my best to follow you
> but, alas, my pace is so slow and trembling.
>
> Will you not show me compassion—
> you, the friend of the poor and the humble?
> Will you not stop for a moment
> and have mercy on this poor pilgrim—
> and help me at least to bow down at your sacred feet
> and adore you?
>
> —Swami Paramananda*

*This meant something to me at the time, but unfortunately I don't know where I found it!

October 22, 1970
Bangalore, India

Dear Friends,

A day of peace and grace with the arrival of Joseph and Gurunathan. Joseph is a twenty-three-year-old Down's syndrome boy with a round, smiling face—a wonderful mixture of Jean Claude and Jean-Michel. He seems delighted to come to a "happy home." He is Catholic. His mother, who is a widow, very protectively said, "He is incapable of receiving Communion because he has no head." He speaks a little English and makes himself understood through gestures and laughter. Gurunathan comes from a very orthodox Hindu family. He is twenty-five, speaks little and resembles Raphaël when he was younger. He has a wonderful smile. He neither speaks nor understands English, only Tamil. His father has died. His mother does everything for him, washes him and shaves him. His brother, an ex-captain of the army, is a man with good common sense. They say Gurunathan is very pious as he goes from temple to temple (he will be able to go to the temple next door to Asha Niketan).

After showing them their bedroom, Ron and I took them to the garden where we worked for an hour and a half clearing the land and digging. We have to prepare for tomorrow's vegetables. Joseph and Gurunathan are happy. Neither one had ever worked in his life but they both put all their energy into it with a lot of joy. They are truly happy to be here.

At 6 p.m. we played with the football that I bought this morning. Anthony joined us. He is the little seven-year-old son of Harisam, our gardener. Harisam is a poor, thin man without much strength. He must be about forty but he looks much older, suffering from malnutrition. He lives in one small room with his wife, son and daughter who will soon be leaving to get married. Anthony's eyes are full of life; his smile is happy and radiant. He does not go to school. He speaks Tamil. It is obvious that Gurunathan likes him. The gardener is making our two new arrivals feel very welcome.

After a little gardening we played with the football. Gurunathan is quite clever. He has good coordination and catches the ball quickly. Joseph throws the ball in an amazing way. Gurkha, the night watchman, joined us and was happy. We played until dinner. Gabrielle had prepared the meal. We sat cross-legged on the ground. Gurunathan and Joseph were much more at ease eating with their hands. I was really handicapped in that. While our two new arrivals were eating quite quickly, I was having trouble sitting there on the ground!

Then we went up to our prayer room. Gurunathan lit a candle and some incense. We sang the Our Father and the prayer of L'Arche, united with all of you. We gave thanks to Jesus for bringing us Gurunathan and Joseph. Both are excellent founders! Joseph sang hymns and songs alone. We could not quite understand the language. His mixture of English and Hindi words made the songs quite incomprehensible. He sings a bit like Jean Claude Lepottier. Then Ronald supervised their showers and put them to bed. It was very peaceful.

I feel happy with the poor beginnings of Asha Niketan. It is so like the beginnings of L'Arche where I did not know anything at all. I have that same feeling today. I have the feeling also that the Holy Spirit is leading and guiding us. Gabrielle was truly inspired by the Holy Spirit when she chose Gurunathan and Joseph. They are wonderful!

Tomorrow, a Jesuit priest is coming to say Mass at 6:15 a.m., so I am going to bed early. Joseph is still in the shower. I can hear Ronald trying to get him out. That makes me think of André in Trosly. Alleluia! In two days' time, Dilip will be coming to join us from Bombay. I am happy that Asha Niketan is beginning with him. He is the poorest of the poor, without any family, without anything. Nobody wants him; he is rejected everywhere he goes. If we were not there, he would be on the streets. Pray for him, that Jesus may welcome him and that he may find a home here. Alleluia!

Friday, October 23

We need to have a car for the shopping since Asha Niketan is a little outside the city. We are thinking of buying a car but they are expensive. This morning we found a used car, a Fiat, without any hand-brake or horn, for a thousand dollars, with seventy-six thousand kilometres!

This morning we had Mass with Father de Mello, SJ, a man of God I met last year in Bombay. Then we had breakfast all together. Ronald is taking care of the work this morning. This afternoon it will be my turn. Ron and Gabrielle will buy a record player and some records with the money that L'Arche gave me before I left. Our boys need music and singing.

Pray for us. Everything is working out well because the Holy Spirit is with us. We need a lot of trust and peace.

Here are a few texts from Mahatma Gandhi that have touched me:

"I must follow my path with God alone as my guide. He is a jealous God. No one is allowed to take away from His authority. We should present ourselves to Him with all our weakness, our empty hands and in the most perfect surrender. Then He will give us the strength to stand up firmly against the world and He will protect us from all evil."

"With all the disappointments and suffering I see each day, if I didn't sense the presence of God in me, I would become completely crazy."

"Unless we have truly died to ourselves, we will not be able to conquer the evil in us. In order to be worthy of the only freedom that is worthwhile, God asks us for total renunciation. And when, in this way, a man completely loses himself, he finds himself in a new way at the service of all that is alive. This new life becomes his joy and his rest. He has become a new man, never tiring in his work at the service of God and of His creation."*

Saturday, October 24

This is the second full day with Gurunathan and Joseph. Joseph makes me think of Jean-Michel at work. He needs work that is more precise than the garden. Guru, however, is really making progress (if what his brother told us is true), for he has a certain capacity for work in the garden as well as with the dishes. He seems to understand quite well what has to be done. This afternoon Guru and Joseph did the dishes by themselves.

Ron and Gabrielle went out to do the shopping. I dug in the garden with Joseph and Gurunathan as we collected the weeds. It was hot as there was a bright sun. I like manual work. Then we cleaned up the house and prepared the evening meal: vegetable soup, rice, carrots and cold beans from last night. I was tired after the morning (especially with that hot sun!). We had a siesta and around 4 p.m. Gabrielle and Ron came back with the record player and many other things. Yesterday I went with Guru, Terry and his friend Harondaz on foot to do the shopping in a small marketplace.

Tomorrow evening Dilip is coming from Bombay with a young fellow who is accompanying him. Pray for him. He is truly poor. I am happy that Asha Niketan is being founded with someone like him. It feels like the beginnings of L'Arche and like my time in Fatima with people who were very poor and simple. I recall going to the market, talking with people, looking at smiling faces who were so open and kind.

---

*Again, these texts meant much to me at the time, and still do today, but almost thirty years later I can't recall where I found them!

Every morning and every evening our little family gathers together to pray for about a half hour: readings, prayers, silence and much peace. Joseph sings "Ave, ave, ave Maria" and "Alleluia." Guru does not talk or sing but kisses the floor at the end. This evening we listened to the tape from La Merci. We feel very present and deeply united to everyone there. Do not hesitate to send tapes. It is good to hear your voices and your songs. Pray for me. Pray for us all. Jesus is good. He is watching over us.

Thursday, October 29

So many things have happened since the last time I wrote. Joseph and Guru are very much at home now. They are starting to do a number of things all alone. This is their home and their own families are happy they are here. Dilip came from Bombay on Sunday, with an assistant from the Cheshire Home who had kept him until now. He repeats word for word whatever we say to him. He works little. When we gave him a paint brush, he licked it! He has a very simple, open face and is quite lovable. He easily gives you his hand and does whatever you ask of him. When our doctor came on Tuesday he said it would be good for him to go for a while to a general hospital where there is a psychiatric ward. I took Dilip there in the afternoon. The doctor welcomed him and immediately prepared a shot of a hundred milligrams of largactil. When the nurse arrived with the needle, poor Dilip became very frightened and tried to bite her. The doctor tried to force him to stop. We had a wild Dilip on our hands. Yet he had been so peaceful at our place. A lot of spectators came to see what was happening. We tried to calm things down. I took him, without having the shot, into the psychiatric ward. There we were welcomed by six nurses who, one after the other, tried to give him the shot. I stayed with him a while but finally had to leave. I felt terrible.

It is true that Asha Niketan is not really the place for Dilip, at least not for now, and yet we can't simply put him back into the streets. But will it work in the hospital? I went back to the hospital two hours later; Dilip was sleeping. They had forced him to have the shot, perhaps for his own good. I went to see him again on Wednesday and he was peaceful under the influence of drugs. We will continue to visit him often with the hope that one day we will be able to welcome him back. I can understand why Dilip is like that. He is all alone in the world, rejected everywhere. Isn't it better to live in a world of hallucinations than to live in a world of pain and violence? Who can bring him back to reality? Is it not too late? At any rate, he needs a warm welcoming reality, a gentle and kind reality, a reality full of care.

Good news about the work! There is truly a hand guiding us in all things and watching over this poor foundation. Sunday morning we had a visit from the director of International Instruments Limited, who said he would give us work. On Monday we are going to visit the factory, a fifteen-minute walk from here. He promises to give us work for a thousand rupees per month. If that is true, then Asha Niketan will become self-sufficient in a month or two because our expenses are scarcely more than a thousand rupees per month. Three factory managers are coming to visit us on Tuesday. We will look at the plans for the new workshop all together. I am touched to meet people who want to co-operate with us in many different ways. The Holy Spirit is watching over us in an amazing way and giving us hope.

The garden is taking shape. Ronald and I have dug up a large area. It was hard in the hot sun, but it was good. Joseph, Guru and Harisam, the gardener, worked with us. Here many workers earn seventy-five rupees a month. In our house the cost of food per person each day is about two rupees. We don't eat much: some rice, a few vegetables, a banana and each day either an egg, a bit of meat or a piece of fish. What can a worker, with his wife and two children, eat with two rupees a day? A kilo of rice costs more than one rupee. It's not surprising they have so little strength. They are so courageous.

I have never felt so well. I can eat Indian food although sometimes it is a little hot! I sleep well on a wooden bed with a thin cotton mattress. I love the schedule of the day. We go to Mass at 6:15 a.m. Following Mass we have a half-hour prayer in the community with Joseph and Guru. There is breakfast, work, lunch at 12:30, siesta, work, dinner at 7:15, prayer and we are in our rooms by 9:00. The rhythm is quite slow, poor and close to nature. We eat with our hands as we sit on the floor. There is no television or radio, not even a newspaper, no books, just fresh air, healthy food, work, prayer, rest and a deep unity among us, and the shining faces of Joseph and Guru. There is also suffering as we carry the pain of Dilip and all the other Dilips throughout the world.

Yesterday I walked to the hospital, five kilometres away. I walked slowly, looking at all the men and women along the way with their dignified faces and their children laughing and playing. India has 550 million people, eleven times the population of France. So many believe in God, pray and live in abandonment. They are not permeated with materialism. There is suffering in them but there is such depth. I love to walk through the streets in these poor areas, praying for those who are living in such poverty. It makes me think also of what we in the West have done with the Gospel.

I feel more and more taken by India and by Gandhi, one of the only men who has tried to find a spiritual solution of peace, love, prayer and simple work for a whole country. I have been rereading what he wrote on prayer, on the love of God and on humility. I would especially like to live it! I sense all that is happening within me. I feel impatient. How urgent it is for men of peace to rise up in our world. The spectrum of violence is so present. We must react quickly with the folly of works of peace that completely surpass our own capacities, without fear of the violence that can strike us and our world. We are called to oppose violence with nonviolent action, based on trust in the Holy Spirit. Although I sense within me a divine impatience, I also know that I must become poorer and trust more fully our Father in heaven in order to do things that are even more foolish. I have the feeling that we must move quickly to live the Gospel more fully, everywhere, without criticizing anyone, without judging, but living more poorly, accepting misunderstandings and violence and loving those who criticize us. We need to live each moment in the hands of God, trying to create unity through our nonaggressiveness, drawing others into this life of poverty as we create communities which will be a link between the rich and the poor.

Jean

November 2, 1970
Bangalore, India

Dear Friends,

Life in Asha Niketan carries on. The days are peaceful. I feel so at home here, so close to people. Gabrielle has things in hand. The Holy Spirit is inspiring her and Ronald is radiant. It is a real grace having him here! Joseph and Gurunathan are happy and radiant. Gurunathan has put an image of his god in the prayer room (his brother said that they are all images of the same God). I love the way Guru kisses the earth in adoration.

We are waiting for work from the factory. For the moment we have work in the house and in the garden. We planted tomatoes and soon we will plant cabbage, spinach and banana trees. Today I made the meal: beets, rice, tomatoes, onions and an orange. Alas, I cooked the rice too much! It is still in my stomach like a lead weight.

Yesterday it rained heavily. Water was coming into the house. We had to change Guru and Joseph's bedroom; their beds were soaked. I could not help but think of the thousands of poor people living in the little huts made of wood and banana leaves who must have been soaked too. The problems with the bathrooms in Le Val are nothing compared to the rain that was coming through our roof—Alleluia! But here where everything is so poor, it is normal. Harisam, our gardener, and his family took refuge on our veranda. Think of all those poor people who have no verandas! My bedroom was dry!

A few evenings ago I walked through the streets looking at all the poor and simple people, their shelters, their restaurants, everything so simple and poor I couldn't help thinking of all the wealth in our countries. I was moved by the eyes of the children. I was the only westerner but I was happy to be there. Mothers, women in general, are so dignified here with their colourful saris. Jesus and his Holy Spirit must love these people so much; they are a poor people. As I walk by, I smile at each person. There is no hatred in their eyes as they easily smile back, especially the children. The last time I came to India I just passed through; on this visit I have time to live here, to be more integrated into their way of life. That is such a grace! I feel such a change in myself, a desire to become much poorer and less aggressive, more gentle, nonviolent and more welcoming. You must pray for me that I will be faithful. Sometimes I feel a great force in me, a desire to speak about the Gospel. Other moments I feel so very poor. I must become more confident in the Spirit. There is so much to do, so many poor people! But the Holy Spirit is there. We must pray hard and ask him to call forth many, many workers throughout the world who will come to befriend the poor and the weak.

I am anxious to get back to Trosly! I leave Bangalore on November 11. I would also like to stay here! I would like to go to Africa and to Cairo, but above all, I want to remain peaceful, living fully each present moment, humbly offering to Jesus my poor hands, head, heart and words.

Deeply united,
Jean

February 19, 1971
Ottawa, Canada

Dear Friends,

I am in Ottawa for a weekend retreat with 125 students plus some former retreatants. There is a strong bond among us all as there are so many friends with whom I have been united for a long time. The Little Sisters of Foucauld are a peaceful, prayerful presence here. Today I gave three talks and tonight there will be a time for questions and answers, followed by midnight Mass and all-night adoration. Tomorrow there will be two talks in the morning. I have a feeling of hope when I am with these young students from seven Quebec and Ontario universities. I sense their thirst for authenticity, for the Holy Spirit and for Jesus of the Beatitudes.

Yesterday morning I arrived in New York after two nights on the bus from Montreal. I spent the night at Village Haven, a house of rehabilitation for girls who have been on hard drugs. New York always overwhelms me—it is so big and dirty, and in the poor neighbourhoods the faces of people are so sad. I went to see Dorothy Day, a woman of peace, dressed very poorly and living in a disadvantaged section of the city surrounded by poor people. She is such a woman of peace. I was happy to see her and Brother Joe, a Little Brother of the Gospel, with his sparkling eyes and radiant smile. He told me that in this section of the city there had been ten murders in the last month. In New York last year there were thirteen hundred murders! Many people are trying to get money to buy drugs.

February 22

I am in a plane somewhere between Montreal and Toronto. I think that it is the twenty-second of February but I have lost all notion of time and space! I keep moving, arriving and leaving. I meet marvellous people and the circle begins again. Last evening I spoke to a group of a hundred men in the prison of Montreal. It is a very harsh prison, with old-style cells. The men are very frustrated—this is the first talk they have had! I spoke for forty-five minutes, then there were questions for another forty-five minutes. The dialogue was funny at times, tragic at other times. These men are so truthful; it was a blessed time. My experiences in the two prisons have touched me deeply. Each time I go to Montreal or to Kingston I hope to visit them again, for no one else seems to visit them. And Jesus said, "I was in prison and you visited me."

The retreat in Ottawa was very good. The Little Sisters of Foucauld were there, a praying presence. We are preparing four retreats for next summer—two in French in Montreal and Quebec City, and two in English in Edmonton and Chicago. I hope that some people from Trosly will come to Canada this summer to see for themselves what the Spirit is doing here.

At the end of the retreat I visited Madonna House, a community of some forty-five permanent members, twelve priests and thirty visitors and trainees (they have houses in Peru, in the West Indies, etc.). It is a very young, lively Christian community. Their prayer and liturgy are very beautiful and alive in the Spirit. They all live off the land and their sixty cows. I was happy to be there but unfortunately my visit was very short. I spoke in the evening and after my talk the group burst out in song. I feel a strong union with everyone here. Catherine Doherty, a woman of seventy-two years, founded Madonna House.

I am told that in the United States there are ten thousand "communes" of young people living together. Not all are under the sign of the Gospel, but many are inspired by the Gospel. A new world is being prepared by these young people.

Dorothy Day, a woman carrying the suffering of the world, impressed me very much. I think also of Little Sister Magdeleine, Mother Teresa, Catherine Doherty, Marthe Robin and Little Sister Monique, all tremendous witnesses of Jesus.

Daybreak is well, searching for its own identity. Steve is well. God is watching over that little community. The boys are so open and marvellous. They have Mass all together every two days. There is much peace and a very deep desire to live in love. It is good to see these communities trying to live their vocations. I hope that others from Trosly will come to see what is happening here. There are many friends here who love us and pray for us.

This trip has changed me but I do not know in what way. Perhaps there is a greater openness in me and a desire to be nearer those who suffer at Trosly. I sense a new freedom as fears disappear. I am anxious to get back to be with everyone and to carry the burden of each day. I believe that I have never had such a full schedule. In the evening I am quite tired, so it is impossible to write much. Early in the morning I pray and there is much peace. I feel so united to each one and have the feeling that we are only at the beginning, of what I do not know, but of many things.

Your poor brother in Jesus,
Jean

November 18, 1971
Bangalore, India

Dear Friends,

Zizi and I arrived in New Delhi Sunday evening.* We had some difficulty with our tickets for Bangalore, but with time and patience everything worked out. I had to relearn patience, learn how to wait again, not to be in too much of a hurry and just be open to each event. In the West we are so conditioned by efficiency and good organization that we forget patience and availability. We slept in the airport that night; the benches were comfortable and we were tired. I was happy to sleep at the airport where there are so many other people waiting for their planes. The place was filled with men and women from northern India, men with their long beards, beautiful turbans, peaceful and wise faces.

The plane arrived in Bangalore at 7:20 a.m. Ron, Gabrielle and Guru were at the airport with Mr. Sawhney, our board president. What a joy to see everyone again. The renovations at Asha Niketan are wonderful: a long veranda with eight or nine bedrooms. About a hundred banana trees have been planted. The garden has been cultivated and the buffalo are happy (one of them is expecting a little one in January and the other gives us four litres of milk daily). Guru introduced me to each new person: Saroja, with her little son Karnaga; Srinivasan, a little rascal who dances and plays and is terribly unstable; Krishna, the gardener; Narashingha, who has been deeply wounded in his life, no family and five years in a psychiatric hospital; Mohanraj, who in many ways is the least handicapped and can assume certain responsibilities; Cham, who works in a school not too far away; Somasundra, forty-two years old (they say he is a real tyrant at home but wonderful here); John, a

---

*Zizi is Elizabeth Pascal, wife of the current L'Arche international coordinator, Jean-Christophe Pascal.

very inhibited forty-five-year-old man; and Srinderan. Ron is very present and gentle with each one. You would think Judy had been here for years. The community is very united and quite strong, but at the same time, like all our communities, it is fragile. The boys, especially Srinivasan, have their crises, and that is normal because they have suffered so much.

The year has been difficult. There has been pain in the community, especially the pain of the death of Kannan.* However, through all the suffering, the Spirit is at work. Jesus has truly been watching over this little community. The morning and evening prayers are very special moments, a time when the whole community puts itself before the Father and for about twenty minutes the boys sing in Tamil with Krishna and Saroja. They also know certain songs that we sing in Trosly (without understanding the meaning of the words). I love these times of prayer, just as much as the mealtimes where everything is so poor, simple and joyful. We have a per diem of about one rupee, eighty paisa. There is rice, vegetables, fruit, porridge, sometimes fish but never any meat. Yes, I love the poverty and simplicity here. We hope that in the future the community will become financially autonomous. Right now, the results of our factory work and the fruits of our garden work are not great but

---

*Kannan's death was particularly moving and terrible. We had just started Asha Niketan in Bangalore and one day Kannan went missing. The community searched and searched for him, but couldn't find him. Then Ron Pickersgill found Kannan's towel beside the community well, dived into the well and brought up the young man's body. Gabrielle contacted Kannan's father straightaway and afterwards put a huge net over the well. What was amazing was the father's reaction: he said that when a work—meaning the Asha Niketan community—was of God, a just man—his son—will die. His father recognized that Kannan was a just man and simply accepted the reality of his son's death. The father believed his son's death gave life. But for the assistants, mostly Canadians and Germans, his death came as a big shock: there weren't many core members at that time, yet one had died due to lack of supervision. It was a terrible beginning to the community, but we all learned and grew from it.

hopefully these will increase. Ron is going to teach relaxation and breathing exercises to the boys every day. Yesterday we had the first lesson. Everyone seemed happy. I'm going to try to do a little each day with the boys. (I'm not sure I will continue when I'm back in France!) Another special moment is our recreation: songs, dances and games from 6:00 to 7:30 in the evening.

Guru has progressed a lot over the year. He is at the heart of Asha Niketan, so attentive to each one, not very efficient as far as work goes, but very reliable in welcoming people. There is much to say about Asha Niketan, and yet in some ways there is nothing to say except to give thanks to Jesus for the way he watched over the birth of this new community. It is alive and radiant and progressing. It is like a sign of the love of Jesus for each one, especially for the poorest, a sign of how present his love is for those who have been deeply wounded by society. Yes, I have a deep feeling that the Father is present, protecting us, helping us, making up for our awkwardness and inspiring us in our desire to share our lives with those who are wounded. I have a deep sense that the Holy Spirit wants L'Arche and so makes everything possible as long as we give our hands, our heads, our hearts and especially our confidence to God to serve as instruments. Gabrielle and Ronald are poor but at the same time very open to the Spirit. They have truly been instruments of God.

The day before yesterday, a huge rat, about twenty centimetres long, ate Judy's sandals! Yesterday, a big, long cobra came to the window. Ron tried to take a picture of it. What a strange animal the cobra is! Judy said that she felt mysteriously hypnotized and attracted by it, and yet she felt repulsion and fear. I did not see it. I thought I would tell you we do have a few exciting events here! People in India say that cobras are present to protect a place and not to attack it. But you must not attack them unless you are sure you can kill them because they can take revenge. They recognize an aggressor. Perhaps we need a snake charmer!

Last night we had a meeting of the board of directors. There will be two more before I leave and also the official opening with the state governor. I am happy to be here to serve Asha Niketan, Gabrielle, Ron and Judy. Pray that I may be poor enough to be an instrument of the Spirit of God. I remain close to each one of you, sensing that I am here for all of you.

Jean

November 22, 1971
Kotagiri, India

Dear Friends,

Right now I am in the new Asha Niketan in Kotagiri, in the mountains, two thousand metres above sea level. It is colder here than in Bangalore. When the sun is hidden one needs a sweater. I left Bangalore at 6 p.m. to come here. The train was crowded though I had a reserved seat with a wooden bench for the night. When I arrived in Coimbatore the next morning, my body was stiff. I am not used to sleeping on hard wood! But I was happy during those twelve hours of the trip, praying, reading Tagore (a Bengali poet), feeling close to many people, very peaceful and free. I am truly happy to be here; I have no particular fears nor desires, only an openness to accepting each event with gentleness.

At 5:20 a.m. I arrived, and took the rickshaw to the bus station where I had an orange drink. Then I took a three-and-a-half-hour bus ride into the mountains. At one moment the driver stopped, got out of the bus and prayed in a temple, leaving half of a coconut as an offering. Tom met me at the bus stop. Tom and Mira have a good, solid stone house which they are renovating. I met Samuel, an eighteen-year-old man who is epileptic and handicapped. He does not talk very much but has a beautiful smile. He has suffered a lot as he has always been considered an "idiot," but he can do many things. The next day Martin arrived with his parents. He is much more handicapped; he had convulsions when he was a child. He is also eighteen, very peaceful and quiet. I think Samuel and Martin could be very happy in this new community with Tom and Mira. Daisy, also eighteen, comes from an orphanage not too far away and works with Mira in the kitchen.

Martin just came for a day. His parents stayed and slept in our house. They all left the next day, quite happy. Martin will come back next Sunday. It will be difficult for him as his parents love him very much and have surely spoiled him. It will be the first time that he has left his parents. Samuel, who is more resourceful, comes from Kotagiri. He will start as a day-worker and later come to live in the community. He is quite rejected by his family. Both Samuel and Martin belong to the Church of South India. I think that Asha Niketan–Kotagiri will be a very peaceful, contemplative home. Kotagiri is a quiet mountain town where there are many convents and missionaries. Our house is located on the outskirts of the town, which is silent both day and night. Mira and Tom plan on welcoming eight boys by September 1972. We worked on the per diem together. There will be a small workshop, some gardens and a chicken coop. The property consists of a few acres of land, but on a slant. I don't know if they will be able to do much with the land since only a small portion could be cultivated. We could build a small house with five or six rooms where assistants and others could come to rest and pray. I pray that this new home will gradually become a place of prayer, a little community of peace.*

Jean

---

*Asha Niketan–Kotagiri had to close one year later, when Mira and Tom returned to the United States.

November 28, 1971
Bangalore, India

Dear Friends,

   There is much peace in our little Asha Niketan. I can hear the boys outside. In an hour all the parents are coming for tea. This evening, I leave for Madras (I will spend the night at Father Ceyrac's house). Then tomorrow I fly to Calcutta where I will probably visit the refugee camps. Friends from Caritas–India called me and invited me to go there. I will see Mother Teresa and Brother Andrew.* I hope to be able to go up to the border of East Pakistan. I sense deeply that the Holy Spirit is asking me to make this trip. I was touched to see how everything worked out so quickly. There is a deep peace in me and a thirst to know the plight of these ten million refugees. It is one of the greatest horrors and catastrophes in the history of humanity. The news coming from East Pakistan is tragic. A liberation army is being organized and terror reigns. The Indian army is ready to attack. We are on the fringe of war, a war that with the participation of the world powers will certainly produce dire consequences.**

   I felt I had to go to Calcutta for all of us, to take into my own flesh a little of that suffering and perhaps also to arrange sending

---

*Brother Andrew co-founded, with Mother Teresa, the Missionaries of Charity Brothers.

**These were the beginnings of the Bangladesh Liberation War. After the Pakistan elections of 1970, when an independence movement in East Pakistan swept to a majority in the Pakistan parliament but was not allowed to govern, huge civil unrest erupted and an estimated ten million refugees fled into India. In March 1971, Indira Gandhi expressed India's support for East Pakistan and then secured the USSR's support. The United States backed West Pakistan in opposing independence. War broke out between India and Pakistan five days after I wrote this letter, and no one knew at the time whether the United States and USSR would enter with nuclear weapons. In the end, the war lasted two weeks and resulted in the creation of an independent Bangladesh.

them some Canadian doctors and nurses. I will be in Calcutta only for about thirty-six hours, unless something unexpected happens. I really depend a great deal on the prayers of each one of you.

Jean

November 29, 1971
On the plane between Madras and Calcutta, India

Dear Friends,

In Madras I was met by "Uncle Pierre" (Father Ceyrac).* It was good to see him again. I slept at his house and attended his Mass in the morning. I feel close to him. We visited a school for children who are blind, deaf and dumb. We also visited the Home for the Dying with Mother Teresa's sisters. I am always very impressed by these houses of Mother Teresa, with the shining faces of the sisters, the suffering faces of the sick, the old and the dying. There were two young adolescents with cerebral palsy. The house is so poor and dilapidated with not even a radio! But one feels such warmth, such peace, a presence.

I am now on the plane to Calcutta. We are flying over the Bay of Bengal. To the left is the coast of Orissa where there was a tidal wave a month ago: more than twenty-five thousand people died during the night and five million others were affected. Mysteriously we are all brothers and sisters. In a half-hour we will land. I feel so poor coming to this city of poverty to visit the refugee camps,

* "Uncle Pierre" refers to Father Pierre Ceyrac, a Jesuit priest who has been in India since 1936. He is Odile's uncle. Odile became committed to L'Arche in March 1969. She succeeded me as director of L'Arche Trosly in 1980 and later became the coordinator of L'Arche communities in Europe and the Middle East. As such, she was a member of the international council.

the slums, Mother Teresa and Brother Andrew. The war is closer there, only sixty-five kilometres from the border. I see in the newspapers that tomorrow there will be a blackout in the city. I feel very moved as I come close to Calcutta, which at this moment is the centre of suffering in the world with its ten million refugees and its vast slums. It is like a huge wound in humanity as a result of terror, injustice and inequalities. It is a place of death, but at the same time a place of life, true life, which rises up from death, for Jesus has transformed death through his death; he transformed death into life. I am anxious to arrive. I am a bit frightened to see all that misery and yet at the same time I feel mysteriously attracted to it. I feel held and carried by all of you and I carry all of you in my heart.

Jean

December 3, 1971
On the plane between Madras and Bangalore, India

Dear Friends,

My two days in Calcutta were very full! I arrived Monday at 4:30 p.m., took the bus for the city and then had to walk about one hour (the taxis were on strike) to Caritas–India. There were huge crowds in the streets. I have never seen such crowds—like an enormous anthill. The city seemed so heavy and oppressive and I did too! It was not terribly hot but there was a heaviness. There were so many poor people in the streets, sleeping on the ground. It was dark and a mist blanketed everything. The trains and buses were overcrowded. Children ran after me, asking for money or wanting to shine my shoes (sometimes they are beaten if they do not bring home enough money). A young girl, draped in a blanket, with big eyes and a beautiful pure face sat on the ground, begging. It was a long walk through those streets. I was tired and very moved.

I arrived at the Caritas–India office, but in spite of a phone call, a letter and a telegram, they were not expecting me. They told me that Mother Teresa was back. I called her and immediately went to her place. I was happy to see her again. I stayed and ate at their mother house and novitiate with a few sisters and some two hundred novices. After evening prayer, Mother Teresa asked me to speak to them. I was happy to talk about Jesus with all these women who are serving the poor in Calcutta. I stayed afterwards to pray in their chapel—a big empty room with an altar at the end of it. You could hear the trains passing by along with all the other noises of the city.

The next day I went to Mass and had breakfast with Mother Teresa. Then I left for Dum Dum, a forty-five-minute ride by jeep. There we found a large plot of land where the sisters have built a hospital for some of the refugee children—from six months to five years old, all suffering terribly from malnutrition. Their legs were like skeletons, their faces like old people, their eyes sad. Some never smiled at all. One four-year-old boy really struck me with his big, sad eyes. His mother had died of cholera and his blind father had left to try to find his ten-year-old son in another camp. I was told that this little boy sensed when his father needed him to take him to the toilet. He is waiting for his father to come back.

There were about sixty beds for elderly refugee women who had left the camps and for men who had come from the Home for the Dying. The women were sick and sad and spoke of all they had lost and of their misery. The Sisters of Mother Teresa have such serene, smiling faces; one senses strength in them. Amongst the men, I met two mentally handicapped brothers, about thirty-seven years old. Their ninety-year-old mother was dying and the brothers have no other family. They speak English as their father was an English soldier. The Sister asked me if we could take them into one of our houses. They seemed so kind and gentle. It's sad to see them with nothing to do, just sitting on their beds all day long.

Maybe Tom and Mira could welcome them.* There was another man with only one foot, sitting next to a blind man who was praying. The man without a foot had a beard and shining eyes. He said to me, "I cannot walk nor see but we are both children of God." I greeted each one with "Namaste,"** trying to show by the way I looked at each one that I loved them. It is difficult to pass by each one without really remaining there with them. Their faces are so beautiful, no revolt, just a certain surrender and peace.

Afterwards, I visited the community clinic for the area; the doctor was a refugee. They also gave out food to children. Then I went with Mother Agnes to visit the refugee camp about five kilometres from the city. It is a huge camp with some 200,000 people! You can imagine the crowds and the difficulty in distributing food and organizing a water and sanitary system. The Indian government has done a remarkable amount of organization but the suffering is tremendous! I saw a children's hospital run by a young English doctor, assisted by a few medical students, refugees from Dacca. Five hundred children die each month. Many arrive in a pitiful state from Bangladesh! The old as well as the young are dying. There is not much cholera in this camp. They are beginning to organize schools with teachers who are refugees. A maternity ward and hospital function well. Everything, however, is very rudimentary. The framework of the small buildings is bamboo; the walls and mats are made from straw. When the rains come, everything falls apart. As far as food goes, there is just the bare minimum. The cold weather is coming. Voluntary organizations bring in clothing, blankets, etc. Some of the small bamboo huts

---

*They were welcomed in Asha Niketan–Kotagiri. Later, when this community closed, they went to live in Asha Niketan–Bangalore.

**This common greeting among Hindus in India has a spiritual connection. Literally, the word means "I bow to you," and it recognizes God within the person you are greeting.

and the straw mats used as walls are drenched in the stagnant waters. Disposal of water is a big problem.

There is a tremendous flow of beggars who have nothing else to do but wait for their rations. Each one has to do his or her own cooking. Each one or each family is given four kilograms of wood for the week, just enough to boil four litres of water. They try to get a little extra. Some are beginning to work but there is no way of paying them, so they have no mostivation unless they are doctors, nurses or teachers. In the whole camp I only saw two other foreigners, an English doctor and a French doctor (a nun). There is a whole mass of people with nothing to do but beg. Soon there will be discord and disputes; in some camps this has already happened. People are lost. They hope, of course, to be able to go back home, but when? How long will they have to stay here? This is just a small camp with 200,000 people. There are 9.8 million people in other camps or on the road. People estimate that there are some 3 million refugees outside the camps. Soon there may be trouble with the local population. Calcutta is already a city of beggars and these refugees receive food freely; it is not given to people in the slum areas of the city. There are only Hindus in these camps, no Muslims or Christians.

I left the camp tired and deeply moved. I had seen so many suffering faces: an old man who had just died, hundreds of undernourished children in a pitiful state and several in the hospital in misery. At the same time I feel a certain peace. I did not see any revolt or hatred. There is such an extraordinary force and capacity in Hindus to accept situations, to remain peaceful and do the best they can. The last thing I saw as I left the camp and went back to Calcutta was long lines of refugees coming into and going out of the city on foot. Those who were leaving carried pieces of wood on their heads. They had found these in the city and would use them for heating. Hundreds went looking for more wood because the nights were getting colder. You can imagine the fights that could arise with the poor people in Calcutta who are already in such need of wood themselves!

There is a lot to say about the political situation, about Bangladesh, about the risk of war and the role of India and of Pakistan. There are these millions of people suffering, trying to survive, with nothing to do; how long will this last? Yet, we, in our countries, continue to live in luxury while there are so many poor people here living in utter poverty. What to do? It is not a question of sending volunteers. India does not want foreigners in the camps. It is better for the refugees that they organize things themselves and work together. Send money? Yes, perhaps, because India is really draining its economy to keep these refugees alive. Each refugee costs two francs a day; that means about 360 million francs per month, and for how long? There are still more refugees arriving every day! Yes, these refugees are like a huge wound in the heart of humanity.

After a quick lunch at Mother Teresa's I went with her to the children's home, not far from the convent: 190 children and many tiny, premature babies. They had all been abandoned, left in the streets or elsewhere. Then, with Mother Teresa, I visited the Home for the Dying where there are fifty men and ninety women in two big rooms. I was moved by this experience. There is such peace in and through all the pain, sickness and suffering. On the way out I met an old woman. Her rags barely hung on her body. Mother and I helped her into the house and Mother Teresa asked the sisters to bathe her and give her a bed. It is wonderful to see how anyone and everyone is accepted in this house, as long as they are sick or dying or in need. Often the sisters can do very little, but they are kind and attentive to each one (there are only three or four sisters for 140 dying people). They have some help from volunteer workers. They welcome people with love and with a smile. The poor are so much better off here than in the street; they die in a place of peace, surrounded by love and care.

The Home for the Dying is very poor and primitive, without any of the usual facilities for such a home, but it is in keeping with the city of Calcutta and with the poverty of India. The sisters are there, smiling and seemingly untiring. Since the opening of this house twenty-four thousand people have been welcomed and twelve thousand have died. That means that twelve thousand others have gone back into the street to beg again.

Mother Teresa took me to visit the Bishop of Calcutta. After fifteen minutes with him, Brother Andrew, who is superior of the Missionaries of Charity Brothers, came to pick me up. He is an Australian priest, dressed very poorly. I stayed with him until my departure time. I like him a lot. He feels so poor in front of the responsibility he carries (ninety brothers working in different houses). He is courageous and I have the feeling that in the future we are going to work a lot with him. He took me to a small centre which he and a psychiatrist have opened. There are twelve mentally retarded and mentally ill men in a small house on the outskirts of Calcutta. Three of the brothers work there and one is a little like Ronald. We had a meeting together for more than an hour. There is such a mixture of people welcomed there: some young mentally deficient boys and some mentally sick boys with violent tendencies. The neighbours are very worried. The brothers have little experience in this domain but are very courageous.

We went back to the brothers', had a quick meal and a piece of cake (it was Brother Andrew's birthday), and then we visited another home of the brothers where they take in children, orphans and mentally or physically handicapped people who are living in the street. There are about fifteen of them in one bedroom. The brothers all sleep in the next room, which is normally the dining room. I was very touched by their material poverty as well as by their poverty of heart. I still have much to learn about how to live poorly.

Afterwards, I went on a motorbike with Brother Andrew to visit the Sealdah Train Station in Calcutta. It took us fifteen minutes to get there; the bike broke down but we were able to repair it. At the station there were masses of people sleeping on the ground: entire families, children, old people wrapped up in blankets with a few pieces of paper for a bed. There was also a crowd of young people who had been abandoned and who had learned early in life to beg. They were everywhere, sleeping on the ground, or in a corner, or on the ticket counter. Two of the brothers work in the station, getting to know these young children, helping them and giving them necessary care. I slept that night at Brother Andrew's. The next morning at 5:45 Brother Andrew said Mass and we had breakfast together before he drove me to Mother Teresa's. Then I caught my plane for Madras and Bangalore.

During these last forty hours I have seen so much. It is as if I am a bit intoxicated from fatigue (I have not slept much) but also from the emotion of seeing all those faces in Calcutta. Brother Andrew told me that he has been there for six years. He said, "Once you know Calcutta, you can never leave it!" Strange effect this enormous mass of poor people has on you—a city of death and life. Brother Andrew said it is the triumph of life over death. The huge crowds of poor people are so alive, smiling, laughing, sleeping, crying—a city where there is tremendous love between people and where the poor share so beautifully with each other.

As I leave, I feel as if I lived a dream, but a very real dream! I have been touched by Mother Teresa, by Brother Andrew, by the refugee camps and by the mystery of Calcutta. Is it possible that Jesus will come back in Calcutta, rising up from the "tomb of Calcutta"? I thank the Holy Spirit for allowing me to live those forty hours there and I sense that I will go back. Maybe we could organize some helpers for Mother Teresa and Brother Andrew? But one would need a certain amount of planning to arrange for lodging, food, etc.

There is just so much to do there, so many wounds to care for, so much purity and so much poverty—another world!

Tomorrow is the official opening of Asha Niketan in Bangalore. The governor of the state of Mysore is coming. Many invitations have been sent out. But war may break out today. They say that nine military airports have been bombed by the Pakistanis. Many in India say that war is inevitable and that they are already in a state of war with ten million refugees. But war would be a catastrophe! What would be the consequences—another world war? I pray that the Holy Spirit will inspire people so that war can be avoided and a solution can be found for the refugees. I pray especially for a real revolution of the heart to begin, where we will learn to share and to love.

Jean

January 22, 1972
Trosly-Breuil

Dear Friends,

Now that our communities are becoming numerous, I am thinking of sending this type of letter to each community every few weeks. I no longer have much time to write at length to each one to give you general news. At the same time, I really feel it is important that we keep in touch with one another, giving each other news of our communities.

There is still nothing definite about the house at Canterbury, but I really feel that within a short time everything will be arranged. Geoffrey and Ann are working in a hospital for the mentally handicapped, just waiting to move into the new L'Arche. Thérèse has to give three months' notice before leaving her position; she too is ready.* I feel very much that the home in England will be born in prayer and will begin very much in the spirit of the Gospels.

I discover more and more that it takes months, even years to build a community. It is not done overnight but takes time and suffering before we can enter into the security and peace of real community, where there is deep trust and union. This suffering comes from the fact that we must learn to die to our own particular ways (formed by our individualistic style of life and education) if we are to enter into this unique community consciousness where we are "one," thinking in the same way, desiring the same things. The sufferings of a community are the sign that the Spirit is deepening and calling. They are also a small participation in the sufferings of the world, which create division and segregation precisely because of the lack of community. They are also a participation in the sufferings of the handicapped, with whom we must in some ways be identified.

In the various homes in Trosly there is much peace. We just finished our weekend of reflection with all the assistants, where we dealt with various problems of work and organization. In many ways it was the best we have ever had. There were some seventy assistants at the meetings. The discussion led by Maurice and Mary on "satellite villages" and the structure of houses in towns around Trosly was particularly interesting. Everyone seemed to appreciate the afternoon session around work. In a week's time we will elect three people to the Community Council. I feel that the system of government we have adopted has been quite satisfactory. It is precisely because we have this council, which means a real

---

*My sister, Thérèse, had studied medicine at Cambridge. She was working as a clinical hematologist at St. Thomas's Hospital in London when she began the task of setting up the first L'Arche community in England. It opened in 1973, near the city of Canterbury. She later coordinated communities of L'Arche that she had helped to create in the United Kingdom and Ireland. She did all this while also working as a palliative care doctor at St. Christopher's Hospice in London.

sharing of power, that I feel free to leave Trosly and go to Canada, India, etc. It takes time to discuss small points, but I feel that the three hours every Tuesday morning for the council meeting are beneficial and permit us to make wiser decisions than if I had to make them alone.

This year we will be making four different pilgrimages: Lourdes, La Salette, Fatima and Poland. For a long time we have wanted to go to Poland. Josiane went there in November and prepared for a group to be at the national pilgrimage of Our Lady of Czestochowa.

I am happy to be leaving soon for Canada to be with Steve and Ann. Pray for that.

Jean

February 1972
Kingston

Dear Friends,

As soon as I arrived in Montreal, I went to the Little Sisters of Jesus. At 7:30 p.m. I went to the Bordeaux prison, where I had my first meeting with a group of twenty-five men. Then I gave a talk to one hundred prisoners. I spoke to them about L'Arche, India and rejection. I was touched by the many questions that poured out from the pain and anguish in their hearts.

The next morning I was driven by car to the prison in Kingston where I gave a talk. All work was cancelled that day so that the men would be free to come to my talk. We had about two hours together. I was touched once again by their pain and also by our society's hypocrisy towards prisoners. We are often harsh and quick to reject them. At the same time I am struck by the infinite beauty and capacity for love that is hidden in the heart of each human being.

From there I went to a women's prison, where I spoke about the relationship between a child and its mother and in particular about the many children I had seen in the streets of India. After the talk I met each one individually and was happy to be with them. The majority were in prison for drugs and were serving long-term sentences.

That evening I went to the house where a chaplain and a couple with five children live and welcome people coming out of prison. We had a Mass at 9:30 p.m. with many people and we experienced a deep sense of the presence of Jesus.

On the following day I had a radio interview and then a talk with six hundred students, all future teachers. I spoke about rejection and read some of the poems of Tagore. I then left quickly for the Collins Bay prison. As I had been to that prison last year, some of the men already knew me. They were very warm, kind and welcoming. Before the talk I met with a group of twenty men. They told me that my books were circulating from cell to cell. The atmosphere was very relaxed. There again the authorities had stopped work for the day so that all those who wanted could come to my talk. Once again I was touched by the way the men listened so attentively as I spoke about love and tenderness, about the little child in each one of us who thirsts to love and be loved. I spoke also about how violence and hardness can often be a way of hiding and protecting that little child. Many of the men had already made a retreat and were part of a prayer group. A few came up and asked for my address so they could write to me. It is a real grace for me to be able to meet and share with them. I think of Jesus who was condemned to death, and how the first person he welcomed into the Kingdom was the "good thief."

On Thursday I visited the hospital in Smiths Falls, where there are two thousand children and adults with a mental handicap. It was a joy to speak to the personnel, the parents and the handicapped adults. I visited with some of the handicapped people in their dormitories. Some of the faces of the boys and girls were so pure and radiant. It was difficult to see all those people locked up in that institution, even though there was a good spirit in the hospital and staff were trying to do all they could.

On Sunday evening I left for Ottawa in a snowstorm. A three-day retreat began that evening for about one hundred retreatants: young people, married couples, priests and religious who had made some of my previous retreats. They came from Quebec, Montreal, Ottawa, Sudbury, Toronto, Edmonton, Chicago and Cleveland. I knew most of them quite well. Those three days were very full with two talks a day and times of personal prayer and sharing. The Bishop of Edmundston* was there and said the final Mass. There was a deep unity among us. It is good to recognize and love brothers and sisters in Jesus.

I am on my way to Chicago for a mini-retreat and a visit to one of the biggest prisons in Illinois. I am sorry I have not written more, but time is limited. I feel close to each of you. Thank you for carrying the weight of each day. Pray for me. I am trying to live each present moment without looking at the future. There are many people to see, many wonderful things to contemplate in the hearts of each one.

Jean

*Fernand Lacroix was the bishop of Edmundston, New Brunswick, for twenty-three years and was very close to Faith and Sharing for much of that time. He died in 1994.

February 11, 1972
On the Toronto–Montreal plane

Dear Friends,

This morning I left Cleveland at 7:00 a.m. and arrived at the Toronto airport, where I met a few people while I was waiting for the plane to Montreal. I met Leonore de Costa, an Indian living in Canada who feels called to Asha Niketan. I am very happy that the Holy Spirit is preparing some Indian women to be at Asha Niketan.

My thirty-six hours in Cleveland have been quite moving. I went there especially to prepare the August retreat, which will take place in the black ghetto. I feel that Jesus calls me more and more into the poorest neighbourhoods to announce his Good News. When I first arrived in Cleveland, I felt so poor and a bit insecure. I knew that I would be spending my whole time with the poor but I was not sure how I would talk to them. At the same time, I had confidence that Jesus would show me what he wanted me to say.

I met Rev. Wright and his wife. He is a Pentecostal minister and he and his wife have worked in the Hough area for many years. Hough is one of the most disadvantaged black neighbourhoods of Cleveland: twenty-five thousand inhabitants, much crime, unimaginable poverty, broken-down houses, drugs, delinquency and many handicapped children. Rev. Wright and Willie, his wife, are very prayerful people and I was touched by their welcome, their humility and their simplicity: "Father Jim told us that you were a friend of Jesus. We are going to tell our people to come and listen to a friend of Jesus." Their church, a meeting hall, is very poor and the heating system does not work.

In the evening we had a large gathering with the people of the neighbourhood. I spoke of Jesus for half an hour. Then Rev. Wright spoke with all the fervour of the Pentecostals, radiating such a deep love of Jesus. He is truly a witness to Jesus. I feel close to him. Others shared simply and lovingly about their encounters with Jesus. Willie sang "Oh, How I Love Jesus." She prays when she sings. I could sense how people were touched. Father Jim and I felt very peaceful. The auxiliary Bishop was with us for the first half of the evening.

The next morning, after early Mass with Father Jim and Sister Sue, we visited Dorothy Gauchat's house for thirty-five profoundly handicapped children. It is a place of great peace and joy. At 10 a.m. we went to Our Lady of Fatima parish, where I gave two talks in a big shabby hall. They showed the film on Mother Teresa of Calcutta. I feel that the seeds have been planted. Rev. Wright and his wife, plus another black pastor, Rev. Skipper, and Father Jim are going to meet each week to pray for the retreat, which we will call "Let's Celebrate Jesus." Each day I will speak in a different church or hall. People from outside Cleveland can come and stay with the people of the neighbourhood. I feel very drawn to this type of retreat. I have the impression that the Holy Spirit is preparing something here.

In the evening there was a large gathering of two thousand young people in a theatre. The film on Mother Teresa was shown. There was singing and then I spoke on "Insights into Peace." I could sense how much the young are thirsting to do something worthwhile for Jesus. The meeting, film, songs, etc., lasted three and a half hours. It was beautiful to see so many young people touched by Mother Teresa.

We arrived Sunday in Chicago and went directly to the Cenacle,* where we had a one-day retreat for former retreatants. There were about one hundred priests, religious and lay people. At night, I stayed with Father Paul Lachance and the Franciscans; they live in two apartments in a deprived neighbourhood. Of approximately 100,000 persons in the neighbourhood, 12,000 have been

---

*Cenacle is an interfaith retreat centre in the heart of Lincoln Park in Chicago.

in a psychiatric hospital, perhaps the same number in prison. The next day I was supposed to visit a huge state prison but was told at the last minute that it was not possible. It is difficult to enter the prisons in the United States because there is still much suspicion. I spent the morning visiting the neighbourhood with Father Paul. In the evening we had Mass in the brothers' chapel. It was very peaceful and prayerful, like the atmosphere in a Byzantine liturgy. The Little Sisters were there and also a young man who had just been sentenced to one year in prison for having burned draft cards. His trial was a witness of peace. He has appealed to the Superior Court, which is why he is still free (and probably under police surveillance).

The next morning I left quite early for Jefferson, where I had a meeting regarding catechism and the spiritual life of handicapped people with some three hundred delegates from all over the States. Before I arrived, they had shown the films on L'Arche and on Faith and Light.* I spoke for an hour and a half on the faith of handicapped people. I was warmly received. They were open and very receptive to what I said about the poor and the weak and their openness to Jesus and the Holy Spirit.

We have just landed in Montreal. Alleluia! I am not too tired. My heart is at peace as I try to live the present moment without thinking too much about the next moment. I trust that Jesus is holding me and I try to rest in him. I know that you are praying for me. I can sense how deeply the community is carrying me and I feel so united to each one.

Jean

---

*I speak in detail about Faith and Light later in this book, specifically in Part 3: Faith and Light and L'Arche.

February 21, 1972
Montreal

Dear Friends,

A snowstorm has blocked everything and the snow ploughs are on strike! It is difficult to get around the city.

I went for a meeting in Beaconsfield. We got lost and arrived forty-five minutes late. The meeting was in an English-language high school, with students, professors and parents of handicapped children. They were very warm and welcoming. I spoke about prisons, hospitals and ghettos, and how Jesus came to liberate us and to introduce us to a world of compassion and tenderness.

Then I went to the maximum-security St. Vincent de Paul prison, where there are 350 long-term prisoners. There were about 250 in the gymnasium who came to listen to me. I spoke to them about the child in each one of us and about Maximilian Kolbe.* There were moments of deep silence. At the end, we had some discussion which at times was quite intense. I sensed how deeply wounded these men were and how much they needed attention and understanding. However, one must not be too naive! Afterwards, many came up to shake my hand and to thank me. I asked them if they would accept me if I came back in August. They applauded. They have few visitors. I feel close to them and want to visit prisons

*Maximilian Kolbe was a Franciscan friar who was arrested by the Gestapo and sent to the Auschwitz concentration camp for hiding almost two thousand Jews at his monastery in Poland. In July 1941, a man from Kolbe's Auschwitz barrack vanished, prompting the camp commander to pick ten men from the same barrack to be starved to death to stop further escape attempts. One of the selected men cried out, lamenting his family, and so Kolbe volunteered to take his place. After three weeks of dehydration and starvation, four of the ten men were still alive, including Kolbe, but the Nazis wanted their cells so they executed each man with an injection of carbolic acid in the left arm. Kolbe was canonized by Pope John Paul II in 1982 and declared a martyr of charity.

more often. Many people are frightened and do not visit them. Jesus helped me to be quite comfortable with them, at peace and without fear.

From there I went to the Carmelite monastery, another kind of prison, "a prison of hope," as Dédé called it.* I spoke to them about different types of prisons and about Jesus, the condemned Lamb of God.

Then I left for Ottawa where we had a gathering with some two hundred French-speaking students from Quebec, Montreal, Ottawa and Sherbrooke. It was a bit crowded but there was a very good spirit. I gave four talks in my forty hours there! One can sense a new spirit that is coming to birth, a real desire for prayer, the Eucharist and silence. One senses how much the Holy Spirit is at work, preparing people for a new way of life, different from the one our modern societies propose with values of wealth and comfort. Some people gave their own personal testimonies—it was very beautiful. The whole weekend was peaceful. A quiet revolution is taking place and many people are experiencing it. People told me about the Council of Youth meeting in Cap-Rouge, not far from Quebec, where five hundred young people desiring to follow the Gospels gathered in a spirit of prayer. It is the same Spirit that is blowing everywhere. New things are coming to birth. There is a new breath of hope everywhere.

Because it snowed the whole weekend it took us two hours to

---

*This expression arose when Dédé, a core member from our Le Val community, and I were speaking with some Carmelite nuns in Lisieux, France. The sisters live in an enclosed community, so we were speaking to them through a grille. During a pause in the conversation Dédé looked at the sisters and said that they lived in a "prison of hope." It was a very moving moment. Lisieux is a place of pilgrimage, particularly to revere Saint Thérèse de Lisieux. Although she was a Carmelite sister, Saint Thérèse realized that she could be holy and express her love of God through the "little way," through small acts of kindness; this "little way" is a spiritual path that is open to everyone.

drive back to Montreal and two hours to cross over the city to St. Charles Hospital for physically handicapped people. We had a meeting with friends and about twenty of the patients; we sang and shared. I was truly happy to be there with them.

The days go by so fast! In Ottawa I felt completely exhausted, but this morning in Montreal, after a good night's sleep, I have new strength. The Holy Spirit is good to me, giving me the strength to continue this way. I sense so strongly that if my words carry a certain force it is because the community in Trosly and all the L'Arche communities are with me. I am just the spokesman for all that is being lived in our communities. I am encouraged and sustained by our communities that are praying for me. I feel so poor—especially at certain moments when I no longer know what to say or when Jesus puts me in rather impossible situations. However, I continue to trust more and more in the work of the Holy Spirit. I believe that the Holy Spirit wants to use our communities to bring a message of peace to our world.

I am anxious to get back home to share with you the weight of each day's work. Some people have told me that I look more tired here than when I am in Trosly! It is true that the life I am living here—like a pilgrim or a bird flying here and there—is a bit out of reality, the reality of carrying the pain and responsibility of each day. Yes, I am anxious to get back and to share the daily load, to be with those who have been carrying this responsibility day after day.

I feel deeply peaceful. Jesus is good. Pray hard, very hard, for all that Jesus wants. Pray that I have the strength to speak as he wants me to speak, in spite of my poverty.

Jean

August 17, 1972
Cleveland

Dear Friends,

The first three days in Cleveland are over. The activities are surrounded by peace, simplicity and poverty. I am moved by the seeds
which are being planted. Upon arriving Saturday, we had a meeting with the leaders from seven disadvantaged neighbourhoods of
Cleveland where the "happenings" will take place during the week.
There were fifty people, some infirm, some elderly, a few priests,
religious and black pastors. What united us all was our desire to
announce and celebrate the name of Jesus. We ate together and then,
outside, on the street, the first "Let's Celebrate Jesus" event started.

There were about two hundred people from the neighbourhood,
a few children, some street people, old women, some black families and some Pentecostal ministers. Together we celebrated Jesus.
It was very simple: we talked about Jesus, the one who heals us,
loves us, our brother and good shepherd. It was the first time that I
had the joy of speaking outside in front of a crowd of people passing in the street. Cars would stop to look and to listen. It was the
first time that I was able to announce Jesus to those who are very
little and very wounded, who do not even dare to enter a church.
It was simple and poor as in Bethlehem. Joy and hope seemed to
be born in the hearts of some people.

At the exact same moment, in another part of Cleveland, Father
Bill Clarke was giving a retreat to about sixty people. They are
praying day and night with us so that hearts would be touched.

Sunday, I went with Father Jim O'Donnell and Steve to a prison.
There were 530 men in that prison. We were told that only five or
six would come to our meeting but thirty came. Most were black
and non-Catholic. Father Jim and I spoke to them about Jesus, the
Saviour who heals us, awakens the child in us, frees us from evil
and calls us even today to tenderness. These men were beautiful

as they listened with so much silence. We felt very poor. At one moment Jim and I tried to sing, and you know how terribly we sing! Happily one of the men came to help us out.

From there I took time for Mass and quiet adoration. Afterwards, I went to a home for forty elderly men. Some of them were 94, 102 and 104 years old. The young ones were 75 years old! There also we sang and shared the Word. I told them how much I needed their prayers, how much the world needed them, and that their fidelity was an encouragement for us, for they had kept the faith while waiting for the Bridegroom: "Behold the Bridegroom comes." Then I went to visit an elderly woman in the Hough area. She is 84 years old and bedridden in a decrepit house in a very poor neighbourhood. She looked at me and said, "You know, I have walked with him for fifty years; I know Jesus." She had such a beautiful radiant face. I looked at her with much joy and at one moment she cried, "He seems so happy to look at me; yes, he sees God in me." I was so moved.

That evening in a park the "Let's Celebrate Jesus" festival was held. Three or four black pastors spoke. The group was composed mostly of poor people with a majority of blacks. I spoke again, happy to share and to pray with them, happy to announce the Good News to the most blessed.

On August 14, after a meeting with the team coordinating the neighbourhood of Glenville, I had two television interviews. The second was the most moving interview that I have ever had. The interview lasted about half an hour; it will be shown on the Cleveland station on September 10. At one moment, the interviewer said to me, "I don't have peace. You seem to have peace. Tell me what peace is." So I spoke of peace as presence, welcome, the fruit of union and love. Then we spoke of other things, of the place of the wounded in the world, and after twenty minutes, he said to me, "I am beginning to sense a deep peace inside. I don't know what is happening. Is it you who have given me peace? I don't understand.

How do you give peace? Do you have a mysterious power?" I said that I think that it is Jesus in me. He seemed to be very touched. All that happened through the medium of television. There was a very great peace, and that peace came from the fact that so many persons were praying with Father Clarke and at L'Arche.

This afternoon I went to another house for elderly men. It was more difficult than yesterday. It took a while for the men to open up, to relax and to pray together. From there, I went to a house for reforming alcoholics founded by the Franciscans. We ate, then shared and prayed together. It was good to share our weaknesses and our hope in Jesus.

In the evening, a "Let's Celebrate Jesus" event took place in a crime-ridden neighbourhood. Like all the other evening events, it was held outside, near a main street. While I was speaking there was a car accident. One of the priests went to administer the sacrament of the sick. There was lightning followed by ambulance and fire-engine sirens. We read passages from Scripture; we sang and then I spoke to all the people. It was a very moving and simple evening. At the end the rain began to fall heavily; most of the people scattered but about fifty of us gathered under a tent with open sides. We started to sing and dance as we did in the square at Lourdes. There were two policemen who found refuge under the big tent; one of them joined us in the dances and prayers. Little by little the rain stopped and we went home. The celebration of rain was very beautiful.

The next day was the feast of the Assumption. We were in a neighbourhood of mostly simple, poor people, some Polish, some Puerto Rican, some Appalachian. In the morning, we visited a number of families with sick people. I was with the pastor. At eleven o'clock we had a very humble encounter with a group of elderly men and sick persons where we prayed and shared and spoke of Jesus. Nothing was planned for the afternoon. We met young people who played and sang, but there was nothing organized. In the evening, "Let's Celebrate Jesus" was held in a park with approximately one thousand people. There was a group of thirty deaf-mutes and a group of persons with cerebral palsy from Erie. At the end of the evening there was a procession with candles. Brother Pearce, a Pentecostal, was there, a very simple man who has lived near the people in the neighbourhood for years. His face lights up when he speaks of Jesus or when he hears someone speaking of him. Before the celebration in the park, there was a meeting with some pastors and the most affluent lay people from five different parishes and churches, a real encounter of unity in the name of Jesus.

Wednesday was in a way the most moving day. There was a big meeting with the auxiliary Bishop, since everything was taking place in the parish where he lives. Then there were three meetings with prisoners and a meeting with 150 delinquents, all sentenced by the judge for acts of theft or similar crimes. These encounters were followed by a visit with elderly men and profoundly physically handicapped people. The prisoners moved me the most, especially the women with their great thirst for prayer. At the end of the encounter we remained a good half-hour, praying and singing. I felt that these women were touched by Jesus and had a great thirst for his tenderness.

In the evening we were not able to have the celebration outside because it was raining, so it was held in a big church. It was a neighbourhood which was half white and half black and there were many young people. The evening unfolded with a sincere desire to celebrate Jesus, Prince of Peace, the one who comes to heal us, our shepherd, brother, beloved friend. Every night we see some faces which we have seen the evening before, people who follow the celebrations from place to place, people who want to celebrate Jesus.

Father Clarke continues to animate the retreat for those who come every day to the neighbourhood church, to pray for long hours before the Blessed Sacrament. This union between the church of prayer and the announcing of the Word to the poor is beautiful. This union which is growing among Christians who ignored each other, who are from different churches but who believe in Jesus, is also beautiful. It is good to see so many priests and religious begin to know each other and share their desire to work and pray together for Jesus. A real current of hope is coming to birth to announce the Good News to the poor and for Christians to be united in the name of Jesus and to celebrate Jesus all together. Alleluia!

Jean

November 25, 1972
Calcutta, India

Dear Friends,

We have been here since Thursday evening. What a city! A city of life and death! Crowds and crowds of people. So many poor people, entire families sleep on the pavement. Little children know home as a bit of pavement! There are old people, physically handicapped people and beggars. These huge slum areas are full of mud and dirt, and nine thousand people are living in the streets. There are thousands of lepers. Life goes on in spite of all the dirt and lack of food; children live and grow; people do what they can to find a little food in order to survive. Yet they seem to live harmoniously together. I have not seen any fights. The look on their faces is peaceful; there is no hatred. Bengalis are a kind and peaceful people—poets. You would think that with all the crowds of people there would be a lot of tension. Maybe the tension is there, but one does not notice it right away.

At the same time, Calcutta is a city of misery and death. Yet there is such tenderness: faces filled with beauty; the beautiful eyes of the children; wise, old, white-bearded faces; young girls with clear, limpid eyes; young people laughing; people helping one another; swarms of people milling the streets—it is a mixed-up world and yet at the same time I feel that there is hope!

The last time I came to Calcutta I was a little frightened because of the war. This time there is no fear in me. I feel at home, happy to be here, happy to be on the street, watching people, travelling on the overcrowded buses. There is a deep peace in my heart, a peace that I have rarely known. I am discovering the beauty of Calcutta, the beauty of the poor. It is difficult to explain.

As I was on my way home this evening, I saw a tent filled with light. Some very wealthy people were having a reception; one could see them from the sidewalk. As I came closer, I saw some women dressed in saris embroidered with gold. There was lots of food and many chauffeur-driven cars. Then I looked again at the street, at the many people in rags—Lazarus and the rich man. I felt disheartened by the contrast.

When we arrived at the airport, we called to see if we had a place to sleep—Gabrielle stayed with Mother Teresa's sisters and I at the Archbishop's house. In order to get to the house, I passed by two poor people sleeping on the pavement. Then I was given my room with a bathroom. The Bishop came to my room; he is a good man. He wants to give, or rent to us, a school, a presbytery, a church basement, many things. I am struck by his offer. Jesus really seems to want us to come here quite quickly! The very first day we were offered these places. This morning we visited a presbytery right in the heart of the city, all kinds of people around, crowds at the gate (talk about integration!). The house is not big but we could welcome ten boys, and there is a church basement we could use as a workshop for about thirty people. The house will be free in January and the basement will be free in three months. Things move quickly! We have the feeling that we must answer the call. Gabrielle is peaceful and quite at home here in Calcutta.

The first morning we spent a lot of time with Mother Teresa. She is founding a home in Yemen and she is talking about Belfast, New York, Amman and Jerusalem. Wherever there is pain and misery, that is where you find her sisters. Mother Teresa is very peaceful. Gabrielle and I visited the Home for the Dying with her. A man had just died; his face was peaceful. Two others were dying. Yet there was so much peace, so much beauty in the faces of the people as well as in the faces of the sisters and the brother who were working there.

This evening Gabrielle and I spent time with the brothers. There are thirty-two novices, wonderful young men mainly from Kerala and Bihar. We had a simple meal: potatoes with curry sauce, bread and water. The brothers are very simple people. We had a moment of prayer together. Then we met two psychiatrists. One is an Englishman from the hospital in Ranchi, about 150 kilometres from Calcutta (the other psychiatric hospital for Calcutta). The other psychiatrist is Bengali, a poet, a wonderful man. We spoke about Asha Niketan. There is practically nothing here for mentally handicapped people so they would be happy with anything we could do to help.

We must entrust all this to Jesus and to his Holy Spirit. Ask that everything be as he wants and that Gabrielle and I be poor instruments. There is so much to be done here. Through the grace of God, we can perhaps put a small drop into the mouth of this humanity thirsting for water. Other Asha Niketans may follow. We must get things started. There is so much goodwill, many people ready to do something, ready to give and to give of themselves, and Jesus is there ready to help, to give us everything, as long as we walk with him and in him, as long as we move step by step in the Spirit, as long as we have a whole network of prayer carrying us. Prayer is like a spring of trust and love, a source of accumulated energy, peace, silence and gift. The more we journey into unknown lands, the more we journey into Asia and into the mountains and the ghettos, the more we need houses of prayer like Emmanuel in Trosly where people pray and protect us from attacks of the devil and from making mistakes. At the same time, their prayer can draw the gifts of God upon us, inward gifts of light, love and strength, as well as material gifts.

Tuesday morning, November 28

It seems clear that the Holy Spirit wants Asha Niketan in Calcutta. Things are clear now with the Bishop and the Vicar General; the house will be free in January. The Bishop will speak to his council on Thursday. The Bishop said he found our arrival was providential. To celebrate the twenty-fifth anniversary of his priesthood, he said he would do something for the handicapped people and that he would collect money, but he did not have any clear idea what he would do with the money. The house he wants to give us, or rent to us, is quite big and right in the heart of the city.

Yesterday, Gabrielle and I had lunch "en famille" with the governor of Bengal and his wife. They are Leonore's cousins. They are Catholic—it is quite amazing that a Catholic be named governor of a province like Bengal. I am told he is quite an exceptional man. His wife, Mme Dias, has accepted a position on the board of directors with others who are not Christians. Gabrielle and I will come back to Calcutta on December 15 for a board meeting. Jesus is good to give such support. In Ambleteuse, things were able to begin because we knew the local prefect; here it is Leonore's cousin who is governor. Yes, when God wants something, he arranges it! Gabrielle and I are happy with this new foundation in the heart of the city of Calcutta. We are happy to be close to this vast world of suffering, with the presence of Mother Teresa (just a few minutes away from our house), Brother Andrew, Father Laborde and so many others working in this city. On Sunday, with Mother Teresa, we visited one of the hospitals (two big tents with fifty beds in each one) she founded for lepers:

about one hundred people, their faces, hands and feet eaten up by the illness, but there was a radiant joy in their beings. They sang and danced. It is strange how beautiful the face of a leper can be even though humanly it is so disfigured. It is the light and peace in the eyes. We had Mass all together. The Rector of the seminary offered it for Mother Teresa and for L'Arche. We in L'Arche must be convinced of the necessity of remaining poor. Of course, we do need competent people, but even more than that, we need the dynamism that comes from love in poverty. How quickly the gift of self and the creativity of poverty can slide into sterile professionalism.

I was shaken by the poverty I saw. It is so easy to reject the poor. So many times I have done it simply because I did not quite know what to do. It is easy to reject someone begging for money to buy a coffee and yet we easily stop and have a coffee ourselves when we really do not need it; our stomachs are full and our pockets too! We always want to be "reasonable" and refuse any extreme situations or gestures; yet if we want to follow Jesus, we have to follow exactly what he says! I spoke to Mother Teresa's novices and sisters, about three hundred of them in all. It is easy to speak about Jesus, Jesus in the poor; but to go out into the streets and come face to face with people in rags, people with empty stomachs, is another matter. Pray that I may learn how to live with the poor and never let my heart be closed up in my own comfort, well-being or flattery. Pray that Jesus may keep me continually in anguish in front of the poor.

On the plane to Bangalore

We are on our flight back. This morning we were with Mother Teresa's abandoned children. The Bishop said Mass. On the way home, there was a thin man in rags sleeping on the sidewalk. Mother stopped. She saw that he had chains on his arms. He must have escaped from somewhere. Perhaps he had been confused and someone attached him with the chains. Mother Teresa called an ambulance to take him to their Home for the Dying. Keep Calcutta in your hearts.

United in Jesus,
Jean

December 18, 1972
Calcutta, India

Dear Friends,

Gabrielle and I have returned to Calcutta. We stayed at the Archbishop's and visited the Home for the Dying with Mother Teresa. The city is full of beggars, naked children, entire families sleeping on the pavement, masses of misery! I have the same feelings I had last time I visited. What humanity!

Last Tuesday, before coming here, Gabrielle and I went by plane to Changanacherry in Kerala, sixty kilometres from Cochin. The Bishop had invited us; he is starting a school for handicapped children and wanted to talk to us about his project. I do not know if we helped him or gave him any good advice, but I was happy to visit Kerala. It is like a huge garden with coconut and banana trees, like a fairy-tale land. Here and there you may see an elephant in the street. Changanacherry is a small town of some forty thousand inhabitants, living in small wooden houses. It is another face of India, very simple and human. Eighty per cent of the people of India live in villages like that; India is not its cities. Calcutta is not India. India is its villages with little houses and families united in prayer. We visited twelve families with handicapped children; they are simple people who accept their children. I was happy to know India with its villages, but I must not exaggerate either by saying there is no poverty here. We visited five hundred children who are given milk and bread every day because their families are too poor to provide for them.

I have just come back from Mass at Mother Teresa's. I am happy that our last Mass in India was with her. I am trying to live each present moment as I leave this world of India and Calcutta. I am happy to be wherever Jesus wants me at each moment, but there is a deep desire in my heart to become poorer. I still feel how much I am part of the class of people who are rich and have power. When I come back to Trosly, I will have my own bedroom, my own bed, clean sheets, my own security, a symbol of power. Outside in the streets, I see all these little people living there and I realize I am incapable of living like them. My need for security is evident. These two worlds co-exist in me and around me. I need to be transformed by the grace of Jesus, by the Holy Spirit, to become poor, not exteriorly but interiorly. We are held by the Holy Spirit, transformed by him and find our security in the love of God. If this is not so, then these divisions between rich and poor will continue until they burst out in violence, hatred and destruction. Unity must come, but it can only come if the rich leave their security in order to live a security that comes from God and brings them closer to the poor and to the weak.

Sometimes I feel a bit like a hypocrite, talking so much about L'Arche, as if I am trying to present myself as a "good" person who is "devoted" to work for the mentally handicapped. All I talk about and am called to say is how much we feel called to work towards a silent, hidden identification with the poorest and the weakest. However, I know that it is also important to work in and with society, to give talks, to handle money, to act in society, to use our contacts, to preside over board meetings, to meet governors, etc. Pray for me.

Jean

December 19, 1972
On the plane from India to France

Dear Friends,

We are flying over Italy. The sun is shining and the sky is blue. There is slight fog, which like a veil both hides and reveals the earth below and the beauty of creation. One feels the warmth of the sun; it is like paradise with no end to the horizon. We are far away from Calcutta. Yet just yesterday there were all the naked children in the streets, the beggars, the slum areas. On our way to the airport we saw a little child giving half of her orange to a beggar. Soon it will be Christmas, the time when the little child was born in Bethlehem so that the poor would know the Good News and receive the Spirit and the joy of God.

The scene below is exhilarating: I have never seen such beauty! A warm, bright sun, the earth so beautiful, the reflections of the Mediterranean, the sky so blue. Now we are beginning to see the Alps—strong, solid, rigid—and yet my eyes are still full of all the misery I have seen, the Home for the Dying and the abandoned children. Now we are high above the Alps, the snow reflecting the light of the sun. I did not sleep a wink all night. I waited seven hours for the plane in Calcutta. Then I arrived in Delhi at 9 p.m. and had to register with Iraqi Airlines at 3 a.m. I was frightened that if I went to sleep on the bench, I would not wake up in time, so I lay down on the floor. It was cold and I did not sleep at all. The plane left at 6:30 a.m. The beautiful spectacle will soon be ending; the sun is setting and darkness will soon be covering the earth, the world enfolded by night in all its deep silence and tenderness.

It was when the earth was completely enfolded by darkness that Jesus came, poorly, without any great light, without any noise, and the first to come to him were the poor shepherds, probably a bit handicapped. Then a little later, there was the massacre of the innocents. Jesus came to announce the Good News to the poor and he wants to live in each one, even those who are hidden in the slum areas, or perhaps especially in those who are in the slums! The tenderness and love of Jesus arising from his poverty are infinitely more beautiful than the spectacle of light and earth.

Jean

February 5, 1973
Montreal

Dear Friends,

On the day of arrival, Frank, from Maryfarm, came and drove me to his little farm. Many renovations have been made and the house is now ready to receive two or three men and women from the big institution in Smiths Falls. They are quite isolated from the city. In winter this aspect of isolation takes on greater significance since communication is sometimes difficult. This difficulty was felt by us the next morning when we left at 5:30 for Kingston. There was so much ice on the highway that we skated in the car for about two hours!

Arriving quite late I went immediately to the university where I was able to talk about L'Arche by speaking on violence and nonviolence. I spoke of the violence of those who have been so wounded that they either act out in violence or remain depressed. Many questions were asked. In the afternoon I visited the women's prison and I shared with them for half an hour.

From there, I went to the big maximum security prison for men. More than one hundred were assembled in the gymnasium where I spoke. One of them stood up and in a very violent manner cried out that I could not understand all the suffering he had endured in his youth. He began to explain in very coarse language all that he had suffered during his childhood, especially having been sold as a homosexual at the age of ten to bring money to his depraved family. His violence and his coarse language left the hall in a great silence. All that I could respond to him was that he was right and that I could not perhaps understand him. I could not understand all the terror of his suffering. I spoke with him a little afterwards.

This weekend convinces me more than ever of the need for L'Arche here in Canada, and indeed, in the world. How much Jesus needs to use each one so that the Kingdom may grow. Ask sincerely that I be his instrument during the month of February in spite of my poverty and also in spite of my fatigue.

Jean

February 11, 1973
Ottawa

Dear Friends,

After the weekend spent in Montreal, I went to Halifax and then to Quebec. In Halifax there were some eight hundred students. So many want to find a living Christianity, close to the Gospel. In so many there is a thirst for prayer and for community, and a desire to go out to rejected and wounded people. In Quebec, it was mostly encounters with people in the St. Sauveur neighbourhood. I met with thirty priests coming from eighteen parishes and with the directors of different movements, all this in view of preparing the August retreat. We will have a celebration with handicapped people, various encounters in hospitals, in homes for old people, and at the Refuge for those out of work. There will also be con-ferences. All this will be prepared by animators who will stay in houses for street people, where they will share short films or tapes to begin discussions, etc. There will be announcements in the local churches. There is a team of marvellous people preparing this week of prayer. We will try to touch especially people who do not usually go to church, who constitute probably the great majority of people in the lower part of Quebec.

Right now I am in Ottawa. The weekend at the university was a "happening" animated mostly by Father Louis Raby and the team of chaplains. When you see some six hundred people at the Eucharist, singing, crying out to Jesus, announcing him, praising him, you realize how much we are in a world in pursuit of love and peace. I was very struck by the quality of listening of all those students.

I have never had such a busy month of February. I had hardly time to read letters and much less to write them! There are days when I just go from talk to talk, but at the same time I feel a great hope, since many people seem to be opening up and committing themselves more to the poor and to Jesus.

Keep me and each one in your prayers. If at times I am a little tired, I know that there are many people who are praying. I also meet people who wish to come to work at L'Arche, or who wish to do something similar in Canada. Pray for them.

Jean

March 8, 1973
Trosly-Breuil

Dear Friends,

This is my last letter about my trip to North America.

In Erie I also gave talks, visited a centre for the handicapped and a prison. I was overcome at the sight of more than a hundred men living in inhuman conditions in the prison. The cells were dark and the men watched television through the cell bars. Some of them have been there for more than a year. I was so distraught to see them behind the bars that I could hardly speak. The director of the prison did not want me to meet the men all together, because he was afraid of the tension and possible revolt. The men were like lions in cages. I suffered very much with them as I went from area to area, speaking with small groups who wanted to share with me. I had deep encounters with these men, innocence in the depths of their being and capable of antisocial gestures sometimes inspired by evil. Once they find deep peace, the innocent in them sees the light of day. I was overwhelmed by the eyes of these men, who have many years of captivity before them, without friends except for other prisoners. We must pray for the world of prisoners. In reading the Acts of the Apostles we hear how many times the apostles were in and out of prisons.

The month has passed by very quickly and I am happy now to go back to my brothers and sisters in Trosly. From my trip I sense a new hope, as many people are thirsting to do something beautiful, to work for universal peace and to follow Jesus in his Beatitudes. I will return to Canada in June for a retreat with people from the United Church, the Anglican Church and the Catholic Church. Pray for this retreat, a time where we will meet together as disciples of Jesus in a common search to live more fully the Beatitudes.

Jean

November 17, 1973
Asha Niketan, Bangalore

Dear Friends,

The transition from L'Arche in Trosly to Asha Niketan was so gentle that I hardly realize I am in India, perhaps because for several years now I have been more attentive to community and to people than to places. I find the same love and unity here as in Trosly, though there are different ways of expressing them.

When I got to Asha Niketan, everyone was in bed. I called John Uncle.* What a joy to see each other again. I took all the mail and packages out of my suitcase. There was such a deep feeling that we are one family, truly united, born together through the same grace and for the same work. I was tired because I had not slept much; the long waits at the two airports had been hard, as I couldn't sleep, pray or work and felt cut off from my own surroundings. After the joy of being together again it was a real joy to find my little room and bed!

Yesterday was a day of peace, prayer and rest. I sensed the same peace in the community as a year ago and a deepening of the community. Each man here continues to grow, very gently. There is nothing spectacular to say about the year. But then L'Arche doesn't do anything spectacular; its work is to bring life, to help people grow a little more each day in love and peace. In a world where there is so much harshness and individualism, strife and war, we are simply there as a sign that love is possible on this earth, that people can live together and love each other, a sign that God is present, hidden in the hearts of each person, and that Jesus is present and loves us. What Asha Niketan is doing is so little compared to the enormous suffering and the number of handicapped people in India. We could get discouraged and want quicker, more efficient solutions. However, Asha Niketan is called to be a sign of what the world could become if each person tried to live as a child of God, open to the Spirit, with Jesus as our older brother.

Community life in Asha Niketan is simple, much like the hidden life of Jesus in Nazareth. Asha Niketan is a tiny isolated foyer with little support from outside. There are difficult moments, like now when there is no work from the factory. It is a life where each

*This is what the core members called John Sumarah, a leader of the community at the time. My nickname was "Tall Uncle"!

person is indispensable and where each one is called to grow, day by day, in the freedom of their giving and their love.

Perhaps what is new at Asha Niketan this year is the presence of George, Ramakrishna and the other Indian assistants. Mitran and Saroja were already there last year and the movement is growing. George is very precious. He comes from a poor family in Kerala and brings a sensitive presence, the presence of Jesus in himself. Yes, the "nothingness" of Asha Niketan moves me, as the community lives a simple life in poverty.

Dr. Reddy spent three hours with us last evening; he is a man of wisdom. He understands what is essential and is preparing the expansion of Asha Niketan with both prudence and audacity. There is a group of people who want an Asha Niketan in Madras, another group in Bombay, and then there are the properties in Kerala. India will be called to prepare other foundations in other Asian countries.

The more L'Arche grows throughout the world, the more we have to be fearless, putting ourselves entirely in the hands of our Father, confident that he will give us the strength, the light and the love to make our communities places of life and freedom, witnesses to the truth and the tenderness of God. I remain so close to each of you, feeling so poor, hidden in each one's prayers.

Jean

November 20, 1973
Bangalore, India

Dear Friends,

I have returned from Calicut in Kerala. Dr. Reddy and I were met by Mr. Pramanand who took us on a drive of more than four hours across Kerala. Kerala is like a huge garden, with tall, majestic coconut trees everywhere. I did not feel entirely relaxed because we would often overtake vehicles on the curves. I just abandoned myself to Providence—no one else was going to help us arrive safely! Luckily I was sitting in the back seat, wedged between Dr. Reddy and Mr. Pramanand.

Calicut, with half a million inhabitants, is a large city full of coconut trees. It is on the Arabian Sea and is very different from Bombay and Madras. We have been offered a large property of about sixty acres, some fifteen miles from Calicut. The property is on a hill near a village overlooking the sea—extraordinarily beautiful, full of silence. It belonged to Mr. Pramanand's father. The family had to leave in 1969 when there was a Communist government in Kerala. The story of this property is quite a long one. Mr. Pramanand's father first saw it in 1938 when the English requisitioned, without compensation, his machinery and his factory in the south of Kerala, which at that time was making soap. He had no money, but he wanted to buy this new property. The first seven acres cost 500 rupees; he agreed to the price, still without any money. On the morning of the day fixed for him to buy the land, he received a letter and 521 rupees from a man in Mangalore (in Mysore) whom he did not know. The man said he had had a dream in which he was told to send him the money. Mr. Pramanand's father bought the land and little by little began to build this new factory, which closed in 1959. He believed that the land belonged not to him, but to God. After the death of his father, Mr. Pramanand had been looking for a work of God to which he could give this property. One day while travelling by train he saw a newspaper lying beside him, which he picked up and read. There was a long article on Asha Niketan–Bangalore. He wrote directly to Gabrielle and a few months later Dr. Reddy, Gabrielle and John visited the property.

Mr. Pramanand is a good and just man who fears God (in the

sense that the Old Testament prophets did). I also met Dr. Vijayan, director of the psychiatric hospital at Calicut and a friend of Dr. Reddy (it was good to hear Dr. Reddy explaining the benefits of L'Arche to him), and two other men who could serve on a local committee. It seems quite possible that we could have a house built and opened there in a year's time. We will start with seven acres and Mr. Pramanand is ready to give us more land if we need it.

Yesterday morning, we went to the beach at six o'clock. The Arabian Sea is calmer than the Mediterranean and only ten minutes from the property is a beach of fine sand where you can walk out in the water for a hundred yards. It is not, however, a good idea to go any farther, because a few sharks are swimming about gracefully, and as you no doubt know, sharks are fond of human flesh. Some fishermen arrived in their little boats, which they had probably made themselves. The men's faces were strong and beautiful. As the sun was coming up gently over this warm and peaceful sea there was a deep silence, just the voices of the fishermen and the birds and ourselves walking in the water, and the sound of the tiny waves rippling onto the beach. It was all so simple and so true, all so natural, nature in all its beauty and peace.

The fishermen were like the fishermen in Jesus's time. The world has evolved and has often destroyed nature's beauty and silence. Yet the deep yearning for the infinite is still present in the hearts of human beings. The sharks are a reminder, however, that not everything is beautiful, and that danger and struggle also exist. We stayed there for about an hour, but I could have stayed many hours as my heart was so full. However, we had to go and have breakfast, and visit the lawyer and the psychiatric hospital. I went to the women's section, where 150 people are shut in, without work, some of them in solitary confinement. I saw them from a distance, sad and broken faces like in any psychiatric hospital.

I was happy with the trip, happy to see how God is calling good and just men who seek his will to work together in Asha Niketan.

Pray hard that the Holy Spirit will show us what he wants and that we will be faithful to his signs. I leave tonight for Madras, where another group of Hindus is calling us to found an Asha Niketan. Tomorrow night, I leave for Calcutta, by air if God wills it (there may be strikes), or if not, by train. I feel more at home in India than ever. The grace of Asha Niketan–Bangalore is extraordinary—a little miracle. The community could have sunk so many times. Those of you who know its story and its sufferings know how many times it could have disappeared, but the Father has watched over it. He has always sent people to be there and sustain it. It carries on, stronger and more fragile than ever.

Now after only three years in India there are four important invitations for new Asha Niketans. People offer us their properties. Throughout India many priests and bishops have come to encourage us. What a mystery! The Asha Niketans are going to evolve a lot in the next two or three years. One feels that they are on the brink of a great expansion and deepening. It is important that Trosly prays a lot, that it carries this mystery and that we at Trosly remain strong in our faith.

Jean

November 25, 1973
Calcutta, India

Dear Friends,

I arrived in Calcutta on Friday evening. They had fixed up a little room for me in a storage shed in the garden behind the house. It is like a little cell, with a bed and a table.

Let me tell you about the happenings during the night. About three o'clock in the morning I heard a noise at the window, a tiny window with iron bars. I saw the outline of a man's head; perhaps he wanted to come and see what was in the shed. I leapt out of bed shouting, "Jayoo"—which means "Go away" in Bengali. I saw him making off but still did not feel very secure. There are three little windows in my cell, and I kept watching to see if my "friend" would come back. Half an hour later he did come back, as silently as a leopard in the night. He looked like he was about thirty years old and was dressed in rags. He came very near, and I had the impression he was crouched under one of the windows. I felt uneasy. Another person seemed to have joined him. I shut one of the shutters quietly, put my shoes on and waited as silently as my friends. From time to time I opened the shutters and looked out of the little window, but I could not see anything. Occasionally, I went back to bed and asked Jesus to help me understand what I ought to do. It seemed better not to go out since there may have been two or three of them. I waited. Then around 4:45 a.m., I opened the door without making any noise and went out, trying to walk quietly. No one was there—Alleluia! I looked around with a torch and saw no one. Finally, I decided that my friend must have jumped over the wall to get into the cemetery next door and that he must have been on his own, and that the noises I heard must have been rats playing peacefully among the dead leaves! How easily our imagination comes into play!

I went out and took a tram to go to Mass at Mother Teresa's, but I took the wrong one! I had to get off and go back to the station near Asha Niketan. There was a crowd of poor people in the street, many of them lying on the ground. I went into the station in the midst of this mass of people in rags: men, women, children, old people. Many of them were still asleep; some were waking up, going to look for water to wash their children. Some mothers were breastfeeding their children; other people were eating crumbs. More prosperous travellers were arriving to catch their trains. A few men argued and shouted, and a policeman arrived. Little by little these hundreds of thin people disappeared, who knows where.

There were just a few children left sleeping, the ones who make up the "gangs" who live in and around the stations.

I went into a church not far from the station. It was large and deserted, and had a marble floor. There were about twenty people at Mass, which was in Bengali. There was such a difference between the station full of poor people and the empty church with a few well-dressed people like myself. I felt a bit crushed. I was happy that I could not understand any of the sermon. My only consolation came from knowing that Jesus was crucified, poorer than the people in the station and on the streets, and that he died naked on the cross, and that he gives us his crucified body. I think that I have never been so grateful to Jesus for the Eucharist, his crucified but risen body. I was grateful also to my friend, the robber, who woke me up and thus I went to the station. Pray for him.

I will try to go back to the station every morning and every night. Perhaps my prayer will simply be that of being with those poor people. I was ashamed to look them in the eyes, afraid to have a contact with them in case they would come and ask me for something. St. Peter said, "I have neither silver nor gold. I have only one thing that I can give you, stand up and walk in the name of Jesus." I have money and I cannot say, "In the name of Jesus, stand up and walk."

These people who are so poor show me my own poverty, fear and lack of faith. I am grateful to Jesus for he gives me the strength to bear and accept this distress, this poverty, this misery. Yes, if Jesus helps me, I shall turn back and look at them, so that at least I let their faces and their ravaged bodies instill themselves into my eyes and my body. Perhaps one day Jesus will give me greater strength and faith. I begin to thirst and hunger for real poverty.

The lack of solitude is difficult for the community here. We at Trosly and everywhere else must support them. Our presence in Calcutta is so important. The climate, the enormous crowds of people and the exploitation in Calcutta are difficult for the community. There are mobs of beggars, and some of the men cut off their children's arms so that the children can beg for them. There are people who buy up rice and stockpile it, then wait till the prices rise and sell it for a profit. The prices spiral here; they have been rising throughout India for a year and have doubled for certain commodities. The price of petrol has doubled since the Middle East crisis. There is a lot of disquiet in Calcutta because of these price increases.

Calcutta is not India. India is the villages, united families, faces which are poor but smiling with peace. However, Calcutta does exist and is a sign, a symbol. Thanks be to Jesus that Mother Teresa is there, along with her sisters and so many others like the Missionaries of Charity Brothers. A doctor at the hospital said to me yesterday, "What you are doing is good, but I'm not sure that you will succeed." What he said is true. But we must trust in Jesus and accept our share in the struggle against all the evil and injustice, and carry in our flesh the anguish of rejection and indifference. By living and sharing our lives with the poor in our communities we will be witnesses that Jesus is alive and that he still has friends who want to follow him, disciples who believe in his name and believe that there is hope.

Jean

November 27, 1973
Calcutta, India

Dear Friends,

It is strange how much I feel at home in this city. I was a bit frightened in my little cell at night, but even that fear is disappearing! In fact, the night after the happenings I was awakened again around 4 a.m. Two men were hurrying past my window; they were stealing bits of metal and bars of iron from around the tombs in the cemetery. They went off with their loot, then came back for a second helping, as good as the first. Perhaps this represented food for themselves and their families for several days. It reminded me again of how secure and comfortable my life is.

I go to Sealdah Station twice a day. There is a huge crowd of some fifteen hundred people there, using newspapers for beds and a few jute sacks for blankets. Some are nearly naked and the children so thin. Some seem to be quite disturbed but are better off at the station than at the psychiatric hospital. In this immense crowd there are only a few beggars. Around 10:30 at night the cleaners come to wash the floor. The man in charge arrives shouting and throwing water everywhere on these poor people lying on the ground. They get up and scatter in all directions, hopelessly taking their few belongings with them. I understand the man who washes the floor; he has his work to do. However, these poor people have nothing. I am beginning to recognize a few of them, because they are there day and night. I feel powerless, but I want to experience the anguish of this powerlessness, asking Jesus to pull down the walls in my being which prevent me from seeing my wounded brother and sister.

In every street in Calcutta there are the same scenes. What an incredible city, each person fighting for life, each person inventing ways of subsisting, trying to earn a few rupees. I am really astonished to see the resignation in the eyes of these poor people. I dare not say "the peace," but there is no hatred. The children smile. Here as nowhere else you see so clearly Lazarus and the rich man of the Gospel. Thanks be to God there are the Missionaries of Charity Brothers and Sisters, and Father Laborde and many others. In all this misery they are there, working, struggling, hoping, thanks to the strength of the Holy Spirit in their lives.

They recognize that the gift of Asha Niketan will be different. In a few months we will have the basement of the church ready for some forty day-workers who will work and earn a salary to help them live. At the moment, Asha Niketan has work from the Philips transistor factory. We will also need a house outside of Calcutta. It is too difficult to be at the heart of this city all the time: the air is polluted and there is not enough space, everyone is crowded in the house.

Continue to carry in your hearts all of us here in India.

Jean

December 1, 1973
Calcutta, India

Dear Friends,

I have just spent an hour with Mother Teresa after Mass. I am struck by her sense of urgency. She is back from a trip to New York, London, Rome, Gaza, Yemen, Ethiopia and Amman. She has a keen sense of the suffering of the world and the poor, and she has a real creativity in responding to their needs. She has been looking for a helicopter to take food into the rural areas of Ethiopia, and for a way to help the Arabs and Israelis exchange their dead. She has seen the prime minister of Israel and the governor of Gaza. She is preoccupied by the hatred in the hearts of the Arabs and the Jews. She speaks about the suffering in London and she speaks about her Home for the Dying here in Calcutta, which has never been so full. Many people in Calcutta are hungry because of the rising prices. She wants to see Mrs. Gandhi. Nothing is impossible. She has abandoned herself to God. She has aged and her face is full of compassion. She is one of Jesus's "bulldozers"; nothing stops her. At the same time she is so little, a real instrument of God.

She never speaks of her community or of structures, but only of the poor. She was in Rome for the meeting of the major superiors, but says, "I said nothing; they were talking about structures all the time and I didn't understand any of it. My spirit was elsewhere." She says this without a hint of criticism; I have never heard her be the least critical of anyone. L'Arche is certainly very different from her houses. We create little communities where we live with wounded people to bring them to freedom—internal freedom, freedom from rejection, freedom to love and, for some, freedom to work; we can only welcome a small number of people. She is there to give what is essential to people who have nothing, the starving and the poorest, and she refuses no one. There is no compromise in her poverty and her truth; she goes directly to the essential. I feel so poor beside her and I rejoice in her beauty and her radiance. She shows me how much I do compromise, and that is good for me.

Yesterday evening during the retreat there was the official opening of Asha Niketan–Calcutta. The governor of Bengal came and so did two hundred other people. The chairman of our board, a neurosurgeon, spoke, and then the governor spoke of the violence which could erupt in this city and of the importance of little communities like Asha Niketan working for peace. Our tiny Asha Niketan has been launched! How amazing to see how we have been recognized and supported so quickly by the public authorities. It is a real sign of God for us.

Jean

PART THREE
1974 ❧ 1988

FAITH AND LIGHT AND L'ARCHE:
BLOSSOMING IN COUNTRIES
STRICKEN WITH POVERTY AND PAIN

It's at this point in the story of our life together that L'Arche's vision began to spread, first to India and then to other faraway places.

In 1969 the creation of a community in India seemed like a crazy thing to do! What did we know about India and the needs of the disabled there? But as you see in the letters, my journeys to India not only opened up L'Arche communities (called Asha Niketan, or "homes of hope") but they opened me up to other religious traditions and a whole new world. I discovered immense material poverty, but what dignity! And from our first Indian community in Bangalore sprang the energy and enthusiasm to start communities in Haiti, the Ivory Coast, Honduras and elsewhere. Today we reflect a lot on how to create a community, but in those early days they just began—God was truly present in these amazing adventures!

In some ways my role was exciting and exhilarating: travelling to far-off places torn by poverty and war, or governed by hard dictators, was stimulating and marvellous. Without realizing it at the time, I seemed to be in all the "hot spot" countries right at the moments of great upheaval: in France during May '68; in India during the Emergency Period; in Quebec during the Quiet Revolution; in Latin America at the height of the repression of the Church; in South Africa during apartheid; in Lebanon during its civil war; in the USSR in 1989, on the eve of its collapse; in the

West Bank during the first Intifada; in the Philippines at the birth of democracy there; and so on. People called out to us during these periods of change and upheaval and we went to them. Each time I felt as if God had prepared the way and I was simply an instrument called to pull things together.

Even in the so-called rich countries we were expanding into—Canada, Australia, Ireland, the United States, Britain—we found poverty. Poverty can be material, but it also exists when you're in a situation where you are lost and don't know what to do. Many parents of sons or daughters with handicaps don't know what to do; they don't know why this has happened to them and their children. The idea of poverty is: I am lost. It's a "lost-ness." And there are all the other forms of lost-ness: immigrants who come to a new country; young people caught in a culture of drugs, alcohol and casual relationships; those who have fallen into prostitution; prisoners, alcoholics, the depressed, the unemployed and so on. Poverty is so vast! And some people live all their lives in this lost-ness, on the margins, not knowing what to do, not having a particular faith, not having access to professionals or resources.

The poverty and pain of the intellectually disabled is both particular to them and common to everyone, everywhere. For so long the isolation and rejection of the disabled was supported by legal and social frameworks: they had few rights and could be locked up in inhumane conditions, denied education, ridiculed, sterilized, neglected and shunned by their families and seen as misfits, mad, errors of nature, subhuman and even dangerous. They are marginalized and lost in societies that prize intellectual capacity, competition, power and social standing. But they are people of the heart and they cry out for relationship! And don't we all, fundamentally? We are all lost, unworthy, lonely or sad at times in our lives.

This is the poverty of the Beatitudes. The Sermon on the Mount is at the heart of the Gospel message, and it's destined for the humble, the poor, the weak and the vulnerable: the little ones, the insignificant ones of this world, those who are always left behind. It's a message of hope and love and healing. And the disabled announce Jesus and the Gospel message by their very presence. He calls his disciples to become servants and friends, not masters, and, as his friends, to become friends of the weak and the poor. He calls them to become "like little children": trusting, open and filled with wonderment and thanksgiving.

The public ministry of Jesus is easy to recognize, and his rejection, torment and condemnation by his own people is mirrored in the situation of the intellectually disabled. But we mustn't forget the mystery of Mary, his mother. Her presence at Nazareth with her fragile child and at the cross is very important to L'Arche: she was present with Jesus, she believed in Jesus and she offered herself with Jesus. She never left him and stayed with him throughout his persecution, trials and death. She is our model of compassion, of being present to people until the very end, of staying and living with them through all their lives, through their psychotic disorders or their physical disorders or whatever their anguish and poverty. Mary welcomes the body with compassion. It's a very simple thing—not doing anything big, showy or important, just learning to love each other, to be friends with people in the neighbourhood, to live in communion and in community.

In the early letters I wrote of our pilgrimages to sites of Mary. We'd have these great convoys and off we'd go! They were important reminders of Mary's ministry, but also opportunities for fun and adventure. Journeys and celebrations are so important—for keeping up our spirits, for opening up our hearts and minds to other realities, for breaking up the routines of our everyday life. And the idea of pilgrimage, of travelling together to a holy place, is common to most religions. Leaving our familiar routines, meeting new people, facing fresh challenges and needing one another along the way healed divisions, cemented old bonds and created new ones. Our trips reinforced what we were trying to live.

But for some reason, in these letters I neglected to speak of one of our biggest and most important pilgrimages: the Faith and Light pilgrimage to Lourdes in 1971. It was phenomenal! It was a hundred times more than we expected, and although we were planning a one-time thing, it became so much bigger than we thought. So there again, do what you think is right, and see where the Spirit leads!

Faith and Light was started because so many parents of the intellectually challenged had no support—they were lost, not knowing what to do or where to turn. Marie-Hélène Mathieu, who had founded an organization to support parents of disabled people in France, came to see me in 1968 about Gerard and Camille Proffit and their two children with severe disabilities, Loïc and Thaddée. The family had gone to Lourdes, a place of spiritual consolation and support especially for those who are sick, disabled and in need, but unfortunately they weren't welcomed with love and understanding. They had a hard time finding a hotel that would accommodate the family, and when they did the hotel told them they couldn't eat in the dining room: they had to eat in their room so their sons would not disturb other guests. Gerard and Camille were deeply hurt by this and turned to Marie-Hélène, a woman with experience helping the disabled. Marie-Hélène and I thought of organizing a special international pilgrimage to Lourdes for people with disabilities, their parents and their friends. We created an organization, contacted parents' associations and wrote to the various church authorities in Lourdes. At Easter 1971, twelve thousand pilgrims from fifteen countries came to Lourdes!

We lived four days of intense personal encounters and community celebrations. We sang, we prayed, we met and talked together. Everything was organized so that the weakest and most vulnerable were not only included but at the centre of all the events. For once they were the guests of honour, the privileged ones, the ones welcomed in a special way. On the final day we had a huge fiesta on the esplanade.

It was a time of joy for all the pilgrims, but perhaps most especially for the parents, who no longer felt alone. It wasn't just a pilgrimage of individuals, but of communities. Groups from various cities and regions came into contact with one another, then lived together in the same hostels or hotels at Lourdes. We suggested these groups stay in contact, and suddenly Faith and Light turned from a one-time pilgrimage into an international organization. Over time and after many meetings at the regional and international level, a charter and constitution were created outlining Faith and Light's vision of support for families whose disabled children live at home. Today there are fifteen hundred Faith and Light communities in eighty countries, and the bonds with L'Arche remain very strong: sometimes L'Arche communities give rise to a local Faith and Light group, and sometimes a Faith and Light community will give birth to a L'Arche foyer.

Faith and Light opened me up to parents in pain, especially parents of sons and daughters with disabilities. Centres and schools for people with disabilities had opened in France and Canada and other wealthy countries. But in Eastern Europe and in developing countries, these social structures just didn't exist, so for many parents Faith and Light became a wonderful source of hope: parents were not alone, their children found friends and families found community. Faith and Light, like L'Arche before it, took me not only into new worlds of pain and discovery, but also into countries searching, peacefully and sometimes not so peacefully, for greater human liberty and dignity.

February 15, 1974

Dear Friends,

I am on the plane between Miami and Cleveland after two full days in Haiti. Haiti is a country of about five million inhabitants. The Spanish came to the country in the fifteenth century, bringing with them slaves from Africa. They put the Indians in such work conditions that they all died. Later on the French took over from the Spanish. In 1804 there was a revolution; the slaves gained their freedom and Haiti became an independent country.

Most of the Haitian people are very poor. More than eighty percent of the population is illiterate. Many are discouraged. A rich elite try often to leave the country to find more interesting and remunerative work. It is easier for the wealthier, who have the means to travel. The poor never have enough money to travel. There are seven thousand Haitians studying in universities, and only one thousand of them are studying in Haiti. There is not much industry in the country because those who do have the means tend to leave the country. There are few opportunities to develop the country and to raise the standard of living.

I was welcomed by Father Jacques Beaudry and Sister Micheline Vinet. Jacques is responsible for the Community of Sainte Marie which was founded about ten years ago. It is in a neighbourhood of Port-au-Prince which has approximately one thousand inhabitants. It was once a very poor neighbourhood—a slum on a hill outside the town. The community has built a school, a small road, a church, toilets, etc. So it is no longer a slum; it has become a real community divided into four areas. Each area has a community council made up of three elected persons and three persons chosen by the elected people. Together they are responsible for health, education and recreational activities in the neighbourhood.

It is the first time that I have seen such a community. It gives an idea of what humanity could have been if it had opted for community life instead of individual material progress. There are, of course, difficulties. Jacques is continually faced with the question of material progress. The community is in danger of judging poorer neighbourhoods. Some people in the community want to leave in order to have a better material life than their parents.

On my first day in Haiti I met approximately six hundred students from twenty schools and the university. I spoke for an hour on the divisions of the world and the hope of youth in the struggle to create a world of peace and justice. As there were no questions after my talk I suggested that we sing. Some students came up on the stage; they found drums and we began to sing in Creole and clapped our hands to rhythmical songs. Then the students started asking questions. The meeting lasted for about two and a half hours. There are not many countries where you would find so many students willing to spend a whole afternoon together like that. In the evening I met with three hundred religious men and women of Port-au-Prince.

The next morning, about twenty of us gathered for prayer in the community. Then I visited a school for physically handicapped children and another little school for twenty-five mentally handicapped children, both schools supported by Dr. Bijoux, a psychiatrist. Afterwards I visited the psychiatric centre, which I found rather depressing; people were there with nothing to do, just walking up and down the hallways.

I also met with one hundred priests and seminarians who were interested in questions around social structures and how to be present to the poor. That afternoon I visited a large slum area of some eight thousand people. Four years ago the houses in another area of the city were completely destroyed and all the people were transported to this swampy area. One priest spends all his time trying to set up small schools there and to consolidate the shacks made of wood and tin. However, one of the greatest difficulties is that there is no work for the men. This slum area with its dirt and suffering reminded me of the slums of India. I was struck by the smiling faces of the people.

I visited another psychiatric centre just outside the city. One hundred and eighty patients live in small houses on a big piece of land surrounded by a great wall. The patients are there, waiting, without knowing what they are waiting for.

Perhaps the best moment of my stay was the evening Mass in the community. There were about eight hundred people gathered in the little church. By 5:30 p.m. it was full; we left at 8:15 p.m. I spoke at the Mass and Father Jacques translated into Creole. Most of the people were poor and simple from the local area. The liturgy was very beautiful; there was an intense presence, prayer and joy difficult to describe. We were truly living the parable of the poor invited to the wedding banquet. It was a real celebration. At the end of the Mass we continued to sing, and clap our hands, as people danced in the church. There was such a unity among all of us. Many came to greet us after Mass. I felt truly "at home" with them, a real community of the poor.

The next morning, we had prayer and Mass at five o'clock followed by a meeting with the community councils of each area. I was interviewed on radio and television and then left for the airport. Everything happened so quickly. Now I am in the United States, another world! When I think about Haiti, I think of all those people displaced from their own native land, living poorly, frustrated because of their great poverty and misery. But at the same time, I remember their great thirst for community and for Jesus.

I do not know what the Holy Spirit wants for the future. I spoke with Father Jacques about the possibility of having one or two retreats and of creating a L'Arche community of peace and reconciliation. So little is done for handicapped people.

Jean

February 28, 1974
Ottawa

Dear Friends,

From Vancouver I visited all the houses close to us in the Federation of L'Arche. In Vancouver, Shiloah is beginning with Judie Leckie, in a large house the United Church has lent us. In Victoria, there is a small community, L'Étable, with Sister Margaret O'Donnell and many friends. I went there Friday night after the retreat with Bishop Remi De Roo, who said Mass in their chapel. I am touched by the poverty and simplicity of L'Étable, which will probably soon ask to enter the Federation.

Marymount in Calgary is another small community with a board of directors. It is not yet part of the Federation, but its founders, Pat and Jo Lenon, and their three children have been in contact with L'Arche for at least three years. After the retreat in Edmonton they felt called to give up everything to follow Jesus. So, they sold their house, left their well-paid jobs and moved into a rundown house. With Lynda, who helps them, they have fixed up the house and welcomed Émile and Gerry from a nearby institution.

I visited Shalom in Edmonton, a community of forty people full of life. I met with the board of directors and visited the four houses and the workshop. It is a very united, happy and prayerful community. I was impressed by the quality and dynamism of their community life.

Sister Marie Paradis has opened Rosseau Court, a community of fifteen people in Winnipeg in a house given to us by some good sisters. The members of the board of directors are all people who made my retreat. The official opening of the house took place in the church next door with Cardinal Flahiff, Bishop Baudoux of St. Boniface, the municipal counsellor who represented the mayor, the minister of labour, the president of the local parents' association and many others. It was an ecumenical event. There were about

eight hundred people in all. I have never seen such an official opening of a L'Arche community!

All these community projects in western Canada are growing,
evolving and deepening. I can sense how much they want to live
in the spirit of L'Arche and be part of the family of L'Arche. There
are, of course, many difficulties, but there are competent people
ready to work. It is beautiful to see how the Holy Spirit is calling
people forth who truly want to follow Jesus. Let us pray with them
and for them.

Last night we started the "Prison in Canada" weekend here
in Ottawa. It comes at the end of my visits to three federal prisons: Stoney Mountain (Winnipeg), Millhaven (Kingston) and
Drumheller (Calgary). There are some 170 people from different
walks of life: ex-prisoners, chaplains, prison visitors, rehabilitation officers, judges, lawyers, psychiatrists, prison directors and
administrators. One can imagine the work involved in organizing
such an event. So it is quite a miracle that it is happening!

The meeting started with a short introduction I gave on the pain,
anguish and fear prisoners can have and how difficult it is for them
to have a positive image of themselves. Then we broke into small
sharing groups, each with ten people from various backgrounds.
The goal of these three days is to help people committed to prison
work to meet and share together. We will see where the Holy Spirit
leads us from there.

Only the Holy Spirit can do the work of reconciliation and help
each one of us listen to others in truth, without barriers. I myself
need to have the peace of Jesus in my heart as I animate these
meetings in prisons.

Jean

March 7, 1974
In the plane for Prince Edward Island

Dear Friends,

The weekend "Prisons in Canada" ended peacefully with a desire in us all to continue to work together. At the end of our meetings a prisoner came to me and said, "I've been in this prison world for thirty years and after this weekend I know now that some people are truly interested in us."

I am shocked by the fact that in Canada we manage to have an openness towards the handicapped, and to make steps forward in that field (even though quite slowly), but we are regressing in regard to the prison world. Everybody agrees that today prisons only increase hate and frustrations. Official statistics show seventy-six percent recidivism, which means that once one enters into the world of delinquency, it is difficult to get out. Prisons are not therapeutic. They are overpopulated, there is not enough work, there is much fear and a real danger of outbursts on the part of the guards. There is talk of building new prisons as it appears that there are no serious alternatives in Canada.

From Ottawa I went to Toronto for a conference with the United Church of Canada. My heart was so full of all that I had lived in the prisons. I met a judge there who had just condemned two men to life in prison for drug trafficking. It is of course vital to stop those who commit this murder of youth, but we also need to find a system which rehabilitates and heals drug traffickers.

On Monday we had a meeting of the L'Arche communities in North America: Shalom, Rosseau Court, Maranatha, Daybreak, Hearth, Alleluia House, Maryfarm. The L'Arche family is growing and deepening with its difficulties and sufferings. Our need for this Federation is clear. We need the support, strength and encouragement of each other. We all experience the same difficulties: an overload of work involved with new foundations, contacts to be made with the minister of health and local officials, welcoming visitors, creating community, helping the handicapped to achieve a greater autonomy, trying to live ecumenism, etc. But we also share the same joys, moments of real celebration and the same call of Jesus.

The L'Arche houses in Canada are preparing for their pilgrimage to Canterbury. Two hundred and nineteen people will be coming to England and then to France! It will be an important time of unity. Let us pray that it will truly be a time of celebration and renewal.

We will arrive soon at Prince Edward Island. I remain close to each of you, especially those who are suffering. I am glad that I will soon be back in Trosly. My health is holding out well, thanks to Jesus, even if from time to time I feel tired. I am sure that is my lot in life.

Love,
Jean

March 19, 1974
Trosly

Dear Friends,

I am happy to be in Trosly with our big family. During my absence, the longest ever from Trosly, Antoinette Maurice and the community council have managed quite well with the daily problems of a community of almost three hundred members! Let me give you some news of my last week in Canada.

My stay in Prince Edward Island lasted barely twenty-four hours with a talk at the university, a visit to a home for handicapped children and visits to a workshop and a prison. In the evening I gave a public talk. The next morning I had a meeting with the various government agencies, as well as with teachers and doctors, on questions concerning L'Arche and the handicapped. Then I left for Toronto to visit the Maranatha community in Stratford.

Maranatha is a wonderful small home run by Charlie and Marjorie Pickersgill.* I was particularly impressed by the unity and peace in the home. We celebrated Mass together and enjoyed a joyful meal. That evening I gave a talk at the Stratford Theatre and then left for Toronto.

In Toronto we had an ecumenical retreat and two days of prayer and unity with brothers and sisters from the Anglican and United Churches. As in all ecumenical retreats there was much pain, but Jesus helped us to live the pain as an offering for all the divisions, hatred and refusals of the past. Deep union can only come gradually, through suffering and through a real deepening of our lives in the spirit of the Beatitudes. Unity can only come about when we are all transformed by the Holy Spirit. We must work more and more towards this unity through prayer and through work with other followers of Jesus. Unity around the Eucharist can only come little by little, when the time is ripe and when the Holy Spirit brings that unity into being.

Many friends from Daybreak were there. There is new life in Daybreak. A new house, Avoca House, has been opened in the heart of Toronto. Another new home will be opened on the grounds of Daybreak. A bakery, run by Kathy Barton, will soon open, and they will start cultivating the farm this summer.

On Sunday evening I visited Alleluia House in Ottawa. Before that I gave a talk at a festival for couples on the four seasons of love. Each one of our communities also experiences four seasons:

---

*Charlie and Marjorie are Ronald Pickersgill's parents. You'll remember Ron from my letters from Bangalore, India, a few years earlier.

the fatigue of fall, the pain of winter, the joy of spring and the radiance of summer when the fruit begins to appear.

The following morning I left for Kingston, where I had a meeting with about a hundred men in a federal prison. It was not very easy as I could sense all their pain and frustration. But I felt it was important to go there and to be with them. Then I gave a talk at the university, followed by dinner and another talk at the faculty of medicine. I left the following morning for Maryfarm where I visited Frank, Anne-Marie, their children, Gordie and Stuart, and the whole farm of about ten cows and calves! It is a small community, full of life. My brother, Benedict, came to say Mass; it was a little family celebration. Then I left with Benedict for the Trappist monastery in Oka.*

Thursday morning I was at Archambault maximum security prison. One hundred and fifty men, watched by armed guards, were there in the gym. I felt the extreme pain of these men who had committed serious offences and who were now experiencing the emptiness of life in prison, which leads to frustration, hatred and aggression. In their hearts, however, there is always the hidden cry for tenderness. The discussion which followed was lively and often rather poignant. There is such truth, such a cry, in those who have been imprisoned, a cry expressed through their aggression and sometimes through their tears.

After Archambault, there was a meeting in a CEGEP with about thirty very aware young people. We spoke about the crisis in

---

*This is my eldest brother, Georges (or "Byngsie" as we used to call him). He had been a soldier in the Canadian Army during the Second World War, and when the war in the Pacific ended he thought he might join the priesthood. He went on retreat to the Cistercian Trappist monastery at Oka, Quebec, and felt called to life as a monk, living in simplicity and silent contemplation. He joined the Oka monastery and took the name Benedict in 1946.

Quebec.* Then it was off to McGill University where I spoke to four hundred students.

After that, I attended Mass in Guy Bouillé's parish, Ste. Cunégonde in Little Burgundy. About nine thousand inhabitants live in this area of Montreal, most of them on some form of government assistance. They are quite simple and poor, carrying the many burdens of marital problems, violence and alcoholism, but also much courage and beauty. I will be giving a retreat in this parish.

That evening I met with about three or four hundred people from the neighbourhood. We danced and sang, and then I spoke for a little while. The following day, with André Patry, I spoke at the Bordeaux prison to a group of about sixty prisoners. I was struck by the way they listened. One man told me, "When I was outside, all I could think about was pleasure and money. It's only because I was knocked over and crushed that I'm now beginning to understand what peace is." Do we have to be "crushed" in order to realize what peace is? I also saw Réal Chartrand there.** He looked well. When we met it was like two brothers seeing each other again.

Then I had a meeting at the Université de Montréal, where there were fewer students and more members of religious orders than

*The 1960s and '70s were a turbulent period in Quebec. The Quiet Revolution of the 1960s saw a wide rejection of past values and a turning towards secular, urban, liberal, "modern" mores. Then, in the 1970 October Crisis, an extremist nationalist group kidnapped the British trade commissioner and murdered a Quebec cabinet minister, leading to the imposition of martial law. In the years following, the extremists went on trial, the provincial government fell, new laws made French the official language and the influence of the Church plummeted dramatically. When I wrote this letter, Quebec society was still feeling the aftershocks of so much change and crisis in such a short period of time.

**Réal Chartrand killed a police officer after an armed robbery and was sentenced to hang in 1972. He was a superman for escaping from prisons! We met at various times in my prison ministry. After serving seventeen years of his conviction, mostly at a psychiatric prison, he obtained full parole.

at McGill or Loyola. I felt I was not able to reach the world of French-speaking students, whose preoccupations are very different from those of their English-speaking counterparts. They may be more discouraged when it comes to politics as they have a greater sense of broader issues. Students in Quebec have always maintained considerable hope in local and regional politics.

After that, I went to see the Little Sisters of Foucauld; many friends were there. Then I was off to Cowansville the next day to visit another prison. That day, Lise St. Arnaud had her little Paula baptized inside the prison. I was happy to be the godfather. The ceremony was simple and beautiful. This little Paula was like an image of each one of us, for we are all little children in search of love and peace. Each one of us is imprisoned, more or less, by our selfishness, behind the bars of our fears. The fifty prisoners present were so touched by this ceremony.

I still feel the emotions of these five weeks in Canada. We don't always grasp the incredible despair of people in our world, and also the thirst of so many young people who are looking for authentic life and authentic love. The communities of L'Arche are a sign of hope for many, a sign that love is possible in this world. It is true that our communities all have their difficulties—the greatest difficulty usually comes from assistants who feel discouraged, or whose own problems can prevent them from being truly loving and persevering. There can also be a fear of commitment and of dying to their own selfishness in order to rise up spiritually. At the same time, however, in each one of our communities one can sense how open people are and striving to grow in love. I was truly impressed by the incredibly deep thirst in the hearts of those young students. More and more projects must be created where youth can find work and a way of life which are in harmony with their dreams. Modern life and the professional world often crush their dreams for love. They become discouraged and no longer believe that love is possible and so they give up.

I feel more and more committed to the vast world of people in prison. I cannot do much for them but I carry them deeply in my heart! If I had been born in other circumstances, perhaps I might be behind bars today, full of frustration and anger.

I have just read Solzhenitsyn's talk when he received the Nobel Prize in 1970. I was touched by what he said. It is well worth reading if you can find it. He has a truly prophetic vision of our world and knows what he is talking about since he suffered a great deal in the camps in Siberia. Blessed are those who are persecuted.

Jean

May 31, 1974
Bouaké, Ivory Coast

Dear Friends,

Françoise, Dawn, Seamus and I arrived here Wednesday. We caught the bus at Abidjan at 6:00 a.m. but did not leave until 8:15 when the bus was finally full. You can imagine how glad we were to see the last passengers arrive! Debbie and Gus had lunch ready for us upon arrival at Bouaké.

Since our arrival we have been visiting from home to home, meeting with people who are open and willing to form a board of directors. This morning the mayor promised us two and a half acres of land, so Gus is preparing to build a house to accommodate eight handicapped people, and a workshop for another ten day-workers. This morning we also visited the psychiatric hospital. We met Saturday, a small, smiling old man with no family. Nobody knows his name, so the hospital called him Saturday, which was the day he arrived in the hospital. We also met Carton, a young man suffering from epilepsy. Hopefully we can welcome them both around June 10, the official opening day of L'Arche in Bouaké.

It is astonishing how quickly everything has moved! When people heard that a group was coming from L'Arche, they had expected an old experienced married couple and a woman, the model social worker. And then they saw Debbie, Gus and Dawn arrive! Since they are so young, people want to protect and encourage them, even though some people might not be sure that this project can be taken seriously. Imagine when Gus met "M. le maire" and said, "Bonjour le maire!" Dawn is convinced that he said "Bonjour ma mère!" This morning both Françoise and Dawn said, "Bonjour monsieur le sous-préfet" to the prefect (local authority)! O la la! But he seemed completely charmed, and talked at length with Dawn! All the authorities are open to us and seem happy to welcome us, in spite of our mistakes.

Before long, Dawn will go to Man, a town three hundred kilometres west of Bouaké, to prepare the foundation of a second home in the Ivory Coast. We felt it would be important to have a second house quite soon, so that the two could give support to each other. In God's time, perhaps a third community will begin in the Upper Volta, almost a thousand kilometres north of Bouaké. We have decided not to start a house in Abidjan. More and more we are convinced of the wisdom of this decision since it would be difficult for us to maintain our own identity in that enormous city. The needs are tremendous and there would be so many influences that would try to force us to create something big and important, and to welcome especially the children of the more wealthy people. Here in Bouaké we can welcome the poorest and the most abandoned.

It is a real joy for me to see Gus, Debbie and Dawn again and to see their peace, their strength in all their weakness, their desire to follow Jesus and to listen to the Spirit. We all realize the importance of this first community on the African continent. We already have many friends in the neighbourhood. An old Muslim man and his children come each day to visit. Monica's family and a young handicapped woman live nearby. A Canadian couple lend their car and bring food. The Christian community of priests and nuns, the Bishop, the Protestant Minister and the director of a nearby school all give us their support.

Bouaké is different from Calcutta and Bangalore. One does not see the great poverty of the Indian cities. The minimum salary for men is about 340 francs a month. There is much unemployment since people come from many neighbouring countries looking for work. Prices are high. The people on the street are open and welcoming, especially at Bouaké. Many are poor and live very simply, but there is joy and peace. We are not aware of any serious tension or discontentment.

Yes, I am happy to be here, my first visit to black Africa. Life seems so authentic, so human, in spite of the fact that Bouaké is a big city of 120,000 people. In many ways it is like a big village. There is much land. The region in which Bouaké is situated is bigger than Belgium, but has a population of one million, of which ten percent are Christian, thirty percent are Muslim and sixty percent are animists.

Wednesday evening I spoke to a large group at the cultural centre. The conference had been announced on the radio. It helped that I had been previously on television in Abidjan and also here in Bouaké. Dawn introduced me. She has a gift for speaking in public; I had to stop her before she said everything! Last night we had Mass and supper with the Benedictine Fathers. It is good that the monastery is close.

Yes, Jesus is good. He is watching over this newborn L'Arche, and guiding it step by step. Continue to pray for us all that we be faithful to the Spirit. Sunday is the feast of Pentecost, Alleluia! Thanks be to Jesus for his Spirit which we need so much!

Jean

August 12, 1974

Dear Friends,

Let me tell you about my time in British Columbia. I arrived last Saturday in Vancouver and was met by the communities of Shiloah and L'Étable. Both are self-supporting; all the members work outside the community and share their salaries. Both want to be open to poorer people. At Shiloah I was impressed by the number of people who sense they have been called there by Jesus. When someone comes to a community because he feels called by the Holy Spirit, he brings a stability and strength which help to carry difficulties and sufferings.

The next morning I visited twenty men in the federal maximum security prison; people from L'Étable and Shiloah came with me. I hope they will be able to continue to visit there.

Then the retreat began in Nelson, organized by Bishop Doyle, the Catholic Bishop. It was, I believe, one of the most peaceful retreats that I have ever had, despite the number: about 550 people from the Catholic, Anglican and United Church traditions, with one Anglican and four Catholic bishops. One of them, the Bishop of Spokane, Washington, lives in a small house in the poor area of his city, works in the garden and spends much time in prayer and welcoming the poor. You sense in him a great simplicity and a presence of the Holy Spirit; what a grace to know him! At the retreat there were also about sixty people from our homes in western Canada. There is such a desire in each one to be faithful to the Spirit and to grow in the love of Jesus and the Beatitudes.

I felt deeply united with the Anglican Bishop and the regional head of the United Church. One evening all three of us travelled together by car and shared for nearly three hours. We are united in our hearts and in our desire to follow Jesus, in spite of all our poverty and failings.

I thank Jesus so much for that retreat and the unity he gave us. Twenty years ago the different churches were fighting among themselves; ten years ago they were hardly speaking; and now we are able to live and pray in unity even though we are not yet united in the Eucharist.

Have a good vacation. Love to you all in the Alleluia of the ten years of L'Arche!

Jean

August 23, 1974
Quebec

Dear Friends,

I am happy to be in Quebec, where I am giving a new type of retreat in a hospital for 450 patients who are elderly or chronically ill, many bedridden. Some come to my talks in the auditorium; others listen to them through loudspeakers in their rooms. A number of people from the neighbourhood also come to the talks. They would not be able to attend a retreat elsewhere because they have to stay close to their families. Every evening I give a talk outdoors where there are about eight hundred people. I like this kind of retreat, which is more accessible to poor people.

Besides the talks for the retreat, I have television interviews, visits to the prison and meetings with parishes. Last night I went to a drop-in centre. It can be tiring to go from talk to talk, but Jesus gives me strength.

A conflict broke out with a group of social workers. A group of Christians deeply committed to a poor neighbourhood became angry and revolted against the wealth of the Church. Working-class people in poor neighbourhoods without many resources often lose their faith, while those who have a more comfortable lifestyle continue to practise their faith but do not follow Jesus, the poor one, prince of the Beatitudes. The social workers were afraid that my talks were only going to confirm people in their piety as an escape from commitment to the poor; they were frightened I would just confirm people in their comfortable way of life. I can well understand their concerns for in many ways I share the same anguish. There can be a real tension sometimes between a commitment to the struggle for greater justice and an attitude of docility to the Holy Spirit. In the commitment to the struggle for justice, there are elements which are purely human; in the docility to the Spirit, there is the danger of a certain verbalism and escape into piety. Those who commit themselves to work for greater justice are truly committed to the weak. Many of these social workers are close to wounded people. Through our openness and docility to the Spirit we are called to grow and to become committed in the ways Jesus wants.

The criticism of these social workers was quite strong. At one moment they said, "It is easy to attract people with words, to confirm them in their piety; however, Jesus was crucified because of his commitment and because of the struggle he led against the Pharisees." We must learn how to commit ourselves to a struggle for justice, but at the same time how to be docile, and to let the Holy Spirit guide us and lead us. Jesus will bring us to the cross when he wants.

Pray that I may be faithful; that is the only thing that counts. It is true that we can easily turn away from the truth of Jesus and be seduced by prestige. Pray that I remain poor and never fear doing what Jesus asks of me. Pray also for these social workers, for I can understand so well what they are saying; I feel close to them. Pray for the 450 patients and old people in this hospital. I am happy to preach the retreat to them.

Pray also for the Church in Quebec, that the people may be authentic in their commitment to Jesus, that they do not try to escape into a certain piety but remain open to the Holy Spirit and to their wounded brothers and sisters.

Stay close. I remain very close to each one.

Jean

November 15, 1974
Calcutta

Dear Friends,

What a joy to be with our community in Calcutta again! Asha Niketan is like a haven of peace at the heart of this mass of suffering.

Things have deteriorated considerably in the city of Calcutta since last year. At the station there are more people sleeping on the ground. There are long lines of people (most of them coming from Bangladesh) waiting for food that the Sisters of Mother Teresa give out. People in the villages around Calcutta, who have no food because of the drought, are obliged to leave their home, their land and any goods they have, and come to the city, hoping to find food and a better life. Prices are going up and the poor remain without shelter and without food. Before I leave Calcutta I hope to visit the villages and perhaps Bangladesh. The whole situation in India obliges me personally, as well as our communities in India, to deeply question our way of living.

Here in Calcutta, a city which is a sign of the sufferings and divisions of our world, we all feel our house must become more and more a place of prayer, of peace and trust in God. Calcutta is a reality in itself but it is also a sign of something much deeper. It is like an abscess on the body of humanity revealing a serious infection coming from a lack of love, the fear of being committed to the poor.

I went to Mass this morning at Mother Teresa's and I had breakfast with her and Gabrielle. She looks very tired; that is not surprising! She told me how happy she was to have visited L'Arche and she asked about the different people she had met.* I feel close to her. This evening I begin a two-day retreat with the Sisters of Mother Teresa. Sunday evening there will be another two-day retreat in the sisters' new house for the dying and homeless. These two retreats will be a moment of real grace for me. We will all be staying in the Home for the Dying during the second retreat, eating and sharing with them.

The whole situation in India disturbs and distresses me more than ever. It confirms all I said in my report at the Conference in Nairobi. When will we in the West understand? What sign do we need in order to wake us up and help us realize that we must learn to share, to live as brothers and sisters? Is it too late? Perhaps we simply have to let the logic of indifference, rejection and hate take its course towards explosions and violence. Here so many of the poor and hungry already live the horrors of suffering, hunger and total insecurity. We in the West are still living in an illusion, not realizing that the intolerable has already begun. Yes, it is evident that love and sharing are the only realities that make sense and that only Jesus and his Spirit can communicate this love which leads to a total sharing and giving of our lives. It is so obvious, and yet so difficult to do. There is so much selfishness in me, but I have confidence in Jesus. I also have confidence that when the explosion does come it will be a grace for all of us. But we must prepare for it now through more prayer and through a love which

---

*Mother Teresa and I were honoured in Washington by the Kennedy Foundation and then we gave a talk together in Toronto. It was there that I invited her to come visit us at Trosly. She arrived in October 1974 with Sister Frederika and spent a morning and had a meal with about a hundred of us from the various L'Arche houses of Trosly. It was a big event!

is more total, more completely given to the brothers and sisters given to us by Jesus.

Help me to be faithful to the Holy Spirit during this trip. I carry with you all the joys and difficulties of the daily routine. I pray with you. Thank you for being there.

Jean

November 18, 1974
Calcutta

Dear Friends,

From Friday to Sunday evening I gave a little retreat to the sisters and novices of Mother Teresa at the mother house. There must have been about 150 sisters in all. These young women from all over India have left their families to follow Jesus. One can feel how open they are to the words of Jesus. Mother Teresa was with us and it was a real grace to share the Good News together.

Now I am in Tiljala, at Mother Teresa's new house for the dying and homeless. There are about forty of us here on retreat; half are Missionaries of Charity Brothers, twelve are from Asha Niketan, plus a few other people. Some of the sisters, their helpers and people living in the house also come to my talks, which are given in the little chapel. The retreatants are divided into five groups. Right now three of the groups are helping the sisters with the sick and the dying while the other two groups meet to share and pray. This evening these two groups will be with the sick and the dying while the other three will have time to share and pray. At noon and in the evening we eat all together some rice and curry, the same food that is served to the people who live in the house. At night we all sleep on the floor. It is very simple and beautiful. It is difficult to express the joy and the peace that is in me and in everyone here.

I have never been in a place more favourable to announcing the Good News. At the heart of Calcutta, the most suffering city in the world, there is this haven of peace and of grace where there is a strong presence of Jesus. I wish each one at L'Arche and in all our communities could be here with me. I carry each one of you in my heart so that we can all benefit from the grace of this retreat.

Two days later

The retreat goes on with its joys and sorrows. No one sleeps very well because of the noise of the trains. We are right next to the railway tracks and the train drivers like to blow their whistles at the arrival or the departure of a train. Then there are the mosquitoes which are small and quite annoying; they love to attack just when we are about to fall asleep!

The whole community of Asha Niketan–Calcutta is here. The men seem very happy. They benefit a great deal from everything: the presence of the Missionaries of Charity Brothers, the larger community we form, the talks and the little group meetings. It is good to see them so peaceful and happy, praying and sharing with everyone else here.

About ninety men are in this house for the sick and the dying. I met Khudabash again, the young vagabond whom Gabrielle welcomed to Asha Niketan. After several weeks he went back to his life as a beggar; then the sisters took him in. He is radiant, with a big smile. He does not talk but occasionally makes some noise in order to express something. He speaks a lot with his agile and expressive hands.

Later, back in the community

Many of us are feeling quite tired and Gabrielle and Ted have a fever. Bryan and I have no strength. Thank God for Maria Delores who is here to take care of us all, as well as Marlene and Philomena who are running the house. I am sorry I have not written before but I had only enough strength to do what had to be done. Last night I gave a talk to students and professors on "The Revolt of Youth." I am happy to have this contact with the Bengalis; it is important for the future of our houses. Tomorrow evening I will give another talk: "A Man for Others." God willing, I will be feeling better. One has to make a real adjustment food-wise and sleep-wise! But I am taking things easy and Maria Delores is giving me a special diet.

Ever since the retreat I find Calcutta more difficult. The crowd, the trains, the dirt; perhaps it is simply the fatigue which gives me this feeling of aversion. I must try to live with it; it will pass like everything else so I try to offer it to Jesus very poorly.

Yes, Asha Niketan is a real folly in the heart of Calcutta, yet it is Jesus's folly and it is important that we offer ourselves as a sign of the power of the Holy Spirit.

Jean

November 25, 1974

Dear Friends,

After ten days with my brothers and sisters in Asha Niketan–Calcutta there is a mixture of joy and pain in my heart: joy because the little community is growing and deepening; pain because I felt so poor, without much strength in that huge city of suffering.

I found the community beautiful with a surprising harmony among the men there, each one bringing his grace and his peace. There are three "brothers" there, Modhu, Shankar and Kashi, who were all found in the streets of Calcutta about three years ago by the Missionaries of Charity Brothers. Kashi was in a particularly bad condition: he was found lying under a tree in the rain with an empty plate at his side; he was dying. Modhu spent several years

in Mother Teresa's Home for the Dying. The three are very handsome now, full of life; their faces burst with smiles and with joy. In
Asha Niketan they have found a family and are obviously happy.
Shankar is perhaps the least handicapped of the three, perhaps not
handicapped at all. It seems he could make much progress. Modhu
has very special gifts of kindness, service, joy and simplicity. He is
always smiling.

Then there is Baroon, the clown of the community. His family
lives in Calcutta. Baroon has Down's syndrome and has been very
well brought up by his family. He is a joy to everyone. Dienesh
suffers from epilepsy; he also suffers from not being with his own
family. He must feel rejected. He has a hard time finding his place
in the community, perhaps because he has difficulty accepting himself and his condition. Noel, on the other hand, Armenian by origin, is very much at home. His family is in Calcutta but his mother
lives in a home for the aged. He is easy to get along with and is
peaceful and prayerful, and is a source of unity in the community.
Peter, a day-worker, rejected by his father, lives with his ninety-
year-old grandmother. He also has a lot of difficulty in accepting
the suffering of his past and thus has difficulty accepting himself.
It is interesting to note that the three who have lived without any
families, who were found in the streets, seem to be suffering less
than the others (except for Baroon and Noel), who have lived with
their families but who feel rejected. I have rarely seen such great
harmony in any of our communities. Of course there are the usual
tensions, but fundamentally there is a deep peace.

The day in the community begins at 6:30. Ted does some relaxation exercises with the men for about forty minutes (those who wish
can go to Mass in the church next door at 6 a.m.). There is a community prayer followed by breakfast (tea, bread and bananas). Then
everyone does a bit of housecleaning and goes to the workshop until
noon. At present there is plenty of work furnished by the Philips
factory (preparing and assembling electric wires, used in transistors).

Lunch consists of rice, vegetables, curry and half an orange. Siesta lasts until three o'clock and then back to work until six. After this a shower, recreation, a lighter meal than at noon, and the evening prayer before going to bed at about nine o'clock. Everyone seems to like this rhythm of life, which is simple and consistent.

Our house, a former church rectory, is like an island of peace glued against Sealdah Station, the most active train station in the world. This little island is at the heart of a mass of humanity (poor people sleeping on the ground, the Sisters of Mother Teresa giving food to several hundred people daily, and beggars and vendors selling all kinds of things). In this part of the city I did not see any other Europeans or Americans in the ten days I was there. There are mainly little people, struggling for survival, struggling to get into the buses and trams, running here and there, and yet one does not feel any great tension. There is a kind of simplicity, almost a good-naturedness. This time I was much more overwhelmed by the crowd; it was even difficult for me to go into Sealdah Station. I was full of irrational fear and felt very poor, with no energy. I felt more like shutting myself up in the house without seeing or hearing anyone or being pushed and jostled by the crowd. I felt so tired, especially after the first four or five days of intense retreat. I wasn't sleeping and I had the classic intestinal problems.

As I had little desire to go out I spent more time with the community. Basically, this moment of "depression" was good for me. Perhaps it made me closer to the poor. Perhaps I was also a little afraid of not being able to fulfill my mission in regard to the community in Calcutta—to listen to each one, to be present as a poor person, to give advice if needed, to be a reminder of the grace of Jesus and to try and share our call, our vocation, the specific role of L'Arche and of Asha Niketan. Perhaps with the grace of Jesus and with time and age, I am beginning to realize that I should no longer make decisions, but rather listen, sometimes awaken and call forth ideas and commitment, suffer with, be the friend and the brother who loves. I wanted to pray more but it was difficult; I was more easily distracted. I feel that my role is above all to pray, to remember that we can never live and love without the oxygen of prayer.

As I leave my heart is at peace, happy to be seeing my brothers and sisters in Bangalore again. Perhaps there will also be some mail for me there, giving me news of Trosly. I keep in my heart all the daily difficulties and especially those who are suffering. I have heard nothing about the strike nor the political situation in France. I confide everything to Jesus and to his Holy Spirit.

If Asha Niketan–Calcutta is growing and becoming stronger, their biggest suffering and search is to find a meaning to their life at the heart of this city. They have welcomed seven handicapped men when there are so many people without any shelter. They have a tiny bit of a garden in this city where land is so precious. So many people are without work, food or shelter; there are so many handicapped people who have nothing; how can we justify our life, which resembles in many ways the life of other L'Arche communities in other countries?

It was John Sumarah* who said when he came to Calcutta that "Asha Niketan should be primarily a place of prayer." And it is true. Asha Niketan has no reason to be there unless we are a place of peace, love and joy, which come directly from the heart of God. But at the same time, after visiting the Home for the Dying, and also the home of the Brothers at Noorpur, I feel more strongly the vocation and role of L'Arche. The Sisters and Brothers are able to welcome great numbers of people who are wounded in their minds and bodies. They save them from hunger, from physical sickness, from the horrible degradation of an animal-like existence and from the mockery

---

*John has been involved with L'Arche since 1971. He lived and worked in L'Arche communities in India and in France, and when he returned to Canada he wrote his doctoral dissertation on the therapy of L'Arche. He edited the first books of my letters.

and jeers of those who pass. They give them a roof, food and medical help administered with much love. But Jesus asks something else of us at L'Arche: to live with the poor, to be with them, to share, to suffer and to rejoice with them so that they become our brothers, our sisters. He asks us to be concerned for the growth of each one, and for that we are called to establish personal bonds of love with each one, which little by little become permanent. We must become parental figures for some, and older brother and sister figures for others. At L'Arche we are not merely employees who fill a function, but brothers and sisters who have heard a call from God to live poorly with the poor, with those whom God sends us. We are there to receive them with a love that comes from God so that they may discover that they are loved in a personal way.

The different aspects of our community life—personal growth, pedagogy and welcome are difficult to harmonize, but that is our vocation. Jesus will give us the necessary strength and light. We must continue to make an effort and sometimes go to the very limits of our strength, but in the end it is the Holy Spirit who brings about real community. Living in Calcutta I felt more than ever how much our lives and our communities are in the hands of God. God sends the handicapped people to us and it is God who inspires men and women to come to live with us. God alone can create unity and true love and compassion. In Calcutta I felt so strongly how much the Eucharist and the cross of Jesus are at the heart of our prayers and of our lives. The crucified and risen Jesus is our hope in this world where there are so many crucified ones and so much despair. Jesus is the suffering Lamb of God, the innocent one, rejected, persecuted and put to death in order to take away the sins, injustices, exploitations and hatreds of the world.

I remain close to each one of you, and especially to those who are suffering.

Jean

February 10, 1975

Dear Friends,

As I fly back from Bouaké I marvel at what the Holy Spirit has accomplished so quickly in our community there. In December 1973 Françoise and Dawn made their first trip to Africa to look at possibilities for a L'Arche community. In February 1974, Dawn, Debbie and Gus left for Bouaké, where Dom Denis Martin welcomed them at the Benedictine monastery. We had decided not to stay in the capital, Abidjan, which is more European, but to begin in Bouaké, which is smaller, more spread out and with a more relaxed African way of life. I would not say that everyone knows one another, but at least there is a great simplicity in human relationships.

Last June when Françoise and I arrived with Seamus the community had already put down roots. Now nearly eight months later we have a committed, competent board of directors, and the community has welcomed Seydou and N'Goran, from the local psychiatric hospital. Both had been town beggars in the streets of Bouaké. Seydou was unable to walk or to work. N'Goran wandered about eating what he could find; he had already been committed a number of times to the psychiatric hospital for delirious outbursts. Both of them are more mentally sick than mentally deficient. Seydou is particularly intelligent and speaks a little French, but has no family. Now both work in the fields and are obviously quite happy in our community. Everyone is amazed at their progress. Our first two African brothers are truly remarkable. It is important that we all welcome them into our hearts and carry them in our love of Jesus.

On February 15 construction will begin on our new African-style house, which will be able to welcome twelve handicapped men and women and six assistants. It will be built on the land which the mayor gave to us.

The number of friends has increased considerably. Neighbours come often to the house just to talk and share. Monseigneur Agré, the Bishop of Man (three hundred kilometres from Bouaké), is very desirous that we begin a little house in his city. We do not quite know yet what Jesus wants, but it is possible that we will say yes to his invitation in September.

In a little more than a year's time, L'Arche is firmly established in the Ivory Coast and recognized by the authorities. Jesus does things quickly! Everyone knows that we in L'Arche are not people equipped with diplomas, titles, age and experience, but it is through our unity, our faith, our poverty, our self-giving to the poor and to Jesus that the Holy Spirit has been able to accomplish things. We can truly be grateful for all that God has brought forth in this little community on African soil. It is so important that we be with them in spirit, that our hearts beat in unison with our brothers and sisters there. Africa is a poor continent. It lacks certain cultural riches found in Asia and South America, but it has something unique and special. It is a continent where personal relationships are amazingly simple and true. It is also a continent which is seeking its own identity, torn between an attraction towards Western materialism and its own ways and spiritual traditions.

Jean

February 24, 1975
Port-au-Prince, Haiti

Dear Friends,

There is really so much to share with you after these first four days in Haiti—where to begin? It is beautiful on top of the hill where the retreat house of the Community Sainte Marie is located. You can see and hear all of Port-au-Prince. In the distance, the sea puts an end to the city lights. This evening, as every evening, the sound and rhythm of drums and songs reach us from many different directions. Haitians love to sing and dance.

Friday evening we went to Bel Air, which, like Brooklyn, is one of the poorest areas in Port-au-Prince. Tiny streets wind around houses that are as big as one of the rooms in our houses. There is no electricity or sewage system. Streets at night are lit up only by glowing candles here and there in the houses and by the light of the moon. Fortunately, the Haitians go to bed early! The odours that spring from the area do not at all conform with its name "Bel Air"!! The population is very dense. In certain homes people have to take turns sleeping as the house is so small.

I was happy to tell the people in Brooklyn about the Good News Jesus came to announce to the poor. They listened in silence, moving from prayer to song with ease. One has to hear them sing with all their hearts and their rhythm "Moé sé yon pov" ("I am poor"); the church walls vibrate with their singing. In spite of their poverty and suffering they never miss a chance to sing and praise "Papa Bondie." Here one can understand so easily Jesus's compassion for the tired and famished crowds, how he invited the crippled and the lame to a banquet and promised eternal life to the oppressed and freedom to captives.

Nadine, Robert, Father Jacques, his choir and I went to a prison where I spoke to the prisoners and Father Jacques ended the day with Mass. The prisoners (both men and women) gradually moved closer and listened. Those who understood French responded by nodding their heads. The others waited for the translation into Creole by Father Jacques. Jesus was so present.

We also had meetings with the minister of social affairs, the minister of health, psychiatrists and others in preparation for a community of L'Arche. There is much hope.

Jean

March 4, 1975
Port-au-Prince, Haiti

Dear Friends,

I gave another three-day retreat to young people between fifteen and twenty-five years old. Most of them came from the "privileged" class, which has the privilege of a good education. They are quite well off but they are sincerely searching to know how to become committed socially as well as on a religious level.

Much peace and hope have been born in the hearts of people during the two retreats in Haiti. There was such a simplicity, joy and deep communion among us all. In the hearts of the young people there is such a thirst to know the living Jesus and his message. Their enthusiasm may seem a bit superficial. The seed of the Good News must deepen and take root in daily life. But there was something so beautiful and true in the retreats. Many young people in Haiti are worried about their future. There is often a lot of suffering in their families and they dream of leaving the country. They are thirsting for a message of hope.

Yes, I really see it is Jesus's hand that is leading us to this country which, in many ways, is rejected and despised by the richer, stronger countries. It has suffered from the more powerful nations and from colonization. Haiti wants to lead its own life, freely. I am happy we are going to begin there instead of on the islands that are more developed but which have no real identity.

Nadine, Robert and I leave Haiti much richer and much poorer than when we arrived: richer because of all we have seen and heard, poorer because of the poverty and simplicity of the people here. There is much hope for L'Arche in Haiti, and Robert is open and ready to follow Jesus in this adventure of L'Arche–Haiti. This new little community will have a special character of its own.

We sense deeply how little we had anything to do with all that has happened in these last ten days. It is as if everything had been

laid out beforehand. All we had to do was to be vigilant, to follow events, to open the doors that we were led to and to continue
walking, discovering something new all along the way. Step by step
we have felt the hand of God leading us. Yes, Jesus truly wants the
presence of L'Arche here. It will be a community that is small, poor,
open and very welcoming.

Jean

March 11, 1975
São Paulo, Brazil

Dear Friends,

Here we are in São Paulo. Last night we went to dinner at the
Canadian consulate. Amongst the invited guests were Adolfo
Pérez Esquivel, who coordinates a nonviolent movement in South
America, Hildegard Goss-Mayr, an Austrian who also works with
nonviolence movements in Latin America, and Mário Carvalho de
Jesus, who for twelve years has been struggling for social justice for
the working class; he was formerly president of the National Front
for Workers.* We did not have much chance to speak with them
during the meal but we sensed their deep commitment to Jesus and

---

*Latin America was in deep turmoil in the 1970s and '80s. Five years after this let-
ter, Adolfo Pérez Esquivel won the Nobel Peace Prize. His organization, Servicio
Paz y Justicia, is based on a Christian view of life and calls for an end to repression and terrorism through nonviolent means. Hildegard Goss-Mayr and her
husband Jean were later very influential in the 1986 nonviolent People Power
Revolution in the Philippines. Mário Carvalho de Jesus was a Brazilian lawyer
who had led and won a three-year-long strike of nine hundred workers in a
cement factory. I didn't realize it at the time, but the incident I recount in this letter became a powerful rallying point for the nonviolent and liberation theology
movements in Latin America.

to social justice. All three had just come back from a conference on nonviolence in Buenos Aires. They are seeking to create a well-coordinated and effective movement for nonviolence which can become a possible alternative to all the violent movements. Adolfo spoke to us about the situation in Argentina, which has greatly deteriorated—three hundred political assassinations in the past year—as groups from the extreme right confront leftist groups.

After dinner we sang some Spanish, Portuguese and Creole songs and we wet our feet in the garden pool of the consulate. We felt very far, materially speaking, from the meal we had eaten that noon in the favela or slum area of this same city.

Mário's wife phoned us this morning. After the meal last night, Mário, Adolfo and Hildegard went to the airport to pick up their luggage, which had arrived on another plane from Buenos Aires. They had not yet returned home so she was afraid they had been arrested, for Mário has already been in prison three times. Father Gabriel, with whom we were staying, immediately informed Dom Paulo Arns, the Cardinal of São Paulo. We did not get to Mário's house before that afternoon. When we arrived we found the three of them there. They told us that when they arrived at the airport, the police were waiting for them. They put black hoods on them and took them to prison where each one was questioned in a separate room from midnight to 4 a.m. They were forced to stand up the whole time, with the hoods on their heads. The police were verbally very brutal: "I want to drink blood"; "priests should all be killed." They tried to find out if they were Communists, and questioned them about their books and about the nonviolent movement. At 4 a.m. they were allowed to meet together and to rest. They prayed together and then decided to start a fast for, as Mário said, fasting is a source of liberation for oneself as well as for the oppressor. He recounted that Jesus prayed and fasted to drive out evil spirits. Mário explained the difference between a hunger strike and fasting, the former being a form of provocation while fasting is a violence against oneself in order to help the other: "The oppressor is still our brother; we must help him to liberate himself." At 6 a.m. the police brought them coffee, but they refused as they had decided to fast for three days if they were not released. As soon as the Cardinal could, he advised all the embassies and the Brazilian and international press. At 8 a.m., he sent his auxiliary Bishop to demand their release by eleven o'clock. I think they were released just a short time before our arrival at Mário's. Meeting them was a real gift from Jesus. Perhaps we will understand later the reason for our meeting. It is difficult to express the peace, serenity and grace that flowed from these three people.

Saturday afternoon we met once again with Cardinal Arns.* He spoke very simply about the situation in Brazil. He noted five different points: the government in Brazil is a military government and does not understand the complexities of politics; the government refuses the participation of the people; when it constructs a road or builds a school it does so as if it were a gift and not the right of the people; the government refuses to follow the law and the constitution regarding arbitrary imprisonment—the government censored, for example, the pastoral letter the Cardinal wanted read in all the churches of São Paulo last Sunday, peacefully requesting that arbitrary arrests stop and that the rights of individuals be respected; there are grave social injustices; too many people live on unacceptably low salaries.

It is impossible to tell you all that the Cardinal shared with us about the contradictions of the regime. Is the government playing

---

*Cardinal Paulo Arns was a fierce opponent of Brazil's military dictatorship and one of the country's most popular clergymen. He often visited political prisoners, speaking out against the abuses of the military. At the beginning of his term as Archbishop he sold the Pius XII episcopal palace, a mansion standing in its own park, and used the money to build a social station in the favelas, the poor, marginalized areas outside the city. Today he is known for being the pastor of the poor, speaking of God from the viewpoint of the economically poor and oppressed.

a double role? Is it really seeking to improve conditions? There seems to be no logic to the arrests. Last week four people were arrested: the president of the order of Brazilian architects, two well-known lawyers and one very popular journalist. No reason was given, and no one knew where the "accused" were being taken. What is certain is that the secret police are brutal and torture their victims. They are terribly frightened by Communism, but at the same time there are all kinds of contradictions. It is difficult to understand who is behind the secret police and what their goal is. The Cardinal told us that any form of tyranny is incompatible with the Brazilian soul. Ever since the military regime has been in power there has been a real change in the people towards a more Christian humanism, which had been rejected earlier. The Cardinal spoke to us of the strange mixture of liberty and tyranny in Brazil, but it is far from the tyranny you find behind the Iron Curtain. Here people can speak out quite freely. There is so much else to share with you but it would be too long and perhaps imprudent to do so.

I felt such deep peace and gentleness in Cardinal Arns. This Franciscan Cardinal, less than fifty years old, is so loved by other bishops and by everyone else. He is a true follower of Jesus, courageous in the face of the difficulties with the regime. Our visit with him gave me a greater sense of the role of the Church, the universal Church, in defending the individual rights of people. I will not forget Dom Paulo for a long time and I have a feeling that this is not the last time we will meet.

Today's events plus the meeting with the Cardinal are in line with the feeling of liberty that reigns here, for you cannot in any way compare Brazil with a country like Czechoslovakia where tyranny reigns. What is happening in Brazil is nothing like what Solzhenitsyn reports is happening in Russia. For example, I spoke twice on television, on a live broadcast without any censorship on the part of the station personnel. I could travel and speak to young people without any restrictions. There is a spirit of freedom, but still a fear of the police and of the regime. Yet there is a terrible gap between the rich and the poor, a form of oppression with very low salaries for the poor and constant intimidations that prevent workers from obtaining their rights. Brazilian people seem to be quite free—they can meet together and there are no laws forbidding group meetings as in Poland—but there is a certain economic oppression. It is difficult, of course, for us to synthesize the social, political and religious situation in Brazil after such a short visit, but we can say that there are many contradictions.

At São Paulo, there are 580 favelas right next to this immense, extremely wealthy city with its skyscrapers and freeways. The look of sadness on the faces of the rich contrasts with the peace and openness of the poor families in the favelas. Mr. Joachim, who welcomed me in the favela, said, "We are ashamed of our misery." Five or six times a day his wife, about fifty, goes down to the well (the only source of water) two hundred metres from the house. She carries water back on her head. His son leaves the house at 5 a.m. to go to work and comes back at 8 p.m.—four hours travelling standing up. He earns about one hundred dollars per month. The minimum salary is sixty dollars. Within the favela each house has its own personal history and its own particular suffering, like the family with fifteen children where one child works, two go to school and the other twelve stay at home. Another woman in the favela, mother of five children, went to work for the first time the other evening. Her husband is alcoholic and only comes home once or twice a month when he really has nothing left. One day she came home and found her youngest daughter, ten months old, with her nose and ears bitten by rats.

What can I say about the visit to centres for the handicapped? We visited one centre for twelve hundred severely mentally and physically handicapped children. There was such a deep, silent crying out for affection, touch and authentic relationship. Those in charge did not seem to understand the extraordinary sensitivity and needs of these children. Nadine, Robert and I were very moved to see the faces of these abandoned children, who burst out in smiles as soon as we touched them. I have never felt so strongly how much children can heal us of our egoism when we touch them with tenderness.

We visited the psychiatric hospital, where we were only allowed to look at the patients through a window. One woman seemed completely crushed by the indifference that surrounds her. We visited another psychiatric hospital run by Portuguese sisters which had a more joyful atmosphere. We sang and laughed together with the patients. At Guarulhos, twenty kilometres from São Paulo, we shared with two groups of one hundred young people and sang some Creole songs. The majority were from rather poor families, young people with hope in their hearts waiting for the project that corresponds to the call in the depths of their being. In Brazil there are over forty million young people under fifteen years of age.

With so few priests in the country, lay people take more and more responsibility. Small prayer groups meet regularly every three weeks and group leaders meet with the priest once a month. Often it is pastoral care of the poor by the poor. Many parishes do not have Mass every Sunday, so certain lay people are chosen to lead a Sunday service and give Communion. Since the priests are overwhelmed with all that has to be done, they do what is specifically part of their ministry and let lay people assume responsibilities and live their *charisms* in the community. Some people follow a mixture of spiritism and Christianity. The present Church is a suffering Church, but there is much new life coming to birth (the small prayer groups, the role of the laity, etc.). The bishops, in general, are loved and admired by all and assume their responsibilities with courage. More and more they are seen as the defenders of the poor and of the rights of the people. They speak of Dom Hélder Câmara with immense respect, but he is very isolated and within the country they know little about him as everything about him is totally censored by the media.*

Nadine, Robert and I are trying to discern why Jesus has brought us here. For Haiti it was clear, but here it is both terribly intense and mysterious. Each day we become more and more involved. What does Jesus want of L'Arche here? How can we understand the meaning of so many meetings with people who have touched us so profoundly? How can we explain that my book *Ouvre mes bras*,** translated into Portuguese, was on sale everywhere since the day we arrived? We have the feeling that L'Arche will have its place here. We talked to the Cardinal about starting Faith and Light groups in the parishes, and I told him about the three-day retreat we had with forty Canadian priests and nuns. It is as if all three of us are walking in the dark, trying to walk hand-in-hand with Jesus and letting him lead us where he wants. We feel so strongly the strength and peace coming from our brothers and sisters in Trosly and elsewhere. Help us to walk like little children, with our hearts open to each event.

Love,
Jean

---

*Archbishop Hélder Câmara influenced liberation theologians greatly with his commitment to the poor. He is famous for stating, "When I give food to the poor, they call me a saint. When I ask why the poor have no food, they call me a Communist." I first met him in the early 1990s when I was giving a talk with Secours Catholique—a Catholic NGO devoted to the poor and disenfranchised in France—in the southern suburbs of Paris. Câmara was also giving a talk and so I invited him to come back to Trosly with us for an evening visit and to talk to us about events in Latin America. He had written an opera about the place of the poor and sang it the whole drive back to Trosly! He was an amazing man with a tremendous gift for communicating and for artistry; he was a lot like John Paul II in his authenticity.

**This French book was never translated into English, but much of it appears in my book *Be Not Afraid*.

March 22, 1975

Dear Friends,

As we fly to Paris, we still have the songs of Amaori and Grazia in our hearts. The outcome of our three weeks in Brazil is hidden in the hearts of a few people and above all in the heart of God. Nothing is concrete yet, except perhaps small Faith and Light communities which will spring up here and there, God willing.

We spent three evenings with the Little Sisters of Jesus and Little Brother René. We feel close to the Little Sisters and Brothers. We are really the same family, with the same preoccupations, the same grace and the same calling, though, of course, in a different form. Little Sister Theresinha and Brother René spoke to us about the Latin American situation. Two Little Brothers have just been expelled from Paraguay after having been imprisoned. They had absolutely no political involvement, but were living with the poorest people and were part of a Christian community in a rural area. Anyone who lives with the poor is seen as a real threat by the government of Paraguay and immediately suspected of being Communist. Christians who want to share the poverty of the poorest and follow Jesus's way of life are being crushed. This is why a Little Brother in Chile was tortured and why so many other priests and lay people in Brazil have suffered the same sort of treatment.

It seems clear that the people in power are panicking in the face of the gradual change towards a system of greater justice which would allow the great majority of the working people and, above all, the Indians, to claim and defend their rights. The present government in Brazil is actually trying to stop torture and arbitrary imprisonments, but the power machine is huge and difficult to budge and the government certainly seems to be resisting any fundamental changes in its structure. Christian movements which have any social implications and want to fight for greater social justice are illegal and must act secretly. If discovered, they are immediately charged with subversive Communism and the injustices are sometimes enormous. A young girl of fifteen we met in a restaurant carried heavy responsibilities in her job but earned only twenty dollars a month (probably with board and lodging thrown in). The Little Sisters told us about workers who were brought in from the north of Brazil and are paid pitiful wages. People who are exploited have absolutely no recourse at all.

Rio de Janeiro is a beautiful city with five million people living in huge apartment blocks, over a space of forty kilometres. On the top of one of the mountains there is an enormous statue of Jesus with his arms outstretched, looking out over the apartment blocks (apparently the most expensive in the world) and the immense favelas. Fifty thousand families live in one of the favelas that we visited, which has no church or chapel. And yet an engineer in Rio has one of the highest salaries in the world and earns more than his colleagues in Canada. This dreadful gap between great wealth and great poverty makes you think of Miami or Cannes.

The Little Sisters want us to go to the north the next time we come, where forty percent of the population lives. People often told us that the south is not Brazil, that the people there aren't true Brazilians, that the north is like a different country. Dr. Odylo Costa, a member of the Brazilian Academy of Letters, was telling us that many people there don't have enough to eat; it is dry country. This time, however, we only visited the south, which is richer and more developed.

In the state of Paraná, as in Rio and São Paulo, there are a great number of immigrants from Germany, Italy and Poland. They have been there for about fifty years and have really taken over the country's resources. They have struggled and worked hard and found their place on a new land through the sweat of their brow. There is, however, another side to the coin. This attitude of determination and struggle did not develop an understanding, an openness or a warm heart towards the Indian people or towards those who were weak, poor or handicapped. This explains a bit why you find such a different situation in the South American countries from those in India or the Ivory Coast. Brazil is made up of many immigrants who left their native lands to come here and start a new life in a conquered land. People of India and the Ivory Coast have grown gently, peacefully on their own land, where they are firmly rooted. You find this same situation within the Church in Brazil: from the Portuguese conquest on, people were obliged to be baptized. This meant that in order to survive, the slaves had to combine their voodoo beliefs with Christianity. For centuries the Church there has been on the side of the conquerors. Gradually, through people like Dom Hélder Câmara, Cardinal Arns and others, the Church is beginning to move closer to the people. But this evolution is not without tension and pain. And the Church in Rio has been terribly wounded. The government has tried to crush it by putting many priests in prison; this made some priests defect, out of fear. We in L'Arche are called to remain close to these Christian communities in Brazil, carrying them in our hearts and prayers.

The future is all in the hands of Jesus. I am certain of only one thing: in the contradictions of South America where the extremely rich are living right beside the extremely poor, L'Arche is called be a reality which is poor and close to the poor.

Jean

August 6, 1975
Ivory Coast

Dear Friends,

How happy I am to be back on African soil! The weather is beautiful. It is the rainy season with light breezes. Except in the northern part of the country, where there is less rain, the Ivory

Coast is rich in land and water. There is a rich, dense vegetation: tall plants and immense trees grow everywhere and are right now a stunning green. Life is teeming: birds of different colours singing, butterflies flying here and there and landing on the bright-coloured flowers. There is an abundance of tiny animals everywhere: lizards, ants, mosquitoes, flies of different shapes, and I even had a visit from a scorpion! There are all sorts of fruit trees: orange, grapefruit, banana, pineapple, papaya, guava and mango, whose fruit is not ripe during this season. The Ivory Coast has so much potential!

So much life everywhere! It's as if everything is in motion; we hear the African drums and the chants; there is all the vitality of the faces with bright smiles.

People of the Ivory Coast love to communicate, to tell stories and to welcome others. They enjoy life and know how to take time to meet other people. When they speak they often use proverbs, and at first it seems a roundabout way of talking, not getting to the point. They can feel oppressed by the efficient, methodical way we meet with one another in our overdeveloped, super-efficient societies, where we tend to say quickly "what we have to say" and then disappear. In the Ivory Coast, people will only mention the reason of their visit after a long moment together, taking time to ask news of each one in the family and to talk of this and that. They know how to come together as persons and to share the mystery of each person, rather than meeting for efficiency and for the purpose which unites them (or which separates them). People here can really teach us how to live. I try to learn but I have a hard head!

The rhythm of the retreat here in Man is very slow, which permits much rest, prayer and silence. I was a little disappointed at first to see that more than half of the group are foreign missionaries. There are also ten people from our community and only about ten Ivory Coast seminarians. But this is the little flock that Jesus has given me for these five days and I rejoice with what is given. We are beginning to know each other a little, to love Jesus and to want to follow him together, each one with his or her grace and *charisms*. The young seminarians are very truthful. They speak easily about their family problems. A certain number have non-Christian parents who are totally opposed to their plans of becoming priests. Others have terrible qualms of conscience, for their parents have paid for their education in the hopes that they will become wage earners for the family, even for the village. What should they do? I find them very authentic, these young Christians who must fight to preserve and deepen their faith and their vocation.

Bishop Agré from Man is with us. He has such an open smile, warm welcome, love for his country and for the Church. We have much to learn from him. He introduced Dawn, myself and Mr. Koudou (a board member in Bouaké) to the head of the local government, who is Muslim and comes from the north of the country. We spoke about L'Arche. He is going to give us two hectares of very fertile, beautiful land, only two kilometres from the heart of the city. At the moment this land seems a bit far from everything but in a few years there will be development all around it. We could cultivate the land. There are already many coffee plants. The community in Bouaké is very eager to see another home begin close by, perhaps at the beginning of next year, God willing.

Our little L'Arche wishes to become an African entity at the service of the little ones. Hidden there where it is supposed to be, it will find its true vocation and its place in the African lifestyle and the African Church. Pray much for this community and for this beautiful country and this beautiful people.

Peace,
Jean

September 1, 1975
Paris

Dear Friends,

Since my last letter there has been the retreat in Winnipeg, a visit to Mobile, Alabama, a few days in Honduras, a stopover in Guatemala and three days with Robert in Haiti. My heart and head are so filled with these last two weeks, which have given me a greater sense of what a precious gift L'Arche is.

From Winnipeg I went to Mobile, Alabama, where I visited the community of Hope for the first time. Hope is a little community full of life and projects! They have a beautiful house. (In Mobile it is amazing the number of big, beautiful houses that exist right next door to a number of shacks where mainly black people live.) I was struck by the way everyone in the community wants to live poorly and simply.

Sunday morning, I went with Jan and Cheryl to visit a friend of theirs condemned for life in one of the prisons nearby. We spent three hours with him, in a large room with a number of other prisoners and their visitors. It is one of the most violent, brutal prisons in the States: there have been eighteen murders among the prisoners in the last two years. During these three hours, Jan's friend spoke of the suffering in the prison, the hatred, the fear, the blasphemy and his own personal pain. He himself had met Jesus a few years ago, at a time when he just missed being killed by a lynch mob. I asked him if he was at peace. I will never forget his answer: "Sometimes I feel like I have the peace that was in the heart of Jesus when he walked the way of the cross and everyone around him was blaspheming." When we left the prison around noon we were incapable of speaking for about two hours. We remained silent, a bit overwhelmed by the mystery of human suffering and a real presence of God in these men. This visit showed me once again how much prisoners can bring us and how important it is that we understand them and grasp what is happening. I realize more and more how much the quality of life in a society can be measured by the way it treats its more marginal, weaker members.

The next day Sue and I caught the plane for Tegucigalpa, Honduras. I had been invited to Honduras by a group of missionaries. Bishop Marcel Guérin of Choluteca drove us to his diocese, a two-hour ride through the mountains. He spoke to us about the present situation of the country and of the Church. The big difficulty that the Church is experiencing right now is how to combine announcing the Good News with a real love for the people and a desire to see them get out of their misery and injustices. The government would like to confine the Church to the sacristy and quickly accuses Christians who speak out for the dignity of man and for his social development of being Communists and enemies of the people.

The next day, we were driven to Tegucigalpa, where we met with other Canadian missionaries. At the end of the meeting, Bishop Nicolas D'Antonio of Olancho, an American missionary, arrived. He has been working in his diocese for eleven years now, in the desert-like northeast part of the country. When he first began in Honduras there were only two priests and three nuns for 150,000 people. Since then he has organized the Christian community, brought in sixteen other priests and twenty sisters, and has opened up centres for human development. People became more and more aware of the injustices. Large landowners considered his work subversive and threatened to kill him if he did not leave the country. Last May, he went on pilgrimage to Rome. He was supposed to come back on June 14 but at the last minute decided to return only on June 27. On June 25, his house was ransacked and two of his priests and thirteen lay people, one of whom was a "delegate of the Word of God," were killed. Under pressure from the Church and especially from university students, the government was obliged to act. The fifteen bodies were found at the bottom of a well, forty metres deep. All the priests and sisters were evacuated from the area by army helicopters to the capital, where they are still waiting to go back.

Bishop Nicolas is impressive, a man full of peace and good humour. He knows that he is still in danger of death but is not afraid. His life has already been given fully to Jesus. He told me simply that torture frightens him but that the Holy Spirit would give him the necessary strength.* The next morning, he celebrated Mass with Sue, Nadine and me. His presence made me realize even more the particular suffering of this country; perhaps there is less material poverty than in Haiti but it is much poorer in other ways. Bishop Nicolas helped us understand more the mystery of Jesus's teaching, which also disturbed certain people. That is why Jesus was put to death. It is so important that we remain close to our brothers and sisters in Honduras as there will surely be more persecution of those who announce the message of Jesus. At the same time the Church of Honduras has been crowned by its fifteen martyrs. All this means that the retreat that I will give at the end of this year will be very important and must be prepared in prayer. I confide this very strongly to the prayer of all our communities.

At the airport of Port-au-Prince, Robert was there with Helen and Jean-Robert. What a joy to see one another again! After a quick meeting with the board of directors at the psychiatric centre, we went to Kay Sin Josef, the name given to our L'Arche there. It is a little house with three bedrooms, a large veranda, a small kitchen, a washroom and a toilet. Robert wants Kay Sin Josef to be truly integrated into the Haitian way of life (he already speaks Creole amazingly well). As in the majority of houses in Haiti there is no gas or refrigerator. Cooking is done on a wood fire (it takes

---

*He found out later that a bounty of one thousand dollars had been placed on his head. I met Bishop Nicolas a few years later in New Orleans, where he is working with refugees.

time to make coffee!) and one fetches water from a well in the garden. In the evening we gathered together around the candle on the veranda for a long moment of silence, singing, offering our hearts to Jesus, asking that he keep us faithful to the call to live with the poor wherever we are. We must pray for Robert and for all that is happening in Kay Sin Josef.

Jean

November 29, 1975
Honduras

Dear Friends,

Nadine and I have been in Honduras only six days, but so much has happened in that short time. We have the impression that we are watching a jigsaw puzzle being assembled; day by day new pieces are being added, and as Nadine said, we know that the puzzle will never be finished. As long as we live, we will continually discover new pieces, new dimensions to the mystery.

At the end of my first talk at the retreat I said I would be happy to meet anyone who could help connect us with professional people or with parents of handicapped children. A young man came up saying his father was the director of the ministry of health. A doctor came and told me he works for the social security. A woman came up who has many contacts in town. And so we had a meeting with the minister of health and with some professionals. There is real interest in L'Arche and a great desire that we come here.

I have seen L'Arche come to birth now in many countries and it is wonderful to observe the same pattern of events here. Our Father, who loves the littlest and the weakest, prepares the path for anyone who comes. It's as if everything has been prepared by God our Father, who watches over the poor and the weak and

helps those who want to give a home to the homeless and to welcome the rejected. In one week much has been accomplished. It is
evident that it is not Nadine and I but Jesus working through us
and even through our deficiencies to manifest his love for those
who are weak. The prophecy of Isaiah (ch. 58) comes alive: "If
we try to break unjust yokes, to liberate oppressed people, to feed
the hungry and to give homes to the homeless, then Yahweh will
answer when we call and say 'Here I am.' He will guide us constantly and in the heat of the desert he will refresh us."

And again from Isaiah (ch. 40, v. 29): "Young people get tired
and fatigued, young men stumble, but those who put their hope
in Yahweh find their strength renewed, like eagles they have wings,
they run without lassitude and walk without fatigue."

That is true—even though now and again we do feel quite tired,
just enough to make us realize the folly of what we are doing, Jesus
gives us strength. Here we are, in Honduras, in Central America,
talking about Jesus and about L'Arche. It's a bit crazy! Isn't it mad-
ness? But there are many signs that show that this is where we
should be, and the puzzle is coming together. The fatigue makes us
put all our hope in God because we know that we can do nothing
all alone. If God wasn't there, everything would be totally absurd.

The retreat is an open retreat: people come for the talks and
go home to eat and to sleep (except for sandwiches we share at
lunchtime). Last night we had a fiesta with many children from the
nearby slum area. We sang and danced then we prayed by candlelight, "L'Arche style."* In a country where there is much oppres-

---

*The way we pray at L'Arche is influenced greatly by Brother Roger and Taizé.
After dinner and washing dishes at Le Val, for example, we gather in a circle in
a darkened room, with a candle and a figure of Mary at the centre. One member
of the community reads a short passage from the Bible, usually from Psalms.
After the reading we sit in silence, reflecting on the message, meditating on what
it means to us personally. Eventually someone might ask that we pray for a sick
family member, a travelling assistant or whatever concern weighs upon them or

sion by the rich it seemed strange that Jesus called us to announce the Good News not just to the poor but also to many wealthier people. But this is the community Jesus gave us for the week and we will see where it will lead us.

One of the most moving moments of our stay here was a visit to the mental asylum for the chronically ill: 250 men and women living in abominable conditions. Some of them were totally naked, a few were locked up in solitary confinement; the roof, the beds, everything was broken. There was a smell of urine, and rats all over the place. In one corner there were twenty empty coffins stacked up waiting for future clients. The personnel were watching television. I don't blame them! What can you do in such conditions? There is no work, nothing to do all day long, the men lie on their dirty beds. It is a hole of despair. Many broken people would not dare to get violent for then they would be locked up. The government has built a beautiful new hospital, which will be opened next February. But it is far out in the country, nearly an hour's ride by car. Nobody will be able to visit them there! And the beauty of the pavilions (eighty men or women in a pavilion) will be quickly destroyed by their despair. This beautiful hospital will be like a big cemetery. How difficult it is for people to believe that the so-called mad person is a person, loved by Jesus, and who is suffering deeply and yearning for respect, love and joy.

Amidst all the oppression of this asylum, Nadine and I experienced the mystery of joy and love in the hearts of these people (some have been living there for thirty years and longer). Each one wanted to touch us; each one was so open to a smile or a simple

the community. Then we choose a song and sing it together, one person leading on guitar or keyboard or with just a strong voice. Afterwards, we take some time visiting with the others in the room, chatting and laughing over the day's events, before we bid each other goodnight. I felt very close to Brother Roger and his ministry. He died in 2005.

touch of affection. In each one there is a craving for love. What a mystery lies hidden in the heart of each person!

Yes, L'Arche has a role to play in our world and in the Church, but only to the degree that we who are responsible do not fall into the pitfalls of seeking our own power and security; only to the degree that we allow the little ones, the wounded ones, to develop, to express themselves, to assume responsibility, to be themselves without fear; only to the degree that their simplicity confounds our complexity and hypocrisy and that we do not close ourselves up in pride but remain humble.

Jean

February 15, 1976

Dear Friends,

It is difficult to describe my joy at being back with my brothers and sisters in Calcutta. As some of you know, I was a bit fearful of this journey to India with the change of culture, food and way of life. I was basically fearful of the fatigue. However, the weather is cool. I sleep seven hours a night, sometimes a little longer, and have an hour's siesta. I eat well and have time to pray in the little oratory beside my room, where we have the real presence of Jesus. My little room at the back of the garden is an oasis of peace and silence, apart from the sound of crows and the noise of the trains.

Asha Niketan–Calcutta began three years ago when Kashi was welcomed by Gabrielle. What a long way we have come since then. The community is quite stable and peaceful. The daily rhythm is simple, healthy and at the same time it gives security to the men we have welcomed: 6:30 a.m. yoga, followed by community prayer, breakfast, housework, then the workshops, the midday meal, siesta, and work until 6 p.m. After work there is time for recreation, the evening meal, prayer and bed. I find that everyone is well physically and spiritually. Everyone feels that the time has come to start a new house. Tomorrow I am going to see a house that we might buy at Dum Dum, next to Mother Teresa's property. We could move in there within three or four months.

In each one here there is such a love for this mysterious, over-populated city where so many people live on nothing in the streets. I also feel a deep love for this city. I am happy to be here, to be on the trams, to walk along the streets, to watch the people. In front of Asha Niketan there is a group of refugees from Bangladesh living on the street, doing their cooking, looking for fleas in each other's hair, the men sometimes playing cards. When you pass by them to get into our house, their eyes greet us with smiles: much kindness and respectful greetings. Unfortunately they are going to be put into refugee camps soon as part of a project for "cleaning up" the city. In the long run I do not know whether this is a good thing or a bad thing. For the moment it is sad. I am always struck by the peace and serenity on the faces of these men and women on the crowded trams and in the street. This is not simply passivity or an unhealthy surrender. It is a peaceful acceptance. It is so different from the anguish and feverish anxiety which so many people in Europe and in North America carry on their faces in their search to have more and in the frustrations of each day.

On Saturday, Gabrielle, Martha and I had Mass with Mother Teresa's Sisters followed by breakfast with Mother Teresa. She was in good form. She told us all sorts of stories with such humour, stories inspired by her childlike faith. I try to give a lot of time to the community and also answer invitations here and there.

With love to all,
Jean

February 28, 1976

Dear Friends,

I am in Bangalore, it is Sunday afternoon and everyone is resting here at Asha Niketan. Outside the sun is very hot, but inside it is quite cool. I arrived here by train on Friday afternoon after four good days at Kottivakkam. Yes, our community there is, along with L'Arche–Haiti, the poorest of all our L'Arche communities: ten people live in a space that is surely no larger than the dining room, living room and office of the L'Arche house in Trosly. The house is at the heart of the village. In the back there is a little garden where tomatoes are growing and a water pump where we wash ourselves and the dishes. There is a thatched roof which covers the workshop and protects it against the sun. There is not much privacy at night: each one spreads out his or her mat and mattress on the floor in the dining room or in one of the two other little rooms. Marielle's bedroom is small and is also her office—all that is a part of the poverty of India. I loved my stay and felt so happy with our little family there.

Sunderan is a ray of sunshine. He had spent more than twenty years in a psychiatric hospital. Jayakumar is so funny and lovable. Shankaran, who arrived in September, has made much progress. He smiles and takes care of Ramesh, Mr. Baraton's son, who also has made a lot of progress. They are the four pillars of the house and living with them are Dominique, Gerald, Sukumar, Unni and Marielle.

What can one say about this little Asha Niketan, so simple and poor, which has welcomed four poor men—two of them can hardly talk at all and the language of the other two is not quite coherent. Living conditions are difficult but God is very present there. Madras is a place where there are only two seasons: the hot season and the intolerably hot season!

Tuesday evening we had the official inauguration of the Asha Niketan–Kottivakkam. Only the people from the village were invited plus some members of the local board. All the village children were there (perhaps because they had heard that there would be some candy!) and about thirty adults. The president of the village presided over the ceremony, which consisted of a few speeches, some garlands and some songs. Everyone is quite open to our little community and to the wounded men, and we already have quite a number of friends. The Swami (priest) from the temple came to pray with us and to share a meal with us afterwards.

About five minutes from the house we have bought a piece of land with fifty coconut trees on it, so there is some shade. It is more peaceful because it is farther away from the loudspeaker in front of our present house that blares out Indian music from morning to night. In a few weeks or months we hope to begin building a house. The plans have been made. We must wait for permission from the local government.

Peace to each one,
Jean

April 8, 1976
Paris

Dear Friends,
I am still in Cochin Hospital with a bit of fever.* The day I arrived back from India things went a little wrong inside: temperature and diarrhea. After a few days, the doctors thought it wiser

---

*I spent two months recovering in the hospital and took another three months to rest. I was doing too much, and my body was crying out for rest!

to put me in the hospital for a few tests. They discovered what they thought was amoebic hepatitis. But once they got rid of the amoebas, there was still fever and a secondary infection that they have to treat. They say that with the quantity of medicine they put in me there just could not be one live amoeba in my body! But as there was still fever and diarrhea we had to begin all sorts of tests again to find out who was still there! They have put me on a common antibiotic but under heavy doses. My temperature is going down, and thanks be to God, the diarrhea has stopped and my appetite is coming back. I have lost quite a bit of weight. I have some very beautiful photos of my intestines, liver, etc., which will help me to get to know myself inside and out.

I feel a bit stronger, particularly as there has been an "airlift" between Trosly and the hospital: people bringing me little bits of steak, sole meunière, artichokes and all sorts of nourishing delicacies which are intended to put a little meat on my bones. I think it is working although I have not weighed myself lately. Nobody dares tell me when I might be able to leave because every time they did before, my fever shot up! So just to avoid the bugs knowing anything about it, I will probably just slip out on five minutes notice and fool them all! I am being well cared for here. The doctors and nursing staff are highly competent and have the most modern equipment. My roommate, Saco, is a young worker from Mali who keeps me close to my brothers and sisters in Africa. The fact that Martine Laffitte, who was our doctor in Trosly, is one of the head doctors has certainly helped a lot and gives me great security.

I will need a time of convalescence after this. I am not quite sure where as yet. I am just living day by day, waiting to see when I will be able to leave and how I will be then. I have been in bed for nearly four weeks now, three weeks in the hospital. I will have to learn to walk again, then to trot, then to run. Right now just going up and down the corridor in the hospital puffs me out. So I imagine it will take time.

As each day clocks by it seems more and more evident that the doctors will not let me go to a tropical country in May. I will not be present for the International Council meeting in Bouaké (but, hopefully, I will still go there in August for the retreats). You can imagine how disappointed I am not to be with my African brothers and sisters and not to be present at the council meetings. God willing, my strength may come back more quickly and the doctors may still allow me to go. At this point, however, it seems to me that that would take a real miracle.

Jesus is really teaching me day by day what confidence and surrender are all about. I give thanks for that. And Jesus arranged for other instruments to give the three Katimavik* retreats that I was supposed to give (in Trosly, Belgium and southern France). He was really present in each one of them in such a beautiful way. I have been absent from Trosly for two months now, but things are running smoothly in the community. There is a deep unity and love as everyone takes on more responsibility. I give thanks also for that. So this is to tell you that I will be even more present at the International Council meetings than if I were there physically. I will be offering my absence and the slight difficulties I have so that there might be peace, love and wisdom in the hearts of each one, and that the burdens carried by our African brothers and sisters might be lightened by the strength of Jesus. I pray that each one during the council meeting will be filled with new wisdom.

---

*Katimavik is an Inuit word meaning "permanent place of meeting," like a community hall. For us in the early 1970s, it was definitely a coming together to meet with Jesus and amongst ourselves. It was oriented towards young people: if we called it a retreat we knew no young people would come! So for a Katimavik we'd sit on the floor and for a retreat we'd sit in chairs. The name Katimavik came from a man who was attending these youth retreats: when the Blessed Sacrament was exposed, he called it a Katimavik. It was a beautiful thing, and it's a beautiful name. (Our Katimaviks are totally separate from the organization Pierre Trudeau later established in Canada and from the Intercordia movement.)

Jesus is giving me a new form of wisdom, an understanding of what it means to be an "assisted" person. After twelve years at L'Arche as an assistant, I am now experiencing what it is like to be on the other side. It is teaching me a lot and it has been a real time of retreat, prayer and offering—a time also of detachment, not to be the one who has power, but to be weak, to put myself in the hands of God and wait and believe and trust.

I have been reading a book by Père Peyriguère, a disciple of Charles de Foucauld who spent about thirty-five years as a hermit with the Berber tribe in the mountains of Morocco. He was there as a sign of Jesus the Healer, for he opened up a dispensary. For many years he was the only European who was able to penetrate that part of the world. He was a man of prayer with deep trust in Jesus; it helped me to read about him.

I have also been reading Bruno Bettelheim's *A Home for the Heart.* I feel we have much to learn from this man and his deep respect for the wounded person. He himself spent time in a concentration camp, so he understands what oppression is and how quickly "assistants" can become like oppressors without realizing it. He also has important insights into architecture and the way of welcoming people. I feel he complements a lot of what we say at L'Arche. He is not a deeply religious man and his aides are more technicians than people called to long-term commitments. At L'Arche we are called to create a real family and to grow together. But the technical and human aspects of Bruno Bettelheim's work can teach us a great deal.

In my heart I give thanks for this time of illness. I give thanks for many people who have been giving me support, praying for me and helping me live day by day this new life.

The Bishop from Beauvais wrote me a beautiful letter in which he said, "God is free with the one He loves. Goodbye to Katimaviks, meetings, visits! Why, Lord, when they would have done a lot of good? But Jesus wants to show us that He does not need us. And

I am sure that finally everything is for the good of the one who loves God."

And so, my sabbatical week, months, year has perhaps begun! Alleluia!

Jean

April 27, 1976
Paris

Dear Friends,

I am writing once again from the hospital. Alleluia! Since my last letter many beautiful things have happened. My temperature shot up, nearly breaking the thermometer, and then a few days later shot down so that the mercury hardly peeked its head up at all. Of course, this worried the doctors and made them suspect that there must be a cause to all this. After Holy Thursday there were a few days of peaceful normality. Since then, however, my temperature has been popping up and down within more reasonable limits! But the doctors still believe there must be a cause and are giving me tests and X-rays, taking blood out of me and inspecting everything that comes out of me, hoping to find the mysterious bug that is working in a very efficient but hidden way. I wanted to write mainly to tell you that I have gained back some strength. I have not put on much weight though and am still not able to take part in a basketball game! But my appetite is good and my heart is at peace. Every day I take a few walks up and down the 150-metre corridor and I go down to the basement chapel for Mass.

Through all this Jesus is teaching me patience. The doctors have no idea when this will all be finished nor when I can leave the hospital nor whether I will need a long period of convalescence. Jesus is teaching me just to live day by day, happy to be where I am for the moment, happy to fulfill the vocation of today. There are, of course, moments of anguish, but I quickly ask Jesus to chase them away and to fill my heart with thanksgiving and trust. Is it not St. Paul in his letters to the Philippians who says: "Rejoice in the Lord always, again I say to you Rejoice." I have much to rejoice about, in particular the love of my brothers and sisters all over the world. There are so many who are supporting me in this new vocation which will last the time it will last. Père Thomas has been particularly good; his quiet, prayerful presence helps me to be abandoned, quiet and silent interiorly. I do not think we have ever had so much time together in our twelve years in L'Arche!

Thérèse, my sister, came over from England to consult with the doctors here. She was impressed by the way I am being treated, the competency and the "non-panic" attitude of the doctors and their reflection. I am deeply grateful to the doctors and the nurses and to everybody for their kindness. I strongly recommend the Cochin Hospital if you ever fall sick! Saco, my roommate, has become a real brother. He shares everything his friends bring him and when I have a high fever or terrible backache, he gives me a massage. On the wall just opposite my bed, they have put up a banner I received from some leper friends in Bouaké. It reads: "A brother who helps a brother is like a fortified city."

The hospital beds were too short for me and I was very cramped. One of the nurses said, "We'll give you de Gaulle's bed." I laughed but it was really true: they gave me the bed that was built especially for General de Gaulle when he had an operation here. It is a simple hospital bed but it is much longer, thank God!

For the moment, everyone is telling me that "rest" is the message of the moment. I feel that too. So I am sad not to be able to see many brothers and sisters whom I would love to see and who I know would love to visit. But this is the sacrifice Jesus is asking of me. All this is certainly new to me after twelve full years of activity and meetings with people. Pray for me that I may benefit from this time of inactivity, that it may be a time for the discovery of a new activity, the discovery of Jesus living in my heart and saying to me, "Abide in my love." Sometimes, on sleepless nights, I think of men and women in their prison cells. I think of all the lonely people and I realize how spoiled I am with so many who love me. There are very few people on this floor who have the flowers and special help I am getting—so many lonely people hidden in hospitals, in prisons or in apartments and rooms—so many rejected and wounded people. Let us pray together for them. And let us give thanks for the love and peace that Jesus has given us, which unites us and which we are called to share. At the heart of this unity and peace are all our Raphaëls in whom Jesus is hidden—Jesus, who is the source of peace and joy.

Peace to you,
Jean

August 4, 1976

Dear Friends,

Last Friday night Claire and I arrived in Man (Ivory Coast) after a good trip despite a big rush between planes at Abidjan airport.

In the afternoon, we visited the new house, which is almost finished. It is situated two kilometres outside the city. The local government has given us this large and beautiful piece of land covered with fruit trees, and Aroona, originally from Upper Volta, has begun a vegetable garden on a small area of this land. The house is big and will easily accommodate a community of twelve to sixteen people. It is African in style with large verandas, obviously, larger than the other houses of the area.

Maria and Brigitte have been here since March and really struggle with their role as house builders. They have had to oversee the construction, buy the materials and sometimes dispute or fight with the workers, without receiving much support from the architect or the building contractor. Those who have had the experience of building houses will understand part of their difficulties. When you are in Africa, you have to constantly negotiate prices and fight to get things done. Truly they have been courageous because they had hoped to have more support. Neither one came to Africa to build houses, which puts them immediately into the situation of the rich who build and the boss who gives orders. And this situation has lasted for four months, so I can understand their fatigue.

The more I speak to the people of Bouaké, the more I am aware of how much our communities suffer from a lack of identity. Many people ask us: Who are you? Are you sisters? Missionaries? Do you belong to some organization? We find it very difficult to answer these questions. They would like to put us in some sort of category so they could feel more secure. And our houses will be welcoming men and women from different religious backgrounds: animists, Christians and Muslims. Here as everywhere else, the big question is that of spiritual nourishment. How to keep hope alive during the gloomy days when we see only difficulties and misunderstandings? At the heart of all our communities there are Amouens and Seydous who give meaning to our lives and who bring unity to our homes. In order to live community life with people who have been rejected we soon discover our need for a love that comes from God. We need to grow in trust that God is our Father and that he wants our communities to be poor witnesses that love is possible.

I feel at ease in the Ivory Coast and know I have so much to learn from the people here. Pray that I benefit from my stay here to come back a bit changed, a better follower of Jesus.

Love,
Jean

August 21, 1976
Abidjan–Paris plane

Dear Friends,

I am in the Abidjan–Paris plane and my heart is a bit heavy to leave Dawn, who saw me off at the airport, to leave our two communities of Bouaké and Man. I like the Ivory Coast, the only country that I really know on this vast continent, but I am anxious to visit and learn about Upper Volta and other countries of black Africa. In the bush-taxi from Bouaké to Abidjan yesterday, I was beside a young Senegalese Muslim woman, the mother of three children. She had a very beautiful and dignified face. She displayed such nobility that it is difficult to imagine how the West could look down on such a person. Often, in India or in Africa, I feel clumsy and heavy with all my culture and pride when I am in the presence of these simple people, moulded by their traditions; they have often had difficult lives and known material insecurity, but have remained peaceful, confident and dignified.

On the way from Bouaké to Man with Dawn and Maria in our Citroën jeep, we stopped in a small village. We visited Marie, a forty-year-old woman, the mother of many children including thirteen-year-old Kouadio who, since he is unable to go to school, wanders all day around the marketplace. Marie immediately brought out some chairs from her small wooden house, sent Kouadio to catch a hen to give to us and brought us a basket full of tangerines. We could not stay long because we had to continue our journey. As we got back into our car, a child selling guavas arrived. Marie bought ten and gave them to us. By this gesture, this poor woman who, in order to support her family, normally sells fish that she fries herself in the market, had given us many days' wages. This is African hospitality. They do not give the small surplus but rather the essential, even what they need. How can one not feel poor and selfish after such acts?

We met also two young Protestant girls who have been living in the village for four years, learning the language (which is used by an ethnic group of only twenty-five thousand people) and writing it down, because up until now it has been only a spoken language. They are there to translate the New Testament. This will take them at least ten years. In the Ivory Coast there are fifteen similar teams, each inserted in a village in different linguistic areas, learning the language in order to translate the words of Jesus for those living in these villages. The Holy Spirit works wonders in inspiring young people like these. I was delighted to see them, and I feel I have much to learn from them. Fortunately, we are in an era of ecumenism. What a suffering it is to be divided in the body of Christ. The disciples of Jesus have so much to share with each other.

At the heart of our community in Bouaké is twelve-year-old Amouen. She was found in the market by the police and placed in a psychiatric institution. The other patients said that she was possessed by a devil. She speaks only a few words and drags one leg. She suffers from epilepsy and she must have had a hemiplegia when she was small: one of her arms and one of her legs are paralyzed. Nobody knows anything about her past or her origins, but she has found a family in L'Arche. She ran, jumped and laughed during the retreat and blew out the candles awkwardly after Mass. During my stay in Bouaké she caught a virus and had a fever of forty Celsius, which lasted many days. We were all worried. Fortunately, Dr. Coulibaly, pediatrician and vice-president of our board of directors, prescribed injections and intravenous antibiotics. It is something to be with a child who is suffering and who grips one's hand with gentleness, her eyes calling for help and yet not complaining and occasionally even showing a bright smile. She is really a gift of God to our Bouaké community. It would be marvellous to have an Amouen at the centre of each of our communities! The child brings a grace, a tenderness, a sensitivity which adults do not show in the same way. At the same time, however, a child has many needs.

Amouen needs clear and precise references; she needs to be loved with tenderness and yet to be educated with firmness.

Amouen has touched the heart of N'Goran, a twenty-five-year-old man who used to wander aimlessly around the marketplace and who also spent time in a psychiatric institution. He too has changed during the two years with us. He feels at home and has found security and peace here. There is a strong and beautiful relationship between him and Amouen.

I would like to share more about each member of L'Arche–Bouaké: Seydou who is now in charge of the henhouse; Gilbert who likes to ring the bell at Mass and who knows when to begin the songs, but who does not like to work and is afraid of any type of authority; Kouadio, a big man of the Bade ethnic group, who likes to wander around the neighbourhood (like Gilbert) and who also does not want to work. After one of my conferences, he came and said in Baoulé (of course, I needed a translation), "I did not understand what you said but I know that you are a man of God and that you say beautiful words. You will not die like other men and my wish is that your family will multiply and fill this whole room" (the room was very big).

Then there is Mamadou, who comes to work each day but lives with his family from Upper Volta. He was very excited to see Dawn and me when we visited him. August is vacation time, so the non-residents stay in their families. Monique also lives outside; she is very handicapped, capable of doing very few things and lives in a poor family. When we visited her with Chantal and Geneviève, her mother insisted that we eat with them. I was a bit afraid of what seemed to me to be a unhygienic way of preparing the "banana foutu" and the fish sauce. I thought of my recent amoebas! But, praise to the Lord, I was able to eat normally with a little smile and a big thank you after it was finished. During the entire month I had no health problems, and I return from Africa rested and with healthy intestines!

Each time I visit one of our communities I sense the ties that unite us and it is difficult to leave. Fortunately, when I leave here I am going back to Trosly where I will be with other brothers and sisters. We will continue to try to help each other to be faithful to the call of Jesus, to follow his new commandment, to be truly present (not just in words) to the poor and the weak who are entrusted to us and to grow together in hope.

United with each of you,
Jean

December 11, 1976
Tegucigalpa

Dear Friends,

Since our arrival here in Honduras I have felt completely incapable of writing. Perhaps it is because everything has been quite peaceful, simple and seemingly unimportant. Our time has been spent meeting with men, women and children in the area; each one is engraved in my heart. Perhaps it is also because I felt so terribly poor and encumbered by my own riches and culture, living with these people in Suyapa, in their utter simplicity and openness, with their welcome so full of tenderness and expectation. My stay in Suyapa makes me question our way of living; it makes me more aware of the pride and hypocrisy in me.

Suyapa is a poor section on the outskirts of the city where about a thousand families live in small shacks made of planks. In each one there is a simple earthen floor, one or two broken chairs and a few boards that are used as beds. There are not enough for everyone and there is certainly not enough room for everyone to sleep. Pacita, who welcomed us, found us a place to stay in the back of a small grocery store.

The fact that no talks or meetings had been scheduled in the city gave us time to get to know Suyapa. It was truly a gift of God and the grace of the moment. In retrospect, we see now that it would have been impossible to go up to Suyapa just to give talks. It was important to have time to live with the people of Suyapa, to meet them in their homes, to play and laugh with the children (and even with the adults).

Most of our time was spent in that way, with many unpredictable, personal encounters where we felt that a certain trust and friendship was growing. Yes, we began to love these people and they began to know and love us. That is why it is difficult to speak and write about our time spent at Suyapa.

I personally feel I have a lot to learn from Latin America. Nowhere else in the world have I felt with such force the gap that exists between the rich, those who possess, and the poor, who live in total insecurity. Latin America is made up of many different races: Indian, African, Spanish and others. It is a place where everyone is baptized and where the Church has great difficulty in finding its way between military and totalitarian governments, which are often terribly brutal, and Marxist revolutionary movements. Yes, in Latin America you really sense the difference between the culture of the rich and the culture of the poor. Is it possible to create in Latin America small Christian communities which could be like yeast in the dough and at the heart of which would be the poorest and the most rejected?

Everything I see here makes me really question our L'Arche communities and the double culture of the "assistants" and the "assisted" that can exist, the danger that can arise when the "assistants" possess power and security, and benefit from the "assisted" in order to gain a certain prestige. The more I advance in age, the more I discover how much I must grow more deeply in humility, which Jesus alone can give me. In order to do that, I need a truly loving and demanding community. I also need to live with and listen to the poorest and weakest ones. How easily we can fall into hypocrisy and verbalism. L'Arche can only exist if the "assistants" die to the culture of our times so that others can leave their culture of sadness and despair and be reborn; together we can create a new culture, which is also the oldest culture, founded on love and a faithful commitment to one another, a love that is ever new and renewed in and through Jesus.

We must continue along the road and see where it leads.

With much love,
Jean

April 28, 1977

Dear Friends,

I have been in Australia a week now and Eileen Glass has been keeping me busy with quite a heavy schedule: a retreat in Sydney, a few public talks, a day of talks in Canberra and now a retreat in Melbourne. In many ways Australia is like Canada: an affluent society with large open spaces. The people seem to have a great spirit of adventure. It is a huge country, but a lot of land is desert and even elsewhere the land is hard and a challenge to cultivate. They say there are three sheep for every Australian! It is a land of birds and everybody has been telling me about the kookaburras, which have a deep raucous laugh.

I am surprised by the number of people here who know about L'Arche, often through Bill Clarke's book.*

People came from all over Australia for the retreat and I sensed a great yearning for Jesus and for the truth. Many were keen to

---

Enough Room for Joy: The Early Days of L'Arche, by Bill Clarke, SJ. This book is now available through L'Arche, at pubs@larchedaybreak.com.

start communities like L'Arche. I am afraid Eileen is going to have her hands full because things are surely going to develop here, although we are not sure what. It was good to be with Eileen again and to sense the deep unity between us all.

We spent a morning at Father Ted Kennedy's place in the inner city of Sydney. His presbytery and the convent next door welcome Aboriginal men and women who are down and out. The Aboriginal people in many ways are similar to the Canadian Indians. Australia belonged to them before Britain colonized it. They are an extra-ordinarily wonderful people with a deep sense of community and a deep love for the earth, which for them is sacred. When the British came, they killed many of the Aboriginals or put them on reserves; their culture was more or less eradicated. They are obviously bitter and resentful towards the white man. In many ways they admire the power of the white man, but they despise his insensitivity and his yearnings to possess. The Aboriginal people have no interest in possessions. When they have money they spend it to visit some of their people who are far away. In Australia today there are about 150,000 Aboriginal people out of a population of about 13 million. They are a small, deeply discouraged minority. Father Ted Kennedy and his community are there to welcome and to be present to these men and women. In many ways it is a broken situation because those he welcomes are broken people, but there was such a good feeling there. I felt very much at home. How is it that people who are totally down and out and seemingly in total degradation can give such peace? During Mass we could hear them outside singing and shouting as they drank their wine, as we too drank the new wine, the blood of Jesus.

It was good to meet Enid and the Bundeena community. A number of them visited Trosly during this past year. Ten years ago Enid and her husband met Jesus and welcomed into their home a broken person who was in deep need. Since that initial community they have grown to 120 people who are deeply committed one to another. They live a "covenant of love," which is a promise to follow Jesus and to be committed one to another. They have a deep sense of community and welcome people in dire need. They are evidently filled with the Spirit and search in many ways to do the will of Jesus. I must say I was impressed by their openness and their commitment. They have an interesting four-month training course for those who wish to live in community: some basic teaching on human relationships, living together and the Word of God. Some of their community were with us on the retreat, as were many of Ted Kennedy's community. The Little Sisters of Jesus were also with us on the retreat. They too have fraternities with the Aboriginal people. Some of Mother Teresa's Sisters came also. And then there was Mum Shirl, a most beautiful Aboriginal lady who visits her people in the prisons. She has an immense heart filled with love for her wounded people. She was one of the treasures of the retreat and did us all much good by her truthfulness, her simple directness and her love for people.

It has been good for me to meet so many wonderful people, to sense how the Spirit is guiding and calling people forth, religious, lay people and married couples. It is difficult in our culture and in the comfort of our Western civilization to create communities filled with the spirit of the Gospels, yet there is such a yearning for that. Australia is a country that is isolated from North America and Europe, isolated behind its own boundaries from the vastly overpopulated Asia just to the north. Certainly, if communities of L'Arche are called forth here, they will be linked in some way to what Jesus wants of L'Arche in Indonesia, the Philippines or Malaysia.

Peace,
Jean

May 8, 1977

Dear Friends,

At the moment I am in Christchurch in New Zealand with Eileen. A retreat begins tonight for 150 people. After about a week in New Zealand and ten days in Australia, I am just beginning to feel what it is like to be in this part of the world far from Paris, London and New York, close to Indonesia, China, the Philippines and the Pacific islands. In many ways New Zealand is like Ireland (except that there are high mountains covered in snow at the moment). It has a population of three million people living simply but comfortably. It is poorer than Australia but perhaps more human because the cities are smaller. The climate is rather like the English climate but perhaps more changeable. They say here that there are four seasons in one day, sometimes in one hour. As it is a small island with contours rather like those in Nova Scotia, there are beautiful views of land and sea. In many ways it is a land of dreams on which graze sixty million sheep! There is a great fear of immigration: few people from the Pacific islands and Asia are allowed to come in. The actual standard of living and the European culture must at all costs be preserved! But Australia and New Zealand are south of Indonesia with its millions of inhabitants, and to the east there are all those overpopulated islands without means of subsistence.

The original people of New Zealand are the Maoris (today there are 250,000 of them). They resemble Canadian Indians except that more have been able to adapt themselves to the European culture and are integrated into it (with all the implications of the loss of their own culture). The Maoris, the Aborigines and the Indians of Canada have a deep love of earth and nature: the earth is their mother and they live in deep communion with her and with the universe. Land is not just for production. The Maoris were uprooted from their soil and in their heart there is bitterness.

In each city here there are the poorer quarters where one finds the Maoris and the immigrant workers from the Pacific islands, who are the lowest on the social scale. The Maoris and the people of the islands are extraordinarily sensitive people.

I gave conferences in the four largest cities here—Auckland, Wellington, Christchurch and Dunedin. I spoke about "The Marginal Person: A Problem or a Prophet?" Most of those who came were already converted and convinced—religious and priests (already a little bit familiar with L'Arche because of Bill Clarke's book), a few parents and professionals, and people seeking a new style of community life. I found them deeply interested and open with many questions. I felt that many New Zealanders are seeking new formulas, new living styles, without being stifled and pulled apart by the structures and crises which one finds in the United States, or the political influences of the Latin American countries. They are also trying to find their place among the islands of the Pacific.

I became more aware of the beauty of the universality of the Church and of the place she plays and could play in the future of Asia and the Pacific. Christians in China, Vietnam and Cambodia have been crucified. The present Chinese and Vietnamese political dynamism* will continue to penetrate Asia, bringing forth closed and totalitarian regimes. They have an amazing dynamism and enthusiasm to propagate their belief in the Marxist system. They are ready to give their lives. Will there be sufficient Christians ready to walk with Jesus in the path of the Gospel, to spread the message of the Good News of the liberty of the children of God? Maybe it will be the martyrs of China, Vietnam and Cambodia who will

---

*One month before I wrote this letter, the Vietnamese regime began expelling ethnic Chinese from its border areas. These people, called Hoa, were prohibited from entering the civil service, working for public enterprises, engaging in retail trades or farming, or moving from one place to another. The repression of this group became so intense that within a year of my letter hundreds of thousands were fleeing Vietnam. They became known in the West as the Vietnamese boat people.

give birth to these Christians. We must pray for the arrival of a new springtime in the Church.

Love,
Jean

July 7, 1977

Dear Friends,

I have just come back from Belfast where I spent three sacred and providential days. I was struck by the despair of the city, the number of partially or completely destroyed homes, vacant houses, windows walled in with bars, burning cars in the streets, armed vehicles with English soldiers ready to shoot and large barricades everywhere dividing one neighbourhood from the rest. I was impressed by the number of people who had either seen people killed before their own eyes or had lost a husband, a son, a nephew or a cousin in a bombing. I was struck by how calmly these people speak about such tragedies, how the children still play in the street and how life goes on as if nothing had happened.

What most impressed me, though, was the courage of the mothers of Protestant or Catholic families who are ready to die for their children and do not let the terrorists intimidate them. The presence of God in many people gives new strength and courage in the face of so much adversity. Everywhere I witnessed the signs of war, destruction and the delinquency resulting from them, but everywhere I went I met men and especially women full of courage and a deep faith in Jesus, who continue to work for peace.

I met Mairead Corrigan, one of the founders of the peace movement. She, herself, has lost three nieces. I also met Peter McLachlan who is on the executive committee of this peace movement. He is a former member of Parliament and a Christian, quite involved in social and political affairs. My stay was organized by Sister Anna, an Anglican who lives between a Catholic and a Protestant neighbourhood. She has a real gift of hospitality and lives in a spirit of poverty inspired by the Gospels. She knows everyone and is present in all their suffering. She truly works for peace. I met with several people who would like to see an ecumenical community of L'Arche which would truly serve the needs of one of the mixed neighbourhoods. However, I leave all that in God's hands. If something is to be born, it will come about very slowly and humbly.

Keep in your hearts the harsh reality of Northern Ireland, but also the presence of God, which is there in the hearts of many simple people and the hope which comes from their faith and courage in spite of all the signs of terrorism.

Pray that I remain faithful.

Jean

August 27, 1977
Ouagadougou, Upper Volta

Dear Friends,

Sunday afternoon, I left Bouaké by car and went to Man for three-and-one-half days.

Life in the community in Man is simple as in Bouaké, but they have fewer visitors as they are outside the city. Henri, Kouadio and Aroona have been working on the land, building a water tower, a chicken coop and a little park for the four sheep. They have lots of projects to help them work towards more financial autonomy. Living these few days with the community, and listening to Maria and Michèle, helped me to realize how much Poyé has progressed since the last time I saw her. The little "crazy" girl who used to sleep and eat anywhere in the village is becoming a responsible young lady, learning how to do the cooking and her own washing. Her mother died and her father left the village for Abidjan; there was only her old grandfather to take care of her but he just could not handle her and did not know what to do. After six months at L'Arche–Man, Maria took Poyé back to her village to see her grandfather. Her grandfather sees her in a different way now, as someone capable of making real improvements. He accepts her more and has asked us to send him news regularly. Perhaps one day Poyé will be able to go back and live in her village. Yes, L'Arche is beginning to discover its vocation in the Ivory Coast.

Before I left Man, Bishop Agré asked me if I would come and give a retreat next year in a Wobé village with representatives from the various nearby Wobé villages. I, of course, accepted his invitation with great joy for it is always a gift for me to announce the Good News to the poor, to those who have never been able to follow a retreat; they listen to the words of Jesus with such open eyes and hearts. Each time I give a retreat like that I realize more and more the truth of the parable of the wedding feast which the king gave for his son: people who were rich, in a comfortable position, were too busy to come and refused the invitation, while the poor, the lame and the blind jumped for joy and accepted the invitation. St. Paul reminds us that God did not choose the strong, the wise, those with high position, but the weak, the rejected and those whom the world looks down on. Maria was really happy with this invitation to go into a Wobé village for she feels that the vocation of L'Arche–Man is to work in close liaison with the nearby villages.

All along the way back to Abidjan I was struck by the good conditions of the roads, especially from Yamoussoukro, and by the large amount of construction that is going on in that town, the president's hometown. It will soon become the new capital of the country. One sees huge machines brought in from France to build beautiful highways. And yet just outside the city one finds little villages that do not even have drinking water.

I left Abidjan for Ouagadougou, where Geneviève, Chantal and Veronica, Chantal's little sister who is visiting for a while, were waiting. Ouagadougou is very different from Abidjan. The Muslim community is thirty percent of the population. Christians are ten percent, but are quite active and fervent. Ouagadougou is at the heart of the Mossi people, about 2.5 million people in all throughout the region. It is by far the largest ethnic group and has kept its hierarchy and its leader, which is like a parallel government with an emperor at the head. L'Arche is located in the Tanghin neighbourhood, on the other side of a dam, about seven kilometres from downtown Ouagadougou. The downtown areas are rather poor with few houses that have a floor above the ground floor. Tanghin is truly like a big African village. Houses are made of earthen bricks; each house has a little yard and one rectangular hut with several little round huts (one per wife for the Muslims and animists), with a straw roof, and all of that is enclosed by a wall of about 1.5 metres high, made of dried mud. In the lanes here and there you find people selling oil, bread and different types of food. There is no electricity and people fetch water from a well in the lane. You get to know people quite quickly, especially if you are two metres tall! Chantal and Geneviève do quite well in Moré, the local language, and in the various ways of greeting people: "How's the family?" or "Is everything all right in the yard?" or "May God give you peace," or for an elderly person, "May God grant you one hundred days and may that be only a sample of the rest to come." People greet each other, stop and talk; they have time.

During Ramadan children come and knock at the door and sing until someone opens the door and gives them ten francs. Then they put their masks on and dance! The women in the neighbourhood come often to see what the "nasaras" ("whites") are doing and they speak with Geneviève and Chantal. There are visits at any hour of the day. We have two rectangular huts, each one with two bedrooms. We do the cooking outdoors on a wood fire (so it takes a while to make a cup of tea). We eat outside underneath an "apatam," a shelter with a thatched roof, because it is too hot and humid inside underneath the aluminum roof.

In our house we hope to welcome two five-year-old children who are living at the orphanage and whose mothers died at birth. Their villages could not take care of them: Jean-Paul had encephalitis and Jean-Noel, whose legs are paralyzed, has a slight mental handicap. With others in the neighbourhood we would like to begin a little school. In Upper Volta there are quite a few schools and centres for those who have physical difficulties but nothing for those who have other handicaps. Chantal and Geneviève told me that they have often seen children in the marketplace in great distress while others hollered at them and treated them as crazy!

During the week we made many visits and everywhere we were welcomed so warmly, starting with none less than the president of the republic, then the secretary of state for social affairs, the director of health services, the auxiliary Bishop, and so forth. A lot of my time was spent trying to set up a board of directors. We had the impression that everything had been prepared ahead of time by Providence and that we were there simply to harvest what had already been planted. The board was really wonderful in its openness and enthusiasm. L'Arche has truly been blessed by God with the support of such a group.

In the evening after the board meeting, Father Berrens stayed and said Mass and shared a meal with us. It was an evening of thanksgiving. During the meal, lightning and thunder announced an approaching storm. Around midnight it started to rain and rain and rain. Around 3 a.m. I was awakened by the water that surrounded my mattress on the floor. I started picking things off the floor and putting them on shelves or benches. Then I sat down on a chair, put my feet on a stool and waited for dawn to come. But the water continued to rise. I decided to go outside and then

I discovered that a part of the wall had collapsed, which was how the water was coming into the house. I found huge cracks in the walls of the house where I was sleeping. So I woke up Chantal, Geneviève and Veronica and in the rain we began moving things out of the hut into another hut.

We worked until dawn and then Chantal and I decided to go into town to get Father Berrens to come and help us. It seemed quite evident that we would not be able to stay in that house much longer. In order to go into the city, one has to cross a little road which separates the two dams. This we did, water up to our knees and with quite a strong current which made walking difficult. When we came back with Father Berrens and his car, it was impossible to cross back. The water had risen and the current was even stronger. There I was on the city side of the dam, but my baggage, passport and plane ticket were on the other side and my plane was leaving at 10:30! I missed it, of course. It was only the following morning that any car was able to pass. Chantal and I decided to cross over the water in order to join Geneviève and Veronica. So we got into a little boat that looked really fragile, but thanks to a good man who paddled we made our way to the other side. Chantal said I was white with fright. The boat rocked from right to left and a little boat to our right capsized and the two occupants had to swim! But we arrived safe and sound. I could not help but think of the text of Isaiah (but not with enough faith): "When you cross waters, I will be with you and rivers will not drown you."

In my last letter I spoke to you about the drought here in Upper Volta and now it is the floods. That is Africa, a continent of extremes: too much water or not enough. Unfortunately, the results are often the same: the harvest is spoiled.

During the month I was able to work on my book on community life, the one Claire wants to call *My Bathtub Is Full!* It is progressing little by little. I feel it should be finished soon, perhaps by December. Every day I am learning a little more about community, especially here in Africa where people have such a deep sense of belonging to an ethnic group or to a village. Pray that I do finish the book.* May the peace of Jesus lead us all towards more truth in our life together and especially with the poorest.

Love,
Jean

October 6, 1977
Sorel, Quebec

Dear Friends,

I am in Sorel, Quebec, about thirty miles outside of Montreal, for a meeting with all the L'Arche communities in the eastern region of North America and a few observers who hope to be a part of L'Arche in the future. How happy I am to see everyone again! It has been two years since I have been in Canada. Our communities have deepened; a few have been battered by storms and are moving towards more peaceful waters. There is a deep unity among them. L'Arche as a federation of communities, as a real union between communities, is becoming a reality of mutual support and trust. Yesterday Wolf Wolfensberger spoke to us about the necessity of evaluating our communities, what that implies and the fears people may have in view of such an evaluation. I learned a great deal from that. I feel our communities are open to an evaluation by people coming from the outside to help them be more truthful. It is easy to "use" handicapped people, consciously or unconsciously, in order to prove a message rather than to put the message at the service of people; it is easy to forget that the message is the listening to and being at the service of people in need.

---

*This book became *Community and Growth*.

Before going to Mobile, I made a brief visit to Tegucigalpa. Régine and Nadine took me to the new house at Suyapa, just opposite the church of Our Lady of Suyapa. It is an ideal house, in the middle of the town, next to a little bar that is used quite a lot, especially on Saturdays and Sundays. It is quite big, made of wood, without any luxuries; cooking is done on a wood fire and one has to walk five hundred metres for water. There was, of course, a meeting with the board of directors and then a visit to the San Felipe asylum where Nadine introduced me to the friends she hopes to welcome into the new house: Rafaelito, a young man with eyes that call you forth; Castorina, a blind girl; Marcia with her big smile, moving about in her wheelchair; Myriam who looks so small and fragile in her bed; and Teresita. What a beautiful family that will be! There will also be a school for three young people from Nueva Suyapa.* But the house cannot welcome the first three until we receive approval from the government. We are expecting it any day now.

My heart is full of thanksgiving for the great diversity in our L'Arche communities throughout the world, but the reality is the same: through our life together we create a sense of belonging to one another and through our mutual trust we grow together in truth. It is so easy to build illusions and prejudices and to hide behind them. We must help each other to live this truth which flows from the heart of God.

Much love,
Jean

---

*Suyapa and Nueva Suyapa are actually two different villages. Suyapa is the older village and is lower on the hillside. After a typhoon swept through the area, people built their huts farther up the hill and this new settlement became known as Nueva Suyapa. Nadine lived first in Nueva Suyapa but then founded the L'Arche community in Suyapa.

November 14, 1977
Asha Niketan, Kerala

Dear Friends,

A torrential rain has been falling for hours. The little Asha Niketan built so ingeniously by Chris to protect it against the heat is becoming inundated. I found a little dry corner where I can write this letter. At Mass this morning, offered by a Jesuit priest from Kerala, we recited the psalm: "May all the rivers clap their hands joyously for God." Yes, they are truly clapping them joyously! Aravindo (twenty-three years old) is beside me profiting from the same dry corner. Viney (twelve years old) comes and goes; Gnanam and her two small children, Gomatri and Abirami, are in the kitchen (the driest place in the house) preparing the meal. Gnanam's husband, Subbaiyan, is "at home," a little house built of stone about two hundred metres from here. Unni should be with him. They make up this new Asha Niketan family, perched on a hill with a striking view of the coconut plantation and ten kilometres away, the sea! The community has begun to work on the ten acres of land. They have planted thirty-five coconut trees, some tapioca and they collect the cashew nuts from the trees! They have built a shelter for six cows which they hope will come soon. It seems to be the most solid building of all! There is another house which will be the prayer room as well as the room for yoga and meetings, with an adjoining room for meditation. If the roofing had been put up we would have taken refuge there.

I thank God for our Indian communities and for my visit to India at this time. Is this my ninth or tenth visit? I am happy with the way of life here, the culture, the simplicity and the tenderness of the people, and the beauty of nature. I dare not say anything about the climate! Yes, my heart is happy here (I must admit though, for those who do not know me well, that I am always happy wherever I am and that I find the people I am with at the present moment always the most beautiful). In India, and most especially here in Chris's community, we live close to nature. (There is no electricity and we get water from a huge well.) I feel often weighted down by all the habits of our Western culture, a culture which uses a quantity of artificial things and no longer knows how to benefit from nature nor how to live in communion with nature. The community life here is very simple, close to the simple life of many Indians. Since it is a bit isolated I think it will become a place where assistants from the other communities will come to rest and pray. It is really an ideal spot for that, a real gift from God.

In Bangalore I was very busy at the Asiatic Congress on Mental Deficiency. For many it was a time of renewal and encouragement. At the same time, as at any congress of this kind, there is the usual problem of remaining on a superficial level. Each one wants to speak about his success, and then very quickly professionalism takes precedence over a more human approach to people. On Wednesday, the delegates visited four centres in Bangalore, of which Asha Niketan was one. We were told that the first bus would arrive at about 11:30 a.m. But at 9:30 while I was quietly in my room I heard quite a lot of noise outside and there was the first busload of people! There were four busloads that morning—more than two hundred people! There is not much to see at Asha Niketan; it is a home like any other. We divided the people into groups of fifteen and each one was welcomed by a few members of the community. For about half an hour we shared about our community life. It was really good. With my talk and then this visit quite a few people have come to know the gift of L'Arche.

The community of Bangalore is at a turning point because assistants are asking very important questions about commitment, about what they wish to live and to witness, about poverty and the responsibility of one for another. For a long time Bangalore could not do more than respond to the immediate needs of each moment of each day. Today there is deep unity which will allow them to go farther with the demands of community life.

I sensed this same turning point at the regional meetings in North America. There is a growing maturity in all our regions; we are asking fundamental questions. What is L'Arche? What has to be done so that it may develop and deepen in its specific grace? It is a time of commitment and responsibility. We must pray a lot for one another and for our international meeting in April. Jesus has entrusted L'Arche to all of us. He wants us to be faithful to its grace, so that L'Arche may become what the Father wants of it and not simply a good professional centre, or a community where assistants are united amongst themselves but not with the poorest. Yes, I have the impression that our meeting in Châteauneuf is truly desired by God at this time so that together we may take a step forward in fidelity.

Jean

February 3, 1978
Port-au-Prince

Dear Friends,

I am in a Foyer de Charité, a retreat house, giving a retreat for about 150 people, mainly young people from high schools and colleges in Port-au-Prince. Father Jacques Beaudry and the Foyer de Charité were at the roots of L'Arche here three years ago. At this retreat there are twenty-five people from L'Arche! Three years ago we would not have believed that we would be so many! Yes, we give thanks to Jesus!

Since I arrived in Port-au-Prince last Saturday, Robert has not allowed me to be idle! First, I want to give you news of everyone here. In the Thor neighbourhood there is the Kay Sin Josef plus two other houses. There is also a workshop where they take coconut fibres and make carpets, and in a few months there will be a little school and a fourth house.

Jerome is the head of the Brooklyn workshop where Jean-Robert works now. Fifteen physically handicapped people work there making wicker mats and baskets which are sold in Canada. Each person earns a salary which, though very low, is much appreciated in a neighbourhood like Brooklyn, one of the poorest in Port-au-Prince.

Last evening I went to Brooklyn to give a homily at the Mass held in the school. There were about three hundred people. They are so terribly poor; they have only Jesus. They reacted with such spontaneity and simplicity of heart, after every two or three phrases, Amen! Amen! Robert translated into Creole.

In three years L'Arche–Haiti has grown. The material development (opening of new houses and workshops) does not, however, speak of the real growth—that of each one towards stability and peace.

At present the project of L'Arche is to strengthen contacts and deepen the insertion in the neighbourhood, and above all to interest more of the people in our activities and to work more closely with the families of the handicapped.

There is a new community of L'Arche starting in Chantal, near Les Cayes, in the southeast of the country.

During the first days of my visit all the assistants of L'Arche–Haiti came together for a time of reflection and prayer. The most essential thing at the moment is to help the Haitian assistants commit themselves and discover the gift of the handicapped person.

At the moment my heart is full of Haiti and all the graces that L'Arche has received here. I dream about our meeting in Châteauneuf in April.* I look forward to seeing everybody and liv-

*I express a lot of excitement leading up to this meeting, and then never write about it in my letters! It was a great meeting of all our communities.

ing this experience of unity together. It will be a time to give thanks
to God all together, time also to be renewed in our hope and in a
greater desire for faithfulness. Yes, Jesus has given us a gift—the
gift of the poorest—and he wants this gift to bear much fruit.

Jean

February 15, 1978

Dear Friends,

The plane has just taken off from Tegucigalpa. My eight days
in Honduras have passed too quickly, with barely enough time to
get accustomed to hearing Spanish and to know our new L'Arche
community.

I met Lita a year ago. She was just sitting there in her own
excrement in a small hut in Nueva Suyapa. I thought she was seriously psychotic: she did not look at us and seemed closed up in a
world of sadness. My diagnosis was much mistaken! Today she is
a happy, smiling girl who has started to work with her one good
hand. She is eighteen (but looks only eight or ten), and suffers
from cerebral palsy; she does not speak and has no use of her legs,
but she manages to get about pretty well on her bottom! She is
well integrated into the family of Casa Nazaret (the name of our
house) but still has a good relationship with her own family. She
goes home every weekend. Her mother came to breakfast with us
on Monday. She is changing her attitude towards her daughter,
becoming gentler and warmer. Nadine works closely with Lita's
family. We must help families to discover and adopt a new attitude towards their children. We have to be careful. Our presence
here could encourage families to want to "get rid" of their children, to put them in the hands of the "rich foreigners" who have
the means to cope with them. But if a child is cut off from his or

her family and put into another milieu with foreigners, he or she may be even more wounded and the wound may never heal. Lita is very relaxed and with Nadine and Régine she is learning many things. With her good hand she serves soup, does the washing up and often, both before and after meals, she turns on the transistor which Nadine bought her. Casa Nazaret is like all the other houses of the neighbourhood.

I met Marcia in the San Felipe asylum. She must be about seventeen or eighteen and moves dexterously in her wheelchair. She is more resourceful than one can possibly believe! Despite her handicaps (both physical and mental) she can do many things. Yesterday she brought wood from the yard into the kitchen. She is always happy and full of life and very stable despite her ten years in the asylum and complete breakage with her family. Yes, Casa Nazaret has been well founded with Lita and Marcia and also Dona Maria who is a real treasure. When Nadine first arrived in Nueva Suyapa she lived with Dona Maria and her family for six months. Now she comes every day to help us and is truly part of the family. She often bursts into laughter at the antics of Nadine (and there is no shortage of them)! Dona Maria brings with her all her wisdom and experience from life in the poor quarters of Suyapa. She is teaching Nadine and Régine how to roast coffee, make tortillas and a thousand and one other things. Above all she has a sense of welcome and love for people. She is the mother of Ana Luz who, with Sandra, welcomed Nadine and me in Suyapa two years ago for a "Celebration of the Word of God." What a long way we have come since then! Régine is completely at ease, chatting in Spanish with everyone who comes into the house (the doors are always open!). The children come and go looking for water (there is a tap in the yard for nondrinkable water); they play in the house with Marcia and eat tortillas. Yes, Casa Nazaret is truly becoming a part of this neighbourhood. Nadine and Régine try to remain poor so that their lifestyle neither shocks nor wounds the neighbours.

We are very lucky. Father Carceres, the parish priest, has become our friend, and has given us this house, a kind of wooden barn that Nadine has made into a house. It is next door to a café. The clients of the café (which does not sell much coffee!) relieve themselves against the walls of our house! This is all part of the local colour and integration into the neighbourhood.

Nadine, like Robert in Haiti, kept me very busy. I gave talks at the psychiatric hospital, and for parents of handicapped children in Suyapa and in Nueva Suyapa. I spoke on television, and on the radio, and had meetings with the board of directors, the Bishop of Tegucigalpa, the minister of health and the psychiatrist responsible for mental health. Then we had a three-day retreat with one hundred young people. My talks were translated by Father Rivas, a Cuban. I felt so at ease with him. He seemed to know what I was going to say before I said it!

I sense that Jesus is guiding this new L'Arche. There is still plenty to be done but the roots are good and solid. In Latin America there is so much struggle and violence, so much division within the Church and such a gap between the rich and poor. Maybe L'Arche can be a tiny sign of peace and reconciliation.

Jean

April 27, 1978

Dear Friends,

Eileen and I flew from Melbourne (Australia) to Brisbane this morning. Here in Brisbane, thirty-six hours of meetings, talks, television interviews, etc. Tomorrow evening we will fly to Papua New Guinea for ten days.

In Melbourne I gave a five-day retreat with two hundred people in a former school-residence-prison for delinquent boys. We were crowded together, some sleeping on the floor. The Brothers of St. John of God took care of all the material organization. This atmosphere of poverty and closeness to one another helped the group to live the retreat quite intensely. The fact that the majority of the participants were people who are living in community with marginal people also helped. People in the little groups shared deeply from the start and the prayer was also intense. I was very moved by this experience, sensing a deep call in many people towards an authentic Christian life, close to the poor. I wonder what Jesus is preparing here for L'Arche and for Faith and Light. I am struck by the welcome I have received here. Last night at one of my talks in Melbourne there were seventeen hundred people!

I have the impression that Australia is ripe for many things. Is it because it is one of the last countries in Oceania where the Church can exist in all freedom and therefore men and women have to be prepared to be witnesses of the Gospel and of the poor? Is it because in Queensland (where Brisbane is located) there is a rightist government which is terribly frightened of Communism and of foreigners and which risks persecuting the Church one day and those who are close to the poor? Australia is an amazing and enormous country: 13 million white people, quite well-off, taken up with a very materialistic life, and a small number of Aboriginal people (150,000), the majority of whom have not been able to live in the structures which the whites have created. Australia is also frightened of the large Marxist and Islamic population to the north and buries herself in work, efficiency and wealth. However, there are also a lot of people who still have a spirit of adventure and a desire to follow the Gospel. We must pray for this country, for Eileen and for the L'Arche community that may come. I will write again, at more length, after my visit to Papua New Guinea.

Much love,
Jean

May 11, 1978
Sydney

Dear Friends,

My heart is still full of my visit to Papua New Guinea which is a country like no other I've seen. The first Protestant missionaries arrived in 1840; then French Catholic missionaries came in 1880. At first the missionaries stayed on the coast because of the jungles and the mountains; little by little they penetrated into the island and discovered new tribes. Today new tribes and villages are still being discovered in the heart of the country, in the mountains and jungles. In fact there are 717 tribes, each with its own language! Most of these people are living in the jungles, living off fruits and roots, fish and wild animals. Within one hundred years, the country (whose population is about 2.5 million) has become Christian.

The Australians were responsible for the country from 1918, when the north (New Guinea) passed from the hands of the Germans to the Australians, until 1975 when Papua New Guinea acquired its independence. It is strongly marked by this Australian era but less than other countries colonized by either England or France. However, the people live the same contradictions or ambivalence one finds in other countries in similar situations. The missionaries and the Australian government freed the people from the fear of sickness, ignorance and sorcery and gave them access to culture, to science, to the benefits of medicine, to a real Christian life. But at the same time the colonists brought with them their culture of power and wealth, which sometimes tore from the heart of the people their deep values. The people of Papua New Guinea are Melanesian. They are a gentle people, family loving, living more through personal relationship than through efficiency. The 717 languages now constitute what is called the Wantok system (Wantok means "one talk" in pidgin). They take care of their families, the old and the sick; each tribe is autonomous in its primitive traditions (about good and evil spirits), in exercising justice, etc. Today, one of their greatest concerns is how to preserve the benefits of their primitive culture and the Melanesian sensitivity, in front of the powers of the materialistic and scientific culture coming from the industrial countries.

What a joy to meet the Servants of Our Lord, a religious order comprised entirely of native women founded in 1919 by a French missionary, Monseigneur de Boismenu, and Marie-Thérèse Noblet. I sensed a great simplicity and special grace in them.

I also met the Little Sisters of Jesus at Port Moresby and at Lae. Their fraternities are hidden in the poor neighbourhoods, where they are living, loving witnesses of the presence of Jesus. The Sisters of Mother Teresa brought us to a few villages where we were welcomed by dancing and singing and where I spoke about L'Arche and about wounded people.

At the general hospital of Lae we visited a ward where there were ten men with physical handicaps, simple mountain men, so alive and radiant. They touched me by their acceptance of their situation and their deep peace.

At Kieta, after two days of retreat, the Bishop brought me to a little village where people did not even speak pidgin. The Bishop asked me to give the homily (it was he who translated it into their language) and after Mass we had time for questions and answers. These simple people asked many essential questions around life and death.

I do not know if one day there will be a L'Arche here. At the moment the question is not even being asked. But the Holy Spirit has given us a network of friends and I hope that this friendship continues to deepen. Papua New Guinea is an island which, by its very situation, is at the heart of Asia, between Australia, Indonesia and all the islands of the Pacific. It may either grow and develop according to its own dynamism and become a place of truly human and Christian living, or it may become a place of struggle between

Marxism and capitalism. Whatever happens I have left a large part of my heart there!

Eileen and I returned to Sydney, Australia, on Monday. We stayed in the Bundeena community, an ecumenical community founded by Enid Crowther about fifteen years ago. One hundred and fifty people are committed to this community, which consists of a number of small houses which welcome people in need. I felt very close to them. The grace and presence of Jesus is profoundly among them. They have a "community training program" for those who wish to prepare for community life. They have much to teach us, not just from their own experience of Christian community, but also because of their contacts with other dynamic Christian communities throughout the world. They told me about communities in Europe and North and South America which I had never heard of.

In Sydney, our friends from Bundeena community prepared a public talk for about two thousand people. I met with professional people and was interviewed on television and radio. We have many friends now in Australia, and Eileen is surrounded by these friends. The seeds are planted; we must wait until they grow to see what kind of fruit they will bear.

As for me, I feel humbled by the way people receive my words. Jesus seems to use them to touch and unite hearts, even though there is a gap between the reality of what I am announcing and what L'Arche is living. But I trust that whatever happens will be the work of Jesus, not my own projects. The works of Jesus are much bigger and more beautiful and often on another level.

Love,
Jean

June 29, 1978
Belfast

Dear Friends,

I must say that I have a great love in my heart for the people of Belfast. Since my last visit, eighteen months ago, many things have changed in Belfast: life is calmer, barriers have been taken down in certain areas and there are fewer tanks in the streets. However, the destruction remains and the hate, fear and prejudice live on. I came here to give a two-and-a-half-day retreat. Many of the retreatants told me that they did not even tell their families they were coming to the retreat because they would not have understood.

There were about seventy people, half Catholic and half Protestant. For almost everyone, it was the first experience of prayer and sharing their faith with Christians from another tradition. A Presbyterian deaconess said that it was the first time she had ever shared her faith with Catholics. She was astonished to see that Catholics love Jesus as she does. Some Catholic nuns also admitted how amazed they were to see young Protestants praying long into the night. One of the most moving moments of the weekend was the Sunday morning liturgy when we came together to give thanks and to sing. Jesus was truly present. We were living Jesus's promise: "Wherever two or three gather in my name, I will be there among you." The retreat was a small way to help bring home peace to the people of Belfast. We must continue to pray for them. Next April there will be another retreat.

I also gave a retreat in Cork and was present in Kilmoganny for the official opening of our first L'Arche community in Ireland. It was absolutely amazing. Kilmoganny is a village of 150 inhabitants. Alva Fitzgerald, the director, spent one year in Trosly. She told me that almost everyone in the village came to help with the work on the house: painting, cleaning, putting up curtains, etc. Paddy and Nellie are the first two people to be welcomed. They both come from Kilmoganny or nearby and everyone knows them. They can no longer live with their families because of the advanced age of their parents. In fact, Nellie's mother died just a few days before the official opening. She was very much loved in the village and when she died everyone was really happy that L'Arche was there for Nellie.

L'Arche–Kilmoganny is truly a model of insertion into the local community. Shouldn't each L'Arche community be mainly at the service of the local community, welcoming mainly the people from the village or neighbourhood rather than taking people who are from far away?

The opening ceremony was on the national television. The house was donated by a lady who owns one of the local pubs; she also included some acres of land which we can cultivate.

The retreat in Cork with about 150 people was also a time of grace. In many respects the Irish have remained quite simple and open to Jesus. During the retreat I felt a deep unity among us. Pray that this retreat will bear all the fruits that Jesus wishes.

Love,
Jean

August 19, 1978

Dear Friends,

Dawn and I are travelling by train to Ouagadougou. It has been a heartening and colourful trip thanks to the friendly Muslim Voltaïques who fill the train. We have already shared much together. As it is the holy season of Ramadan, the month-long Lent of Islam, they begin to eat only after the sun has set, having abstained from all food and drink since sunrise. Many respect this; their faith is beautiful.

I have just spent three full days in our community in Bouaké. It is a true L'Arche community with all the inherent fragilities, strengths and, of course, celebrations. Today at noon we had a celebration. After a meal of chicken and rice we all got up for some dancing and singing. Mamadou sang "Allouette," Kouadio (with such a serious face!) danced, deftly moving his body to the rhythms of the music, while Amouen busied herself running from person to person. It was a real L'Arche celebration filled with laughter and joy. It was then we felt how much L'Arche here is a united family.

The arrival of Christiane makes the creation of the little school possible for our three children and seven children from the neighbourhood. The board of directors is excited about the school project and, besides giving plenty of encouragement, plans to finance it completely. This will be the first school for handicapped children in Bouaké, and if it works out well others will follow. The idea is to create small schools for about a dozen children, well integrated into the small towns. Close ties to the children's families can be maintained, making it possible to work closely with them at all times.

There are many changes going on with respect to assistants, changes which are not always easy, and yet at the same time God did send us Marcelline, twenty-three years old, who has been at L'Arche–Bouaké for almost a year now and wants to stay. She is Baoulé and so, of course, speaks the language of her people. This is especially important as Bouaké is situated in the Baoulé region of the Ivory Coast and several members of the community are of that ethnic group. She also speaks Duala which is more or less spoken in all the large markets. She works so well with the children. L'Arche, after an initial period of foundation, has found its own rhythm and is starting to put down roots.

I spent four days in Man, two and a half of which were spent in Trokpédro, a small Wobé village about eleven miles from town. Trokpédro has about four hundred inhabitants, with no electricity and only one small store. The first Christians from the region were from this village and there is a church and a room available for a priest, a Polish priest who comes only once a week to celebrate Mass. Bishop Agré had chosen this village for a retreat because of its location in the heart of the Wobé region. The retreat was attended by the villagers but also by some catechists from neighbouring villages. The first morning I found myself in front of an audience of about 120 persons, few of whom were young people. I had to explain what a retreat was. Thomas, a catechist, translated into Wobé. Everyone listened but there was little reaction. It was clear that I was being sized up! After my first talk we met with the elders and the catechists to draw up the program for the retreat: morning prayer at 6:00, conference at 8:30, Mass with a long homily at 10:30, followed by lunch together, rosary at 2:00 p.m., group meetings at 2:30, meetings with group leaders at 3:30, a talk at 4:30 and then, after supper, a time of dialogue, questions, etc., at 8:30. As you can see, I didn't just idle away my time!

Little by little, through meetings with group leaders and the questions that were asked, I began to grasp the underlying problems: conflict between traditional customs and Christian beliefs and way of life, problems around the traditional practice of polygamy (what to do, for instance, when a man who has three wives, each of whom has borne him children, asks to be baptized?). To be a Christian in an African village is not always easy. One needs a strong inner force to say no to certain customs and one must be ready to be persecuted.

I was a little afraid at first but the Holy Spirit helped me in my weakness. The retreat ended with the Mass of Mary's Assumption and a last meal together, which was followed by a bangi ceremony. Bangi, a fermented drink quite similar to beer which comes from a young palm tree, is used by most peoples of southern and central Ivory Coast as the traditional ceremonial beverage. Two tall glasses can make your head spin and put you to sleep! We all drank from the same "calabasse" and then what was left over was poured on the ground as an offering to and out of respect for one's ancestors. Some of the people told me that they admired the fact that even though I come from a country with airplanes and submarines, I believed in God. God must therefore exist. I was then presented with a large boubou, a traditional African garment. Then I spoke, asking God to send rain for the coffee and cocoa crops of the village and to help each one to lead a Christian life.

In the evening, before dinner, I visited some families (where, of course, we drank bangi together). What bonds of secure relationships exist among all of them! What simplicity! It seems that in the letter I wrote from Papua New Guinea I said the people there "lacked culture." Karen, who lives close to the Aborigines of Redfern (Sydney), brought this to my attention. I must have meant to say "intellectual culture" for it is true, as Karen says, that a culture is a way of life, a way of viewing all the important events of life from birth through death. In any case, for me the culture of people is not of central importance: beyond any culture and in all cultures there is a heart, human relationships and a sense of truth, of justice, and God's love. However, I do regret having said what I did for it could easily be misunderstood. The Wobé do not have an "intellectual culture" either but they do possess a deep sense of truth that all mankind desperately needs today.

During this time in Man we felt how much the people, and the local board of directors especially, hope that the house in Man will be reopened.* We have many friends and L'Arche–Man is called to work in some way with the surrounding villages.

My visit to Ouaga was very full. Chantal welcomed Karim (six years old) the tenth of May. He had been placed in the orphanage of a Protestant mission in Ouaga because his mother had died at his birth. When he was about two years old he must have had

---

*The house was eventually closed permanently, and the property was sold.

meningitis, and the few members of his family who visited him occasionally completely abandoned him. The orphanage could no longer keep him for he had been there for six years. Besides that, the staff was not prepared to deal with a child who sometimes needed to be tied down in his bed. Now, however, things are much better for him. He has received much from the love and attention of Chantal, Elizabeth and Martine. Both Elizabeth and Martine are Mossi. They also welcomed Denise, a fifteen-year-old girl who was chased from her village because of her epilepsy. She had become a beggar in Tanghin. She seems quite happy even though she remains quite unstable and could decide to leave at any moment, preferring her freedom in poverty to a life in community. There are also a few day-workers: Dieudonné, fifteen years old, who comes and goes all day long according to his desires; Awa, fifteen years old, fragile, epileptic and yet so beautiful, who lives just two hundred metres from the house; Fati, nine years old, whose home I visited, two hundred metres from our house where she lives closed up in a small hut without windows; Francis, six years old, who also had an illness when he was four and as a result is very handicapped.

L'Arche–Volta is well integrated into Tanghin where everyone seems to know Chantal, whose knowledge of the local language, Moré, is sufficient to get her through most situations. I love the simplicity of Tanghin. The houses, made of sun-dried mud bricks, are joined by walls made of the same material which create large courtyards where virtually the whole family life goes on. There is no electricity, of course (though the centre of the city is just three miles away), nor running water which means the community needs to get their water from Brother Laurent's well. Brother Laurent lives in a small house just nearby.

Friday morning the auxiliary Bishop, Monseigneur Compaoré, came and celebrated a sunrise Mass in the courtyard of our house. This very religious and yet simple man seems to understand

L'Arche so well. We prayed together for the cardinals gathered in Rome to elect a new Pope, hopefully a Pope of the poor!*

My visit to Ouaga, where I made contacts with Muslim families, and my stopover in Niamey (Niger) have made me realize how much L'Arche has a role to play in Muslim countries. Muslims often shy away from Christians, fearing all forms of proselytizing, and as a result they are not always at ease with missionaries. It is terrible when such barriers stand between cultures. I am certain that L'Arche can play a small role in the coming together of the two religions, for there are handicapped persons everywhere and parents of all religions are often overwhelmed by all the difficulties of their handicapped children. The Bishop in Niamey, a Frenchman, hopes we will come to Niger. Let us pray that there be more contacts between L'Arche and Islam.

United in Jesus,
Jean

December 13, 1978
Tegucigalpa, Honduras

Dear Friends,

I am sitting on my bed in Casa Nazaret; it is early in the morning and in a couple of hours I will be leaving for the airport. My stay in Honduras is coming to an end. Last night Dona Maria came with her children and grandchildren to take shelter in the house. Her husband was dead drunk and had become violent with

---

*About a week after I wrote this letter the cardinals gathered in Rome and elected Albino Cardinal Luciani, the Patriarch of Venice, as the new pope. He became John Paul I, but died just thirty-three days later.

them and might have killed one of them. They slept the night with us. Nadine says they came to us and not to one of their immediate neighbours because they wanted to say goodbye to me. Dona Maria comes every day to do the cooking, but she does much more than that; she is really a member of our community. In a way what happened last night typifies much of the life in Suyapa and L'Arche. The people are poor, very poor; their houses are earth-floored shacks made of planks and there is no sanitation or electricity. There is little or no work for the men. This makes them depressed and pushes them to use the little money they have for drinking. Once they are drunk, they become violent. The poor of Honduras are a depressed people; families are broken, or often do not exist at all. A newspaper stated that sixty percent of the children do not know their fathers. There is deep suffering because of the history of the country and the way the Spanish conquered and colonized the people.

I was impressed to see how much our community is now part of Suyapa. Nadine tells me that this is even more so since last August, when the hut next door caught fire and the fire spread to our house. The roof was badly damaged, but the firemen from Tegucigalpa were efficient and were able to save the rest. However, everyone had to be evacuated. Nadine stayed with neighbours; Lita returned to her mother; Régine and Marcia went to a village nearby. Misfortune often brings people together and particularly the poor—so all the neighbours are much closer to us. I sense this as I walk in Suyapa or Nueva Suyapa. People are more open and friendly. Nadine, Régine, Lita and Marcia are obviously very much loved here.

On the day of my arrival there was a Mass in our main room and the parish priest blessed the house. Then there was a piñata, where children play and candies and little biscuits are given out. About 150 neighbours came with many children, a little sign of how L'Arche is accepted and loved here, and is even a sign of hope for many.

L'Arche–Honduras has not grown much during the year because official papers have not yet come. This time of waiting has been precious for the community; it has helped it to become part of the village. The people feel that we are living like they are—even though our house is a bit bigger than theirs and we have electricity. Neighbours are constantly coming in and out of the house.

I have been very happy here in spite of the handicap of my almost nonexistent Spanish. The rhythm of the community is a slow one. It is a peaceful and gentle community, filled with laughter and close relationships. I feel that the community is appropriately called Casa Nazaret, the house of Nazareth.

These three weeks in this community have been very important. We came here like children, with outstretched hands, with few expectations. The future is now all in the hands of Jesus. I am certain of only one thing: in Latin America, where the very rich live beside the very poor, L'Arche can only be a reality which is poor and close to the poor.

Jean

February 1, 1979
Kottivakkam

Dear Friends,

I am always amazed at how our God watches over me and my trips. The other day when I arrived at Roissy airport to leave for India, the flight I was supposed to take from Brussels to Bombay was delayed; the Brussels airport was closed because of snow and ice. I was able to change my ticket at the last minute and take an

Air France flight to Delhi where I arrived at five the next morning. I had to run in order to catch a connecting flight for Calcutta, and I arrived there at 9 a.m. Everything happened so quickly that I could not really believe I had arrived! You can imagine how happy I was to see everyone again. This community at Sealdah Station has a very special place in my heart. Calcutta has not changed: the trams are still bursting with people; people who have no home are still living in the streets. Traffic around our house is as impossible as ever! The city is still as animated and exciting as ever; and our community is there with its workshop like a little island of peace. Like so many of our communities it is the handicapped men who are at the heart and who give it its stability. Most of the assistants have changed.

The day I arrived I gave three talks in a centre for Christian and Hindu students on "The Life of Jesus." It was the first time I did that and I was happy to do it. It is painful to see that so few know the real face of Jesus. The four days in Calcutta went by very quickly: Mass and a talk with Mother Teresa's Sisters (Mother Teresa unfortunately was not there), breakfast with Cardinal Picachy, a symposium on mental deficiency and meetings with each person in the community. For me, it is such a gift to see how the men have grown over the years. Kashi is so handsome and willing to help everyone; he is really "at home" here. Christopher, who was quite difficult the last time I was here, is more peaceful.

Right now I am in Kottivakkam in our house on the coconut plantation. The sea is five hundred metres away; nights are cool and all day long one hears the birds sing and the sound of the banana and coconut leaves waving in the wind. We are far away from the noise and the dust of Calcutta. But the noises in the house resemble the noises in the Calcutta house! Veeran (nineteen years old, coming from the psychiatric hospital) cries out a few words, or Shankaran sings with his heavy voice, and Ramesh runs back and forth. Yes, all our L'Arche communities are much alike.

I gave quite a number of talks in schools here. We must hope and pray that more and more men and women will come and live with us, God willing. Pray for that.

Love to you all,
Jean

February 12, 1979
Asha Niketan—Nandi

Dear Friends,

My heart is truly full of thanksgiving for this trip to India, for the life and peace I found in our communities. I love this country more and more. My heart is especially full of Kerala and our Asha Niketan near Calicut which I have just left.

Asha Niketan–Calicut covers an area of five hectares where Chris and Subbaiyan have planted a hundred or so coconut trees and thirty banana trees; there were already a multitude of cashew nut trees. There are three cows and a little calf. The team dug three enormous wells and built the house, a prayer room, a stable for the cows and the house for Subbaiyan and Gnanam and their children. Subbaiyan is in charge of the work and Gnanam does the cooking for the house. The foundations for a workshop have also been laid. The last time I was there the building was not finished and the community was only coming into existence. Now the community is full of life with six men—Mitran, Vishwanathan, Ramesh, Prasannan, Lanciettan and Selvaraj—and four assistants—Kanaran, Haneefa, Maniettan and Mani—plus Chris, Subbaiyan and Gnanam. Their day begins at six o'clock, at sunrise, with a short prayer after which everyone draws water to wash themselves and water the banana trees. They have breakfast and then gather the cashew nuts or work the land. Lunchtime comes, followed by siesta until three o'clock and work again until about six o'clock. At seven there is evening prayer followed by the meal and bed. Their days are full. Chris estimates that in five years, when the coconut palms begin to bear fruit, they will reach financial autonomy. But this autonomy will come by the sweat of their brow as they have worked hard on the land. The style of the community is characterized by their simple life, close to nature. It is also a very Indian community: three assistants come from Kerala, three from Tamil Nadu, and only one is a foreigner.

On Friday we all went away for the day. A bus taken at Nandi Bazaar, the village at the foot of our property, took us to a river ten kilometres away. There we took a small boat steered by a man who stood and pushed with a long pole. We slipped silently through the coconut palms; beautiful birds greeted us as we went along. How beautiful it was with the dazzling sunlight and a light breeze. After three-quarters of an hour we landed at a small village. We were welcomed by a group of people intrigued by these two white people with a rather strange community. As we waited for the bus the crowd grew. To give them something to look at, Chris went to look for some oranges so that I could do a juggling act. The crowd continued to grow! Then I took the opportunity to give a short talk which was translated into Malayalam by Mani. I talked about the handicapped person who is a child of God as we all are. It is definitely the way to draw an audience. I did not have as many people at my talk in Bangalore even though it was well advertised! At that moment a man from the village, one of "our people," was brought to us. We made a circle round him and he started singing and dancing. We had to wait there for over an hour for the bus, a providential delay because, as we waited, we talked about Asha Niketan to all these people. Many took our address and promised to visit.

Another moment of celebration: yesterday evening after a meeting with the local committee, we all set off on foot for the beach.

The water was so warm that Chris, Subbaiyan, Gnanam and myself succumbed to the temptation of going for a swim. Four fishing boats arrived to unload their fish. We formed a circle to say our evening prayer and then shared a meal together which ended with a battle of orange peels! It was truly a L'Arche celebration.

I give thanks for all the Holy Spirit has done and is still doing in our communities in India, for all our brothers and sisters there.

Jean

September 7, 1979
Roissy airport, Paris

Dear Friends,

I have been in England for the Renewal since July 15, except for two weeks when I visited different communities and slipped off to Norway and then to Wales to give retreats.

The Renewal has been quite an experience! Only two weeks left and I still do not know if I am renewed! Perhaps I am making progress. Eight weeks with brothers and sisters from seventeen different L'Arche communities is really something. Usually, I only see people during a retreat or a meeting. What joy to be able to spend more time together, to play ping-pong or volleyball, or have a lesson from George Durner to improve my juggling! What joy to have the time to eat together, do the dishes, make the coffee, take a stroll and pray together. We need the support and friendship of one another. In fact, many of us have been carrying heavy responsibilities for a number of years. We have often felt powerless and at times insecure in front of all the difficulties, frustration and tension. We need this friendship to renew our hope.

The intellectual and spiritual nourishment we have received was very rich; sometimes steaks, sometimes just breadcrumbs. Bishop

Stephen Verney's talks on St. John's Gospel touched and nourished me. The psychoanalyst Fred Blum talked to us about the "wounded healer," and Jack Durnam about stress.

Here are a few words and phrases that this Renewal has put in my heart. "Find my centre—that silent centre where Jesus abides." "Pass from one stage in life to another—which sometimes involves a little confusion—but trust, Jesus is there." "Jesus walked serenely and determinedly towards Jerusalem where he was going to die." "To be able to be at the service of our brothers and sisters as an instrument of peace, one has to look after the instrument, sharpen it, clean it, make it more efficient." "In order to assume difficulties and stress, resources and nourishment must be increased." The words of the Gospel which most often come to mind are, "Come to me all you who labour and are overburdened and I will give you rest."

By stopping, each one of us has discovered within himself the things he was running away from, the things he did not want to or could not look at, all these obscure parts of our beings. It is good to discover that one has a right to have these parts and that Jesus came precisely to call Lazarus from the tomb. There is hope. I have the right to be myself in this hope of being able to grow.

We loved having daily Mass—a liturgy full of life and peace. For many of us the little chapel was a real source of life where we could pray and rest in Jesus.

This Renewal has convinced me even more that L'Arche is one of the signs of God, one of the signs of hope for our time. I am more convinced that Jesus is calling me to give my life. And with his grace and his strength, I am also convinced that we all need to grow in wisdom!

Jean

January 4, 1980

Dear Friends,

I am back in Trosly after spending Christmas in Ouagadougou and New Year's in Bouaké. My heart is full of thanksgiving for all that the Holy Spirit is doing in Karim, Binta, Bakary and in each of our communities there. Yes, L'Arche truly has its place in Africa. However, it will still take us a while before we find our way, before L'Arche truly becomes an African reality.

The African countries are torn between the Western culture and their traditional cultures, between a Church that was initially French or English and one that is now searching for its own liturgy and ways of expression. They are torn by many economic, political and religious struggles. For so long they were dominated by white people who had frequently little respect for their extraordinary and beautiful culture.

So, it is not surprising that L'Arche is groping to find its way in Africa. We are neither missionaries nor professionals. "What are you then?" people often ask. We do not know what to answer. We do not want to bring our Western culture; we do not want to create a L'Arche that would simply be an imitation of the one in Trosly or in Daybreak or elsewhere. And yet, most of the assistants who are there come from Canada and Europe, and they have their specific needs both physically and spiritually. So it is not easy.

But I have come back from Bouaké full of hope. We have more and more African friends around our communities, who believe in L'Arche and who want to support us, even if we still do not have many assistants from Upper Volta or the Ivory Coast. It will take time!

Dawn and I spent two days in Abidjan and I think the government of the Ivory Coast is going to cover a good part of our expenditures. This is encouraging news, not only financially but especially because of the acceptance and support this means for

L'Arche by the authorities in the country. Dawn is courageous; she carries the project of L'Arche in Africa deeply in her heart, and now has more friends there who carry it with her.

I wanted to wait until I returned from my trip to wish you all a happy New Year. After spending a very simple Christmas in Ouaga and Bouaké, and then coming back into our rich countries, I feel somewhat ill at ease. The international news about Iran and Afghanistan is worrisome.* So many people in our world are oppressed; so many live in poverty and confusion. And we, in our richer countries, live another type of insecurity: what will this new year bring us?

Jesus came to bring peace, and our world is devastated by war, preparations for war or its after-effects. We hope that our communities will be little oases of peace. But if our communities are to be oases of peace, it means that each one of us must constantly struggle against our selfish instincts. How quickly we can fall into seeking our own comfort and human security. We must die to the values of our culture, which are not the values of loving and giving, but possessing, knowing, dominating.

As I look at our world, my faith in Jesus increases. I know that for me personally, I must root myself more firmly in him and in the Beatitudes. The Beatitudes are the only answer to the forces of war and deceit. I know that the world news is bad and that insecurities and dangers are great. Will there be a war? Will there be an economic crisis, inflation? We do not know. Perhaps we will suffer. Many people on our earth already know deep suffering, hunger

---

*Less than two weeks before I wrote this letter, Soviet troops had entered Afghanistan. They were there for nine years, supporting the Communist government against the Mujahideen rebels (who were backed by the Americans). Also that December, the Islamic revolution in Iran inaugurated its Koran-based constitution, having overthrown the pro-Western dictator the year before. Later in 1980, Iran and Iraq began their own war. It was a terrible period for the people of the region.

and oppression. At L'Arche we must remain peaceful, and keep our eyes focused on Jesus, on his peace. He will give each one the necessary strength.

I always find consolation in this text of Isaiah:

> If you give your bread to the hungry,
> and relief to the oppressed,
> your light will rise in the darkness,
> and your shadows become like noon.
> Yahweh will always guide you,
> giving you relief in desert places. (58:10–11)

The grace of Jesus is powerful, and if we at L'Arche are faithful to the poor, he will be faithful to us. Yes, "Blessed are the merciful, for they shall receive mercy."

God willing, the coming year will be a very full one for me. On January 19, I leave for a three-week visit to our communities in India. In February, I will go to Lebanon for ten days. In March I will be in Haiti and Honduras. In April we have an International Council meeting in Canada. Then, in mid-June, the French Renewal begins.

I am anxious to be with my brothers and sisters in India. I am anxious to go to Haiti and Honduras and am happy to discover Lebanon. At the same time, I am happy to come back to Trosly, so much so that starting November 1, 1980, I will stay in Trosly and will not travel for a year. I feel Jesus is asking me to live what others have been living for a long time at L'Arche, and what I have been speaking about but not living enough. I ask you to pray for this.

Happy New Year to each one. May the year be filled with the peace of Jesus. May he give us his strength and light.

Love,
Jean

January 28, 1980
Kottivakkam, India

Dear Friends,

I have been in India for ten days now after a year's absence. I have spent most of my time listening, sharing, trying to discover better this gift God has given us with Asha Niketan and where he is leading us.

Asha Niketan will be celebrating its tenth anniversary this year and L'Arche its sixteenth! It is a time for putting down roots, a time also for discovering more how to sustain a living hope and dynamism in our daily lives—the deep meaning of our communities in our society.

I spent four days in our community near Sealdah Station. I was happy to see each one and also to share the pain and anguish of Dienesh's absence; he disappeared into the immense city of Calcutta a few months ago. You can imagine how difficult that is for the community.

Brian and I were able to go to Mass one day with the Sisters of Mother Teresa and to have breakfast with them. They radiate an amazing peace and simplicity. They are tired from the number of tourists and visitors they welcome, but each one is seen as sent by God and is welcomed with such kindness and respect. At the same time it is their cross and they suffer from it. The order has grown: there are 250 novices every year in India and in other countries. God continues to send workers for the harvest. Brother Andrew, founder of the Missionaries of Charity Brothers, was in Calcutta for their chapter meeting. I was happy to see him again; I feel close to him and he is close to L'Arche. He told me about their new foundations in Japan, Hong Kong, Macao, Korea, the United States, Guatemala, El Salvador—there is never a dull moment there either! He radiates such humility, so hidden in God. "God will always send us workers," he told me, "because he has such a desire to show his tenderness and love to the poorest." He gave me new confidence for L'Arche. Yes, our communities will always have the necessary assistants because God wants to reveal his tenderness to the poorest. God wants the rejected and the humiliated to have a place where they are honoured, respected and loved.

I am always sad to leave Calcutta; it is a city bursting with life, the crowds of people, the poor living in the streets, the crowded tramways, the noise, but also the smiles, the gentleness and the tenderness.

I spent three and a half days in our community at Kottivakkam (near Madras). I found the community in good shape. One evening, when the moon was shining, we went to the beach to have an evening picnic supper, to sing, play and celebrate Sukumar's birthday. L'Arche is the same everywhere. Perhaps some people find us a bit strange and maybe we are! But there is a joy and a simplicity which warms the heart and gives new hope.

Jean

February 8, 1980

Dear Friends,

As I leave India my heart is at peace and I am very happy with this trip. These past ten years of Asha Niketan in India are a real gift. Of course, there are difficulties in our communities there. But where is there a L'Arche community with no difficulties? Difficulties are our daily bread; they provoke tensions which can be creative and help us grow and discover new ways and paths where God is leading us. We can also learn from past errors and can acquire a certain wisdom from failures. So, there are difficulties, but today I see the fruits of these ten years of L'Arche in India: four communities welcoming more than fifty handicapped people (including the day-workers), some of whom have really found new life and inner peace. There are twenty-seven assistants in all, twenty-one of whom are Indians, and half of them have been with us for more than two years. They are assuming more and more responsibility and one senses in them a real maturity with regard to Asha Niketan and to L'Arche in general. In the same way, one feels that the governing board and the local committees are more and more involved in taking on responsibilities and are interested in L'Arche. Little by little, Asha Niketan is becoming an Indian reality. On the financial level, the average per diem of our homes is twenty rupees—about three dollars per day. About half the expenses are financed by the work in the communities and by money that has been found locally. There are more and more friends around our communities who understand us and who want to help us. Good foundations have been set. Now we must continue to build so that the Asha Niketans can fully respond to their vocation in this immense country of India.

I will not be coming back to India for two years. My heart is sad for I love this country and I love our Asha Niketans. I have learned so much from them. When you are here, you realize that the centre of the world is no longer London–Paris–New York. It is changing and moving towards the Middle East and Asia.

I am going back to Trosly for one week. On February 15, I fly to Lebanon for ten days of talks and a retreat. It is a privilege for me to visit that country. Pray for me that I may be an instrument of God, attentive to the suffering I will meet there.

Love,
Jean

February 22, 1980

Dear Friends,

I am at Feytroun, in the mountains near Beirut (Lebanon) where there is a group of two hundred of us on retreat. I have been in Lebanon for a week. Everything is very stressful; people are full of despair and yet hope. The country is so beautiful and yet so insecure that it is hard to say anything.

In the last five years, newspapers have been full of news about Lebanon, so we are all aware of what they call "the events" here. Lebanon is a small country with 2.5 million inhabitants, Christians and Muslims. This little country has welcomed some 500,000 Palestinians who were driven out of Israel. The various tensions— between Christians and Muslims, between Israel and the Arabs, between Syria and Lebanon, between Palestinians and Lebanese Christians, between landowners (people well off) and the poor class yearning for socialism—have burst out into a real war that has cost 60,000 lives and 200,000 casualties. The problems are so complex that people can say one thing and then just the opposite and both would be true! There are seventeen different religious denominations here: three Muslim sects, one Jewish and thirteen Christian denominations. In Beirut alone there are ten bishops, four of whom are Orthodox. The country itself is rich in water and thus in vegetation, like an oasis, a pearl of rare beauty. And the Lebanese, descendants of the Phoenicians, are very astute in the trade world.

Lebanon is still at war. Soldiers are everywhere: Syrian soldiers, United Nations soldiers, Lebanese soldiers, Palestinian soldiers, Phalangist soldiers and other military groups. They all carry arms, machine guns, and are ready to fire on a car if it does not stop at a checkpoint, which you find every hundred yards. From time to time one hears shooting. The country is more and more divided into zones: the west zone of Beirut is Muslim; the east is

Christian; Zahlé is mainly Christian; Saida is Muslim; and then there are the Palestinian zones like the town of Damour. Militia from each group are in each area controlling who comes and goes into the area. Forty thousand Syrian soldiers are here apparently to prevent war from bursting out once again. But the Lebanese are afraid of being annexed by Syria. During my stay here, there have been some terrible battles in the northern towns where Syrian troops attacked Phalangist towns. People speak about the 10,000 refugees who have fled that area. The Syrians claim that in 1918 Lebanon took over territories which belonged to them.

You can imagine the deep insecurity of people here: war has lasted five years and they know that it could all begin again at any moment. They feel helpless. The Lebanese government does not have any control over the situation; in many ways it, too, is helpless. That is why the different groups have established their own defences and created ghettos. Everyone here feels like a toy in the hands of big powers who want to settle the Palestinian problem, but at the expense of the Lebanese. Some Islamic fanatical elements do not accept this small Christian–Arab "island." France and the Western powers need Arab oil. And what is the role of Russia, Syria and the United States? Throughout the country there are signs of war: homes have been demolished or are in ruins. But there is such a vitality in the Lebanese; they rebuild, life goes on. There are, however, all the consequences of the war: 400,000 displaced persons, 40,000 orphans, thousands of physically handicapped people and families that have been broken up by those who have left the country in order to escape the war.

It has been a deep grace for me to be here, to listen to the suffering and the insecurity people have been living, to speak with Christian and Muslim groups and to touch the reality of war and its consequences. Too often we live in a false security; we are not really conscious of the drama of our present world. We forget the tragedy and consequence of sin and hatred. There were, of course, moments when I was very frightened by the gunfire and the machine guns, but that only forced me to live more deeply the words of Isaiah—"Be not afraid for I am with you"—and to trust in Jesus.

I gave many talks, sometimes five a day. I will spare you the list. But here are a few flashes of people and events that deeply touched me: the young people in the mountains of Zahlé, so full of life and enthusiasm; the welcome I received at Saida University, which is mainly Muslim (Saida is the Arab name for Sidon, where Jesus spent time during his public life); the Fraternity of the Little Sisters of Foucauld, who live in a Muslim area very near the border line in the west zone of Beirut; an ecumenical charismatic community that is very much alive and prayerful; young people in the Focolarini movement. Many young people in Beirut are open to the message of Jesus but do not know how or where to commit themselves. The Training Centre and El Kafarat Centre, both for mentally handicapped people, and in Ber Chabab, a centre for physically handicapped people, are all doing wonderful work in spite of all the difficulties. I gave a conference at the psychiatric hospital to five hundred people on "The Wounded Image of the Mentally Sick." A round-table discussion followed with psychiatrists, a psychoanalyst, a social worker and myself. The therapy of L'Arche draws much interest here. I also participated in a television program that brought together both Christians and Muslims.

We crossed through the town of Damour on our way to Saida: each house in the town had been destroyed or partly destroyed. It is now a Palestinian town. The Palestinians chased out all the Christians after the Phalangists had destroyed a Palestinian section of Beirut. The destruction and the savageness were appalling. I met a young Muslim woman from the west zone in Beirut who would not come into the Christian section for fear of being kidnapped or killed! I visited the ruins of the temple of Baalbek: a Roman temple 360 metres long, built in the year 100 on the ruins of a Phoenician temple built two thousand years before Jesus. Baalbek was a Roman city with 400,000 inhabitants. Civilizations and empires come and go, but humanity continues.

Saturday

We have just learned that the daughter (less than two years old) of the head of the Phalangist movement, the granddaughter of Pierre Gemayel, was killed by a bomb that exploded near their family car. It was probably revenge. A few months ago the Phalangists had killed the son of ex-President Frangié, a Christian. The situation is very serious: the Phalangist army may retaliate with much violence. How quickly vengeance enters into our hearts. It is now Christians against Christians. And we should not simply deplore this event, but we must do all we can to take away any feeling of vengeance we may have in our own hearts regarding our "enemies" within or around our own communities. The only answer to this violence is to live forgiveness where we are, and to humbly hold out hands to those who criticize us. More than ever before our world needs real peacemakers. This war and these acts of violence help me to discover how much I must strive to become more a man of peace in every circumstance, disarming my tongue. So quickly I can use it to destroy and criticize instead of using it to build and encourage.

Sunday

I am in admiration of the Gemayel family and the way they have called for calm, forbidding any acts of retaliation or vengeance. Bachir Gemayel has said that his daughter has joined the martyrs of Lebanon.

The retreat will end soon, and tomorrow morning Marie-Hélène and I will be leaving for Paris. A part of me is happy to leave the tensions here, but there is another part of me that would like to stay, to be with those who suffer and weep. It is difficult for me to come here and talk about trust to people who are living in a state of insecurity and war, and then to leave. It is difficult to preach the nonviolence of Jesus when you yourself are not in danger of death. During these ten days we have made new friends; many want to come to L'Arche or to work for Faith and Light. The bonds between Lebanon and L'Arche have been deepened. After these ten days I will never be indifferent to what is happening here. My heart is deeply linked to a number of these people. It has been a real grace for me to live this time with them.

I was impressed by the number of people who are committed to orphans or physically handicapped people or who are opening their homes and convents to refugees. There are plans for the creation of many little neighbourhood schools for mentally handicapped children. If the situation seems to be one of despair, there are also many men and women who have confidence, and who are struggling and working with and for the poor. In Lebanon they need to see the birth of a number of communities where Christians and Muslims live and work together, communities which do not seek power or riches but which give witness to the Beatitudes, showing that it is possible to live these Beatitudes and that different cultures do not necessarily divide what is essential in the heart of all human beings. These communities would testify by their very being that our God is a God of forgiveness and unity, a God who desires peace. Will our L'Arche communities throughout the world be these communities of reconciliation where we bear witness to the message of the Beatitudes, where we truly love each other?

Pray for Lebanon and for the world.

Love,
Jean

March 29, 1980

Dear Friends,

I have just spent a week with Nadine and all the community at Tegucigalpa, Honduras. The death of Archbishop Romero at San Salvador has shaken the country; people are afraid.* The newspapers are full of the events in El Salvador and Nicaragua. Even in the streets of Tegucigalpa there was a big freedom march, which was an anti-Communist demonstration. The elections in Honduras will be held around the twentieth of April. People were quite affected by the assassination of the Archbishop of El Salvador, for he was a man of peace who identified himself with the poor and who preached nonviolence and reconciliation. He was hated by both the extreme right and the extreme left (which are always quite similar). I was in Choluteca to give a retreat on the day he was killed. There was an official Mass for him at the cathedral and I was asked to give the homily. It was a grace for me to speak of Romero who, like Jesus, was not afraid to speak the truth, again and again. I am full of admiration for the Church of Latin America, which is beginning to flourish in its commitment to the poor and where there are so many men and women full of courage and truth, prepared to risk their lives. The documents of Medellín and Puebla, which reflect

---

*When Oscar Romero was appointed Archbishop of San Salvador, many were concerned that his conservative views aligned him too closely with the government. But when one of his outspoken friends was assassinated, he changed his views, saying, "When I looked at Rutilio lying there dead I thought 'if they have killed him for doing what he did, then I too have to walk the same path.'" Romero began to speak out against the poverty, social injustice, assassinations and torture taking place in El Salvador, and he gained worldwide attention. On March 24, 1980, Romero was murdered by a government death squad while celebrating Mass at a small chapel near his cathedral. The day before, Romero had given a sermon calling on soldiers, as Christians, to obey God's higher order and to stop carrying out the government's violations of basic human rights.

the thoughts of the Latin American Church, are important for us all and for the entire Church.*

Casa Nazaret is good. Lita and Marcia have grown since my last visit. They are happy and work hard at home and in the workshop (where they make little dolls). For a year now, Claudia and Rafaelito are also there—both about ten years old, both abandoned since childhood. Rafaelito has a severe mental handicap and cannot walk. The doctor says he will not be able to grow much. Claudia is blind and quite closed up in her own world. However, each one is very much "at home" and secure in the relationships that unite them with Nadine, Régine, Françoise and Dona Maria. The house is well organized so that the children live in security and find a rhythm of life that permits them to be at peace and to grow little by little. The life in the house is similar to L'Arche–Haiti, poor and simple. The neighbours are also close, coming and going at every moment. And the village children play a great deal with Rafaelito. L'Arche in Honduras is small, but there is wisdom in this slow growth of the community. It allows a few people to live strong relationships that bring security and healing.

Happy Easter!
Jean

*Three years after Vatican II, Latin American bishops met in Medellín, Colombia, to see how they would live out the insights of Vatican II in their continent. Afterwards, they issued a document calling for Christians to express their faith through actions that might lead to a new social order. Ten years later, in 1979, the bishops met again in Puebla, Mexico, and recommitted themselves and the Church to social justice, especially for the poor.

October 19, 1980
In the plane from Tel Aviv

Dear Friends,

The forty-five pilgrims of L'Arche are flying back to Paris after our thirteen days in the Holy Land. You can imagine what this trip meant to us. Many had never been on a plane before and, of course, most of us had never been to the Holy Land. For months we have been saving up for the trip. Everyone says it was really worth it and some have decided to start saving now for another trip in one or two years!

Our pilgrimage began in Bethany, where we stayed two nights. From there we went to Bethlehem, Nazareth and finally Jerusalem for the last five days.

For me personally, each day brought new discoveries. I feel I have learned so much about the Gospels. It is amazing how they come alive when one is in the Holy Land. There is just so much to say and yet so much that cannot be expressed as it touches something deep within us. But here are a few flashes.

I had never really imagined what the grotto of Bethlehem was like. The Holy Land is just filled with grottos; they are huge holes in the rock of the hills or mountains which provide protection from the cold of winter and from the heat of the sun in the summer. During Jesus's time, almost all the houses in Nazareth were grottos. People built a wall and a door at the entrance and they had a house. So to take refuge in such a grotto was not something extraordinary. In fact the grotto was actually preferable to an inn, where there were more people and little silence or intimacy. The grotto where Jesus was born is now a big church and so it is difficult to imagine what that original grotto was like. However, nearby is the Shepherd's Grotto, which has remained as it was two thousand years ago. And in Nazareth, the actual grotto home of

Mary, the place of the Annunciation, is quite visible in spite of the church that has been built around it.

Of course, Lake Tiberias has remained the same; it is truly beautiful. You can easily imagine Peter, Andrew, James and John going out to fish. Jesus spent the greatest part of his life and his ministry time in Galilee, where he was welcomed so warmly by the people, at least at first. Certain towns on the edge of the lake were destroyed in the fifth century by a terrible earthquake. Very little remains of Capernaum. You can see the ruins of the synagogue where Jesus first spoke about his body and blood. You can also see the home of St. Peter's mother-in-law; it is not bigger than ten metres by five metres. People lived poorly and simply.

We had a beautiful day on the Mount of Beatitudes. We sat under some olive trees which cut off the heat of the sun and we spoke about the Beatitudes, the charter which Jesus gave us. Our little group was not much different from that first group of people who listened to Jesus: poor people, open to the simple words of Jesus. Jesus always speaks quite simply; it is we who complicate things. As we crossed Lake Tiberias, we read two texts from the Gospels: Jesus walking on the water and the storm at sea.

Then we left for Jerusalem. In spite of successive constructions of churches, one can still see Mount Calvary and, a few steps away, the place where Jesus was buried. It was very moving to be on the exact spot where Jesus died and to touch the hole in the rock that held the cross.

We often had Mass at the place we were visiting. We took our time, listening to the Word and praying. Sometimes we would find a shady spot nearby and we would act out a scene from the Gospel. We tried to follow the different steps in Jesus's life as closely as possible. Each evening, especially while in Nazareth, we met at the Little Sisters' to talk about the events of the day. We also sang, danced, prayed and met new friends there.

Yes, there would be so much to tell you. For me it was a very deep experience where the Word of God, the beauty of our earth and the history of humanity came together in a new light which made the message of Jesus more alive for me.

We also touched the reality of today's Israel. We saw Jews praying at the Western Wall, also known as the Wailing Wall. Last Friday, we participated in the opening of the Sabbath when people danced, sang and prayed at the Wall. One can feel how many Jewish people continue to live deeply the revelation given to Abraham and the Prophets. I also had a greater sense of how much Jesus was Jewish; how he must have lived the traditions and the feast days of his people; how much he loved and respected them. Yes, there is a deep sense of the beauty of the mission God gave to the people of Israel.

At the same time it is difficult not to be hurt by the political aspects and by a certain temporal messianism. Today what one sees is not a people who trust in Yahweh, but a people fully armed who defend themselves through their military superiority, not always in number but in high technology. One senses an uneasiness and a violence in the country; soldiers are everywhere with machine guns. It is a country that is at war and a country that has wounded the Arab people of Israel. And, of course, the Jewish people have been hurt over centuries. Certain territories were given to Israel in 1948 by the United Nations. Other territories have been occupied by Israel since the war in 1967. Clearly, Israelis fear and mistrust the Arabs of their country.

When we were there the situation was quite calm, but I could sense the tension. Many Arabs, who have been in the country for generations, feel oppressed. The government rules through fear. But it is difficult to talk about this in a letter. It is such a complicated situation and people can make quick judgments that are false or that only increase the poison of hatred. It is more important to try to understand both sides, and especially to grasp the suffering on both sides.

We visited a few centres for handicapped children. My talks in Bethlehem and in Jerusalem were translated into Arabic by Peter de Brull, SJ. I must say I was deeply touched by our new Arab friends, by their openness and their pain. Many are Christians and their families have been Christians for many generations.

We left Israel full of wonder at all the richness there but also more sensitive to the sufferings and the complexity of the present situation. Some of the friends who participated in our evening gatherings told us that we brought them hope. Many feel that their situation is impossible, without any solution. Each year the situation is becoming more difficult. Jews and Arabs who used to live and work together peacefully no longer speak to each other and distrust one another. We must pray for our Jewish brothers and sisters as well as for our Arab brothers and sisters there, and most important of all, we must love them both. Last night was the vigil of an important feast day for the Muslims, the day on which they celebrate Abraham's sacrifice. It is unfortunate that Christians and Jews cannot celebrate with them.

This pilgrimage has been a good preparation for my sabbatical year, which begins on November 1. The first week, I will make a retreat, time alone with Jesus so that he may prepare my heart for this new year. I know that, living at La Forestière,* I will discover many new things. As November approaches, I am more and more anxious to be with Eric, Edith, Loïc and the others. I will have to learn their language, a nonverbal language, and become more attentive to the little signs of their needs and desires. Since I will no longer be responsible for the community, my heart will be freer to

---

*This is one of the L'Arche homes in the village of Trosly, just up the road from the original L'Arche and Le Val Fleuri. It sits on the edge of the beautiful Compiègne Forest, where the 1918 Armistice with Germany was signed. This home welcomes ten very severely handicapped people.

pray. I know that it is only through a more regular prayer life that I will learn how to be more present to those who are poorest in our community. I ask you to pray for me, that I may live this year as Jesus wants, that I may discover more fully what real presence is. For years now I have been talking about it. Now I am asked to live it. Pray also for Odile and Alain who have accepted the cross of responsibility for this year. It is a real cross, even if it is a cross that brings much grace and a special union with God, our Father, and with Jesus, the good shepherd.

Love,
Jean

March 1981
Trosly

Dear Friends,
    This time I am writing not to tell you about a wonderful trip to a faraway country, but to tell you about my own interior trip with Jesus, with and through my brothers and sisters at La Forestière. It is perhaps the most enriching trip, the one that gives me the most peace. I remain closely united to each one of you, to each community that I will not be visiting this year. I miss not seeing you and sharing with you, but maybe I am even closer to you living here at La Forestière, as I am living what you have been living day after day.
    I have been at La Forestière since mid-November. There are twenty people in the house. Chris and Françoise are in charge, with eight other assistants. Loïc, Eric, Alain, Edith and each one we have welcomed into the house have many difficulties and their level of understanding is very low. None of them can communicate

verbally and only a few can walk, but their hearts are very alive and they need presence, tenderness and sometimes firmness. It took me a few weeks to get to know each one and to build relationships. I am learning a great deal from my daily life with them.

In the morning, the assistants have breakfast together at about 7:40, and then at 8:00 they start getting everyone up. I give a bath to Alain, Loïc, Yvan or Lucien. I am discovering how important baths are in creating relationships and also as a source of fun and relaxation. I realize how different the effects of a bath are from a shower. Showers can be violent: people can have trouble standing up and then the soap can slide over to the other side of the room. In the bathtub filled with warm water, the person is sitting down and even has time to play with the soap. After the baths, we get dressed, shave and are ready for breakfast.

Then, when all my brothers and sisters go off to La Chaumière, their occupational workshop (and if there are no meetings), I have time to pray, to write letters or see people. I have to be back at La Forestière before noon to welcome everyone back from La Chaumière for the meal. Each assistant sits next to someone in order to help him or her eat (or to prevent them from stealing from their neighbour's plate!). You should see the size of their eyes when it comes time for dessert! Mealtimes are almost always peaceful moments. It is good to be together. We laugh and are ready for any event that might occur.

After the meal, it is off to the toilets! After this "interlude," we all gather together in the living room, where some have a siesta while others share or play before going back to La Chaumière at 2:15 p.m. Then once again, if there are no meetings, I have free time.

In the last two months, I have written two articles for magazines, on "Compassion" and on "Welcoming the Poor." I will try to send you copies of these. It is good to write. It forces me to deepen and clarify what Jesus is calling me to live. I am beginning to understand a little more what the covenant at L'Arche is, but I still have much to learn. There is still much aggressiveness in me that has to be purified by the Holy Spirit so that I may truly become a man of compassion. Perhaps I am also becoming more aware of my own vulnerability, of what I often call "wounds," and of my defence system and aggressiveness, which are there to protect me from pain. I am also rediscovering that living and working with the weak and the poor is a privileged way for me to enter into the heart of Jesus, into the heart of the Gospel and thus into the heart of the Church.

I am beginning to understand the type of spirituality Jesus wants me to live at L'Arche: the spirituality of Jesus at Nazareth, of the Beatitudes, of Charles de Foucauld. Jesus is asking me to live a covenant with those he has entrusted to me. This covenant is the deep links of the heart that bring us together.

In L'Arche Jesus has given us a small and simple path or "way" of living the Gospel, made up of ordinary daily gestures of forgiveness and celebration. I could say much more, especially about service and communion, two attitudes which we are called to live at L'Arche and which are truly complementary. In our work, meetings, organization, etc., we are called to serve the community and for that we must be competent and efficient. But we are also called to live a deep friendship, intimacy and communion with those we welcome.

At 5:30 p.m. I go to Mass with one person from the house. Then there is dinner. After dinner, we put everyone in their pyjamas and we gather together around the fireplace for a time of prayer, of singing, of silence before everyone goes to bed at about 9:30. Once everyone is in bed, we do the dishes and I am free once again. As you can see, the days are full, as there are also meetings and exceptional events which link us to the larger community. I have been greatly helped by the larger community. People respect my sabbatical; nobody comes to talk to me about community affairs. They are really helping me to live this year at La Forestière, and it is a source of joy for me to see how well the community is managing.

Physically I am feeling well and people tell me I look well! It is a rest for me to live this new rhythm of life, which is the rhythm of Eric, Loïc, Edith and each one. My weekends are taken up in the house as everyone is in the house the whole day. At first I found that difficult but I like it more and more. I am beginning to appreciate the nights when it is my turn to watch over each one. There is something very contemplative in the silence of the night, watching over each one in his or her sleep. Sometimes this silence is broken by unexpected happenings and I do my best to cope with them!

The team of assistants in the house has certainly helped me a great deal. It is not easy to welcome a former director into your house with kindness, simplicity and a spirit of forgiveness. I am learning from them and they are helping me live what I am called to live this year. I do not know if the team of assistants in each house is like the one here; it is a real support for me, especially on days when things are more difficult, and believe me, there are difficult days. Life is not a bed of roses! But in our community life with the poor, we are called to learn how to live difficulties with patience, hope and trust in the heart of God.

And so I am writing mainly to tell you how happy I am in L'Arche. I have never loved nor understood so well L'Arche and its vocation in the world and in the Church. It is a privileged way for me to live the simplicity and the heart of the Gospel, through little things each day, as well as through the anguish, suffering and cross of each day. Pray for me that I may put my roots down more and more in this simple life, that I may understand more and more how the poor are a privileged way for us to enter into the life of Jesus.

Love,
Jean

February 19, 1982
In the plane to Paris

Dear Friends,

I am tired after these three weeks in Haiti, the Dominican Republic, Mexico and Honduras, but my heart is peaceful. Everywhere people spoke to us of the needs of handicapped people, and we met them ourselves in the hospitals, on the streets or with their parents, who were worried and in distress. Nadine, Robert and I felt deeply confirmed in the vision and reality of L'Arche through these needs and callings. We became more conscious of the importance of the "little way" of L'Arche for Central America, where many in the Church vacillate between conservatism (the status quo, which does not speak out against the injustices and oppression), a charismatic vision but without any commitment to the poor, and a political struggle which leads to violence. The way of the Gospel lived in L'Arche, as well as by other individuals, communities and groups, means *living with* the poor, creating community *with* them, listening to their cry and letting ourselves be transformed by them. This *living with* reveals very quickly the egoism, anguish and fears in us all. For the poor call us continually to go farther in our love and in the bonds that unite us. At the same time, their call and these bonds of friendship form and transform our hearts, encouraging us to give ourselves more fully and to live the Beatitudes of Jesus.

The situation in Central America since our first visit to Haiti and Brazil in 1975 has deteriorated a great deal. Today, there is war in Guatemala and El Salvador; the situation in Nicaragua has also evolved with its hopes and anxieties regarding the future. In Honduras, on the government level there is a change that seems quite favourable, but there is much concern and uneasiness in the face of all that is happening in the neighbouring countries. The United States gives them a great deal of military support.

Everywhere people are preparing for war and, as always, it is the poor who suffer the most. The more money put into arms, the less money there is to help the needy. In Central America the Church is often divided, torn between different moral and religious currents. The United States seems to be financing and favouring a number of religious sects which often are a source of division in poor families—and all that in the name of Jesus. In a general way, families that are in a more comfortable situation do not seem to sense the urgency or the evolution of events. These countries are deeply affected by the economic recession and inflation.

We met many people who were discouraged, anguished and incapable of confronting realistically the present situation. Many are simply paralyzed with the fear of terrorism. If someone speaks out against the injustices or illegal imprisonment and torture, he or she is very quietly and quickly warned to stop doing so. If they continue, they are threatened. There are many different kinds of terrorism. Adolfo Pérez Esquivel (Nobel Prize for Peace) says that what hurts him is not so much the evil committed by the so-called bad as the silence of the so-called just. If a greater number would speak out then the injustices might be reduced and people would be obliged to use more just means to resolve problems. But the so-called just are often petrified with fear. Further, in Central America, the Church is not united or prophetic as in Brazil, where the Church speaks out loudly and clearly and cannot be stifled. All this is to say that we met many suffering and anguished people.

It seems evident to me that in order to live in such difficult situations and remain open, dynamic, creative, peaceful and refusing to be governed by fear, one needs to live an intense community life, a community life that is poor and centred on Jesus and on the Holy Spirit. These communities, close to the poor, must become oases of peace and reconciliation.

I spent only a few days in Honduras so it is impossible for someone like me, coming from the outside, from another culture and another way of thinking, to make judgments. There is much pain and anguish everywhere. We must learn how to carry all that, how to live in solidarity with the people there; how to live their suffering and anguish in the degree that Jesus asks us to live it. How closely united we should be to the many Christians—lay people, priests and religious—who dare to speak out and act according to what they believe; we must also be close to those who are petrified by fear, doubt and the immense ambiguity of the situation.

I fly back to Trosly and will be happy to get back to my own house, Le Val Fleuri. After leaving La Forestière, I now share responsibility for Le Val, where I am with many old friends like Jean Claude, Jean-Pierre and others. I am happy to be here and to share my life with each one. Odile was confirmed by the community as its leader for the next three years; Alain shares that responsibility with her. The community is in good hands with those two shepherds! I am deeply touched to see how Jesus watches over us.

Much love,
Jean

November 26, 1982

Dear Friends,

I am on the plane, somewhere between Harare (Zimbabwe) and Johannesburg (South Africa). I have just spent two very full days in this young country of Zimbabwe (formerly Rhodesia). I spent a day in Bulawayo and a day in Harare, the capital. Zimbabwe is a country which won its independence after seven years of gruelling warfare which cost many lives. The white people (four percent of the population) wanted to stay in power at any cost, but finally, in 1979, there was a ceasefire. Robert Mugabe, who had fled to Mozambique during the war, legally assumed the leadership of the country. He is a great man, deeply Christian, who loves his people and wants to create a socialistic and humanistic regime.* I was happy to be there. One can sense an air of peace and fellowship in the country. I was invited to Zimbabwe by a Jesuit, David Harold Barry, who lives in Silveira House near Harare. A few years ago he met Bill Clarke and Daybreak. Ever since then he has been dreaming of a L'Arche community for his people in Zimbabwe, and so we have corresponded over the years.

During my visit, several people spoke to me about John Bradburne, an Englishman who lived a life similar to Benedict Labre's. The last years of his life he lived in a small hut at the heart of a leprosarium (eight kilometres from Harare), caring for those with leprosy, praying with them, bringing them Communion and, at times, angrily defending them against those who wanted to steal from them. He lived very poorly amongst them and he was always surprised that those with leprosy welcomed him with such kindness and allowed him to stay with them. He died in September 1979, murdered through hatred. After his death, and especially at his funeral, there were signs that showed he was deeply loved by God. I feel drawn to pray to him, that I, that we all, may remain faithful to our people. He was a poor, hidden servant of those who were most abandoned. He lived with them and little by little, he gave them a desire to live and a desire for Jesus. He really felt that the people with leprosy, often quite disfigured, were precious to the Father, that they were the most important people, that they were signs of God. For him, it was such a privilege to be able to live with them. Is this not the message of L'Arche? Yes, he confirms

---

*Unfortunately, Robert Mugabe did not live up to his early promise, when he led the liberation struggle against the repressive and racist regime of Rhodesia. Since his overthrow of white rule and particularly since assuming the presidency of Zimbabwe, Mugabe has been criticized around the world for mass murder, deep corruption, suppressing political opposition and bankrupting his country.

me deeply in the vision that it is the poor who are most important to the heart of God. They are signs of Jesus and a privileged way to penetrate into the heart of the Gospel.

Jean

December 1, 1982
Johannesburg

Dear Friends,

After twelve days in South Africa I am beginning to get a feeling for the country. How can I describe the situation with some truth in a letter which cannot be too long?

First of all, the country appears to be quite normal. Everything seems to be in order. When people arrive, they go through immigration quite easily. People can speak openly and there are newspapers which also seem to speak quite freely against the government. In downtown Johannesburg, you see black people and white people in the streets. Everything seems to be peaceful and normal—a city like others. But once you scratch the surface a bit, you discover an enormous world of suffering and oppression. There is a radical separation of the whites and the blacks. A whole system has been set up by which all the black people of South Africa will soon become "foreigners" with practically no rights. It is a very subtle, Machiavellian system. In the country there are about ten African ethnic groups. So the government has decided to create ten "homelands" within the territory of South Africa, one for each ethnic group. These homelands are supposedly independent or will become so. They have been created in artificial ways, in different areas that are not even linked together. The land is generally small and poor. Four of these homelands have already been given their independence; none of them have been recognized on an international level. They are poor and can only survive with money from South Africa. It is the South African government which trained, named and bought the leaders of these homelands. There is rejection and exploitation of the black people in the homeland who do not belong to the dominant ethnic group.

The principle behind all this is that each ethnic group should have its own homeland. This is a way, of course, for the government to divide the different ethnic groups. Once an ethnic group or one of these homelands has been given their independence, all the members of that group, no matter where they are living in South Africa, lose their South African nationality. They become foreigners! And, the government has forced more than two million of these foreigners to move to their new homelands. It is hard to imagine all the difficulties, impossibilities and injustices of such a system. Families are divided as husband and wife sometimes belong to two different ethnic groups! People are forced to leave the homes where they have been living for years. And, of course, these laws do not apply to the white people of Dutch, English, Portuguese, etc., origins. They can stay in South Africa and they get the best of everything: the most prosperous cities, fertile land, etc. The presence of two million Indians and "coloured people" is a problem for the government. They can stay in South Africa but they are allotted their own areas in or near the city.

The white population (about five million people) is sixty percent Afrikaner, of Dutch origin. The Afrikaners, or Boers, fought against the colonial power of England and lost the Boer War but, in the end, won politically. Now they have all the power in the country and will do anything to keep it! They are a religious people, members of the Dutch Reformed Church, which is quite rigid with a theology of separation and elitism. It has just recently been banned from the World Council of Churches because of its separatist theology. However, just lately more than one hundred ministers of this church signed a document condemning apartheid.

I visited one of the homelands, about one hundred kilometres from Johannesburg, Bophuthatswana. There are, of course, no borders. The black people from this homeland come into the city to work. In Bophuthatswana, I visited Winterfield, a slum area where blacks who are not from the ethnic group of Bophuthatswana live. They are the poorest of the poor, rejected, living in little huts. I visited a school: fourteen hundred children with eight teachers! The classrooms were huts with tin roofs; they were stifling hot!

There are some black cities close to the white city of Johannesburg. Soweto is one of the most well known because of the riots five years ago in which many young people were killed. These cities are poor and overcrowded. Amongst the black people there is a middle class that is just beginning to appear. They have their own houses and cars and are quite well off. They are comfortable with this situation of division and separation. In a way, it is easy to buy people with money and privileges.

The government continually creates new laws which make life more difficult for the black people: making it illegal to live or stay for any time in an area that is not their own; imposing fines on white people who welcome or house or give work illegally to black people. Marriage between people from the four different groups (white, black, Indian, "coloured") is illegal. But this desire to completely separate people of different races is impossible, because they need cheap labour in order for their products to be competitive. It is not possible to totally regulate the lives of human beings. And so the police impose fines, they hit people and they force people to move, but they cannot put everything in order. Many people are crushed and oppressed in the process.

However, there is hope, for many blacks and whites are co-operating together. Many are working together, where they can, and creating community. Churches speak out in truth. The Anglican Bishop, Bishop Tutu, is the general secretary of the South African Council of Churches. He speaks with much force. The Catholic

Bishop of Durban, Father Denis Hurley, is also a man who is not afraid to speak out and denounce injustice on every possible occasion. But the majority of people are wedged in; they do not know what to do. They are taken in by the system. There are, of course, a good number of "silent" whites who deplore the system but at the same time take advantage of it. You find the same reality all over the world. Who can throw the first stone? We are all so mediocre; we are all easily frightened. In order to have the strength to do something, you must be part of a loving community and on the path towards greater transformation in Jesus. But it is still painful to see many Christians amongst the rich. The Catholic Church as well as the Anglican and Methodist Churches are made up of eighty percent black or "coloured."

In these two weeks in South Africa I began to grasp the situation a little, but I am also fully aware of the fact that I spent most of my time with whites. I barely touched the reality of the blacks. However, those I was with are in opposition to the government and are trying to do all they can to denounce the injustices.

The Methodist Church, who knew me through the Church of the Saviour in Washington, DC, invited me to South Africa. My program was organized by Rev. Peter Storey, the Chairperson of the South African Council of Churches, Rev. Trevor Hudson and Helen Muller. My talks were held mainly in the Methodist church at the heart of Johannesburg. I stayed with the Little Sisters of Jesus. It was a great gift to be with them each evening for a meal before going out to give a talk, to have a home away from home, to have their chapel and their prayer which helped me so much. I spent eleven days in Johannesburg and three days in Cape Town. During that time, there were two retreats, two seminars, and several talks and visits (especially to the centres for handicapped people).

My talks were centred on Jesus and his Good News or on L'Arche and the person with a mental handicap. I felt very welcome. There was such a thirst in people. For many, the mystery of Jesus identified with the poor was something new. I spoke about the suffering of people who have a handicap, their need to find a positive image of themselves and new hope, their need to be loved and appreciated in community. I spoke about the needs of assistants and especially how they must make the passage towards greater compassion. I spoke of the covenant and of the role and place of people with a handicap in society, in community and in the Church. Small groups of people are beginning to meet in Cape Town and Johannesburg as well as in Zimbabwe to study the possibility of starting Faith and Light and to be a reference for L'Arche in those countries. My heart is thankful for all that happened. Jesus sustained and inspired me during the trip, and I am not too tired coming back to Trosly. I sense that many people were touched by the mystery of the poor who call us, renew us, and awaken our hearts.

While in Cape Town I had the privilege of visiting a Camphill centre. I was touched by the quality of life there. I was happy to meet the wife of Dr. König and two of his daughters. Dr. König founded the Camphill villages for people with mental handicaps in Europe. There are many of these villages now throughout the world, all based on Rudolf Steiner's principles of education. I had always wanted to meet him but he died about twelve years ago. I felt a deep unity with Renata, his daughter, and her husband, who are the community leaders.

I was happy to be in South Africa, where many wonderful people are working and struggling for justice, living out their faith in the Gospel. They have a genuine trust in Jesus, who came to save all men and women regardless of their race, and to teach us how to love and how to create community. Helen Muller from the Methodist Church said to me, "The great advantage for Christians in South Africa is that their priorities and options are clear." There is no other way for them than to create communities where there is real brotherhood between all races. Jesus came to unite, not to separate. And so they are necessarily called to disobey a system of apartheid.

Pray with me.

Love,
Jean

March 14, 1983
Trosly

Dear Friends,

Our International Council meetings in Port-au-Prince were very intense. While listening to the reports of each coordinator one could feel the heartbeat of our communities. The reports were honest and sincere, presenting the gifts, the pain and the questions of each region.

We were there at the same time as John Paul II's visit to Haiti. It was an important moment for everyone. When the plane landed at the airport, the people applauded and cried out with joy. His sermon was a call to wash the feet of the poor, to be close to them, to share with them. I do not think the members of the government expected such strong words. The Pope really confirmed the Church of Haiti in its orientation to be close to the poor and to follow the path of the Beatitudes.

The L'Arche community in Port-au-Prince is well, with more young Haitians becoming involved. Our homes continue to welcome young people who have been completely abandoned in the asylum of Signeau. I am touched by the quality of life in our homes, by the way they welcome people, by their integration into the neighbourhood. I come back to my own home, Le Val, with a greater desire to live our daily life with all its simplicity, but more aware of the way God is present there.

Soon it will be the feast of St. Joseph. Happy feast day to each one! Let us ask St. Joseph to help us put our roots down faithfully in the day-to-day of our community life, consisting of work, welcome and prayer.

On April 3, I will be leaving for Syria (two days) and Lebanon (April 4–13). Pray for me and with me. We have many friends of L'Arche and of Faith and Light in these countries. Let us pray for them.

Happy Easter to each one.

Much love,
Jean

April 13, 1983
Beirut

Dear Friends,

On Easter Sunday I left for Damascus. Damascus touched me deeply. In the old city there are many Arabian houses with their inner courtyards; there, one cannot travel by car. There are little lanes with houses on the right and left. On the plane I had reread chapter 9 of the Acts of the Apostles, so it was like a pilgrimage to the place where St. Paul was converted. It was in Damascus that St. Paul preached the Good News for the first time.

Syria is a country linked to the Soviet bloc. The military are everywhere and even the schoolchildren are dressed in military uniforms. Christians are an important minority, twelve percent of the population, and the government gives them a certain amount of liberty. The greatest enemies of the government are the Muslim Brothers, a fanatical sect which comes from Iran. Syria wants to be socialist, linked to Russia, rather than linked to Khomeini.

For a few months now, there has been a Faith and Light community in Damascus. I attended Mass with them, where there were seven first Communions. Afterwards we had a celebration and a meeting with parents. It touched me to sense the quality of life in that little community and the commitment of young people. In the afternoon I had a meeting with the religious from the city, and in the evening I gave a talk at Our Lady of Damascus Church.

The next day, we left by bus for Aleppo, which is in the north, not far from Turkey and Antioch (where the followers of Jesus were called "Christians" for the first time). On the way we passed Hamah, a city which was the stronghold of the Muslim Brothers who were planning to take over the country. A year ago the Syrian army encircled and bombarded the city. It is estimated that thirty to forty thousand people died, and the city was destroyed. In Aleppo, the situation is less tense because it is farther away from Damascus. I visited a school for people who have a handicap and gave a talk for priests and religious.

Early the next morning we left for Zahlé in Lebanon. All along the way we saw Syrian troops. We passed through the Bekaa valley. The majority of people in that region are Muslim and there has been a lot of infiltration from Iran. On the walls we saw portraits of Khomeini. Zahlé is a city of 130,000 people, all Christian. Two years ago, the city was bombarded for three months. During all that time the people lived in little shelters. Bishop Iskandar, who welcomed us, led the negotiations. He was like the leader of the city. He is a man of great kindness and wisdom, a real shepherd for his people. Zahlé remains a very insecure city, encircled by Syrian troops and by different Palestinian elements. The inhabitants are frightened to go outside the city as there have been many kidnappings. The people feel as if they are imprisoned. There are two beautiful Faith and Light communities and three more that are beginning. We sang and celebrated together. Jacqueline, who is responsible for the communities, spoke to me about the prophetic aspects of some of her people. During the bombings Jacqueline was in the church crying because two of her students had just been killed. Nadya, from Faith and Light, said to her, "You know, I will pray for those who are bombing us." In the evening I gave a talk and then the next morning we left in a convoy—six cars accompanied by two armed police cars which brought us to Beirut.

In Beirut, I gave about ten talks and led a two-day retreat and a meeting of the leaders of Faith and Light in that zone. There were sixteen communities represented in all, from Egypt, Jordan, Syria and Lebanon. Some of the communities are just beginning. Each community presented itself and one could sense such enthusiasm and real commitment. All the communities are Christian; in one or two, they are looking at the question of links with Muslims.

I found Beirut more peaceful than the last time I was there three years ago. People circulate freely between the east and west sides. French, Italian, American, Syrian, Israeli and Lebanese troops are still all around, but we did not hear any machine guns or explosions. There is a certain feeling of peace, but I was horrified to see the enormous amount of destruction, especially in the centre of the city: hundreds of houses completely blown apart and ruins all around. The Lebanese people are courageous; they immediately begin to clean up and to rebuild. At the same time they have no illusions. Beirut is free and seems more peaceful, but the Syrian troops are right there to the north of the city and the Israeli troops to the south. We must pray for the negotiations and pray too that Lebanon may truly refind its land.

During my talks, people were very open and listening. One can sense a real desire to rebuild peace; people are open to the poor and to the needs of little ones. This morning, just before leaving, I spoke to a group of nine hundred young people coming from schools in Beirut. Most of my talks were in a Christian milieu, though I did speak at the American University, which is in the Muslim area.

Roland Tamraz wants to start a L'Arche in Lebanon. We had a meeting with about ten people who could become the board of directors. They are thinking of having a little workshop on the line that separates east and west Beirut and then, later on, a home. Jesus will shows us what he wants and when.

Let us pray and keep trusting in our world which is so broken.

Jean

May 16, 1984

Dear Friends,

It has been such a long time since I have written to you. I am writing as I leave Sydney, Australia, after two weeks of retreat and visits.

As I reflect upon these past six years in Australia, I think how slowly but surely God has been at work: three L'Arche communities,* many Faith and Light communities and many friends. I sense how many young people are seeking alternative ways of living and of working towards peace. The number of Australians who have lived and worked in our communities in India is striking. The tiny seeds that were sown in 1977 have begun to grow. I give thanks for the life that is there and particularly for those who are the

---

*The L'Arche community in Canberra, known as L'Arche–Genesaret, was founded in 1978, and today consists of three houses and two flats. L'Arche–Sydney was founded in 1983 (and now has three houses), and when I wrote this letter L'Arche in Hobart, known as Beni-Abbès, was well into the planning stages for its own house, which would be founded in 1986.

littlest and weakest and who have found life at the heart of these communities. How I wish I could transmit by letter the joy of sharing with and listening to each one!

During my stay in Australia, I had time to share once again with Father Ted Kennedy. He is living with the Aboriginals in Redfern and has a deep understanding of the Church of Jesus as the Church of the poor. I have much to learn from him. I also met Father Brian Stoney, a Jesuit who lives in a community called Corpus Christi. He works with men from the streets who have a drinking problem. Here is an extract from its charter: "The homeless, destitute and most unlovable alcoholic man is the heart and centre of Corpus Christi Community. It is his home. To give him dignity, a sense of belonging and a heartfelt conviction that he is loved and able to love is the source of our spirit and the purpose of our mission. Our living together and our cherishing of each other are based on our faith in God who loves us while we are still sinful, who embraces us in our utter weakness with open, forgiving and life-giving love." I was deeply moved when I discovered this community founded on covenant relationships like L'Arche. I met and shared with others who feel called to share their lives with the broken and the wounded. So many have lived the experience of meeting Jesus in the "least of the brothers and sisters." Pray that we may all be faithful to these covenant relationships, for they will keep us faithful to Jesus and to the poor and the suffering throughout the world.

The plane will soon be landing in Manila. In my heart I prepare myself for all that will be given to us during these five days in the Philippines.

Much love in Jesus,
Jean

May 25, 1984

Dear Friends,

Chris Sadler and I arrived in Manila the day after the elections. We were welcomed by the Little Sisters of Jesus. Little Brother Bernard (whose bedroom is big enough to give me the necessary rest!) and Little Sister Marlene helped us to enter into the spirit and enthusiasm of the people after the successful election results: the success of the opposition. Sustained and supported by Radio Veritas, the radio of the archdiocese, and other groups, millions of people worked day and night, determined to make these elections just and peaceful. They also prayed. Before the closure of the election campaign, the last meeting of the opposition was replaced by an evening of adoration in the churches. It was moving to see how people reacted to Aquino's assassination.* For the first time, the people were united and determined to work for justice, truth and nonviolence, the ideals for which Aquino had suffered and been killed. In the provinces, the army had to "protect" the voting urns. Consequently, the opposition was less successful and the final victory was declared by President Marcos's party, which had the power of veto or of modification on all parliamentary decisions, and even on the Constitution. The future is uncertain. People are already talking about fraud and about violence in the southern provinces following the massacre of unarmed opposition workers.

---

*Benigno "Ninoy" Aquino, Jr. was a Filipino senator who had fought against the repressive regime of President Ferdinand Marcos. He was jailed, sentenced to death and then sent into exile. He returned to Manila on August 21, 1983, and was assassinated as he stepped off the plane. His death galvanized opposition forces and during the parliamentary elections held just two weeks before I wrote this letter, his supporters took to the street like never before. As you'll read in my subsequent letters, two years later Marcos was in exile and Aquino's widow, Corazon "Cory" Aquino, and her political party, were leading the government.

In spite of all the fear and despair we encounter, an atmosphere of hope born of suffering dominates our visit.

The first morning, we visited a psychiatric hospital in Manila: five thousand people. When I saw the size of the building I was amazed to find it so clean, to see the staff's efforts and to find a chapel. Some faces we saw there still haunt me: young faces behind bars imploring, "Please tell my father I want to come home."

We went to the maximum security section of the national prison, where there are more than three thousand prisoners. I spoke to the group of those condemned to death. We began with a time of prayer. Then two prisoners spoke about meeting Jesus and how that had changed their lives. We met Nonoy, a friend of the Little Sisters, who has been in prison for eight years, condemned to death by a military court without any possibility of recourse. He told us that in prison he had discovered a new meaning to his life; he had discovered a deep covenant with his prison companions and even with the guards and their families. His wife told me that when they were rich and powerful, they used to speak about freedom and justice. Now that they do not have security or money, God has allowed them to accomplish, through suffering, things they had not done before.

As we walked through the prison, we discovered how it had been transformed from a place of violence and frequent murders into a Christian community, a place of peace, friendship, respect, mutual service and inner freedom. We went from surprise to surprise. We saw men condemned to death for murder taking care of their sick brothers in the hospital or counselling other prisoners who wanted to marry; some were involved in catechism or pastoral work in the prison. We met one prisoner who was shaving a guard with a sharp one-blade razor! And we were the only ones amazed by that!

On our way from the airport we passed by Forbes Park, the rich section of Manila surrounded by high walls and barbed wire fences. No one can enter except with the permission of armed guards. Another type of prison! People imprisoned out of fear of losing their wealth. In the first prison, we were invited to share a simple meal with Nonoy and his wife. We celebrated with joy our inner freedom and fullness of life in Jesus Christ. A week later, I went back to visit the prisoners. I felt like I was visiting old friends. I spoke about our hope that a L'Arche community would begin in Manila and I asked them to pray for this. Never before had the words of the English hymn been so true: "I come like a prisoner to set people free."*

In the afternoon, we had a time of sharing with three fraternities of the Little Sisters; some lay fraternities and friends joined us later. I showed slides on L'Arche and felt deeply inspired by the Little Sisters.

The next morning we visited Quiapo Church and the famous Black Nazarene transported from Mexico in the sixteenth century and venerated by the multitudes with all the fervour and devotion that characterize the spirituality of the Filipino people. Then we flew to Davao, on the southern island of Mindanao. We immediately sensed the tension and fear in this region. It was good to see Jing again, a young Filipino who spent two years in L'Arche–Liverpool and then in Asha Niketan–Madras. He was well but spoke of his difficulties on his return home last September. We spent Saturday morning with Bishop Gaudencio Rosales, a friend of the Little Sisters who comes from another province on the island. He is a beautiful person and will certainly be a good friend of L'Arche if and when it is born in the Philippines.

Saturday afternoon, Archbishop Mabutas of Davao brought us to the psychiatric hospital. We had been overwhelmed by our visit

*These words are from a hymn by Sydney Carter, "I Come Like a Beggar."

to the Manila prison, but the visit to this hospital was even more painful. I cannot find words to express the horror. More than 750 people with only three doctors working part-time who never visit the rooms where many young people are locked up, crowded together like flies, practically naked, completely abandoned. There are no windows, no openings to the sun or sky, only bars that open onto a long hallway, where all they can see are the bars, faces and arms of other people like themselves in identical rooms on the opposite side of the hallway. Many obviously had a mental handicap, and some were perhaps child prostitutes whom the police had brought in from the streets. One nurse told us that seventy percent of these people do not need hospitalization but that they have nowhere else to go. I thought how much these people who were smiling at us are human beings loved by God; he is present to them in a mysterious way and prevents them from tearing each other apart out of despair. Chris and I found it hard to see the state of moral degeneration to which they have been unjustly reduced!

In other institutions we visited, especially the one run by the Missionaries of Charity, we found much hope. We met Lucia, a young woman who had been paralyzed by a bullet wound in her back. She was shot by soldiers who had suddenly attacked a group and cried "hands up" in a language she did not know.

The future of the country is full of question marks; the economy is falling apart. Even as I write this letter it has become clear that rejection and oppression of the poor and the weak is increasing. The future of L'Arche in this country is also full of question marks but has been gently but powerfully confirmed by the Holy Spirit; it is already a source of hope and trust. The Filipinos are beautiful people. Their beauty is born from the patience with which they have carried suffering. It is born also from their faith and courage which are giving them the strength to stand up in truth and in love, in front of brute power, to follow the Gospel. If L'Arche comes to birth here it will be an extraordinary gift for the whole family of L'Arche, for the world and for the glory of God. We feel the strength and the blessing of your prayers and we are grateful.

Much love in Jesus,
Jean

August 30, 1984
Orval

Dear Friends,

My ten days in this Trappist monastery in Belgium are coming to an end. It was good to be here. It has been about three years since I have taken time away, time to enter more deeply into silence and to listen to Jesus. In the past three years I have made many Covenant Retreats which nourished me, but I usually was there to accompany others in the retreat. I did not have much time alone with Jesus and his Holy Spirit. Here I have time alone to look at Jesus and to review my life in his light, all that has happened over the years, my relationship with each one, my limits and my fears. I offer all to the Father and try to find my centre, the source of my life, once again and to review my priorities. To do all that I need time, silence and solitude.

Since the beginning of L'Arche, I have not had many vacations. When my community was on vacation, I usually gave retreats elsewhere. Perhaps I have given an image of a man very active, with a great deal of energy, perhaps even hyperactive. Forgive me if I have not taken enough time to rest my heart in Jesus and the Father. In each one of us there is the struggle, as in the Gospel, between Martha and Mary. Martha is very active, annoyed by Mary who doesn't seem to do anything but listen to Jesus; she does not allow Mary to be herself, to be filled with wonder at the words of God, to find all her joy in him. And yet this deepest, most intimate part of our being must grow and develop. It is dangerous to develop only the "builder" part of our being. Of course, vacation is a time for rest, to have a change of air and of activity, to relax with friends. But it is above all a time to awaken and nourish that deepest part of our being where God dwells in silence. This is to tell you that I have had time to breathe deeply in this place of silence and prayer. I have had a good rest, and perhaps I have even gained some weight for the food is good here! The monks make their own beer, which is served at every meal.

I am also taking advantage of this time to say thank you to Jesus for these past twenty years. I think I can truly say they have been beautiful years. We have seen our family grow little by little. We have been linked by bonds of love and tenderness. We now form a large "body," and at the heart of this body of all our communities, there are those who are wounded, poor and who cannot fend for themselves. This body is vital to them. Without it they would die of despair and isolation. For those who are more independent, perhaps this body is not absolutely vital. If they are disappointed or dissatisfied, they can go somewhere else. The beauty of our family is that we find our unity, cohesion and strength in and through those who are poor; they are the raison d'être of L'Arche; they are the ones who give meaning to the covenant we are living. It is Jesus and his Good News which gives meaning to the life of the poorest.

One of the monks gave me a book of Louis Lochet. I would like to quote just a few lines which show the meaning of L'Arche and of our lives. He talks about the first Communion of a young man called Francis who had quite a severe mental handicap: "After Mass, we got together at Francis's house for a meal. While the appetizer was being served, different people were commenting on the ceremony. It was a beautiful Mass and the priest had spoken well. In the midst of all this joy, the godfather came out with this unfortunate comment: 'But it's a shame that this poor, innocent one just did not understand anything at all.' It was just what he shouldn't have said. Immediately, the parents' sadness stifled the joy and threatened to completely swallow it up. Francis knew what they were talking about. He came close to his mother and wrapped her in his arms, and said simply, 'That doesn't make any difference. God loves me just as I am.'"

Our world cannot tolerate the poor. Someone who is in need and who cries out disturbs those who are comfortable, satisfied with themselves and their condition in life. It is true that God has chosen what is weak, foolish and despised in this world in order to confuse the strong, the wise, the esteemed. Not only has God chosen them, but he has identified himself with them. Jesus *is* the poor. When we welcome a little one, we welcome Jesus: "Whatever you do to the least of my brothers and sisters, you do to me" (Matt. 25:40).

During these ten days of silence I try to open my heart more fully to this apparently foolish message of the Gospel. The words of Jesus truly give me life, light and inner warmth.

I also say thank you to Jesus for all those who have carried the daily life of our communities over these past twenty years and all those who carry L'Arche in their prayers and sacrifices, people hidden in monasteries or in hospital beds or in prison. We will only know in heaven how much these people have been a source of strength and a gift for our communities.

Now I must look to the future and move step by step in the footsteps of Jesus, following Jesus hidden in the poor. Sometimes I have the impression that L'Arche and Faith and Light are just beginning. Many people with a handicap still live in impossible conditions, many are pushed aside and suffer utter loneliness. I ask our Father in heaven, our Father full of goodness and tenderness, to give each one of us the grace to be faithful, the grace to love, the grace to be compassionate like Mary at the cross, the grace to be close to fragile bodies like Mary in Bethlehem, the grace to become like little children, full of wonder, thanksgiving and trust and ready to take risks.

A new year has begun in Trosly and I am happy to be with my people at Le Val Fleuri. It is my place in the community, the place where I live out my covenant. I feel united to all of you throughout the world who are beginning a new year in L'Arche.

Love,
Jean

December 24, 1984

Dear Friends,

I am on my way from Ouagadougou to Paris. The plane is four hours late. That means I will miss midnight Mass. These last twelve days in Bouaké and Ouaga have been very full.

My last visit to this part of the world was four years ago (except for a stopover in Bouaké on my way back from Zimbabwe and South Africa in 1982). My heart is full of all I lived in L'Arche–Bouaké: the joy of seeing N'Goran, N'Dabla, Amouen and each one; the joy also of meeting Innocente, so small, so poor, whom the community welcomed two years ago. She is truly at the heart of the community. Each person loves to come and take her in their arms. She laughs with her eyes and her mouth and shakes her head with joy.

After that first week in Bouaké, I went to Burkina Faso (this is the new name for Upper Volta). On December 19 Elizabeth, Hervé, Tipoko and Karim met me at the airport of Ouaga. I was happy to see this beautiful country once again. It is a poor country, part of which is in the Sahel. Our community is located on the outskirts of Ouaga, in a neighbourhood called Tanghin. We are a bit isolated, on very sandy land at the beginning of the Sahel. People tell us, however, that soon others will be building homes around us. Our community consists of ten buildings built in a big courtyard (African style!). Congratulations to Pierre Lippe! There is a well forty metres deep which provides us with water. I don't have to tell you what a gift water is in a country like Burkina Faso!

Karim, the first person we welcomed into the community seven years ago, is very well. Before going to bed at night he goes around the table and kisses each one. He truly feels at home. Wendkuni seems to be more stable now. Sambo, a little eight-year-old fellow, is quite disturbed. The police brought him to us. He had been abandoned in the streets of Ouaga. The latest arrival, Tipoko, about seven years old, comes from the family of the leader of Tanghin. Martine is an assistant who has been there from the beginning. She is married to Alphonse who takes care of the gardening. Delphine has been there for four years, and two new assistants are there for a trial period. There is also a school for the children of the community and four others from Tanghin who come for the day. That makes quite a wonderful little family!

While in Ouaga, Monique and Dominique from the movement Aide à Toute Détresse had invited me to visit the old men and women in an open shelter not far from our community. In this shelter there are about a hundred old women who have been rejected by their families and by their villages, as well as about fifty old men who have a physical or mental handicap, or who were former beggars. Monique and Dominique asked me to come and speak to the men since they have been terribly rejected, excluded, treated as mad. I was a bit apprehensive but I trusted. When I actually found myself with them I was deeply moved. With the help of an interpreter, each one introduced himself, gave his name and how long he had been there. For some it had been ten to fifteen years. Then I spoke to them about L'Arche and told them the Gospel parable of Lazarus and the rich man. The majority of the men were Muslims. Behind the brokenness of their bodies and the tattered clothes there was such beauty and innocence. Their eyes and their smiles were beautiful. One old man told me he was there because of a motorcycle accident and that he was just waiting to go to heaven.

His eyes were so beautiful, without any hatred, fear or bitterness. I felt the presence of God in that shelter. These men were truly amongst the poorest, the most outcast of humanity, the Lazarus who will be received immediately into the bosom of Abraham. I went there with Elizabeth, Delphine and Tipoko from our community. Tipoko is very small, poor and unable to talk. Each man shook her hand with such warmth and tenderness. It was beautiful to see them together.

After sharing with the men, I went to pray with the old women in the shelter. It was very quiet and prayerful. They were sitting on the ground, in a circle. Jean Tapsoda, who was translating, stayed with me and thus missed Mass. "Jesus in the poor is my Eucharist tonight," he said. This Christmas Eve is the first time in my life I will miss the midnight Mass. I offer this little suffering with all the poor people in that shelter and with all our communities which will not have midnight Mass tonight.

Christmas is here. It is truly a day of celebration for us. It is a great day of celebration for the shepherds, for all the poor of our world. I am always deeply moved as I think of Jesus, Mary and Joseph, how they lived in that cave, hidden from the powerful, in a country where there was hatred, war, inequality and oppression. They were living a great mystery of fidelity and tenderness. God was present in their midst. Who in that Jewish culture could believe that the Saviour was there, hidden in poverty? We are also called to live this mystery of the presence of Jesus in a very poor and hidden way.

You know how close I am to each one of our communities, asking Jesus to keep us faithful, to help us welcome and live our covenant with the poor. Merry Christmas and a blessed New Year.

Love,
Jean

March 24, 1985
Trosly

Dear Friends,

I have just returned from the International Council meeting in England and my heart is full. But in this letter I wanted mainly to give you news of my last two trips. I am sorry to be a little late in writing to you.

I was in Poland from February 14 to 24, at the invitation of the twenty-five Faith and Light communities there. They are very alive with many committed young people. At the end of my stay, I gave a retreat in Czestochowa to some 250 people in Faith and Light, mainly parents and young people. Czestochowa was covered with snow, but our meetings were filled with warmth. In addition to my talks, there were group meetings, evening celebrations, times for prayer in front of Our Lady of Czestochowa and fiestas! It was truly a joy for me to announce the message of Jesus there.

Since October, I had been deeply touched by the life of Father Popiełuszko, the thirty-seven-year-old priest who announced time and again the truth as he saw it. He often said he was frightened but he did not let fear paralyze him. He continued to denounce every lie. And so the Polish police seized him, tortured, mutilated and finally killed him by throwing him into the Vistula.* During my first night in Warsaw I went to his tomb at St. Stanislas Church, which has become a place of pilgrimage. Even with all the snow there were many crowns of flowers covering the tomb. When I

---

*Father Jerzy Popiełuszko was a staunch anti-Communist who had close ties with the Solidarity movement. At the time churches were probably the only places in Poland where people could gather together and hear a vision that was different from the government message, and his sermons were famous for announcing the Christian and Solidarity vision. More than 250,000 people attended his funeral in November 1984. The Catholic Church opened the process to beatify Father Popiełuszko in 1997.

think of Father Popiełuszko, I think of all those who want to follow Jesus, who are put in prison and tortured because of their faith in Jesus, and often because of their deep belief in the presence of Jesus in the poor. They are determined to follow Jesus to the very end. Father Popiełuszko helped me to realize more than ever how great the struggle is in our world between the forces of evil and the forces of love. Hatred always seeks to stifle confidence and love in people's hearts. L'Arche is also a place of struggle between love and hate, between good and evil, first of all in each one of our hearts! By welcoming and sharing with people with a mental handicap who have been rejected, scorned, crushed, we too enter into a struggle. It is not surprising that the forces of evil rise up against our communities, trying to discourage and destroy us. But Jesus will always be with us as long as we remain in truth, without compromising with the forces of deceit, comfort and wealth.

After my visit to Father Popiełuszko's tomb, I spent a day at the Warsaw seminary with three hundred seminarians. I was touched by their beauty and by the way they welcomed me; so many young people wanting to follow Jesus. The Church in Poland is highly structured in order to confront the forces that try to suppress the struggle for freedom and the spiritual life. It is a Church prepared to struggle but perhaps less prepared to listen to the poorest and the weakest, to discover in them the presence of God. I was deeply touched, though, by the way these seminarians listened and by their receptivity to the message of L'Arche, to the Gospel as it is lived in L'Arche.

After a day with friends in Krakow, I went to the University of Lublin, a Catholic university which the state accepted in 1947. I gave talks to some three hundred students in psychology, pedagogy and sociology on the place of handicapped people in society.

Poland, right next to Russia, is like a thorn in the foot of the "big bear"! It is a country that knows great suffering and real poverty. There are many courageous people, but there are also many discouraged people since Solidarity has been crushed.* It was important for all of them to know that in the West there are also people who struggle and people who are not too naive with regards to the "big bear"!

I came back to France and after a week at Le Val I left for the West Bank with Odile Ceyrac. The International Council has asked us to continue to follow the project of L'Arche there. Marie-Antoinette David has been there for one and a half years now, learning Arabic and working in a small centre for people with handicaps. I gave talks in Haifa, Jerusalem and Nazareth. I must admit that the majority of people in the audiences were Europeans or Americans who live in the Holy Land and have a great love for it.

But the Holy Land is also a land of war and of enormous tensions which I cannot speak about here. The Jewish people have suffered for so long and especially during the war of 1939 to 1945. They are a people who wanted to have a "home." But in finding a home they have thrown out another people, the Palestinians. Yes, Israel is a land of suffering and tension.

We are moving towards the creation of a L'Arche community that will be Palestinian. We have contacts in the Palestinian–Christian world on the West Bank. We spent time in Bethlehem and in Bethany. We were able to set up a board of directors around Jacqueline Sfeir, a professor of pedagogy at the University of Bethlehem. She understands the different dimensions of L'Arche: a home where people with a handicap can find life and be happy; a work of peace and

---

*Solidarity started as a Polish trade union in 1980, but it quickly grew to become a general anti-Communist movement in Poland. The Communist regime imposed martial law in 1981 to try to crush Solidarity, but didn't succeed. After semi-free elections in 1989, a coalition government was formed led by Lech Walesa, Solidarity's leader. Most people attribute the founding of Solidarity to John Paul II's visit to his Polish homeland in 1979: he inspired his people with the freedom of the Word, which sparked a revolution of conscience that led to Solidarity and eventually to the collapse of Communism in Eastern Europe.

unity in a world of war; a witness that it is possible for Muslims and Christians to live together. That is our challenge. If L'Arche comes to birth there, it will probably be in Bethany. It will be small, welcoming a few children, a sign, we hope, of God's presence. However, we remain open to the possibility in the future of a L'Arche community in Galilee. We have no priorities. L'Arche is called to make peace by welcoming those who are weak. There are many Jewish people in institutions who are also crying out to be welcomed, to be loved, to have a home.

The night before we left, we were sitting on the Mount of Beatitudes, near a grove of grapefruit trees. The sun was radiant; we looked at Lake Tiberias, which was just in front of us. Galilee, this land of Jesus, is such a beautiful place! We gave thanks for all that Jesus had done for us. War and oppression seemed far away from this peace and silence. And yet, the reality of war and pain is there just as it was in the time of Jesus.

Pray for our friends in Faith and Light in Poland and for our friends in the West Bank. Let us ask Jesus to give us the strength and the light so that we remain faithful and are not seduced by the power of our rich cultures. May he give us the strength and peace to take our place in the world as instruments of peace and unity.

Perhaps you are surprised at all my travelling this year. It is not always easy for me, but I feel I must follow the call of Jesus. He gives me the grace to announce the Good News, the secret, that he is hidden in the heart of the poorest. However, I cannot announce that unless I myself am rooted in a community, unless I too am sharing my life in a L'Arche home. I give thanks to my brothers and sisters at Le Val Fleuri who allow me to live with them and also to travel in order to announce to others what we are living.

Much love to you,
Jean

September 1, 1985
Trosly

Dear Friends,

I am in Trosly, at home in Le Val Fleuri, happy to be back after weeks of retreats and meetings. If I did not live with Albert, Mark and each one at Le Val, I could never announce the Gospel the way I do. My words would be empty. I want my words to be full of the life Jesus gives me to live.

A new year has begun for us here. Like last year, this year is surely going to be quite full. Sometimes it is difficult for me to set my priorities and to keep my roots in Le Val, but the people in the house help and encourage me. They send me off on missions and I know they pray for me when I am away.

What can I tell you about these last few months? Visits to L'Arche communities: El Rusc (Spain), Il Chicco (Italy), An-Croi (Ireland), Emmaus House, Kara Foyer and L'Arche–Frontenac (Canada), and in the United States, The Ark (Washington) and the community that is coming to birth in Kansas City. In each place there was the joy of getting to know each person, of sharing a meal around the table, of praying together and of meeting the board of directors. So much life in each community: the laughter, the joy of being together, but also the deep pain in some people. I meet the same suffering everywhere I go for retreats and visits. I am more and more aware of the reality of anguish which is like an inner uneasiness, a feeling of death in the heart. It comes from a sense of being abandoned, of not being loved, of not having any place in society, in the family or in the community. Isn't it surprising that some of the last words of Jesus are "Why have you abandoned me?" It is the primal cry of so many in our world today: "Why don't you love me?" "Why isn't there room for me?" And these questions lead to another one: "Whose fault is it?" "Am I bad or is it the fault of someone else?" We try to find the guilty one, or else we condemn ourselves.

This anguish, the feeling of being abandoned, of having no value, is so painful that we try to smother it or calm it through hyperactivity or unending distractions. We try to forget. We try to fill the emptiness in ourselves through illusory substitutes. Yet the only way to fill this emptiness in the heart is through love, a love that we receive, a love that flows forth from us as from a spring.

I am deeply drawn to Jesus's words: "As the Father loved me, so have I loved you. My commandment is that you love one another." We are all called to drink at the Source of life and to be a source of life. At L'Arche, Jesus invites us to discover this source, his presence in the hearts of those we welcome. They may not always be very capable on the level of production or action or on the level of intelligence, but they have such a deep thirst for relationship. They are a source of life and awaken that source within us. Only living waters of love can fill our emptiness and allow us in turn to be a source of life to others.

That is the essential message of the retreats I gave in Dublin, Washington, Kansas and Sherbrooke. During those retreats I felt the thirst in people's hearts; so many are in pain and cry out because they feel abandoned. Yes, the Good News is truly *good* news for *everyone*. We are loved just as we are, with our poverty and all our wounds. We do not have to prove ourselves.

After the retreats in Ireland, Canada and the States, I had a few days "hidden" in a Trappist monastery in Belgium. Those ten days of rest, silence and prayer were so good for me. It was like a hidden fiesta for my heart. But there too I touched those parts of my own being which are hardened, where there is fear and anguish. But Jesus comes to forgive, to heal and to give us life.

What kept coming to me during that time of retreat was a call to humility. When the Word became flesh, he humbled himself. Jesus humbled himself even more by becoming poor and by living with the poor, by washing the feet of his disciples and by letting others lead him like a lamb to death, and to death on a cross. To follow him means also to become humble and poor, to live with the poor, to live with our own poverty and there to discover the Source of life flowing from his presence.

As I begin a new year my heart is full. I am deeply united to each one in L'Arche and in Faith and Light. We are together on a wonderful pilgrimage, our sacred history. Jesus reveals himself to us more and more each day in the hearts of the poor, within our communities and throughout the world.

Much peace and love,
Jean

December 1985
Trosly

Dear Friends,

I was in Egypt from December 10 to 16. The days were very full and blessed with the grace of Jesus. In spite of my fatigue, Jesus gave me the strength each day to give talks and to meet new people. It was my first trip to Egypt. Egypt is a country full of history. On the Sunday morning as we travelled to Alexandria by car, we passed by pyramids that had been built more than fifteen hundred years before Moses! History seems much closer!

Around the sixth century after Jesus, there were thousands of monks in the desert between Cairo and Alexandria. After Jerusalem, Antioch and Rome, Alexandria is a real cradle for our faith in Jesus and for Christianity. Today in that same desert there are five Orthodox monasteries with many monks. After visiting the pyramids, we stopped in the monastery Deir Anba Bishoi, where there are one hundred monks. The monastery was founded in the fourth century; there are parts of it that date from the sixth century. It is amazing to be in a monastery where people have been praying for fifteen centuries!

This was my first encounter with the Coptic Church. Their Pope, Shenouda III, had invited me to speak in the auditorium of their faculty of theology. There were between eight hundred and a thousand people with quite a large number of Coptic clergy, including about ten bishops. I was able to talk and meet His Holiness Shenouda III for thirty minutes before the talk, then afterwards during a reception. My talk was translated from English to Arabic. I was touched by the opportunity to speak to such an audience. Shenouda III, in his beautiful robes, presided over the evening, which began with a long moment of prayer. I felt that my talk on people with a handicap was something new for the Coptic Church. Several Coptic bishops asked me to keep in contact with them.

The Orthodox Coptic population in Egypt is about 6 million; the Catholic population is about one-tenth of that (600,000); and the Muslim about seven times that (42 million). The Coptic Church is quite powerful and when the government does anything against the Muslim extremists, it feels it also has to do something against the Coptic Church, and so Shenouda III spent several years in guarded residence.

At my two-day retreat there were several Orthodox Church members, including Sister Ruth from the Convent of the Daughters of St. Mary. She founded a small centre for people with a mental handicap. I was touched by our meeting and I think that she too was touched to discover L'Arche and Faith and Light. Her Bishop, Atanasios, encourages her a great deal in her work. There is a Coptic monk who is known in North America as Matthew the Poor. A collection of his writings has been published in book form by St. Vladimir's Press, called *The Communion of Love*. Matthew was a rich pharmacist who entered the monastery of St. Macarius. Ten years ago there were only ten monks in the monastery. Today, there are a hundred, which shows that the Holy Spirit is at work and giving much life. These contacts with the Orthodox Church touched me deeply and I have the feeling Jesus is going to increase and deepen them. We have so much to learn from our Orthodox brothers and sisters. They have a deep sense of what is sacred, of the divinity of Jesus. As I have often experienced, the poor can truly lead us along the path to unity.

Egypt is, of course, a country where the majority are Muslim. My contact with them was mainly through schools. I spoke in several large Catholic schools where more than half of the students were Muslims. I sensed such thirst and expectation in all those young people. It is important for us to create links with Islam. In Islam, there are extremists whom we hear so much about, who are fanatical and ready to wage a holy war against Christians. However, the majority of Muslims are men and women filled with a deep respect for and fear of God. They have such a sense of surrender to the will of God. Let us pray that we may continue to develop links with them.

I gave several public talks. I was moved by the "cry" of parents. It was almost unbearable for them to hear talks on people with a handicap, their beauty, their value, their possibilities, when they themselves are so alone with their child and struggle to help him or her. In Cairo there are only five or six schools for handicapped people, very few workshops and practically no residences. There is a world of suffering that most people seem to ignore or want to ignore. However, I met some men and women, Christian and Muslim, who are trying to do their best to create a few little institutions. I feel very close to them.

One of the reasons for my trip to Egypt was to visit the Faith and Light communities. There are three lively communities, coordinated by Bernadette Labbad, the mother of two children with a handicap. These communities lack young people who are truly committed. Perhaps my talks to young people will help some to discover the grace of sharing with people who have a handicap and of celebrating with them in Faith and Light.

I also wanted to visit the place where tradition tells us Joseph, Mary and Jesus lived when they escaped into Egypt. I wanted to pray there, but I never found it. There are many places of pilgrimage, but none are certain.

I entrust to your heart and prayers the people of Egypt, all our contacts there, the Faith and Light communities and the "cry" of so many parents. We will see what Jesus wants for their future.

Jean

March 8, 1986
L'Arche–Trosly

Dear Friends,

We have just taken off from Manila airport, flying to Bangkok, then on to Karachi and London. I hold in my heart all that I have heard and lived this past week in the Philippines. You will have seen and heard what happened as the Filipino people followed the call of Cardinal Sin, Archbishop of Manila, to go into the streets to prevent the tanks of the troops loyal to Marcos from reaching the troops of General Ramos, who had aligned himself with Cory Aquino. Then there was the subsequent departure of Marcos for the United States. How moving to hear the first-hand details of those who had spent nights praying before the immobilized tanks and to sense the excitement and relief of so many. I arrived in Manila, with Hazel, on February 28, just three days after Marcos had fled. Bishop Rosales and the rector of the Manila seminary met us and drove us to a retreat house about one hour from Manila.

On the way they showed us where the tanks had been blocked by crowds of hundreds of thousands of people in prayer.

In spite of all the events, over eighty people came to the retreat: three bishops, twelve priests and many committed people, many friends of L'Arche, and parents and friends of Faith and Light. It was a deeply moving experience for me to announce the Word of Jesus in the Philippines at this particular point in their history. When I was asked to give the retreat about a year ago, I was asked to speak on the "Suffering Servant." However, the context was very different. During the celebration the last evening, we mimed all together the events of the last few years, beginning with Marcos announcing martial law and the assassination of Ninoy Aquino, and ending with the people praying in front of the tanks, the departure of Marcos and the liberation of the people. All this was done to show the link between what they were living and the history of the Exodus of the Jewish people from slavery and fear to freedom and peace. As you can imagine, it was quite a celebration!

The Filipino people are still in wonderment over the "miracle." A few months ago nobody believed that it would be possible to change the situation in their country. Then, within a few weeks, this remarkable woman, Cory Aquino, rose up and called forth others, gathering them together, calling them to prayer, to truth, to solidarity, to forgiveness and reconciliation, asking that there be no hatred or vengeance against Marcos and his followers. This revolution was a revolution of prayer and love, a revolution of nonviolence which can bring hope to many in other countries.*

---

*After the unrest that followed the assassination of Ninoy Aquino and the parliamentary elections I wrote about earlier, President Marcos called a presidential election. Opposition forces chose Aquino's widow, Corazon (or "Cory"), as their candidate. Marcos was declared the winner of the election on February 7, 1986, but there was general suspicion about vote tampering. Two weeks later, Vice Chief of Staff of the Armed Forces Lt. Gen. Fidel Ramos withdrew his support for Marcos and defected to the opposition. Cardinal Sin called on Filipinos to

There are three Faith and Light communities in the Philippines. They are growing and deepening. The seeds for a L'Arche community have been planted. Jing, a Filipino who spent two years with The Anchorage in Liverpool and a few months in Asha Niketan–Madras, has been working for the last year and a half in a "village" for children and adults who have a mental handicap. He will soon be going back to Asha Niketan for another six months. Every six weeks at the Little Sisters home in Manila, a group of friends interested in becoming committed to L'Arche as assistants or board members or just friends will come together to pray and share.

While I was in Manila I went to the prison of Muntinlupa, where Nonoy Arceo has been for the last seven years (after serving four years in other prisons). I went there with his wife, Nellie, Jing and Little Sister Marlene Karla. I spoke with a number of the prisoners. They touched me deeply as we shared, sang and prayed together. Nonoy is waiting patiently for his release. He and his wife are praying and hoping to get involved with L'Arche when he gets out. It will take a little longer for him to gain his freedom than for the political prisoners. He was framed for murder by the Marcos regime and was tried by a military court and condemned to death. In prison he was deeply touched by Jesus and, since then, has worked to make the prison a better place. Jesus seems to be using him in a special way.

I am sad to leave the Philippines. In these few days I have grown to love the people and the land and have, of course, become quite identified with their joys and their hopes. I love the finesse, the gentleness and the delicacy of the people. It is true that I yearn for L'Arche to put its roots down more firmly in Asia. The Philippines

aid the rebel leaders. Many people answered the call, armed only with prayers, rosaries and statues of Mary. Four days of peaceful demonstrations led to the downfall and exile of Marcos and the installation of Cory Aquino as president. This moment is sometimes called the People Power Revolution.

is a big country: seven thousand islands, seven hundred of which are inhabited, with a population of over fifty million and growing rapidly. In the year 2000, it is estimated that there will be more than seventy million people. Because of the great poverty, little is being done for people who have a mental handicap. L'Arche and Faith and Light certainly have a role to play if Jesus wants to send us men and women to create communities of forgiveness and celebration, helping handicapped people find their rightful place in society and in the Church.

I have not yet told you about the visit Odile and I made to the West Bank last January. We will be returning in June and I will write you more then, but I did want you to know that a community has begun in Bethany. We have welcomed Roula and Ahmad. Marie-Antoinette David and Kathy Baroody started the community together. Marie-Antoinette has left, but Joelle from Le Levain (in Compiègne) has joined the community, and Wadi from Trosly will be joining them soon. Kathy is from the States, but of Lebanese origin, so she speaks Arabic. Jacqueline Sfeir, from Bethlehem, is president of the board of directors. Pray for this little community that has just been born. We believe and hope that Jesus will give them peace and strength to answer the call of Roula, Ahmad and others like them who are waiting.

To be a family spread out over the world, situated in different cultures, is a grace for us but also carries with it a responsibility. We are responsible for each other, for sharing pain and hope, and for being in communion with one another.

Much peace and love to each one during this Easter time.

Jean

June 1986
L'Arche–Trosly

Dear Friends,

I am with Odile on the plane between Tel Aviv and Paris. My heart is filled with love and trust for our community in Bethany, in the West Bank. Our newest community is in a place of great tension, suffering and oppression. It is located in a Muslim neighbourhood, on the edge of the town which touches the desert of Jericho. Last Wednesday was Roula's fifteenth birthday. She was at the heart of the celebration, surrounded by friends and by the family that owns the house and lives upstairs. Since the beginning of the community last November, this family has truly opened itself up to the presence of Roula and Ahmad. It is beautiful to see the links that have been woven between them and through them with other families in the neighbourhood. Roula has changed so much since the last time we saw her in February. She comes from a poor family of Bethany. Her mother just could not cope any more as she has two children with a handicap and six others. The social services of Bethlehem asked us to welcome Roula. In many ways she is poor, as she cannot walk or talk. But in other ways she is rich and her heart is awakening.

The community is so small and in a constant state of insecurity because of the cultural differences and the political situation. However, the community exists and God is truly present there. Odile and I found it hard to leave Bethany. These days have been so good, such a sign of God's love for the poorest and the weakest and for L'Arche. We count on you and your prayers for this community.

In the desert, not too far from our house, there are tents of the Bedouins. They live there with their camels and their flocks. Bedouin women often come into town on their donkeys to get water not too far from our home. A few months ago they spoke with Kathy. They asked her if she was Arab and why she was there. When she told them about Roula and Ahmad they said, "Ah, that is God's work." It was such an affirmation for us. Sometimes we seek affirmation in our vocation from influential and powerful people but often it is not given. God arranges things so that it is the poor who affirm us.

I spent two days giving talks in Jerusalem, Tel Aviv, Netanya and Beersheba. I also visited a sheltered workshop where some people with a mental handicap were working. I was touched by how much our people resemble each other; culture and religion may be different but there is something in our people that is deeper than culture, that is more linked to basic humanity. If we all put ourselves more fully at the service of the weak then we would walk more surely towards peace and unity. In our divided, broken world, it is they who call us to unity.

L'Arche goes against the flow of society, which encourages people constantly to go up the ladder of social success. Jesus invites us to go down the ladder and to become a friend of the poorest and the littlest. We must pray for one another that we will be faithful in living the covenant in our daily lives. We often say that it is not necessary to announce the covenant in a formal way in our own communities, but it is important to announce it each day, at break-fast, by the way we are there which says, "I am happy to be with you. It is God who has united us."

Let us entrust Faith and Light and L'Arche to God. We need God's help so much. God is truly our rock, our source of life.

Love,
Jean

September 1986
Orval

Dear Friends,

I have just spent ten days in a Trappist monastery. Each time I think about my stays in a monastery I wonder why they are so short. I would have loved to spend more time there. My heart was nourished and refreshed by the silence. I had time to pray, time to spend long moments, quietly, with Jesus. It was good to look at this past year with him and to offer him the coming year. It is true that sometimes I worry about my rhythm; I spend about forty-five percent of my time away from my community. Even if I find a little time each day for prayer, it is not the same as having these long moments. Our lives are meaningless if they are not grafted onto Jesus. Neither L'Arche nor Faith and Light will continue to function if they are only the fruit of our own activity, if they are not the fruit of our union with God. L'Arche is countercultural and to live that reality we need a strength and an energy that come from God. If we live in Jesus we will bear much fruit.

Since my last letter I attended an international Faith and Light meeting in the Dominican Republic. There are now more than 650 communities in forty countries. It is amazing to see all that is happening with so little. The poor are being evangelized; they are receiving the Good News. They have their place in the heart of God and in the Church. Communities have begun in Sierra Leone, Zimbabwe, South Africa, New Zealand, Cyprus and the Philippines, to name some countries. They continue to grow and to multiply in Poland, Brazil and in the Middle East, especially in Lebanon. They are like seeds of hope that are spreading throughout the world.

If Faith and Light and L'Arche have grown over the years, is it not because Jesus has a message to give through those who have a mental handicap? It is the parable of the wedding feast. The people who were invited by the king did not want to go or were too busy. The poor came running! Isn't that what is happening today? The rich, the powerful and the intellectual do not have the time to receive the gift of God, to listen to Jesus. But the poor are open and welcome him with joy. They want community; they know how to celebrate Jesus. Pray for Faith and Light and for L'Arche, that they may continue to grow, to deepen and to spread the Good News to the poor.

In August, I spent a few days with the Dene people in Fort Simpson in the far north of Canada and then with the Micmac people in Nova Scotia. I was deeply touched by the way they welcomed me. I spoke to them about Jesus and they in turn shared with me. Their lives and their whole existence taught me a great deal about what it means to be truly human. If we listen to them, we can learn a great deal about our humanity and about the ways God wants us to live together.

During my stay in Canada I was able to meet our three communities in Nova Scotia (L'Arche–Antigonish, Corinthian House and Homefires), plus the community of Irenicon in Boston. These four communities form the Atlantic region, a region full of life and growth. Seeing them filled my heart with joy. On my way back from Fort Simpson I spent a day with our community in Edmonton. What a gift our L'Arche family is!

Jean

February 3, 1987
Trosly

Dear Friends,

I arrived a few days ago from Honduras where there was a meeting of the International Council of L'Arche. When I arrived in Tegucigalpa, Nadine met me at the airport and told me that I was to meet with the Central American bishops. They had visited the Casa Nazaret the night before and asked that I come to speak to them. It was a great privilege for me to share with twenty bishops from Honduras, Nicaragua, Guatemala and El Salvador. I was touched by the way they listened and responded. Central America is a place where there is much tension, and the bishops are naturally preoccupied. I sensed how open they were to the reality of L'Arche, which seems so small in the midst of all the tensions. Our faith is to believe the words of Jesus, "Whoever welcomes one of these little ones in my name, welcomes me, and whoever welcomes me welcomes the One who sent me." It seems so impossible that in welcoming a wounded person with a mental handicap, we are welcoming Jesus and his Father!

This year has been called the "Year of the Homeless," and so in some ways it is the year of L'Arche, for our goal is precisely to give a home to the homeless. Yet how few we can actually welcome compared to all the needs. How little we are doing in the midst of the immense pain and suffering around us.

After the talk, Nadine drove me to Choluteca, in the south of Honduras, near Nicaragua and the Pacific Ocean. As we drove there I saw the mountains where the camps of the Contras are hidden and the border of Nicaragua where the war goes on. Along the road we met quite a number of American military. What a contrast with the littleness of our new community born in Choluteca on December 31, 1986.

Pilar, a Mexican woman, spent two years in Trosly, then a year in Honduras before beginning the community in Choluteca. She welcomed Felipe and Santos. Felipe comes from the neighbourhood; he has quite a physical and mental handicap. He used to spend almost all his time in the streets. He could only walk on all fours. Some people would give him money, others food, and some would throw stones at him. Some people pitied him, others laughed at him. He is quite well known in the neighbourhood! He has an amazing smile and his eyes are bright with laughter as he greets you. Santos comes from a nearby village. He suffers from epilepsy as well as a mental handicap. There is such a beautiful gentleness in him. He was terribly mistreated in his village. At night he frequently screams in his sleep, no doubt remembering his past. The neighbours are close and love the little community as they knew Felipe so well. They often bring fruit, chickens or tortillas to share.

Pilar is helped by a local committee, men and women desirous to have a L'Arche in their area. I am truly moved by the birth of this new community. Choluteca was the first place in Central America where, about ten years ago, I gave a retreat. Since then the Bishop has been asking us to come. The head of the local government, the gobernadore, used to be at the head of the local Catholic radio station. She is a remarkable woman, strong in her faith and in her conviction for truth and justice. So with the Bishop on one side and the gobernadore on the other we have really been welcomed.

It is a gift to be a witness to this community. The house is simple, like the other homes or huts in the neighbourhood. There are four rooms and a little kitchen. One of the rooms has been transformed into a chapel. Jesus in the Blessed Sacrament is there, watching over us as we watch over him. I realize too that this community could never have been born if the larger community in Tegucigalpa did not exist. It is a source of strength. So also, the community in Tegucigalpa can only exist because there are other communities in the Americas, Europe, Africa, Australia and India. We give support to one another; we need one another; we belong to the same family. The birth of a new community is a time of rejoicing for the whole family, so let us rejoice!

I am back in Trosly at Le Val Fleuri. My heart is filled with gratitude and a yearning to be more faithful this year. This letter is perhaps too late for New Year's wishes but I do send you my love and prayers for 1987. Let us pray for each other as we continue to walk on the road that has been given to us. Let us continue to deepen the secret God has confided to us: that he is present, hidden in the weak and broken; that if we welcome them, we welcome God.

In our world there is much brokenness and darkness within us and around us. Let us continue to believe that a light is shining, a light of hope which is the presence of Jesus, hidden in that brokenness. Let us pray for one another and let us pray for our Federation meeting in May, in Rome, that it may truly be a time of renewal of our faith and our hope.

Jean

March 1987
Trosly

Dear Friends,

I have just returned from Bethany. The community has grown. We now have a workshop where we can welcome three men from the Malja (an institution which welcomes some two hundred men and women), and Faduah, a six-year-old girl who lives in the neighbourhood. This growth has brought new life to the community. Neighbours are getting to know us better and are helpful. A man who sells vegetables in front of our house asked his friends

for help and they brought us gifts of sugar, olive oil, etc. Ali and
Fatma, our proprietors, with their six children, invited us all for
a meal.

Bethany is situated on the road between Jerusalem and Jericho.
Jesus told a story about a man who was attacked by robbers while
on this road. A priest and a Levite saw him but passed him by.
Then a Samaritan, a stranger who was "different," came and cared
for him. Jesus gave us this Samaritan as an example of true love.
In Bethany the Gospel seems even more alive, for Bethany is the
place where Martha, Mary and Lazarus lived. It is the place where
Jesus loved to go and rest. In the midst of our world with so many
conflicts, divisions and rejection of those who are "different," our
communities must become places where Jesus can find rest, where
the poor and the little ones can be welcomed and find peace.

Before going to Bethany I was in Nigeria. Bill Scanlon, an
American Jesuit and friend of L'Arche, had invited me. He has a
deep desire for a L'Arche in Benin City. I met a few people there
who really want a L'Arche in their country. The seeds are planted.
Let us see if the time is ripe. Pray for that also.

During my visit to Benin City I had the privilege of giving a
retreat in the prison. There were about four hundred prisoners
plus a few hundred other people who had permission to come
into the prison for the retreat. I was deeply touched by the faith
of these men. I was particularly moved by sixty of them who were
locked up in dark cells, condemned to death. From their cells they
could hear my talks. At certain moments we who were in the
courtyard would be silent and listen to their songs. I visited them
each day in their cells. One day one of the men asked me to pray
for him, "for perhaps tomorrow I will not be here." The next day
I heard that two men had been shot. When I visited the cells, the
seven other prisoners were depressed. One of them looked at me
and said, "Do you remember the man who spoke to you yesterday? They killed him." I reminded them of those words of Jesus

to the man who was crucified on his right, "Amen, Amen I say to you, this day you will be with me in Paradise." Their faces lit up and they said, "Yes, it's true, it's true!" They knew that their turn would be coming up next.

I was also touched by my visit to a leprosarium, where four thousand men and women are living on a large piece of land. In two wards there were people disfigured by the sickness which had eaten away their bodies. Many were blind. They jumped for joy at the presence of Bill Scanlon. There was no bitterness, no anger in them, but rather cries of joy springing from childlike hearts. In that prison and that leprosarium I understood better the message of the Gospel and how it is truly Good News for the poor—how it is the poor who really understand that it is "good news." So often the rich are disturbed by the Good News; sometimes they receive it as "bad news" for they have to change and they feel guilty. But the hearts of the poor are wide open and they receive the message like someone dying of thirst who finds water.

It was good to be with Faith and Light in Enugu and Benin City. I spent a day with the Tiv people in Benue State. Sister Rosemarie Donovan had invited me there. In 1968 she and her sisters gave us the property in Toronto which became Daybreak. I was happy to see her again, living in the midst of the Tiv people, a very poor and simple people. She lives in a small home where there is a chapel with the presence of Jesus in the Blessed Sacrament. It was such a gift to see the love and warm welcome of these people and to see how Sister Rosemarie is their friend, present and attentive to each one.

Jean

June 19, 1987

Dear Friends,

I am flying from Japan where I spent fifteen days with Susan Zimmerman and Hazel Bradley. It was my first visit to Japan, where I discovered a totally new world, the world of the Far East. I am leaving with mixed emotions. I have been touched in many ways and have learned so much. I met many people open to the gift of people with a handicap. A whole new world is opening up to L'Arche and to Faith and Light. I feel close to many new friends.

Japan is a rich country with a population of some 120 million, of which hardly a million are Christian. Tokyo is a huge city where everything seems to run like clockwork. The subways and the stations are wonderfully clean. People look clean. Everybody seems to be working hard. Everything seems structured and well-ordered, and everybody is incredibly polite: the taxi drivers give you cold napkins to wipe your face and hands; the food vendors in the train bow respectfully. The crime rate is very low. One senses that the Japanese are proud to be Japanese and to be from the East. They have succeeded economically; they are amazingly precise in all the details of life and work. The standard of living is high and the yen is strong.

Japanese roots are in Shintoism and Buddhism. I was told that from Shintoism they have a deep sense of cleanliness, and from Buddhism a deep sense of harmony, of order and of tranquility. That is what one sees and feels, a strong sense of the group, where everything is ordered and clean, and where traditions and culture are honoured. One sees few foreigners, and those foreigners who want to become Japanese have to adopt a Japanese name; they must truly become Japanese. We are far from French, English or American society where high value is given to the freedom of the person and of different ethnic groups.

This sense of order and of purity of race does not give much space to "those who are different." You do not see many "different" people in the streets; schoolchildren are all in uniforms; women in offices wear a kind of uniform also. I am told that schools here are even more success- and work-oriented than in the West. People work hard, so family life and leisure activities suffer. Today many countries of Asia are looking towards Japan as a model. This country can become a powerful force for good, or it can create a model of hard work, materialism and rejection of the weak.

One of the most moving moments of our stay was our visit to Hiroshima. We celebrated the Eucharist with Father Joe and then visited the atomic bomb museum. We saw all the photos of that fateful day, August 6, 1945, and we prayed. May L'Arche, in our little way, be an instrument of peace; may we all continue to work to be peacemakers wherever we are, accepting people as they are, not judging or condemning, but forgiving and being compassionate.

For a long time I had been urged by Brother Andrew, of the Missionaries of Charity, to go to Korea. I took advantage of this time in the Far East to spend three days in Seoul with Hazel and Susan. Sister Gerardine, who followed one of my retreats in England some years ago, is now living in Korea in a small home with people who have a handicap. She helped set up a retreat and a public talk.

Korea is very different from Japan. South Korea has a population of forty million. This country has frequently been invaded by the Japanese and the Chinese. It is considerably poorer than Japan and there is much political conflict, as you have surely read in the papers, but Christianity is very much alive there. Twenty percent of the population are Christians and there are thousands of baptisms a year. Many who came to the retreat were interested in Faith and Light, and again a little group was started to translate the documents. Sister Sook, a Korean sister, will be going to the Asian meeting of Faith and Light. The Little Sisters of Jesus were so wonderful and now we have many contacts and many friends there. Seeds have been sown in the Far East. We must pray that the soil will be good and that the seeds will be nurtured. Asia has an important place in the future of the world because of its population and vitality. Will you pray that L'Arche and Faith and Light may truly grow there as Jesus wants, not according to Western ways, but according to the ways of each culture? I feel very small and humbled by all that has happened. It is the work of Jesus: he wants his message of love to be known.

Jean

September 29, 1987

Dear Friends,

I am on my way back from Madrid, from a meeting of the International Council of Faith and Light. There are now seven hundred communities throughout the world with one hundred new communities just beginning. Some of us have been working together now for ten years, and we are amazed to see what the Holy Spirit is doing through Faith and Light. The Good News is being announced to the poor, and many parents and their children are finding new life and hope. However, Faith and Light remains fragile. There are only five people who work full-time in it; the communities are carried by people who have other jobs but for whom Faith and Light is their community of prayer and support.

In August, I gave two retreats in North America: a "popular" retreat in the city of Quebec and a retreat in Chicago with a "mission" every evening in the cathedral. So many men, women and young people are yearning to hear the Good News. What a grace and a joy it is to announce the Good News of the Gospel, the Good News we are discovering in L'Arche and Faith and Light: God is hidden in the poor.

While in Chicago, I received a telephone call from the Apostolic Nuncio in Ottawa telling me I had been invited by John Paul II to the Synod on the Laity. I believe it was the Canadian bishops who submitted my name. I will be in Rome for the whole month of October. I had to cancel retreats I was supposed to give in Poland and in Winnipeg. I am sorry about these changes, but I am happy to be going to the Synod in the name of L'Arche and of Faith and Light. I feel I am going there to represent those who have no voice, those who could never assume a role on the level of the universal Church and yet are at the heart of that Church for they are hidden in the heart of God. I want to go to the Synod like a child, to receive all that Jesus wants to give me and also to give what Jesus wants me to give. Pray for me and for the Synod.

After the retreats in North America, I spent ten days in a monastery in Belgium, time to enter more deeply into silence and prayer. I needed this time of rest for my body and also for my heart.

From September 11 to 17 I was in Bethany. You know that Odile and I are accompanying this new little community. Every six months we visit them, for they need support. Kathy Baroody, who has been head of house there for the last two years, will be leaving the community in order to take time to pray and reflect and to see what God wants of her in the future. On September 2 Françoise Lagand, who has been with L'Arche for twenty years, left Trosly for Bethany. She is studying Arabic and in January will assume the leadership of the community.

All the events in the Gulf these days show how much the world needs places of peace.* So many people live in a situation of war

---

*The Iran–Iraq War was threatening Kuwaiti oil tankers in the Gulf, and the United States sent a convoy of warships to protect them. Kuwait and the United States were allied with Iraq. The US ships suffered a number of Iranian attacks and it wasn't clear if the US would enter the war and the situation would escalate. Instead it helped lead, a year later, to a ceasefire between Iran and Iraq.

today and each day there are new events which endanger world peace. When I was in Jerusalem, Françoise and I visited the tomb of Jesus. I love to pray where the dead body of Jesus was laid. It was there also that his body rose from the dead. It is a place of waiting and a place of hope. For me the empty tomb is full of meaning; it reveals to us that if sometimes our hearts seem empty, we must wait and trust in the resurrection.

Much love to you,
Jean

October 11, 1987

Dear Friends,

I am writing to you from the Synod in Rome. We have general assembly meetings from 9:00 to 12:30 and then again from 5:00 to 7:00, except on Saturdays when we do not meet in the afternoon. We are all here mainly to listen (220 bishops, sixty lay auditors and some twenty experts, mainly theologians). One after another, the bishops give their reports. Eight minutes is the limit for each one. The lay people do not give any report, and I "thank God" for that! It would mean sixty more reports! There is no discussion. The discussion will come next week when we begin meeting in small groups of twenty: fifteen bishops and five lay people or experts.

As I listen to the different talks, I am amazed at the vitality but also the suffering of the Church. We hear about the suffering of people in Haiti, in South Africa, in Eastern European countries, in countries where there is war and in countries exposed to various forms of persecution. We also hear of the suffering in the richer countries where the Church seems so poor, exposed to many contradictions because of the wealth, the confusion of values and the despair of so many people. I find these 220 bishops coming from more than a hundred different countries quite amazing. Each one carries so much! Many risk their lives by announcing the Gospel; many feel terribly poor faced with such enormous tasks. It is truly an experience of the universal Church for me. I am deeply nourished as I sense the pulse of the Roman Catholic Church throughout the world. I sense how much it is a Church that is seeking its way; it is not a Church that knows, that has all the answers. It is a Church that is trying to harmonize daily experience and the signs of God in our world today with the treasure of faith, as it has been revealed by God in Scripture and through two thousand years of tradition. It is good to hear certain bishops admit humbly that they do not know how to put into practice the vision given by the Second Vatican Council.

The Second Vatican Council was a council of hope in a world full of questions and ambiguities. That Council and this Synod have clearly underlined that we all are the Church, that each person has his or her gift to live and communicate to others. All of us, priests and lay people, are called to holiness and to work together in the Lord's vineyard. Certain words keep coming up again and again: participation, co-operation, co-disciples, brothers and sisters. There is a real desire that each man and woman find his or her place in the Church in order to announce the Good News. There is a real consensus of faith, but often in practice there are blockages that come from different attitudes or from fear of relationship and co-operation which prevent this participation.

Although many bishops are talking about the participation of lay people in the decision making and the mission of the Church, few talk about the important place of the poor. The Latin American bishops are the most outspoken with regard to the preferential option for the poor and basic Christian communities with the poor. It is true that the participation of lay people in the responsibility of the Church is a real source of wealth for the Church, but there is the other aspect of going down the ladder in order to live and share one's life with the poor. I sense that that is the call of L'Arche: to live and share with people who have limited capacities and who will never be able to take on responsibility.

John Paul II is at every session. I spend much of my time watching him, especially the way he listens to each speaker. He listens very intensely; he does not say a word. He is truly a model for us.

On three occasions, lay people were asked to speak. Patricia Jones, the sister of Susan Jones from L'Arche–Liverpool, was one of them. There was also the personal testimony of a blind lady. She spoke about the joy of the resurrection and how we should help each person discover to a greater degree the risen Jesus. The bishops seem very happy with the presence of lay people. Communication between us flows easily. There is a good spirit. I sense that this Synod is going to be a turning point for the Church. I am convinced that from this Synod there will be more global awareness of one of the central themes, namely, communion. If there is a deep communion among all members of the Church and a love and trust inspired by Jesus, then we will bear much fruit.

I am writing this after the first week. There are still three more to go! I am living this time like a retreat. I am staying with the Little Sisters of Jesus, and that is also a grace. I try to live the Synod with and for all of you. I want to let all the cries and calls of our world penetrate deep within me. I want to be penetrated by a new love of the Church, the body of Jesus, so that I may be more faithful to the call of Jesus for me: to recognize his face in the face of the poor; to live a covenant with them, create community with them and thus proclaim the Good News.

Jean

December 1987

Dear Friends,

The meeting of the Synod has truly opened my heart, as we touched on many different situations of the Church in the world today. It was nourishing to listen to the bishops' reports from the Eastern European countries, Vietnam, South Africa, Central America, the Middle East, etc.; it gave us a whole vision of the universal Church in its struggles but also with its hopes.

Through these different reports, I sensed a desire for the Church to become more and more the people of God, the mystical body, where all the followers of Jesus, lay people and priests, work together for the Kingdom. One of the key words at the Synod was "communion." The Church is communion and this is lived out in family, in community and in the parish—which is the community of communities. Yes, the Church is and wants to be a family founded on communion.

The Synod confirmed me in the vision of L'Arche as a sign of the Kingdom. But isn't this also a challenge for each one of our communities? It means learning to accept others in their differences and also accepting that our communities can become communities only when people are allowed to exercise their various gifts. However, it is not always easy to welcome differences. So often difference is seen more as a threat than as a treasure. Yes, I sense that L'Arche is one of these new communities that the Holy Spirit is calling forth in the Church today.

I want to wish you a happy, holy Christmas. Christmas is a special feast day for the poor. I love to think of those shepherds who came to worship Jesus in the manger and who found hope close to this little child, and to Mary and Joseph. Many of our communities are hidden, like the family in Bethlehem, but Jesus is there in the weakest and poorest ones, continually renewing our hope.

Jean

April 13, 1988

Dear Friends,

I arrived in Trosly yesterday from Lebanon, via Larnaca (Cyprus). I was afraid the airport might be closed due to the incident of the hijacked plane.* But, thanks be to God, we were able to take off for Paris. Being so close to the hijacked plane, I thought about all the people taken as hostages, locked up in a situation of horror. How many men and women in our world are living in horrible situations of injustice: imprisoned, mistreated, tortured, dying of hunger. When the mass media directs our attention and our sensitivity to a certain dramatic situation, we become emotionally involved with this tragedy. But once it is over, we often forget all those who continue to be treated unjustly. So many poor people, so many people with a handicap, live in inhumane conditions. We do not want to know about it, for it is too much of a challenge to our way of living, too much of a call to change.

I was moved by my visit to Beirut. I had to take a plane from Paris to Cyprus and then a boat to Lebanon. The Beirut airport, located in West Beirut where some extreme groups are operating and could be looking for hostages, is closed.

This was my third visit to Lebanon. When I went there in 1980, I was able to visit West Beirut, but could hear the sound of cannons

---

*On April 5, 1988, a Kuwait Airways 747 was hijacked as it travelled from Thailand to Kuwait with 120 people on board. This happened towards the end of the Iran–Iraq War and was motivated by the conflict. Kuwait was allied with Iraq and was holding Iranian fighters prisoner. The plane's hijackers were Iranian-backed Shiite Muslims who forced the pilot to land in Iran and demanded that seventeen of the Iranian fighters in Kuwait be freed. On April 9, the hijackers forced the plane to Larnaca and killed two passengers to force authorities to give them fuel. On April 13, the same day I wrote this letter, the hijackers flew to Algeria, where they released the surviving passengers a week later. The hijackers were never captured.

and machine guns. When I went to Zahlé, we had to pass through several military checkpoints. When I returned in 1983, there were tanks and armed forces all over the city. Lebanon was really occupied by different military forces. This time I no longer heard the sound of war. In East Beirut, the Christian area, one can circulate quite easily. For the moment people are not living under the fear of a bomb falling on their building. For over a year now, there has been a serious economic crisis. In 1983, one American dollar was worth two Lebanese pounds; now one dollar is worth 350 pounds! You can imagine the consequences. Of course, those who have money abroad really take advantage of the situation and gain a lot from it! The rich become richer and the poor, poorer! For many people, even the most essential medicine is too expensive and thus inaccessible. At one time the country was almost on the brink of a real famine.

On the political level, now the country is controlled mainly by Syrian troops. Southern Lebanon is living in a state of war between the Hezbollah (Shiites who are linked to Iran), the Amal (linked to Syria) and the Palestinians. Christians are also divided amongst themselves. Lebanon is like a grouping of various political and religious clans. Each one is struggling to survive and to increase its influence. For the moment, that struggle has not exploded into a civil war.

Young people view the situation with despair. Those who can, leave, as they see no possible solution within the country. But in this new situation where there is a relative peace, or at least no civil war, there is a spiritual renewal which impressed me. I left Lebanon with a greater sense of hope than before.

I gave a three-day retreat at the Jesuits' place in Jamhour. Those who organized it wanted to limit expenses. Instead of staying there, people were brought in each day by bus. You can imagine the organization required for 650 people (500 of whom were picked up from different parts of the city). There were sixty group leaders.

But everything was peaceful and well organized. Jesus seems to have touched, nourished and strengthened many hearts. I sensed such a thirst for God, a deep desire for a personal encounter with Jesus and a realization of how much we must work to create community, small communities open to the poor and the weak. I also sense in many a desire to renew contacts with their Muslim brothers and sisters in West Beirut. Yes, in the hearts of many young people I heard this cry: "Enough is enough! We have had enough hatred and war! We must rediscover our common humanity. We are all brothers and sisters, created in the image of God."

Each day of the retreat there was a liturgy according to a different rite: Latin, Byzantine, Maronite. I am touched by the oriental rites and by the singing in Arabic. It was a joy for me to be with the Little Sisters again. They have been so faithful for many years and are well rooted in this Lebanese soil.

I went to Beirut also for a zone meeting of Faith and Light. There are fifty communities in this zone—in Lebanon, Egypt, Syria and Cyprus—and the seeds for fifteen new communities. The communities are very dynamic with many committed young people as well as parents. They are a source of support, friendship, strength and peace for many. One senses such life and hope in them.

Perhaps through the Orthodox Church Jesus wants the grace of Faith and Light to spread into Russia during this year, the celebration of the millennium of Christianity in Russia. It would be such a joy for families there to discover that their child with a handicap can become a source of life. Pray with me for that.

The next few months are going to be very demanding for me because of many trips.

Ask Jesus to keep all of us faithful, and to keep our hearts open and receptive to whatever he wants to give us. There is always the danger of our hearts closing up because of daily work and concerns. So easily we can forget the gift of love, which flows from the heart of Jesus and which should flow from the heart of each one of us.

The struggle is great and we are all fragile. We need the strength that comes from Jesus. Pray for me. You know how much I need the presence and support of Jesus.

Jean

April 21, 1988
Trosly

Dear Friends,

At the end of April, Teresa de Bertodano and I went to Zimbabwe for a meeting of the Faith and Light zone in Africa. There were delegations from communities in Sierra Leone, Nigeria, Rwanda, Zimbabwe and South Africa, plus observers prepared to start communities in Ghana, Botswana and Zambia. Faith and Light is growing and deepening in Africa. It was a time of sharing and unity among us. In Africa there is still much to be done, as in other parts of the world, to help people discover that people with handicaps are not to be hidden away or regarded as objects of charity. They are called to become a source of life, if we listen to them and are in communion with them. One of the most moving moments was when parents shared with us their suffering and then gradual discovery that their sons and daughters were a source of life for the family.

I was touched by Zimbabwe, a country that is growing and developing in peace. The war that brought independence was terrible, killing some twenty-five thousand people from both sides, the white rulers and the black liberation fighters. When independence came, President Mugabe announced an amnesty for all. So, today, Ian Smith, the ex-prime minister of Rhodesia, still lives in Zimbabwe and many whites have found a home and a place where they can live and work in peace. Zimbabwe is a country where there is true co-operation between races. Recently the country found unity and reconciliation between the two main ethnic groups, the one from Matabeleland and Bulawayo and the one around Harare. Yes, Zimbabwe is truly a symbol of reconciliation in our world today.

After Zimbabwe, Teresa and I went to South Africa. I feel confused in writing about this country. On one side there is the immense callousness of the South African government in its treatment of the black population (about eighteen million, compared to five million white and seven million Indian and "coloured"). There is no doubt that it wishes to keep the black people oppressed and to prevent them from participating in any decision making concerning the country; the black people have no voice and no vote in legislation. Vast numbers of black people have been forced into "homelands" which theoretically are independent countries; thus the people are no longer officially South African citizens. These homelands frequently lack the basic facilities; they are on arid land and far away from big cities.

On the other hand, I was touched by many white people who feel so powerless to do anything about the situation. South Africa is still in a state of emergency; news is censored; people often do not know what is happening; many feel frightened of approaching townships or black or so-called coloured areas. These white people, like so many of us in North America and Europe, carry their own burdens of poverty and the difficulties of each day. They sometimes feel guilty for being white in South Africa but are unable to do anything about the political situation. I wonder if sometimes we in North America and Europe point the finger at South Africa while forgetting all the injustice in our own countries, the minority groups, the treatment of people with a handicap, etc. How often we too feel powerless, not knowing what to do in the face of suffering and injustice. I am struck by how apartheid exists everywhere. We are all locked up in our own groups whether they be class, language or religion; we have trouble dialoguing with others who are different. Even in community so often we can take sides! I am more and more convinced that Jesus came to teach us to open our hearts to others. He calls us to walk in insecurity, breaking through the barriers of our own group. How difficult that can be for all of us.

We must ask the Holy Spirit to help us fight apartheid in our own lives, communities and countries. This is the only road to peace, that our hearts become hearts of universal brothers and sisters. That does not, however, mean that there is not something particularly evil in the South African situation, where black people are denied their basic rights. We must pray earnestly for them and for all of South Africa.

I also visited Soweto, where there is great poverty, large squatters' camps as well as emergency camps. Soweto has a population of two million. There is a small Faith and Light community there. Those with a handicap go to a tiny workshop, the only one in Soweto.

The townships such as Soweto are so different from the cities with their large spacious suburbs, similar to North American and European cities, where the white people live. In Durban, I had the privilege of staying with Archbishop Hurley, who has been Bishop for nearly forty years and who was president of the Bishops' Conference for a number of years. He remains one of the great figures in the South African struggle for truth, justice and reconciliation. He spoke to me about the mystique of the Afrikaner people and their great trek from the Cape up north, with their Bible, identifying themselves with the Jewish Exodus. The Afrikaner people are about three million; they control the government and its apartheid policy. Their mystique is firm and stubborn, and they are terribly frightened of losing any control. Archbishop Hurley spoke to me of two great figures of the Dutch Reformed Church, Beyers Naudé and Nico Smith, who have broken away forcefully from the apartheid system. One of them is living in a black township near

Pretoria. Since my last visit to South Africa in 1982, the Synod of
the Dutch Reformed Church has proclaimed clearly that there is
no biblical foundation for apartheid. This shows a little progress.
The Churches in South Africa, particularly the Methodist, Anglican
and Roman Catholic, are working together for the rights of every
human being.

There are now thirteen Faith and Light communities in South
Africa. With Teresa I visited the communities in Johannesburg
and in Durban. Each one is attached to either a Methodist or a
Roman Catholic parish. Most of them are interracial, and many
are linked to institutions, trying to create links of friendship with
men, women and children who have no family. It was good to
share with the community leaders, to hear their joys and their pain.
Jesus is truly guiding them.

Jean

May 21, 1988

Dear Friends,

This morning Françoise Lagand and Fabienne Dalbet drove us
to the airport in Tel Aviv at four o'clock in the morning. Odile and
I have spent five intense days with the community in Bethany. The
situation in the West Bank is tragic. After almost twenty years of
occupation, the new generation of young Palestinians burst out in
a rather spontaneous revolt last December, wanting to do away
with this state of oppression once and for all.* Their cry of revolt

---

*This was the start of the first Intifada (or "War of the Stones"). Israel's occupa-
tion of Palestinian territory after the Six Day War had created much tension.
Then in December 1987 when an Israeli truck hit two vans carrying Gaza labour-
ers, rumours spread that it was an act of vengeance for the stabbing of an Israeli

took the Israelis by surprise; the Palestinians have scored a few "victories" which fill them with a new hope and pride, and encourage them to go on with their struggle, to organize a real resistance movement. The Israeli soldiers are omnipresent on the West Bank and respond with brute force. They capture young people in the street; they go into homes attacking and beating the men who are there. They have put many people in prison, where living conditions are horrible, without any trial. They refuse to negotiate but want only to put down the revolt and create an atmosphere of fear. They try to make life impossible by closing stores and schools. There are constant confrontations. The Palestinians refuse to give in; they respond, using only slingshots as weapons.

In Bethany itself, just before we arrived, the situation was very tense. The local school had been transformed into a prison; a young Palestinian had been struck by a bullet right in front of our door. But things have calmed down a little. The authorities are trying to normalize the situation. They say schools will reopen next week. However, just yesterday, we witnessed real confrontations in Bethlehem. The people had discovered the body of a young man who had been killed by a Jewish settler. When they gathered in procession to bury him, the military intervened quite violently and shot another young man.

Marlene, who works at the Malja and who has been close to our community, was responsible for a young orphan for a number of years. He left the institution as he was doing quite well but has completely disappeared in the last three months. Many witnesses say that he has been put in prison. The Israeli authorities, however,

in the Gaza market a few days earlier. Palestinian teenagers reacted by throwing rocks at Israeli military forces and the conflict grew from there. On December 22, the United Nations Security Council condemned Israel for violating the Geneva Conventions due to the number of Palestinian deaths in the first few weeks of the Intifada. The uprising lasted until 1993.

deny this. So every day, Marlene and a few friends light a candle and hold a vigil in front of the police station asking for justice. She is harassed by some Israelis and passersby, but encouraged by others. I admire her courage. She is an example of commitment to people who are poor and defenceless. The Israelis are frightened that these revolts are not aimed only towards independence for the West Bank but question the very existence of the state of Israel. That is why they have hardened their position.

In the midst of this situation our L'Arche community continues to grow and deepen. I was touched by the peace and joy in the community. It is such a contrast to what is going on in the country. However, as you can well imagine, the pain and uncertainty of the political situation weigh heavily on us and on our neighbours. Continue to pray for them.

During my short stay I was able to meet and share with groups of people who are interested in L'Arche in Jerusalem, Bethlehem and Ramallah. There is clearly a growing interest in the message of L'Arche.

South Africa and the West Bank are quite similar. In each place there is great tension. One part of the population wants to impose the law on the others; one group refuses to allow the others to assume full responsibilities as free citizens and to organize and develop the country according to their culture. In all corners of the world the right to live and grow is denied to people with a handicap. L'Arche is called to be attentive and faithful to each one, to give space, a place and a voice to the poorest and the weakest. There is always the danger of our trying to control others, to do things for them, instead of being there to allow the life that is in each person to express itself and to develop. Let us pray that in this world of fear and oppression people may hear the cry of the poor and may make room for them in their lives and in the life and culture of the neighbourhood. Mary, the mother of Jesus, announced the good news in her song: "My soul magnifies the

Lord and my spirit rejoices in God, my Saviour . . . for he has brought down the powerful from their thrones and has raised up the lowly and the humble."

Jean

August 18, 1988
Orval

Dear Friends,

I have been here in the Trappist monastery for three weeks. The silence, rest, prayer, walks and welcome of the monks give me life. I feel like a fish in water. I have not had a month like this since the beginning of L'Arche twenty-four years ago. Before celebrating my sixtieth birthday, I wanted to give this month to Jesus, and I think he wanted to give it to me as a gift! This year will end with the sixtieth anniversary of Père Thomas's priesthood and the twenty-fifth anniversary of L'Arche, an important turning point for all of us.

This month is a time of renewal for me. Jesus called me and asked me to follow him in 1950, when I left the Navy. Then I met Père Thomas who helped me to know and follow Jesus in a deeper way. I have taken the time here to look over the different stages of my life, to see how Jesus has been guiding me and watching over me all the time. He truly has filled my life: "He has filled the hungry with good things." And he has made me hunger. I realize how blessed I am, how happy I am and how full my heart has become. Will you thank Jesus with me and for me?

Sixty years is a turning point, and I am trying to prepare for it. I feel well, in good health; there is still a lot of energy in me but I know that after sixty we begin to lose our strength. So I ask Jesus to help me grow old as he wants. I also want to learn how to disappear, to trust others more, to live with less power and more trust in the grace of Jesus and in the poor, and more centred in prayer. I have a deeper desire to do the will of the Father, to be a friend and servant of Jesus and to let him penetrate more and more into my whole being. Often my prayer has been just that, inviting Jesus to come with his light and his love into the darkest and most hidden corners of my being.

God has done great things in and through our two families, L'Arche and Faith and Light. Many people with a mental handicap have discovered the Good News of Jesus; parents have found a new inner peace and joy; friends have found Jesus and a hidden, loving way of living his Gospel in the fellowship of the weak. When I think of our communities over the five continents, my heart cries out thank you to the Father, to Jesus and to the Holy Spirit. So much life and grace have been given and received. At the same time, I ask forgiveness of Jesus and of all my brothers and sisters for all I did that was not inspired by God, but rather by my own pride or by my wounded sensitivity.

As I look into the future, I realize that there is still much to be done. It is as if we are only at the beginning. Our two families are weak and fragile in many ways; perhaps it is the reality of every community. Perhaps we have to be weak, fragile and insecure in order for God to accomplish his work of love in us. Jesus told St. Paul: "My grace is sufficient to you; my power is manifested in weakness." In our two families there is a lot of space for Jesus to manifest his power!

But there is fragility and fragility! A fragility that seeks its strength and support from God is a good fragility; a fragility that does not, is not a good fragility.

I am more and more convinced that God has called forth these two families for a very specific reason: to remind the Church and the world that God chose the foolish, the weak and the despised in order to accomplish his work of love. The world seeks human and technical knowledge; God wants the heart and love. So he chooses the little ones in order to confound the clever. That is the folly of the Gospels and of God, whose ways are often just the opposite to the ways of culture and reason. Our world is a world of scientific discoveries, materialism, search for money, power and independence; it is also a world of confusion, oppression, tyranny, apartheid, a breakdown of values and the rejection of God. L'Arche and Faith and Light, as small as they are, have a message for the world and good news for the poor and for those who are close to them: God loves them and watches over them. "God has put down the mighty from their thrones and exalted the humble and the lowly."

In a world that constantly urges people to climb the ladder of human promotion, the Holy Spirit is teaching us to go down the ladder in order to find light in the hearts of the poor. That seems crazy and even impossible. It is a secret Jesus has entrusted to us in L'Arche and in Faith and Light, and to many others in our world today. However, in order to live this secret folly, each one of us needs to grow in the love of God. In order to discover Jesus in the heart of the poor and to be faithful in living with them, our hearts must grow in Jesus. To become a faithful friend of the poor we must become a faithful friend of Jesus.

One of my concerns for L'Arche is the rooting of assistants, and I could say the same for Faith and Light but in a different way. Those who have a handicap are there at the heart of the communities; they are more numerous, more mature, more welcoming, more wonderful and more united to Jesus than before. They are the ones who, with Jesus, call us to love and to build community. But they also suffer from the turnover of assistants. And the pain becomes even greater because of the gap between their age and maturity and the youthfulness and sometimes immaturity of new assistants. Is this turnover of assistants quite normal? Surely it is. But at the same time we must ask ourselves if we are doing everything we can to help them put down roots. They will not be able to do that unless we give them the means to deepen their spiritual life and to discover God's plan for L'Arche. Just as Jesus called the rich young man in the Gospel to give everything and to follow him, he invites many assistants to follow him more radically, to become his friend and a friend of the poor.

Celibacy in L'Arche is a fundamental question today for those single assistants who are called to live in our homes day after day with those who are fragile and dependent, and who for the most part are not called to marry. To live celibacy in L'Arche, to give one's life totally to Jesus in L'Arche or, as Jesus says, "not to marry in view of the Kingdom" (Matt. 19:12) presents many difficulties. Some people wonder if it is possible to live in a L'Arche home on a long-term basis. I believe that what seems humanly impossible can be possible for God. I feel this question is vital; the life of L'Arche is at stake.

Two celibacy commissions have been working on clarifying this vocation in L'Arche. In the Roman Catholic, Anglican and Orthodox Churches as well as in some Protestant Churches, there is a whole tradition and support system for those who feel called "not to marry in view of the Kingdom." We must draw from these traditions and try to discover how Jesus wants us to live celibacy today in L'Arche, living as we do a covenant with the people we have welcomed.

The International Council has asked that the twenty-fifth anniversary be a year for announcing L'Arche. Each one of us is called to announce what we are living in schools near us or in churches, etc. We must speak about what is characteristic of L'Arche, our community life with people who are very dependent. If we do not tell others, how will they discover the gift of our people? How will others get to know us and discern a call to live with us? But of course, before announcing it we must live it more fully, and in order to live it we need the strength of the Holy Spirit as announced in the Gospels. To live it implies a quality of love and presence in our houses, and people living it on a long-term basis.

During this coming year there will be two meetings or "covenant journeys" for older assistants in L'Arche, one in Europe and one in North America. They will be a time for us to review and deepen our covenant and to see the orientations for the future. Let us ask the Holy Spirit to come and renew us in our vocation and show us the path to follow in the coming years.

While I was finishing this letter, I had news of Josiane Gueusquin's death in a car accident on the road near Trosly. Josiane had been with us for eighteen years, after being a Little Sister of Jesus. Her death has touched me deeply. She had given much to L'Arche and to me personally. With her death it is as if a part of me has been torn away. Each death is a passage of God which brings with it something very gentle but also very painful; it wounds us, but it also brings us back to the essential and to greater hope in the resurrection. Josiane had such a thirst for God and for L'Arche. From heaven she will surely help us to be faithful as we walk forward into the future.

The days go by quickly. Soon everyone will be coming back to Trosly, and on September 11 I will leave to give a retreat in Yugoslavia. This year will be another busy one. But my heart is full of thanksgiving for the past and full of trust for the future. I have a greater desire to serve Jesus. Pray for me that I may be faithful and that I may let Jesus change my heart and give me a heart that is gentle and humble like his.

Jean

PART FOUR
1989 ❧ 2001

A TIME OF TRANSFORMATION:
MATURING AND FINDING NEW WAYS
OF BELONGING IN EASTERN EUROPE
AND THE MIDDLE EAST

Our primary focus at L'Arche is caring for and creating meaningful relationships with the developmentally disabled. These are the "poor," like Dédé in France, Amouen in the Ivory Coast, Srinivasan in India and Claudia in Suyapa, whose path and growth you come to see over the years in the letters. But there's another set of "poor" L'Arche serves, and these are the assistants.

In the same way that Père Thomas told me to "come and see" when I first asked him to be my spiritual director and asked to come live with him, so it is with the assistants at L'Arche. To be an assistant you can show up, you can apply, you can send an e-mail. And we'll say, Come for a few days. After a few days, we ask: Are you happy? If they're happy, then: Do you want to stay a week? And then after that: Do you want to stay three months or a year? People who think they're coming for only two weeks will stay for two years, and those who think they're coming for two years will stay maybe for only two weeks. And they're followed, what we call "accompanied," to see whether they are happy, because the important thing is for them to feel at home and to be in a place of growth. If people have a harmonious relationship with people with disabilities, then they stay. If they develop fusional relationships—if they become particularly attached to one core member—you see them becoming jealous and closed, and they may be asked to leave because such relationships are dangerous for the core members and for the assistant. The ones who stay are open, full of fun, generous, non-ideological, but with a capacity to live relationships and assume responsibility. Combine these elements with the salt of faith and you have a good assistant. Some of them discover that L'Arche is a real call from God and stay for life. And sometimes the best assistants are the ones who are most lost when they come to us.

Young people have immense inner resources. So often today I don't see these resources being called forth, being tapped. I see some young people hanging out, slouching around: their body is not getting formed, not growing in discipline and strength. They haven't really been told that they are precious, that they have meaning, that they can do beautiful things. And without this sense of their own importance, this trust in themselves, they can abdicate responsibility for their lives and too often fall into drugs, alcohol, boredom and casual sexual relationships. They are lost and unsure of themselves, not knowing where to go or how to make their lives purposeful.

Through my parents' trust I was always made to feel important and precious, and my strengths—a sense of freedom and confidence—arose out of their trust. So when I was a young person, I never had a moment when I didn't know what I was doing. I remember when I arrived in Liverpool from Canada to join the Royal Navy College, Dartmouth. Nobody met me, and I had to find my own way to London. When I got to London I went to my sister's house only to find that she wasn't home, so I just lay down on the doorstep of her building and waited for her to return. And I was just thirteen! This would almost never happen today, when children are so protected from the world and from themselves. We're in a world now that has lost trust, that seeks protection rather than freedom. And then as more and more families break up, where can young people find trust? It's easy for young people to become lost, to harden their hearts, to seek easy comfort in television or video games or drugs, to isolate themselves from others.

My determination and my energy stems from the trust I was given as an adolescent. I felt free to move outside of the "already done," free to search for answers, free to step outside the world of competition and power. When I left the Navy after eight years, I was a fully trained, efficient and disciplined officer. I could lead men, I could wield weapons and I could help direct ships of war. I was accomplished and climbing the ladder of promotion, greater prosperity, success and achievement. There was never a moment when I didn't know what I should be doing; I had direction and duties and responsibilities. I was happy serving in the Navy and travelling to various parts of the world. But I also felt torn inside and somehow dissatisfied. My heart and my spirit were searching for something more. When HMCS *Magnificent* (the "Maggie," as we called her) stopped in Havana and my brother officers went out dancing, I would go looking for a church. I felt called to prayer and I began to read more and more books on spirituality.

When I left the Navy I needed to find a place to be, but there weren't that many places to be without people saying you have to do this or you have to do that. I was entering into a new world where there was no fixed order, and gradually I discovered who I was: first of all that I was loved by Père Thomas and by God, then that I had a mind that helped me to understand, to see the light of truth. I didn't go to Père Thomas just to be nourished; I went to be born, to develop a consciousness of who I was, and that came little by little.

Today when assistants come to L'Arche or when people come to my retreats, many are exploring their own need to find meaning and purpose, to find out who they are. They are looking for the peace that comes with accepting who they are and being accepted by others for who they are. Each of us tends to run away from our lostness, to hide our fragility and vulnerability behind violence or blame or competition or independence. We live behind masks and stifle our hearts. We are, in so many ways, controlled by our fears and compulsions—our fears of rejection, judgment, not measuring up or not succeeding. We live in a world where emphasis in education is given to individual success; where people identify themselves with what they *do* rather than who they *are;* where climbing the ladder of promotion, possessions and pleasure is prized.

And so it is the parents of the assistants who are most often afraid when their children come to L'Arche. The vision of L'Arche doesn't fit with the culture of achievement and success that families value so strongly today. This is especially true in France, which is an intellectual society where young people are educated and formed to fit within the intellectual culture. It's one thing for their children to want to work with street people in Brazil for a short experience; it's quite another to stay in France, to move to the tiny nowhere village of Trosly and to live with the intellectually disabled. It can be seen as a rejection of the parents' culture, their intellectual values, and it's very hard for some to understand.

But young people thirst for authenticity! And L'Arche, as a concrete experiment in living out the Gospel message, strikes the young as authentic—it lives as it preaches, or at least it tries very hard to. You can see this thirst in the letters when I go to Quebec and speak with student groups in the early 1970s, after the Quiet Revolution had changed so much and it wasn't clear who or what students could trust, and you can see it when I go to the USSR in 1990 on the eve of Communism's collapse and so many show up for a spontaneous retreat in a student's apartment. This thirst for authenticity is what drew so many young people to John Paul II and World Youth Day, to Mother Teresa's community in Calcutta, to people like Père Thomas and Henri Nouwen, and to the communities of Faith and Light and L'Arche.

To come to L'Arche, to live and work at L'Arche, is to come face to face with brokenness: first that of the members with intellectual disabilities, then eventually our own. It can create a deep transformation. But it's not a quick transformation: it comes over time, as we slowly abandon the motivations and forces of competition so ingrained in us, and as we travel through the different stages of relationship with a disabled person. I remember a young man with cerebral palsy, his body all contorted; looking into his eyes, I saw peace within him. Someone might ask, how can a man in such pain be at peace? And I'd say that if you just see the contortion, then all you see is the brokenness. There is something deeper than the brokenness. He accepted himself as he was, and I accepted him and appreciated him as he was. Everyone struggles to know whether they'll be accepted in their brokenness. And once we have a true, authentic, accepting relationship with the marginalized and the poor, it becomes easier to accept our own fragility and vulnerability, our own poverty, to open up, to create peace within ourselves and within and across our communities. We're less driven by our compulsions: we aren't as agitated and fearful, we aren't seeking always to control, we listen better to our hearts and to others.

I read an excellent article by Julia Kristeva, a French psychoanalyst, that said to live with people who are irremediably wounded, you have to be in contact with your own irremediable wound. It was Martin Luther King, Jr. who said that people will stop despising others only when they learn to accept what is despicable in themselves. The truth is that we are transformed as we enter into a relationship with a disabled person. We are changed as individuals and as communities by the very person we reject. We are then able to welcome what we reject in ourselves.

I have witnessed many transformations: assistants who were angry and depressed, who had felt the pain of rejection or of not living up to their parents' expectations, or who had succeeded in the world of ambition and "success" but still felt empty, becoming people of trust and hope, open and loving towards others. I can say that we have seen people rising from the dead, people who arrived at L'Arche closed up in their anguish, their angers, and who then discover peace. Instead of pretending to be the best and the strongest, they are free to be themselves, with their gifts, their weakness and their vulnerability. When we are strong and successful we think we can do it alone, but when we are in need or ill or weak we need others to love us just as we are. At L'Arche we experience the security that comes through loving, faithful relationships where people count on each other and where all are open to welcoming, helping and serving each other. Our compulsions and fears gradually dissipate; we trust and assume responsibility for ourselves and for the common good. As the barriers people have built to protect their wounds and fragility break down, and as they humbly enter community life and the communion of hearts, many discover or rediscover a religious faith—not just faith and trust in themselves or in society or in life and the future, but a faith in a God of love. This God is hidden in their deepest hearts, at the centre of their being and at the centre of the universe and of all creation, a God who loves each one of us and is calling us each to the happiness of a deeply human fulfillment.

This capacity for change, unity and peacemaking is L'Arche's greatest strength. But yet, as an organization, it is extremely fragile. In as little as ten years' time it could all collapse, because we depend on people who are called to live in communion with people with severe disabilities, not just work shifts in a forty-hour week. What if assistants don't come? We're always on the edge, always unsure of who our assistants will be—we don't even know who our house leaders in the nine foyers around Trosly will be next year! But this insecurity is also a strength, for we live on intuition, we live on trust. We depend on people seeking the presence of God, and on the presence of God in people, to determine that what we do here has value and is important and good.

The letters that follow show that in so many cases, it is the assistants who have found their vocation in L'Arche who lead us to the "hot spots" of the changing world, drawn there by the call and the needs of the weakest members of our communities. It is through the partnership, intuition and trust of these two groups that L'Arche is continually re-founded in new soil. Their commitment to and faith in what they've discovered at L'Arche is a tremendous grace.

April 4, 1989

Dear Friends,

I am now at the Moscow airport waiting for my plane and trying to assimilate these last five days. I don't think I have ever lived such full days, days of blessings and of surprises. I was greatly helped by the warm and efficient presence of Marcin Przeciszewski, who came from Warsaw to accompany me in Moscow. I carry all that I lived deeply in my heart, but what comes back to me with the greatest force is the immense thirst of so many people to know Jesus. "We are tired of being afraid," one person said to me. The persecution of believers seems to be easing up; people are finding new confidence. They are courageous for they know that persecution against them could begin afresh. The doors of "perestroika"* are opening, but will they close again? Nevertheless, change is evident everywhere. It was extraordinary to be able to hear an Orthodox priest, Father Men, giving a talk in public before a group of 450 people. He spoke to them about faith, about the parables, Lent, and life and death. Someone who was with me looked around the auditorium during the talk and said how astonished he was to see the way these people were listening to the priest; it was as though their whole being was waking up after a long sleep.

It was a privilege for me to be invited to Moscow by the Canadian ambassador, Mr. Vernon Turner, and his wife. It is not easy to get into the Soviet Union without being part of a group or having an invitation. They helped me in every conceivable way, introducing me to the religious authorities and to the heads of social services. With both, I was able to begin a dialogue about people with a mental handicap. I realize that I will have to look

---

*This is the Russian word for "restructuring," and it was a plan by Soviet leader Mikhail Gorbachev to open up the USSR to greater economic freedom. Perestroika was the beginning of the end for Soviet Communism.

more closely at the Orthodox tradition and at Russian literature in order to discover their vision of people who are considered "mad," but who are seen also as prophetic, saying things that others may know but dare not say.

I had a half-hour interview on Moscow television. They are also going to show clips of the American film on L'Arche, *The Heart Has Its Reason.* If all goes well, the interview should be shown on television in Moscow on April 18.* I spoke mainly of the need for love in each human being, especially in the poorest. I spoke of love which is stronger than hatred, of trust which is stronger than fear. Throughout the interview I tried to remain in the presence of God, in order to speak from the depth of my heart, from that place where Jesus lives within me, and thus to speak words from God. That interview moved me deeply.

During my stay, I met many wonderful people, each with his or her own secret and thirst, Christians from the Orthodox Church, the Roman Catholic Church, Pentecostals and Baptists; some have suffered terribly for the name of Jesus. Some said to me: "We're used to living under persecution. Now we have to learn to live in freedom; it isn't easy." When the enemy is outside, Christians unite out of necessity. When exterior pressures diminish, people begin to discover the enemy inside. Rivalries between people and between groups begin to appear. This trip truly confirmed the ecumenical options we have taken in L'Arche and Faith and Light. These are absolutely vital today, a call of the Holy Spirit. Meeting people who have suffered for their faith, and who are ready to suffer more, renewed me interiorly.

I prayed in Orthodox churches where the liturgies are long and the singing so beautiful. I prayed in Moscow's only Roman Catholic church and I prayed with the Sisters of Mother Teresa. I listened a great deal to the work of the Holy Spirit in many men

*I don't know if this ever aired.

and women. I felt their deep thirst, their yearnings. I was truly happy to be among a people who have suffered for their faith, and I consider it a great blessing to be associated with them. Whatever happens, bonds have been created between L'Arche, Faith and Light, and a number of people in Moscow. I am sure this communion will deepen. We must give support to our brothers and sisters in Russia. Peace and justice in the world will grow if each one of us within our own countries becomes more loving and fearless in following Jesus, carrying his or her cross, taking his or her rightful place in the great struggle for love, peace and truth. We must struggle against all forms of oppression and not be dominated by selfishness or by our own darkness and fears; we must grow in love and in holiness. As I leave Russia, I feel renewed with more hope, as well as more realism, regarding the present situation. Pray that we live in communion with one another, and with our brothers and sisters in Russia, in Brazil and in Lebanon, where there is much suffering right now.

Jean

June 24, 1989
Trosly

Dear Friends,

My last letter, in April, was written after my trip to the Soviet Union. Since then I have travelled to Czechoslovakia and Syria. This year I am giving special priority to Eastern European and Middle Eastern countries. I am moved by all that is happening in those countries, where the needs of people with a handicap and their families are great.

Last Wednesday I returned from a visit to Beit El Rafiq, our community in Bethany (West Bank). The political situation has deteriorated since my last visit. Soldiers are on the rooftops, watching everything; Jewish settlers have become more violent. The other evening they came down into the town and ransacked homes and wrecked cars; all this was the reaction to an accident which was provoked by some young people who had thrown stones. This tension, which is felt by our community, makes life more difficult. Siham has been much more nervous than usual; she had to be hospitalized to establish a new balance in her medication. There are nights when they don't sleep. Yet, at the same time, Odile and I found the community united and peaceful. Françoise, Fabienne and Rick are courageous, strong in their weakness. It is obvious that they are sustained by a grace from God. Roula continues to grow and to be transformed by their life together. What a difference between all the political or military tensions and the peace that radiates from her heart!

In the midst of all that is going on, the community is growing. They have rented a new, more spacious house which serves as a workshop. They have also rented the ground floor of another house which will soon be used as a home for four men coming out of an institution. This growth is necessary and will give more credibility to the vision of L'Arche. The two homes will be a source of strength and support for each another.

During our stay, Bishop Michel Sabbah, the Patriarch of Jerusalem, Latin Rite, came to visit the community. He was very affirming. He told us how important it was to have small homes well integrated into a neighbourhood, just like the other houses, and to be able to welcome Christian and Muslim assistants. He reminded us how much small Christian communities are needed, living simply, close to the poor. I told him how close we feel to the spirituality of Brother Charles de Foucauld: to live poorly among the poor, like Jesus. I realize more and more how meaningful the Gospel is for our world today: to live close to the weak, to create community with them, to discover the presence of God in them and with them. This is difficult, even impossible, without the grace of the Holy Spirit. Humanly speaking it is impossible to take the downward path, to continually welcome the weak (within us and around us). In each one of us and in each group of people, there is such a flight from vulnerability, such a search for power and recognition and a desire to prove ourselves. Those we welcome in L'Arche are leading us onto another path, a path of humility. It is a path which leads to unity and truth in a world of war and oppression.

At the end of May I went to North America for two weeks and we celebrated the twenty-fifth anniversary of L'Arche. My time in North America helped me to rediscover the value and the difficulties of our communities there. How I love them! How much I believe in their significance. How important it is for them to be there, a sign that love and sharing are possible, that community and faith are more important than individual success, technology and the search for money. What a challenge for L'Arche! Sometimes it is more difficult to be a dissident in North America than in the Soviet Union! It can be more difficult to believe in the values of love in North America than in Third World countries!

Let us continue to pray for each other and remain united in the love of God.

Jean

August 30, 1989

Dear Friends,

At the end of June, I went to Hungary where I gave a five-day retreat to 250 people, mainly young people. It was truly a joy for me to be back in Hungary after three years of absence and to find people enjoying greater freedom. It is one of the fruits of the

Russian "glasnost" and "perestroika."* When I was there in 1986 I found people crushed by fear and persecution. Today people are standing upright and singing. But what will they do with this new freedom? Will they use it only for economic expansion and greater material comfort, or will they use it to create a more just society where there is more love and sharing, and a deepening of the Gospel values? This is the challenge! Will the Church start dreaming of regaining the structures of power it once had, or will it be the Church of the poor? Faith and Light communities continue to grow and deepen in Hungary and now, in Budapest, the first seeds of L'Arche have been firmly planted. Let us pray.

I am writing this letter from a Trappist monastery in Belgium where, for the last four years, I have made my annual retreat. Last year I spent four weeks here, this year only two because of a retreat in Chicoutimi (Quebec). In the future I hope to be able to spend a full month in silence, solitude, rest and prayer. Jesus welcomed me here with such tenderness as soon as I arrived. It is good to have this time to offer to the Father all of our communities, and each person living in them, especially those who are the most wounded.

So, here in the silence and solitude of the monastery, I have time to pray for each one and to pray for all the L'Arche communities, especially the ones that are lacking assistants or are living in difficult, tense situations. Yes, I pray for and offer up each community that Jesus has given us. I pray as well for all the Faith and Light communities throughout the world, and in a special way for the forty-three communities in Lebanon. People have been suffering

---

*Glasnost, which means "openness" in Russian, was part of Gorbachev's Perestroika plan. Its aim was to combat corruption within the Soviet regime by allowing for greater transparency, freedom of information and freedom of the press. It opened the doors to public dissent and led to the collapse of Soviet Communism.

for such a long time in that country. For weeks now thousands and thousands of bombs have been dropped on Beirut. They need our love and support.

As I read the Gospels these days, I am struck once again by Jesus's words about humbling oneself, about becoming poor, little, like a child, about becoming a servant and washing each other's feet. Jesus invites us to take the last place just as he did. In my heart I have been carrying these words of St. Paul to the Philippians (2:5–8): "Make your own the mind of Christ Jesus, who, being in the form of God, did not count equality with God something to be grasped. But he emptied himself, taking the form of a slave . . . he was humbler yet, even to accepting death, death on a cross." We are called to follow Jesus, to become like him. Jesus strongly insists that his disciples become poor and humble, so that the work of God may be accomplished in and through them, so that they may truly be instruments of the Holy Spirit. I realize more and more that power, and especially spiritual power, can become dangerous: how easily we can abuse it. Human beings have a strong tendency to prove themselves, to say, "See how important I am!" It is difficult to become empty and to let God do his work in us. But of course, we can become poor and welcome poverty only if we have received the richness of God's love; with this love we rise up with Jesus. When I pray for our communities, I pray that L'Arche may be the work of God rather than our own project. If it is God's work there will be surprises for us again this year, for God is a God of surprises; he is always creating anew. That, of course, shakes us up a bit and disturbs us. But through it all God is calling us to grow in trust, in love and in the gift of self. Yes, my prayer is that we truly become poor and humble, with a deep trust which allows us to be audacious in working for the Kingdom of heaven.

In the Book of Judith it is written: "You are the God of the humble, the help of the oppressed, the support of the weak, the refuge of the forsaken, the Saviour of the despairing." (Jth. 9:16).

Yes, Jesus came to reveal the love of the Father to those who are poor and weak and to each one of us, but only if we recognize that we too are poor and weak. Is this not the ultimate meaning of L'Arche? Should not all our efforts to help people grow in independence, to find good work, to live in community and to find their place in society be directed towards this end?

Yes, God has truly chosen those who by human standards are foolish and weak in order to put to shame the wise and the strong. God wants to live in the weak and be their friend. Philosophers are constantly trying to find the source and meaning of all things. God chooses to communicate this freely to the poor and the humble as a gift of his love. Is this not why Jesus invites us to take the last place? Is it not there that we find in the poor and the rejected the treasure of love?

Tomorrow I will be leaving this place of silence that has been so good for me. But I will be happy to be with my brothers and sisters once again and to rediscover the treasure hidden in all our flaws and fragility. During the coming months my time will be quite full: at Lourdes for the International Council of Faith and Light, a retreat in Finland, a retreat and visit with the six L'Arche communities in the Caribbean and in Central America, the Zone Council meeting in Calcutta. I have also been invited by the Academy of Sciences in Moscow to a conference on nonviolence. Help me through your prayers and through the communion that unites us, so that through all these events I may be a gentle and humble servant of Jesus.

Much love to each one,
Jean

October 13, 1989

Dear Friends,

I am writing to you from my little bedroom in the Casa Nazaret in Suyapa near Tegucigalpa (Honduras). My time here in Central America has come to an end.

What strikes one so forcibly in these countries is the tremendous gap between the rich and the poor, the enormous gulf that separates the two as in the parable of Lazarus and the rich man. Yet one discovers so much life and dignity in many of the poor. In Haiti and in the Dominican Republic, they have reached a point of explosion; inflation is running wild. While I was in Haiti there was no bread, and other vital necessities like soap were scarce and thus too expensive for most people. The Dominican Republic has become a real paradise for tourists but a real hell for the masses of people living in the poor or slum areas. One can understand why the Church cries out its preferential option for the poor. It was clearly the option Jesus chose when he came to this earth in order to announce the Good News to the poor! And it is the only right and just option that leads to peace. In Haiti, you see how the country is being eaten away by hatred and divisions; the Church has been terribly impoverished and divided; it has lost its courage and leadership. In the face of all these divisions the people feel lost and confused. Some people are saying that the bishops have abandoned the poor and these people want to bring to birth a new "popular" Church in opposition to the bishops. This causes great confusion in the masses of Haitian people who are simple and poor, a people of faith.

While in Haiti I gave a retreat in Les Cayes. It was especially for people in L'Arche and Faith and Light, but it was open to others. We had hoped that some young people from Les Cayes would come but very few did. They seem to be too affected by the divisions in the Church and perhaps seduced by political programs that seem to be more radical. With the strength of the Church weakened and the voice of the bishops lowered, the country is closer to a revolution. We must pray that does not happen because Haiti is a country where there is so much passion hidden just below the surface. If this passion explodes there will be great suffering, and once again it will be the poor who will suffer the most.

In all the countries I visited, my timetable was extremely well prepared. L'Arche and Faith and Light are now more loved and recognized by government and Church authorities. Perhaps there is a gap between our reputation and the reality of our daily lives: the lack of assistants, the fatigue, etc. It is not always easy to live with this discrepancy. How much we need more people committed to our communities, ready to carry the load with us so that we could welcome more people. L'Arche remains terribly small and poor. And yet, as Nadine said, "Jesus sends us just what we need in order to continue."

I am amazed to see all the life in our communities in spite of all the difficulties: the growth and peace of Luisito in Santo Domingo, Yveline in Carrefour, Germain in Chantal, Juanita in Mexico, Pépé in Choluteca, Claudia in Suyapa. We have many friends and are quite well integrated into the local parishes. In Mexico, after a long time without any expansion, the community is ready to grow. But it seems Jesus wants us to remain poor and small, with "just what we need." Sometimes that is difficult to live day after day and in the face of other movements in the Church that are more active, more militant, more politically involved and which have many vocations. To live with the poor is not always very attractive! And yet that is the "little way" that has been given to us in L'Arche. I pray and offer all to Jesus that he may send us vocations. There are so many wounded people in need of community. There are so many parents in need of support, consolation and friendship.

There is certainly a growing consciousness among Christians of the preferential option for the poor, of the value of those without any voice in our world, who are broken in their bodies, hearts and minds. In Tegucigalpa I spoke to university students in an auditorium that was fully packed. There were many people at the retreats I gave in Mexico and in Honduras. In Santo Domingo many young people came to the talks I gave. Even in Haiti, where few people came to the retreat, we have many friends and good support from the Church. I could say the same thing about the interest professional people have in L'Arche.

I am sad as I leave this part of the world. I love our L'Arche communities here. Each one is a gift of God. What a joy to sense the wider family of L'Arche and of Faith and Light; it is good to be in this large family of the poor and of those who want to be friends of the poor.

Much peace to you,
Jean

November 22, 1989
Madras

Dear Friends,

I always feel so happy in India, really at home there! I must admit that it is a cool season right now. I went to India for the meeting of the Asia–West Pacific Zone Council which was held in a retreat house near Calcutta. It was an ideal place for the meeting with beautiful flowers, big coconut and banana trees, many birds singing and a quiet pond filled with fish. What a contrast from life in the city of Calcutta, where I visited our community. Calcutta is a city of chaos, dust, dirt, people, beggars, shopkeepers, shouting, shoving and overcrowded buses. Yes, that is Calcutta. But it is also a place filled with gestures of love and solidarity among the poor. It is not surprising that this city has called forth people like

Mother Teresa and the Missionaries of Charity and many other men and women who were challenged, converted and inspired by the eyes, the heart and the cry of the poor. Many men and women have discovered the secret of God in this city: God is hidden in the poorest, the weakest and the lowliest.

The big news from Asha Niketan–Calcutta is that in a few days the whole community is moving. They are leaving their house in Sealdah, in the centre of the city, and moving to Tangra, which is about ten kilometres away. Tangra is an area where there are many slums. It is not easy to reach; visitors will have more difficulty finding us there than in the present house which is right next door to Sealdah Station. The board of directors has built a beautiful workshop and a good house on land that was given to us by Mother Teresa. Our neighbours will be the Missionaries of Charity Sisters, who welcome women who have just come out of prison. On the other side, there is a community of brothers who welcome people with drug problems. Pretty special neighbours! That is what is given and it is truly a gift. It takes a real miracle to be able to find land or a house in Calcutta. Moving into a new house is like a new beginning for the community. Each one is looking forward to the change, except perhaps the day-workers; the new workshops are farther away so it is difficult for them to come to work. Marc Larouche hopes that we will be able to welcome some people with a handicap in Tangra to work with us. The new house will allow us to welcome new people. New life will be given to the community. I was happy to see Kashi, Modhu, Bulanie and each one in Asha Niketan. I was also happy to be able to visit Mother Teresa after her hospitalization. She looked so rested and was so radiant! But I have just heard that she had to go back to the hospital. What an amazing instrument of God that woman is! She spoke to me of her desire to start a community in China.

I am convinced that our communities will never be very strong; they are called to remain small signs that love is stronger than war and hatred, that peace and unity are stronger than division. I say so often that Jesus is hidden in the poor and the weak, and in our own poverty and weakness. I realize more and more that Jesus is hidden in the weakness of our communities. But there is still something in me that would like to see one strong, solid community—at least one! But that's not the way it is and Jesus is teaching me little by little that he is there, hidden in the weakness of each community.

From Calcutta, I went to Madras. I gave some public talks and a day of retreat for our communities and friends. There is a whole network of people who have been touched by the poor, who see the poor as a source of life and who want to live the same spirituality: live with the poor and receive from them, and not just do things *for* them.

Jean

November 29, 1989
Trosly

Dear Friends,

This trip to Moscow was short. Just a few days before I left, I received a cheque for a sum of money Josiane had left for me in her will. (Josiane, as you remember, died in a car accident in August 1988.) She loved Russia and the Eastern European countries so much. She often told me that she prayed that I would soon go to Russia. Well, she paid for this trip! It was a sign from Providence—a sign also of the union with Josiane that exists beyond death.

The Institute of Philosophy, which is a section of the Academy of Sciences in Moscow, invited me to participate in a conference on "The Ethics of Non-Violence." There were thirty participants: fifteen Russians and fifteen foreigners. It was quite clear that the

Russian philosophers did not have much experience with nonviolent action in the resolution of conflict. Some of the foreigners, like Jean Goss and Hildegard Goss-Mayr, had much more. This is a very important question for the Russians today as many serious ethnic conflicts are arising. We are already witnessing the nonviolent action for freedom of the people in Hungary, Poland, Czechoslovakia and East Germany. It is a vital question for our world with the danger of a nuclear war where there would be no winners or losers! I spoke about disarmament on a personal level: how our societies are a reflection of the life of the individual in society, the macrocosm reflecting the microcosm. If we can understand the process of disarmament on a personal level, perhaps it will help us to see more clearly the disarmament process on a national level.

At the conference, I realized once again how much nonviolence is a vision given by the Gospels for the resolution of all conflicts. In our communities, as well as everywhere else, there are conflicts. We need to become men and women who have the audacity to penetrate these conflicts in order to bring peace; we must not fear conflict. The fundamental principle of nonviolent action is the desire for truth; we must put ourselves at the service of truth and justice without being governed by our own temperament and fears. This desire for truth does not allow us to belittle the other person. It means that we must speak the truth in the presence of those who are in authority and never allow ourselves to be governed by injustice or falsehoods. It also implies admitting our own mistakes, errors and weaknesses. This vision leads to a greater maturity, but also to a greater dependence on God, as we need his strength to penetrate our weakness.

From time to time I left the conference to meet with professionals in the field of social work, the Sisters of Mother Teresa, parents of people with a mental handicap and groups of Christians I had met during my last visit in April. I also met Ilya Zabluska, a man with a physical handicap who was recently named to the Supreme Soviet, that is, the parliament. I was deeply impressed by him. Russia remains quite poor economically and people are worried. They do not as yet feel they are in a regime of freedom; they are waiting with much prudence. But there are changes. When I was at some friends' homes we were watching the news on television. We saw what was happening in the other Eastern European countries; there were pictures of the Pope. At 10 p.m. there was a ten-minute interview with an Orthodox priest who spoke about spiritual values. There are not many television channels in our countries which would allow a priest to talk about spiritual values at prime time! Yes, things are changing. There was the meeting between Gorbachev and John Paul II in Rome.*

On Monday, November 6, in Tre Fontane (Rome), Little Sister Magdeleine died. She is the founder of the Little Sisters of Jesus. I had seen her in Rome just a few days before. Little Sister Magdeleine is an important witness to the way of the Gospel, which was also announced by Brother Charles de Foucauld: live poorly with the poor, become their friend, see a sign of God's presence in them. Throughout the world our L'Arche communities are close to the Little Sisters and Little Brothers of Jesus; we are the same family! With the death of Little Sister Magdeleine, we have gained another friend in heaven. She loves us and will surely watch over us. She loves Russia and the Eastern European countries so much. Surely she will continue her work in heaven. As a matter of fact, it was on the day of her funeral that the Berlin Wall fell!

Now we are preparing for Christmas, to celebrate the Word that

---

*On November 9, 1989, the Berlin Wall fell. On December 1, two days after I wrote this letter, Gorbachev went to the Vatican to meet John Paul II. It was the first-ever meeting between a Soviet leader and a Pope. Gorbachev promised religious freedom in the USSR, and he and John Paul then announced that formal diplomatic relations between Moscow and the Vatican would be established.

became flesh in poverty and littleness. May we enter more fully into this mystery this year. A very blessed Christmas to each one.

Jean

April 9, 1990

Dear Friends,

My letters often begin with "I am writing to you from the airport," or "I am on the plane between such and such a place." This time I am writing to you from a small village near the forest of Compiègne which is called Trosly-Breuil! I just wanted to write to wish you a happy Easter.

I am convinced that Easter is a special feast day for L'Arche; it is a time of celebration especially for the poor. Jesus rose from the dead with the marks of his wounds: "Thomas, put your finger here; look, here are my hands. Give me your hand; put it into my side. Do not be unbelieving any more but believe" (John 20:27). Each one of us is called to find new life through our wounds. Jesus was born in poverty and weakness and died in great poverty and weakness: tortured, excommunicated, rejected, "a man of sorrows, familiar with suffering, one from whom, as it were, we averted our gaze, for whom we had no regard" (Isa. 53:3). How many people are living that same reality in our world today? In L'Arche we are called to welcome and be close to people who have been crucified, people who are in anguish and who carry within them tremendous pain. We are called to discover a source of life in them. That is the mystery of our life.

I often say that L'Arche is founded on pain, on broken hearts and broken bodies. Our first objective is to welcome men and women, and sometimes children, who are living in great pain and anguish. Some of the pain and anguish might disappear thanks to community life and to the Good News of Jesus, but not all. Many who come to us will never be fully healed; their pain and anguish subsist. We are called to walk with them. So L'Arche is founded on compassion: "Be compassionate as your Father in heaven is compassionate." Let us look at Mary, the mother of Jesus, standing at the foot of the cross; she has much to teach us about compassion.

In Faith and Light we continue to prepare for the pilgrimage to Lourdes at Easter 1991, for the twentieth anniversary of Faith and Light. There will be between twelve and fifteen thousand pilgrims coming from fifty countries. There are now some 850 Faith and Light communities throughout the world. Not all of them will come, for it would be too expensive, especially for those who are far away, but they will all be represented at Lourdes.

Twenty years ago, when we had that first pilgrimage to Lourdes, we wanted it to be a celebration to help people recognize the place people with a mental handicap could have in diocesan pilgrimages. In many countries now this has been accomplished. But today we have an even greater concern. More and more people with a mental handicap are killed before or even just after birth. Much has been done for the integration of our people in society and in the Church, but at the same time there is an ever increasing intolerance. We are hoping that the Easter pilgrimage in 1991 will be a time of thanksgiving and also a reminder to the world that people with a mental handicap are full human beings and that they have a gift to bring to our world.

I am deeply united with you in the hope of Easter, and the hope that flows from our covenant with Jesus in the poor.

Jean

June 1990
Trosly

Dear Friends,

In May I spent two weeks with Odile in Moscow and Leningrad. We were not able to go to Lithuania as planned due to the political situation.* Patrick Mathias, our psychiatrist in Trosly, was with us for the week in Moscow. As I reflect on this visit to the Soviet Union, my heart has mixed feelings: the joy and the hope of seeing the withdrawal of the yoke of oppression, the joy of discovering the beauty of the Russian soul and Russian culture, the joy of sensing such a deep thirst for God in the hearts of the people today, but also the sadness of realizing how much these people have suffered, sadness also in seeing their state of confusion and feeling of helplessness today.

The first thing I noticed was the great poverty in the country; there is nothing in the stores and people have to stand in long lines in order to buy a little food. The economy is in a terrible state. Some things, like bread, cost practically nothing at all. A subway ticket costs less than a penny, the same thing for a phone call within the city. People do not feel like working. Why should they work when you can't buy anything with the money! Few people we spoke with had any appreciation of Gorbachev for, they said, he had not done anything to improve their living conditions. The Communist regime put all the country's money into a vast propaganda machine and the creation of a huge war machine.

There is, however, a new sense of freedom in the air. People can meet and talk to each other. Newspapers are free to publish what

---

*Perestroika, Glasnost, Solidarity and forces of liberation slowly chipped away at the foundations of the USSR, and nationalist feeling within its states began to rise. On March 11, 1990, Lithuania became the first Soviet republic to declare independence from the USSR. In response, the Soviet authorities imposed economic sanctions and political and military pressure on the state. Finally, in September 1991, a new Soviet parliament acknowledged the independence of Lithuania.

they want. People can practise their religion. In certain parts of the country, like Georgia, they are reopening churches. It was easy for us to talk in public to different groups of Catholics, Orthodox and Pentecostals. This time I was able to visit two seminaries of the Orthodox Church, one in Moscow and the other in Leningrad. In each one there are some five hundred future priests! One senses a deep spiritual and theological life; liturgies are beautiful and prayerful. I am getting to know the spiritual tradition of Russia, which is so beautiful and so important with its saints, its monasteries and its icons.

In some people I sensed a certain distrust of the hierarchy of the Orthodox Church, which has compromised with the former regime. We also detected a certain distrust with regard to the Roman Catholic Church and perhaps with regard to the West in general. The Russian Church has such a deep sense of what is sacred. They criticize the Western churches sometimes for having lost a sense of the greatness of God and for being too taken up with political and social matters. Yet, I felt they were touched when they rediscovered the place of the poor at the heart of the Church, the poor as an image and real presence of Jesus. Are there not two dangers that confront all followers of Jesus: either to be too distant from the poor, too closed up in our own spiritual life, or else to be too distant from a union of love with Jesus and his Father because of too much involvement in social matters? Is this not the challenge of L'Arche: to try to find a harmony between an intimate union with Jesus, an interior life in the Holy Spirit, and at the same time a loving presence to and with the poor? We need to ask Jesus and his Holy Spirit to give us the grace to live this unity.

In Moscow, I gave a three-day retreat during the evenings. It was a very gentle experience for me. There was such a unity and love among us, a real presence of Jesus. On Sunday evening, the last evening of the retreat, there were two hundred people: Orthodox, Pentecostal and Catholic. At the retreat in Leningrad there were fewer people; the retreat was held in an apartment but the quality of the silence and prayer after the talks was impressive. Without any doubt the Holy Spirit is at work in this country! Many people are thirsting for Jesus and his Gospel; there are more and more baptisms. We are being called to open our hearts to the movement of the Spirit in Russia and to be in communion with these people. It is important to pray for them and with them, and to be ready and open to receive the gifts the Russian Orthodox Church has to give us.

With the fall of the Communist empire, humanity is entering into a new era of its history. How can we welcome this as a grace, with new generosity and new hope? The danger for us in the West is complacency. We believe that our system is better and fail to see all the untruthfulness, oppression, injustice and selfishness in our own countries. If Marxism arrived on the scene with such force and attraction, it is precisely because there was such a gap between the world of the rich and the world of the poor and because Christians showed so little concern for the poor and for sharing together. Are we not in the process today of creating the same conditions for a new uprising of the poor, especially in Third World countries, through the indifference of richer countries?

Last week I returned from a visit to Bethany and the West Bank. My joy in being with the community was tarnished by the political and military situation of the country and the latest announcement by the new Shamir government of its desire to crush the Intifada. The Palestinian people are crying out to have their own space and political and cultural freedom. Bethany was filled with soldiers. Just before our arrival, there was a curfew that lasted a week. No one had the right to go out of the house, not even to the workshop. You can imagine how difficult that was.

May the Holy Spirit guide us and keep us.

Jean

September 1990
Orval

Dear Friends,

This is my last day in the Trappist monastery where I have had two weeks of rest, prayer and walks in the forest. My heart is full of peace and thanksgiving. I have offered to Jesus all the events of the past year and all the events of the coming year.

As I leave the monastery I feel like a little child; this time of prayer has made me more vulnerable. It is as if Jesus has taken away many of my defence mechanisms and systems of protection. And so I feel poorer, more insecure on the path of this new year, and yet at the same time more confident and more abandoned in the heart of God.

There is such a contrast between the peace of this monastery, the peace I feel in my own heart through the presence of Jesus, and all the preparations for war in the Middle East: the aircraft carriers, the bombers, the jet fighters, the numbers of troops on alert, the arms, chemical weapons, etc. Last year there was hope for world peace with the fall of the Berlin Wall and of Eastern European Communist regimes. But once again the world is reminded of the harsh reality: peace will come only when each one of us is converted and committed to works of peace, justice, sharing and reconciliation. The danger of war is not just in the Middle East! It is in our families, our communities, our cities, our countries and our own hearts. War exists whenever we refuse to listen to someone who is different or when we do away with a child with a handicap, or any child. There is war when there is rivalry, competition and jealousy or when there is depression and lack of trust.

It is important to pray that war will not break out in the Middle East, with all the horrors that will follow. But each one of us is called in an urgent way to become a man or woman of peace and reconciliation wherever we may be. We are called to open our hearts and minds to people who are different from us and who disturb us—to let the Holy Spirit come into our beings and take away our fear of others, so that we may become less intimidated in welcoming others and listening to them.

While in the monastery I read a remarkable book, *The Company of Strangers* by Parker Palmer. He writes about the relationship between private and public life. Today there is a danger that private life becomes focused on ourselves; we forget the stranger. And yet the latter always has some truth to offer. Parker Palmer, who has been living in a Christian community for a long time, points out some of the dangers for communities but also how they are called to give life and be like yeast in the dough of a society. We can all benefit greatly from a careful reading of this book.

In July I went to Romania and Hungary. I was moved by my visit to Bucharest, which was prepared by Piotr who coordinates Faith and Light in Poland. Caritas invited me to come, especially to meet parents of children with a mental handicap. There is much to be done in that country, and like everywhere else, people with a mental handicap are not a priority! I visited a large institution for some three hundred people with a handicap, mostly children. It was a place of great pain and distress, and yet I was told it was one of the better institutions. It is very clear now that in all the totalitarian countries (as in many other places) people tried to do away with those who had a handicap. Their weakness was disturbing and they used up the country's resources, so it was better just to ignore them, or else to let them die, or to kill them. As I went from room to room and from bed to bed in that institution, seeing all the little faces that were looking at me with such a thirst for love, I felt almost physically ill. It was too much. But how to help these people in Romania discover that all these little faces are faces of prophets who are calling us to tenderness and to love, that these faces in search of love are revealing the deepest thirst in the heart of all human beings, that the answer to war is to welcome one of these little ones in the name of Jesus? I hope to go back to Bucharest next March to give a retreat. Pray for this country and for friends there who, in spite of all the difficulties, are working so that the Kingdom of Jesus may come.

From there I went to Budapest, where it was joy to visit the Faith and Light community and Ildiko, who is beginning a community of L'Arche. Hungary is a country in complete evolution. What a change from the last time I went there a year ago. People are breathing a new air of freedom, joy and peace. The question remains: are they going to use this new freedom to follow Jesus and to live in communion with the poor?

One of the greatest concerns Ildiko had for the new foundation of L'Arche was how to get government approval. Last May they had elections and a new government was set up. The new minister of health is a doctor who made my retreat last year (he was not in politics at the time). It was not difficult to receive government approval, and even a government grant! What a joy to see the birth of this community in Budapest!

At the beginning of August, in Edinburgh, we had an international meeting of Faith and Light. The meeting was a turning point for Faith and Light. The mandate of Marie-Hélène Mathieu as international coordinator has ended. Everyone has confidence and lives this new phase in the life of Faith and Light with much peace and hope. It will be marked by the international pilgrimage at Easter 1991, for which all the communities are beginning to prepare. The pilgrimage will be an important international event. I hope that a number of L'Arche communities will be able to join Faith and Light communities for this pilgrimage.

I have just come back from a meeting with a group of young people (fourteen to eighteen years old), the World Association of Adolescents in L'Arche (WAA!!), all children of assistants in

L'Arche. They organized this time of renewal and invited me to come and speak to them about the meaning of suffering. I can tell you it has been one of my greatest joys this year: twenty-two young people with a great love for L'Arche and deep faith in Jesus. At the beginning of L'Arche some people advised me not to welcome families because the children would never want the same options as their parents! This meeting has revealed one of the fruits of L'Arche, a sign of the Holy Spirit. God blesses L'Arche with the gift of people with a handicap at the heart of the community and with the gift of families and their children.

Love,
Jean

December 1990
Trosly

Dear Friends,

I have not written since September. Since then I have been to the Philippines, Taiwan and Hong Kong. It was a real joy for me to visit Punla (The Seed), the L'Arche community in Manila. Jing and Keiko have welcomed Roy, Jordon and Helen. Helen has been with them for six months now; she is blind and her little body is very wounded. In September Keiko was telling me how painful it was to see that Helen did not respond to any relationship. Just recently, however, I received a postcard from Keiko telling me of her joy: Helen smiled for the first time! What a mystery of pain, and also of potential love, is hidden in the heart of Helen and of so many like her.

From Manila I went to Taiwan. This was my first visit with the Taiwanese people. I am just beginning to discover the depth of their ancient culture which, like all other cultures, has trouble understanding the meaning of people with a handicap; so often they are regarded only as a punishment from God. How much they and their parents must suffer from that attitude!

We spent two days in Hong Kong, which is in an important period of change: in 1997 Hong Kong will be part of China. People are feeling terribly insecure; they do not know what their future will be. Many are trying to immigrate, but immigration laws in most countries do not allow families to bring with them their child with a handicap. They are obliged to leave him or her in a hospital in Hong Kong. There are two wonderful Faith and Light communities there and preparations for a third one.

In October I went to North America to give a Covenant Retreat in North Bay. I also visited Daybreak and the Hearth, our first two North American communities, to see the men and women who are truly the founders of our communities. It is true, they have aged, but they are peaceful and radiant. It was good to have time with the community leaders, the councils, the boards and the priests, Henri Nouwen* and George Strohmeyer,** and to feel the pulse of

*I first met Henri Nouwen through Jan Risse, the founder of the L'Arche community in Mobile, Alabama. Jan invited Henri to come with her to a silent Covenant Retreat I was giving in Chicago in the late 1970s. Henri Nouwen was a Dutch Catholic priest who had spent much of his life teaching at universities in the United States. After we met, I invited him to come visit us at Trosly, and a few years later he gave up teaching to become the pastor at L'Arche–Daybreak, assuming a role much like that of Père Thomas at Trosly. He became very important to L'Arche. First of all, he understood L'Arche, as he showed especially in the book *Adam: God's Beloved*. Also, he had what I call the sacrament of the word. He knew how to say things that people would listen to and had a power of the word, especially the written word. And third, he was extremely authentic. He would have lost himself if he had stayed at Harvard or Yale, but he found himself in L'Arche. He helped people to find themselves, to discover a vision. You can see that his vision continues to touch me and flows through my letters even after his death in 1996.

**George Strohmeyer founded the L'Arche community in Erie, Pennsylvania.

those communities. I give thanks for the grace and the faithfulness of our communities in North America.

Now we are preparing for Christmas, a special time of celebration for children, for the child Jesus and his mother and father. Their celebration was simple and hidden in a cave, but it was revealed to a few shepherds, a few poor people. I think of our communities which often feel isolated and poor, in need of assistants: communities that are far away in Third World countries, but also those that are perhaps more hidden and farther away from their own culture, in rich countries that have completely lost the meaning of Christmas. I think of the growing insecurity in the world as we get news of the threats of war, inflation and hunger. Yes, everywhere people are waiting for a Saviour: "Come, Lord Jesus, come and heal our hearts, help us to share and to trust, come and renew hope in the hearts of people, come and open our hearts and homes to those who are in pain." I rejoice when I think of each one of our communities around the table at Christmas, and these words of Jesus: "When you give a dinner, invite the poor, the crippled, the lame, the blind; then you will be blessed." Yes, I rejoice when I think of each one of our communities as a place of peace and unity, a place where God is present, Emmanuel. God-with-us.

Peace to you for Christmas,
Jean

February 1991
Trosly

Dear Friends,

In January I lived an event that marked me deeply: the ecumenical retreat organized by our L'Arche communities in Great Britain. There were seven bishops, about twenty-five clergy and religious sisters from various traditions, plus the leaders of all our communities in Great Britain. I was particularly moved by the long moments of silent prayer we had together before breakfast: all of us, representing different churches, in silent adoration before God, our hearts open to God's forgiving love and God's call to risk loving more. All were connected in some way with one of our communities. We were bonded together in the mystery of the Gospel which has been revealed to us: God is hidden in the weak and in the poor, and as we enter into communion with them, we enter into communion with Jesus and the Father.

On the last day of the four-day retreat the war broke out in the Gulf.* Even though we were expecting it to happen, when we received the news we were shocked, realizing that it was leading to a world conflagration. New seeds of hate are now being sown which will grow and remain for many generations to come. In response to this war we are called more and more to become men and women committed to peace, called to love in a special way those who threaten us. To be a peacemaker is to be a man or woman of forgiveness and of reconciliation.

Just before Christmas, I went to Egypt and Lebanon, where I talked about L'Arche and Faith and Light, sharing the same secret that has been confided to us: God is hidden in the poor and as we enter into a relationship of communion and friendship with the weak and the poor we discover God and love. It seems so incongruous and impossible. Yet I was touched as I spoke in schools where over fifty percent of the students were Muslim and I saw how so many were open to this message of love. But once they hear it and

---

*It was what the Americans call the First Gulf War. Iraq had invaded its former ally Kuwait in August 1990. The UN imposed sanctions, but ultimately authorized a coalition force to expel Saddam Hussein's army from Kuwait. The war started on January 16, 1991, and lasted for forty-four days. Many of the tensions leading up to and left unresolved after the war are at the heart of the current "Second" Gulf War now being led by the United States.

feel the attractive power of this truth, they do not know what to do with it, how to incarnate it into their lives, and so the message dies within them. I was particularly moved by a retreat I gave in Beirut for some 650 people, many of them young. After years of civil war, and particularly after these last few months of war where Christians were killing Christians, a deep discouragement has set in. There is anger and resentment regarding the churches, a feeling of guilt and of being let down by everybody. It was such a privilege to announce the Good News of Christmas in that context. Jesus is present in this world of pain, awakening hearts not to a big ideal of triumph but rather to compassion and love, to loving people just as they are in all their poverty and pain.

There is a tendency everywhere today to want a victorious religion, a successful Jesus, as proof of our goodness and our truth. We forget the true Jesus who was persecuted, abandoned, lonely, who suffered agony, wept and was crucified. We forget that Jesus continues to live today in those who are persecuted, abandoned, lonely, crucified, in agony and in those who weep. They are waiting for friends who will be with them, who will accompany them on this journey of life and whose presence will transform the pain of loneliness into the joy of communion. Beirut is even more broken than before; many buildings are destroyed. Yet in this very city, God is present among the poorest and the weakest and the most broken.

Now I am in India. What a joy to be met by Subbaiyan at the airport. From there we went by taxi to our community, Asha Niketan–Nandi Bazaar.* They had thought I might not come because of the war. I was immediately plunged into the gentle, loving life of the community, its simplicity and poverty, its closeness

---

*Asha Niketan–Nandi Bazaar is about forty kilometres from Calicut in the province of Kerala. I refer to it by all of these place names at different points in the letters.

to nature, the people with all their beauty. I was touched by the simple evening prayer. There, hidden in the heart of Kerala, in this vast country of India, every morning and every night a community made up of Muslims, Christians and Hindus comes together in prayer and in communion with all the other communities of L'Arche throughout the world.

When I am in India, and particularly with our Indian communities, I feel close to God; there is a peace and a harmony in my body, a stillness within me. Perhaps it is the style and rhythm of life, the poverty and simplicity, or the climate, culture and food. I suppose it is a mixture of many things. Maybe it is due to my own poverty and dependence on others when I am here, since I do not understand the language. I have to have complete trust and try to live each event, each moment, in the presence of God and of others, trying also to be a presence of God for others. I want to live each moment as fully as possible for each one of us in L'Arche, to live this gift of love given in a L'Arche community in a world of war where hatred is so rampant. I was moved to tears as I thought of the beauty of this gift: there, under the stars, in the midst of the coconut and banana trees, the ripening cashew nuts and the loud cries of the jackals, close to the wells that give us water, we were able to sing and dance, to work and pray, to forgive each other—Muslims, Hindus and Christians—and together celebrate our common humanity as children of the one eternal Father. It is those who are poor and weak, wounded by rejection, crying out for love and friendship, yearning for a meaning to their lives who were calling us to be there all together.

Not far from there, in the Gulf, guns were spitting out their fire of destruction, sowing seeds of racial and religious hatred that would last for years to come. We all know that no one is going to win this war; the world will be a worse place to live in because of it! And yet, God is present in the midst of all this pain. Like the soil, many hearts are being churned and ploughed in order to receive the gift of God. Perhaps all our countries are going to fall into pits of insecurity that will shake us and call forth in us a true, deep faith.

From Nandi Bazaar I went to Madras, to Asha Niketan–Kottivakkam. Hazel, the community leader, is radiant but tired; she has carried much over these last months. However, there is much life in the community and many friends who give their time, love and support to the community. There was a three-day retreat which was a significant time for me. There were about eighty of us from different churches, a few Hindus, young assistants from four communities, board members, friends and members of Faith and Light. Many people were touched by the presence of our core members at the retreat. "They bind us together in compassion and love," one of the retreatants said. Their very weakness, vulnerability and call for relationship are like magnets that draw us to unity.

I leave India with a feeling of sadness in my heart. I love this country and the people. I love our communities here, so weak and vulnerable, yet carrying within them a deep message of hope and of love. My trip to Pakistan was cancelled; it is not the time to give public talks there because of the war! I feel sad about that too.

I came back to Trosly a week earlier than planned, where I met Françoise and Rick who had just arrived from Jerusalem. Each one is in great pain, with a deep sense of loss. Our community in Bethany has been closed. Let us hold each one in our hearts and prayers. Roula, Siham, Elias and the others have gone back to the institution or to their families; they too are in pain, in a state of shock and withdrawal. On Holy Saturday, Mary, the mother of Jesus, was in a state of loss and grief. She was waiting for the promise of Jesus to be accomplished: waiting, not looking back, not making plans, real or imaginary, for the future, just there, living the present moment in trust and in faith. Let all of us wait in that present moment of trust where we meet God.

We wait also for Père Thomas who has not been well and is resting in the south of France. Let us pray for him quietly and wait for his return.

> Much love to you all,
> Jean

Feast Day of the Heart of Jesus, June 1991
Trosly

Dear Friends,

There is much I have wanted to share with you over these last few months, but I have not had the time nor the energy to do so. Perhaps that was good, for I needed time to live through the grief of my mother's death.*

My mother's passing happened so fast and was so unexpected, in spite of her age (ninety-three). Nothing in the preceding days warned us that she would be leaving. For a few days she complained of an upset stomach and had no desire to eat. On the Thursday before Palm Sunday she had an X-ray which revealed a cancer in the intestines. She was operated on that evening. I was able to visit her around midnight when she came out of the operating room; she was still under the anesthetic. I was with her at the hospital very early the next morning. She opened her eyes and looked at me with the eyes of a young girl in love. She could not speak because she had differ-

---

*My mother, Pauline Vanier (née Archer), came to live in Trosly after my father's death in 1967 and the death of my grandmother, Thérèse de Salaberry Archer, in 1969. Like many assistants who come to us, my mother came thinking she might stay for just six months. In the end, she sold everything back home in Canada and lived at Trosly until her death. She had her own private home in the village, Les Marrioniers (The Chestnuts), and she was a constant, wise presence in the life of the L'Arche communities.

ent tubes in her mouth from the respiratory machine. Quite quickly afterwards, though, she lost all consciousness and on Saturday morning stopped breathing. Everything happened so quickly; that was wonderful for her as she had feared suffering with a long illness, but it was too fast for us, her children and the community.

We brought her body back home to her bedroom, where for two days the community came and prayed. Our final prayer with her was the Eucharist celebrated on the Monday of Holy Week; it was very beautiful, peaceful and prayerful. Her death has left a great emptiness in Trosly. She used to welcome so many people with much affection and showed an interest in everything. She comforted many people, especially assistants. As she could no longer read, she anxiously awaited each visit, but when it was over, she experienced once again the loneliness which often weighed upon her; she was quite often in anguish. But now she has joined my father and Jesus. Her heart that had always thirsted to love and be loved is now fulfilled.

After that final Eucharist, I left for Lourdes to join Marie-Hélène Mathieu and the leaders of Faith and Light for the final preparations for the pilgrimage. The first pilgrims started to arrive on Holy Thursday. In all there were 13,500 pilgrims from the five continents, many from Poland, Hungary, Czechoslovakia, Russia, Lithuania and Romania. We formed a large community of the poor who had come to Lourdes to thank Jesus for starting Faith and Light twenty years ago and for the way he has been guiding it over all these years. There are now about nine hundred communities throughout the world. Many people have found support, a new family and new life from their relationships with the weak.

The theme of this pilgrimage was "Towards Unity," unity between countries, cultures and classes, between people with disabilities and their friends, and between Christians. Faith and Light was born in a Catholic country. Now there are more and more Anglican, Protestant and Orthodox communities. Faith and Light, like L'Arche, has a mission to bring Christians of different traditions closer together. This is done through the cry of the poor and the weak who awaken our hearts to love. Jesus has a tremendous thirst for unity. His last prayer was "Father, may they be one."

One day, at the Grotto, I met some mothers from Moscow and Leningrad. They had tears of joy in their eyes, not only because they had come to France, but because they now had a whole new way of looking at their children. They were discovering the secret of the Gospels and the secret hidden in the heart of their son or daughter: their child is not a disgrace, a misfit or a punishment from God, but a full human being with a gift to be shared with the Christian community and with society in general.

Immediately after the pilgrimage I went to Canada for my mother's burial (next to my father) at the Citadelle in Quebec. The governor general and other officials, as well as many friends, came to the Eucharist celebrated on April 3 in the basilica. Mum was loved by many people. Now we must learn to live without her. I am discovering she is present in a new way, closer to the heart, hidden in the heart of God.

In the following weeks I experienced three important events that strengthened and deepened my vision of L'Arche and gave me a greater sense of thanksgiving for it: a meeting of the Spirituality Commission, a Covenant Retreat and a retreat for young assistants in L'Arche.

It is clear to me that L'Arche will no longer be L'Arche if it does not have a deep spirituality; it will wither and die. In order to live together in the spirit of the Beatitudes with people who are wounded, in order to truly become their friend for the rest of our lives, we need a new force that comes from God, a new love, the Spirit of God. When I preach retreats or accompany people, I realize that assistants cannot imagine committing themselves to community life with those who are weak unless they themselves have had an authentic encounter with God. This encounter takes place at a very deep level of our being, deeper than any psychological instinct or wound of the heart. This personal encounter with God gives new hope and a new vision; it gives the strength to walk through the difficulties and frustrations of life. It frees one from being governed by fear and guilt; it liberates new energies which break the chains of egoism and opens one up to others in love.

This spirituality is quite simple; that is why it is so difficult for us who are such complicated beings! Jesus shows the way when he says, "When you give a dinner, do not invite your friends, nor your family, nor your rich neighbour . . . invite the poor, the blind, the sick and the lame (that is, all those excluded from the temple and from society), and you will be blessed." In the biblical vision, to eat a meal together means to become friends. That is our call in L'Arche: to become a friend of the weak, to slow down in order to listen to them, to live according to their rhythm, to see the light of God in them, to allow them to disturb us. Living in community seems like such a small reality unless we discover within that life a presence of God, hidden and silent, the God of the incarnation, the God of love.

The challenge of L'Arche is to help assistants discover the richness of this spirituality and to give them the means to live it. The Spirituality Commission agreed that the only true way of communicating that spirituality is for each one of us to live it. In order to live it we have to be attached to a source of life, to a church and to spiritual guides. L'Arche is not a church in itself. It is vital that its members belong to a church or a religious body, and that they be helped, guided and sustained by a priest, minister or spiritual guide.

In May, I went to the USSR for the fourth time. We left Moscow deeply moved, having met a number of people who have suffered for many years; they have such a thirst for freedom and for God but they fear the future. The economic and political situation is in chaos. There is little to eat: some bread and cheese, a bit of sausage, potatoes, tomatoes and cucumbers.

One of my greatest concerns today is the contact with the Orthodox Church. I am convinced that one of the sources of salvation and peace in the USSR will be the collaboration between the Orthodox and Catholic Churches; they have much to bring to one another. (In Moscow, Catholics are not very numerous, about twenty thousand people.) However, the Orthodox Church is rather distrustful of the Catholic Church for many historical and current reasons; some mistakes have been made particularly by Catholic movements that have come from the West. Here again, I hope that Faith and Light can bring the message of the weak as a call to unity, to mutual respect and to reconciliation. We must pray hard for unity between these two churches.

I trust that L'Arche and Faith and Light will continue to deepen throughout the world thanks to the prayer of Père Thomas, who prays and offers his life. He is not at Trosly at the present moment, but Jacqueline spent two weeks with him and she tells us how much he remains united to us.

Pray for me that I am faithful to the call of Jesus, that my heart becomes gentle and humble like the heart of Jesus.

Jean

August 1991
Orval

Dear Friends,

My stay in the Trappist monastery is coming to an end. Three full weeks of deep joy: the joy of having quiet time just to pray, to walk, to read and to write, time to drink long moments from the Source of life. The deep joy of offering all to God and of knowing that everything comes from God.

Psalm 91 has been with me in a special way these days. It is a cry of gratitude to God who has protected us and watched over us. God is our refuge, our safety and our stronghold.

I also have had time to plunge into the writings of the prophet Isaiah. His book begins with the lamentation of God:

> Listen, you heavens:
> earth, listen, for Yahweh is speaking,
> I have reared children and brought them up,
> but they rebelled against me.
> The ox knows its owner
> and the donkey its master's crib;
> Israel does not know,
> my people do not understand. (Isa. 1:2–3)

And Jesus wept when he entered Jerusalem and said: "You have not understood the message of peace" (Luke 19:42). Our poor world does not seem to understand. We do not understand the tenderness of God's love. This rejection of God and of the plan of God is due frequently to a lack of knowledge. So often people see God as a judge who punishes or who makes us feel guilty. We do not experience God enough as a God of peace, of tenderness and of forgiveness, "slow to anger and rich in love," a God who leads us to freedom and gives us hearts full of joy.

Our God is a God of love, close to each human being, close to the poor, the weak and the rejected. God yearns to rebuild humanity so that those who are weak, little and impoverished are at the centre and are no longer marginalized, alienated and isolated. God pulls down the powerful and raises up the lowly.

> Human pride will lower its eyes
> human arrogance will be humbled,
> and Yahweh alone will be exalted, on that day.
> That will be a day for Yahweh Sabaoth,

for all who are majestic and haughty,
for all who are proud, to be brought low,
for all the cedars of Lebanon, high and proud,
and for all the oaks of Bashan;
for all the high mountains
and for all the proud hills;
for every lofty tower
and for every towering wall;
for all the ships of Tarshish
and for everything held precious.
Human pride will be humbled,
human arrogance brought low
and Yahweh alone will be exalted, on that day. (Isa. 2:11–17)

We are in a world where human beings seek out their own glory, power and greatness; they build lofty towers and create powerful empires. In so doing, they crush the poor and the weak. But the God of all goodness intervenes in the history of humankind:

The people that walked in darkness
have seen a great light;
on the inhabitants of a country in the shadow of darkness
light has blazed forth . . .
For a child has been born for us
a son has been given to us,
and dominion has been laid on his shoulders,
and this is the name he has been given:
Wonderful Counsellor, Mighty-God,
Eternal-Father, Prince-of-Peace. (Isa. 9:2, 6)

Yes, a child will lead us on the path of peace, communion, forgiveness. These days here have helped me to understand more than ever that the true path for each human being is the path of humility. It is this openness of humility which allows God to act in and through us. Without humility we close up in our own desires, honour and glory. We are no longer servants of unity, reconciliation and peace; servants who allow themselves to be moulded and guided by the power of God, which can only be manifested in and through our weakness, poverty and littleness.

During these days at Orval, I have been offering to Jesus L'Arche, Faith and Light, and Faith and Sharing;* I offer him all of last year and the coming year. I pray that each one of us may become truly humble enough to follow the will of God and not our own. I pray also that we may have the audacity to believe in the Gospel, to become like children, to let God lead us. For that, we need to nourish and deepen our faith.

I am also looking at my priorities for the coming year. I am not old but am starting to grow old! How to remain the founder and yet not cling to the role? How should I be present to the International Councils in order to help forge a common vision, help leaders assume their responsibilities and grow in trust and at the same time not take up too much room?

My first priority remains the same, to live a covenant with Jesus and with the poorest and the weakest (which is not always a person with learning disabilities). And then, through the International Councils, to help L'Arche and Faith and Light to situate themselves clearly and truthfully as ecumenical and inter-religious movements. That is the option we made when we welcomed men and women coming from different religions and different Christian traditions. That means that we are called to create a way of living together where each person can truly grow in the love of God and of his or her brothers and sisters, a way of life that brings each one to

---

* Faith and Sharing is a retreat movement in Canada and the US that started soon after my first retreats at Marylake—a retreat centre and Augustinian monastery north of Toronto—in 1968.

greater inner freedom, so that each one may become more deeply him or herself, in the image of God. Ecumenism means recognizing that the Spirit of God is speaking and acting through our churches. It means helping each community and each person to situate themselves in all truth regarding their faith and to find what they need in order to deepen their spiritual life. It is very clear to me that without a deep spiritual life, without the help of God who is love, L'Arche will not be able to continue. It may be a place where people with learning disabilities can be more integrated into society, but it will not be what it is called to be: a network of communities of love inspired by the Spirit of God where the littlest and the weakest find their place and can exercise their gift.

Each one of us and each one of our communities is called to take this path of love, which is the path towards holiness and wholeness. It means that we must be deeply rooted in the sources of holiness and grace which are our churches and the Word of God, that we must be guided by men and women of God, priests and ministers. Isn't there a danger in our world today of refusing to take any stand or to announce clearly our values and sources of inspiration? We are frightened of being considered intolerant or of being criticized because we hold convictions which may not be acceptable to society as a whole. So, we can prefer to remain in a certain confusion and vagueness. To have convictions does not mean we are going to judge or condemn others. It simply means that we want to serve our brothers and sisters, especially the weakest, in poverty and humility, as Jesus did. It means we want to be open and loving with others and live in communion with them. For that, however, our hearts must be rooted or grounded interiorly in a new force of love. That is why our communities must be clear regarding their spiritual, ecclesial and religious options.

Another priority for me this year and in the years to come is to be more attentive to countries that are poorer and in distress, countries in Eastern Europe and the Arab world, and developing countries. My heart feels drawn to those places where people with disabilities and their families are living in great pain and misery. I pray that each one of us may experience this same grace of attraction to those places where suffering is so great. That does not mean that we should all go there. The Holy Spirit will show each one how he or she is called to live out this concern in a concrete way.

This encourages me to make a very concrete request of you. Our international association, which brings financial aid to communities in poorer countries and which finances our support system, is practically at zero! Fortunately, the Royal Bank of Canada has just awarded me a prize of $100,000 which it will present to me in November. However, that will not be enough to cover all the expenses programmed in the next six months. Do you know people who would be willing to help us? Every little sum is helpful, for small streams become wide rivers! Cheques should be made out to "L'Arche Internationale" and sent to either Joe Egan (at Daybreak) or Claire de Miribel or myself here in Trosly. God has always helped us from the very beginning of L'Arche. I am sure that the Spirit of God will continue to inspire friends to share with us.

Pray that each of our communities may be like a little spring of love irrigating our parched lands.

Much love to you,
Jean

April 1992
Trosly

Dear Friends,

In March I had the privilege of giving a retreat in Czestochowa for people from the Faith and Light communities in Eastern European countries. There were about six hundred people from

Poland, where there are more than a hundred communities, but also people from Moscow, St. Petersburg (formerly Leningrad), Lithuania, Romania, Hungary and Czechoslovakia. I had already given a retreat in Czestochowa in 1983. At that time I said we would not rest until Faith and Light had reached Siberia! Who would have dreamed then of the collapse of Communism?

I marvel at the beauty of these people, their cry for freedom and for God and the power of grace which has brought down the walls of hatred and the oppression of Communism. We must give thanks for the power of grace within the human heart. For a long time the powers of evil seemed to triumph. But God, hidden in the human heart, always emerges. We must continue to pray that the walls of hatred will not rise up in other forms in these countries.

As we were not far from Auschwitz, I went with a group of young people to visit the concentration camps. We walked in silence across the camp grounds, asking God to remove from our hearts the roots of fear, hatred, violence and prejudice which make us hurt and crush other people. We walked silently along the road which formerly led hundreds of thousands of men and women, mainly Jews, completely exhausted and skeleton-like, to the gas chambers and the crematory furnaces. These two camps near Auschwitz are vivid reminders of what human beings can become and what they can do when they cut themselves off from love, when they capitulate to the fear and prejudice in their hearts. In one of these camps, Father Maximilian Kolbe died when he offered to replace a married man who was condemned to the death row. The Nazi regime ended, as the Communist regime did, but at what a cost of lives! We must pray and hope that other forms of oppression will not develop. We must pray that the weak and the powerless will not continue to be crushed. L'Arche and Faith and Light are just one response to these powers of hatred, a response that cries out our trust in the beauty and capacity of love in each person.

I must admit that I am more and more in love with L'Arche and

Faith and Light! I want so much to be faithful to the gift Jesus has given us, the gift of his presence hidden in the hearts of the weak. I have such a desire that the Good News of Jesus, of life shared together in community, be deepened in L'Arche and in Faith and Light. The powers that oppose this Good News are so strong in our world and in our own hearts.

We have noticed that many of our communities have lost a sense of the wider family of L'Arche. Each community is so taken up with its own projects, questions, difficulties and, of course, the question of assistants coming and going. There is a danger of isolation, forgetting the wider family. Isn't this one of the realities of the world around us? With all the insecurity in which people are living, they tend to close up in groups or countries, erecting solid barriers around themselves. They no longer want to allow foreigners in; they do not want to have to deal with those who are "strangers." They don't want to hear about problems elsewhere. But the Holy Spirit is inviting us to put down roots in *one* particular community, in *one* country, and at the same time to open our hearts to others, to other communities and other people in other countries. Our world needs men and women with a universal heart, who recognize our common humanity. It is a gift to have brothers and sisters in diverse cultures, living the same reality, the same family life in different situations. Let us pray for one another that we keep our hearts open and attentive to the needs of people close by as well as far away.

In January I was happy to be in Japan for the official welcoming of Kana-no-ie into the Federation of L'Arche. It is amazing to see how much our communities resemble one another in spite of the differences of language and culture, because those who are weaker are at the heart of the community; they have their place and are held in honour!

A few weeks ago, I visited Père Thomas, who is with his brother, Père Marie-Dominique, in Saint Jodard. It was good to have time to share and pray with him. In spite of his age and the anguish he lives, he remains the same, just as I knew him when I left the Navy some forty-two years ago! He is truly a man of God, a priest of compassion and kindness; he watches over us more than ever through prayer and the offering of his life to the Father. God is truly living in weakness, in his weakness. Jesus was the man of compassion, and he became the man in need of compassion. Jesus came to bring the Good News to the poor, but on the cross he became the poor man. Père Thomas is living fully the mystery he has called so many of us to live since the beginning of L'Arche. For many years he gave us the Eucharist; now he is becoming Eucharist.

This letter will reach you, I hope, for Easter. Jesus shows us the way towards the Kingdom of love. We must know weakness and pain in order to have access to true joy. He invites us, with him, to remain close to people who are weak and powerless in order to enter more deeply into the mystery of compassion and of life.

Love,
Jean

September 1992
Orval

Dear Friends,

Life has been quite full since I last wrote to you. That is nothing new! Ever since L'Arche began my life has been very busy. I give thanks to Jesus for that. I only hope that it is full of Jesus and for the Kingdom, not of me and for me!

In April and May I went to Romania, Russia and Lithuania. I was deeply nourished by these visits. Everything is so poor and yet so rich in vitality. Everything is so full of hope and yet so close to despair. There is much division, even latent hatred, which is becoming very visible now that the iron curtain of Communism has been raised. After years of fear and oppression, it is difficult to find new trust in life, in authority and in each other. It is difficult to exercise authority in a way that gives confidence.

One of my deepest concerns in my visits to these countries is the contact with the Orthodox Church. For a while now it is as if a veil has come down between the Roman Catholic and Orthodox Churches. There is a danger of a rebirth of the same distrust, if not open opposition, that tore Europe apart at the beginning of this millennium. These divisions among Christians rip apart the work of God. How delicate and respectful we must be towards each other. We must always try to see the work and signs of the Spirit in others, rather than to prove our own values or to exercise a certain power over others. The Orthodox Church has suffered a great deal throughout all the years of persecution. The Greek Catholic Church in the former Soviet Union and Romania has particularly suffered. In Moscow a Pentecostal minister said to me, "When we were being persecuted or imprisoned, we were all united. Now that we have freedom, there are divisions. We have to learn how to live in freedom."

In May I spent two weeks in Canada and the United States. I was happy to give a Covenant Retreat in Portland, Oregon. It is good for people who have lived five, ten, fifteen or twenty years in L'Arche to come together to pray and to deepen our common vision. I was also happy with my visits to the L'Arche communities in Winnipeg, Vancouver and Seattle. There is a great deal of life in our North American communities. I was impressed by their vitality and their desire for fidelity; they have much to give to all of us in L'Arche. That does not mean, of course, that there are no struggles. It is not easy to live community in a wealthy society where the values promoted by the mass media seem to replace family and religious values. It is not easy to live the daily life of our communities, sharing our lives with men and women who are weak and powerless, when everything in society urges individualism, power, success, more money.

The Youth Festival in July at Ottrot (France) was a highlight of the year. It was truly blessed by God. The Festival took place in the park of the Foyer de Charité, one of the retreat houses founded by Marthe Robin and Père Finet. It was transformed into a cluster of "villages." There were sixteen hundred people (about four hundred from L'Arche) spread out in villages of forty or fifty people in five tents. In each village about half the people were French, the other half English, Dutch, Russian, Romanian or from elsewhere. One of the greatest joys was the presence of young people from Eastern European countries; buses came from Poland, Moscow, Lithuania and Romania. There were meetings, talks, times of prayer and celebration all together under the main tent. Then there was the life in each village, where we shared meals and community celebrations, and where those who were weaker were really at the centre and could radiate life and transform hearts.

The goal of the festival was to allow more young people to discover the gift of the weak. The men and women from our L'Arche communities fulfilled their vocation, helping us all to enter more deeply into the mystery of God's presence hidden in weakness. Now we are called to follow up this festival by the way we welcome young people into our own communities. We want to help them understand the gift of the weak, how they can become a source of life and a path to God in our daily lives.

My three weeks' stay in the monastery is coming to an end. I was tired when I arrived, as the month of July had been quite heavy. I immediately entered into silence, which is a milieu or atmosphere that gives me new life. I felt like a fish in water and I really drank of the water of silence. I rediscovered time, not as a space too small for everything that has to be fitted in, but time as a touch of eternity, a presence which, like silence, is a milieu, a place for communion and intimacy that always goes beyond time. Now I feel rested and blessed, blessed by Jesus and by the gift of L'Arche and of Faith and Light, blessed by the gift of life and of the universe. I feel ready to go back into daily life, back into the world of struggle and pain, the world of injustice and evil. That does not mean that here in the monastery I have not been in touch with all that is dark and painful within my own heart. I ask forgiveness of each one I might have hurt during this past year. Here in the monastery, I feel as though I am wrapped in the cloak of God's forgiveness, which is a cloak that keeps me peaceful and joyful on the path towards greater union with the Father.

I have been meditating on the life of Jesus, who came to love each person, who is concerned with each person, especially with those who feel lost, excluded, impoverished, abandoned, locked in anguish. He did not come first of all to confirm laws or support institutions (though laws and institutions are important). Jesus came to live in communion with each and every human heart.

Of course, I prayed for L'Arche. Perhaps that is more my role now, to pray. We are at a turning point in our history. L'Arche is no longer a baby, tiny, hidden, insignificant. It is no longer an adolescent which disturbs, advances, is generous and might feel it is better than others. L'Arche is becoming an adult. It is twenty-eight years old! It is quite well known and appreciated by governments and social services; it is well organized with good structures and competent leaders. But the risk now is of falling into the trap of being well organized on the level of finances, administration and pedagogy but forgetting the essential: those who are poor and weak (assistants as well as those with a handicap).

We are all aware of what often happens in the history of communities. There comes a time when rules and the institution become more important than the person, good organization more important than compassion, know-how and competence more important than wisdom, formation more important than transformation, security more important than openness to Providence.

I pray that L'Arche and Faith and Light will always take Jesus as their model: Jesus the man of compassion, the man of goodness, the man who leads us into communion with the Father and with others. I pray that Jesus may help us in the organization of L'Arche so that rules and institution will always be enfolded in compassion. That means that each one of us is called to discover wisdom and truth: truth enlightened by dialogue and tenderness, truth that does not accept unhealthy compromises, which never closes up in déjà vu or illusions, truth that can disturb (as the poor do) and is not frightened of differences, truth that enters with courage into conflicts and always seeks clarity, avoiding all confusion. Let us take Jesus as our model of compassion, Jesus who always puts the person above the law and continually announces the truth.

With the fatigue of July, I realize I have to go a bit more slowly this year: less absence from my community, a bit more rest when I come back from long trips, a few more weekends of silence.

I give thanks to Jesus for last year, for all the graces given and for the people I met. Now I am prepared for the coming year. In the silence of my heart I offer to Jesus all the people and the moments of communion, as well as all that will be painful and difficult. May it all be a source of life.

May each one of us drink abundantly from the Source of life, so that we in turn become sources of life for one another, for others. May we open our hearts to receive the gift of compassion so that we become more and more men and women of compassion. In this broken world of ours, may we trust in the fruitfulness of our small gestures of compassion and reconciliation.

Much love to you,
Jean

December 1992
Trosly

Dear Friends,

I have just come back from the Zone Council meetings in England, where there were thirty-one L'Arche coordinators. I was touched by the unity, the maturity and the vision of the group.

One of the major concerns of all L'Arche coordinators is the commitment of long-term assistants living in our homes. In a community each person is important and has his or her place. However, those who *live in* the house day after day have a vital role; they create a home, give security and weave permanent relationships with the men and women welcomed. The quality of life in each home is essential and is at the heart of community life; it depends a great deal on the assistants living in the homes. Without them, the people with a handicap might have food, lodging and interesting work but they would not have family.

We are discovering more and more the vocation of L'Arche, of assistants who live a covenant in the homes as a vocation of love and of prayer. We believe that people with a mental handicap are a path to God. However, there is sometimes quite a gap between what we are announcing and the reality lived in many of our houses. So often we do not know how to call, nourish and give the right support to assistants. Often they are too busy, too tired or too stressed to be open to the deep presence and gift of people with a handicap. We will take time at the Federation meetings to talk about this. Our greatest desire in L'Arche is to help assistants to put down roots in the life of our homes and to be able to remain there the rest of their lives if this is truly their call. Pray for that.

Each time I come back from a trip I am welcomed so warmly by my people at Le Val Fleuri. It is a big house, perhaps the biggest in all of L'Arche, but we are truly a family. I feel at home there.

Many of us have been here for ten, fifteen or twenty-eight years, like Jean-Pierre Prat. His father started Le Val before L'Arche, in 1960. In March 1965, just seven months after the foundation of L'Arche, M. Prat asked me to take over the responsibility of Le Val. Over the years we have reduced the numbers in the house. Today there are fifteen people with a handicap, six full-time assistants and about ten others who work elsewhere in the community or for the wider family of L'Arche. We are quite a lively community. The size of the house allows us to welcome many people. It is as if the table is elastic! We love celebrations, especially when Patrick, Laurent and Jean Claude jump up and dance.

Just recently, on November 10, we celebrated Gerard's ten years in L'Arche. Gerard invited all his friends for dinner, which was followed by a celebration and prayer of thanksgiving. We spoke about his life before L'Arche, the suffering he had endured, his arrival at Le Val, his steps towards growth, the discovery of his "real mother," his bonds of friendship with Father Roberti and Le Toit in Belgium, L'Arche–Verpillières and Philippe Seux. We read letters from different people who had been welcomed and touched by Gerard over those ten years. Above all, we celebrated Gerard's gifts today, gifts of presence, peace and joy. The next day at Hosanna, our community hall, we celebrated with the others in the community who have lived ten years in L'Arche. Counting the children, about 450 people attended. The evening ended with the final celebration, the Eucharist celebrated by Père Gilbert.

Le Val has been my home for eleven years now. For eight years I was co-responsible and I loved animating the meetings with the house assistants. I can no longer take on that role as I am called to travel rather extensively. However, I do try to take some responsibility in the house. I am happy to have my place at table with Jean-François, René, Didier, Pauline, Luisa, Patrick, Jean-Pierre, Ian, Anne-Marie and each one. We are bonded together in communion. I am happy to have my service of washing the dishes, even if some say I do it badly and give me back plates to be washed a second time! We have the evening prayer in the living room, around a candle that lights up the little statue of Jesus and Mary. Gerard always reminds us to pray for those who have died. Jean-François prays for each one and our communities throughout the world are often present.

Each year, with a few friends and former assistants, all of Le Val goes to a monastery for three days. This November we were welcomed by the Trappist monks in Orval (Belgium). We shared in little groups, had times for mime and times to pray with the monks. I love announcing the Good News of the Gospels to the people in my own house. As we know each other so well, we can touch some delicate questions like our fear of death. I have been bonded to some of the people in Le Val, like Jean-Pierre and Jean Claude, for twenty-eight years now. With others, like Albert, I have a special relationship; every year we go together to visit his parents' graves. Although I am called to travel to announce L'Arche and the Gospels in other places, my life, my joy, my base are here in Le Val. It is the place of my covenant. Olivier and Anne-Marie truly help me as they accept me and all my comings and goings with such kindness and understanding. I sense a deep unity in the team of assistants. I would even say there is a great love and affection among us and that also nourishes me.

Most of my day in Trosly when I am not in Le Val is spent accompanying assistants. To accompany people is to listen to the way the Spirit is working in their heart, to hear about their struggle for truth and the different passages they are making, to be a witness to deep transformations. To accompany someone is also a moment of communion. It is a privilege to accompany people, and humbling also to sense their trust as we enter a little into the secret of their heart. As I accompany people I am deeply affirmed in L'Arche. I see that in spite of difficulties the Holy Spirit is at work unifying and transforming hearts, making the impossible possible.

Soon it will be Christmas and I rejoice. Christmas is a time of celebration for all those who are yearning for a Saviour, for all the poor, for L'Arche and for Faith and Light. The angel announced to the shepherds, men who were poor and rugged, "I bring you good news of great joy, for unto you is born a Saviour. You will find him in a manger, a baby." The shepherds must have been surprised and amazed when they heard that the Saviour was a poor one, a little one! These men must have run towards the cave singing and shouting and jumping for joy. Then they saw him, a little child in the arms of his mother. I can imagine their reaction. The mother is silent, smiling as she looks on. Jesus chose to reveal himself first of all to the poor, in a heart-to-heart relationship with them.

Christmas will be a big feast day for us, an important time for welcoming friends and visitors, a time of joy, of prayer and of meaningful celebrations. To be with Gerard and each one during this Christmastime is truly meaningful. I feel just as privileged as those shepherds that first Christmas night.

Let us pray for each other this Christmas, that we may learn to be more humbly present with those who are weak, to become their friend, to discover in them and with them the gift of communion in the Holy Spirit through our mutual poverty and trust.

Love and Happy Christmas to each one!

Jean

April 1993
Trosly

Dear Friends,

Père Thomas died on February 4. It is only now, two months later, that I am beginning to get over the pain and the shock. Jesus led me to Père Thomas forty-three years ago when I left the Navy, and Père Thomas became my spiritual father. He also formed my mind. He guided me for many years. He is at the source of my spiritual and intellectual liberty. I began L'Arche because he called me to Trosly when he was chaplain of Le Val Fleuri. He inspired and encouraged me to do "something" for people with learning difficulties. Over these twenty-nine years of L'Arche, while I have been called to travel and to give support to new communities and animate retreats, he has always been here in Trosly, at the heart of L'Arche, praying, carrying all in the Eucharist, giving strength and support to each one in the community and to many who came to visit.

Even though Père Thomas had been absent from the community for the last two years, living close to his brother, Père Marie-Dominique, his death touched me deeply. Perhaps I had the childish hope that he would live forever! But the physical and spiritual pain I have felt with his death is important; it is calling me to greater maturity and responsibility, as well as to deeper humility and docility to the Holy Spirit. Père Thomas always encouraged me in all circumstances to ask Jesus to show me what to do. How often I forget! I try to do things myself, relying only on my own intuition, which may come from my own brokenness or need to succeed. But I am sure Père Thomas will continue to inspire me to ask Jesus that all I am and that all I do may be according to the will of the Father.

I have travelled a great deal since Christmas, mainly to give retreats for L'Arche or for Faith and Light. In January, I was in New Zealand, in March in Haiti, the Ukraine and Poland. Each time it was such a joy to speak of Jesus, of his vision for the world and for humanity, and of the new order he came to establish where the rejected and the powerless are at the centre. We are so used to, even conditioned by, a hierarchy where the powerful and the comfortable are on top of the social ladder and the powerless at the bottom, often crushed or perhaps looked upon as inferior. Our hearts and minds need a real conversion in order to discover the new order of Jesus and to live it. I am quite conscious of the struggle in me between my faith in Jesus and in those who are weak, and the need I have to prove myself. I know how difficult it is to accept the last place and to become like a little child.

I was overwhelmed by all the suffering, the poverty, the divisions and the struggles at all levels in Haiti! The country is in an extreme state of pain. Yet I was touched by the serenity, the unity and the love which radiate from our two L'Arche communities there. In a mysterious way our people keep us anchored in reality and give us inner peace in the midst of the chaos.

I was invited to the Ukraine with Odile (zone coordinator) and Patrick Mathias (our psychiatrist in Trosly) for talks with professionals and for a retreat. Zenia, a Ukrainian who lived for ten years in Daybreak, arranged everything. She has been living in Lviv for the last two years and helped create two Faith and Light communities. The Ukraine is poor in many ways, as the Communist domination since 1917 has left its mark. There were six hundred people at the retreat, a sign of their thirst for the living Word of the Gospels and for the new order given by Jesus. People at the retreat were from different churches: Greek Catholic, Latin, Independent Orthodox, Orthodox attached to Moscow, Baptist and Pentecostal. It was beautiful to sense the unity among us. It was the first ecumenical event of this kind in western Ukraine.

From the Ukraine I went to Krakow (Poland) for a meeting of Faith and Light with representatives from Germany and many Eastern European countries. Then I gave a retreat for young people at the Dominican parish. I was happy to have time also with the L'Arche community in Sledziejowice, which is growing and deepening.

I have recently come back from Slovenia (formerly part of Yugoslavia), which has a population of two million. The people of Slovenia are full of life; for the first time in years they are tasting freedom. I sense a great deal of enthusiasm but economic difficulties are also great. I was touched by my visit to two institutions for people with mental handicaps. I was also moved by my visit to a camp of refugees from Bosnia.* When I asked them if they had hope, they said they had none, not even of returning home as their whole village had been burned down. I was struck by the gap between the enthusiasm of those who are enthused with their new freedom and the desire to lead their country towards economic success, and the cry of many broken people—the poor, the refugees, handicapped people—who are seen as a heavy weight and whose cry is difficult to hear. Yes, I was deeply moved by my visit to Slovenia. Pray for the seeds of L'Arche and for the twenty-four Faith and Light communities there.

I wish you a happy, holy feast of the Resurrection! How important it is that we become men and women of the resurrection. The mystery is that Jesus leaves so much pain and confusion in our world and even in our own hearts and our communities. We always want the pain and confusion to disappear. But then Jesus rises up within us and gives us the strength to live it and sometimes even to transform it.

Peace,
Jean

---

*The Bosnian War had started the previous March and lasted until November 1995, when NATO's military forces intervened. The collapse of Communism throughout Eastern Europe created great economic, political and social instability. As the Communist regime in Yugoslavia started to crumble, people began to hold on to old "certainties": suspicions, grudges and hatred for other ethnic groups and religions. It was a very complex conflict: Serb, Croat and Bosnian factions changed sides and allegiances several times. However, by the end of the war, it was clear that Bosnians had suffered widespread killings, mass rapes, ethnic cleansing and torture.

July 1993
Trosly

Dear Friends,

I have just lived three important events: the celebration of the family of L'Arche in Quebec, the twenty-fifth anniversary of Faith and Sharing in Guelph, Ontario, and a retreat for the leaders of Faith and Light in North America. God was manifestly present in these three events.

In L'Arche, in Faith and Light and in Faith and Sharing there is great vulnerability, even fragility. The communities are not strong or powerful. They are founded in weakness and in pain. They want to be Good News for the poor and the suffering. However weak and vulnerable these communities may be, God is truly present in them, not in any great power but in the joy and unity springing from their weakness and childlike, trusting hearts. Clearly, Jesus has brought these three movements into being as a sign in our world today that God is present in weakness and that we are all called to grow in love. We can rejoice and be filled with hope; humanity is not condemned to violence, war, competition and death, but is called to love and to trust.

Perhaps what struck me most was how present Père Thomas was in these three events. He died in such a humble, hidden way last February, but he continues to be deeply present. He led me to the Good News of Jesus, and the Gospels are truly Good News for us all. We are loved. God is present to us. God is Emmanuel, God-*with*-us just as we are, in all our vulnerability.

For me the celebration of the family of L'Arche was like a song of unity. We came from over a hundred communities in many countries, cultures, languages and religions but we were one, united around the weak and the poor. While we are grounded in different religious traditions we believe in the one God of love who is hidden in weakness. Yes, it was a wonderful song of unity.

The twenty-fifth anniversary of Faith and Sharing was very moving. Many communities have sprung up in North America since the first retreat I gave at Marylake in 1968, each one called to announce the Good News of Jesus to the weak and the poor, through weekend or five-day retreats.

Then there was a five-day retreat with Faith and Light leaders in Aylmer, Quebec, near Ottawa. So many parents who have lived through pain, so many people with mental handicaps who have known rejection and the feeling of being a disappointment, and so many friends seeking commitment are united together in little communities of friendship and support. Faith and Light is very alive, growing and deepening. The meeting was like a song of joy. It was like a fulfillment of the prophesy of Isaiah: "I will change the cry of pain and of grief into a cry of joy." Pain transfigured into joy. The stone rejected by the builders has become the cornerstone. Parents are discovering the meaning of the lives of their sons and daughters with a handicap. They are no longer misfits, but people with a vocation at the heart of the Church.

I give thanks to Jesus for all that has been given. I feel humbled and blessed. I feel weak. I feel chosen. Sometimes I feel tired, sometimes full of energy. I feel deeply confirmed in my faith and in my hope. In August, I will be in a Trappist monastery where I will rest and offer myself to God, just as I am, and I will continue to pray, "May your Kingdom come on earth as it is in heaven." However, there is still much work to be done. We must be wise. We must be faithful. We need strength to enter into the struggle against many forces of evil in us and around us. One thing is sure: our God is a God of love who calls us to live and to work for the Kingdom.

Love to you,
Jean

September 1993
Trosly

Dear Friends,

The month I spent at the Trappist monastery in Belgium was very restful. Last year was quite heavy, with Père Thomas's death and the meeting of all the L'Arche communities in Quebec. It was also a year full of hope and of life surging forth in many places. I needed the rest with a more regular rhythm of life and prayer with Jesus. The death of Père Thomas implies a greater responsibility for all of us. Jesus said to his disciples, "It is good that I leave." Jesus had to leave so that each one of the disciples could receive the Holy Spirit and become more responsible in the Holy Spirit. So too each one of us must receive a new gift of the Holy Spirit in order to become more responsible for L'Arche, especially for its spiritual life. L'Arche makes sense only if each one of us is united to God and "seeks to be guided by God and by their weakest members." These words come from our new charter.

What touches me most in the life of Jesus (this was the essence of my time of prayer in August) is his humility, his littleness, his gentleness, his openness, his total communion with the Father. When I see the way he washed the disciples' feet the night before he died, I am moved. He not only wanted to give them words of great tenderness but wanted to touch each of them with tenderness. It was his last good-bye, the last time he would touch them. I began to understand the meaning of this gesture when I was called to bathe Eric, Lucien and Loïc each morning at La Forestière, to touch the body of the weak and the poor with respect and compassion.

God is hidden in all this universe of ours. God is present, so humbly, even though we do not always see him. Creation, however, is bursting with life, light and goodness; and God unifies all things. God is hidden within L'Arche. God is hidden in the heart of each one of us, especially in the weakest and most powerless. The tragedy is that we do not recognize this presence of God and so we struggle to affirm our own selves, to prove that we are right and that others are wrong. Barriers of hatred rise up, as in Bosnia. But God is continually present, in a humble way. And Jesus is the icon of this invisible God, a reflection of God's goodness and humility. Jesus is the humble servant who comes to give like a beggar. I could summarize my month of August with these few words: surrender, humility, risk to love, look at Jesus, advance and trust.

On September 1, I left for Bangladesh, formerly called East Pakistan; it was my first trip there. I had met Bishop Theotonius Gomes from Dinajpur during the Synod on the Laity in Rome in 1987. Since then, we had tried to find a date when I could give retreats in his country. It is a poor country with 110 million people, 90 percent Muslim, 0.3 percent Christian. Dhaka, the capital, resembles Calcutta with all its life, poverty, beggars and beauty. Christians are a small minority and so live necessarily behind walls of protection. I gave an "open" retreat, meaning that anyone who wanted could come to the talks in the cathedral. The retreat was translated into Bengali. Then I gave a "closed" retreat in the seminary, mainly for priests, religious and a few lay people.

We had an important meeting for about eighty people committed in some way to people with a mental handicap. I spoke to them about Faith and Light. Dominic Rosario, the father of a sixteen-year-old-boy with a severe handicap, gave his personal testimony. He spoke about the shock he and his wife experienced when their son became severely handicapped after a bout of high fever and convulsions. Dominic had a low salary and told us that he had to spend most of it on medication. Sometimes he did not have enough left for rice! He told us that he prayed that God would heal his son, and that God had heard his prayer and answered it in an unexpected way: "God gave me a deep peace and a real joy in having a son like Vincent." As Paul Claudel wrote, Jesus did not come to eliminate suffering or to explain it; he came to dwell in it.

For Dominic, God did not eliminate the pain of having a son with a severe handicap, but God gave him new strength to welcome and accept him with joy. Dominic was happy to learn about Faith and Light. I asked him to help start Faith and Light in Bangladesh. He and his wife are going to do everything they can to encourage other families to join them.

From Dhaka, I went to Calcutta for a two-day retreat with our communities of L'Arche in India. I was happy to have time with Françoise and Leo Jalais, who became the community leaders of Asha Niketan–Calcutta when Marc and Geneviève Larouche left for L'Arche in Quebec. Mani, recently named the new regional coordinator, came up from Kerala. It is the first time we have had a coordinator of our Asha Niketans who is Indian. I am amazed at her perspicacity, her clarity and her vision for L'Arche in India. What a joy to listen, to sense all the life in our Asha Niketans. Yes, our communities are truly listening to the cry of the poor.

The retreat was held in the workshop of Asha Niketan–Calcutta. There were about a hundred people from the communities, plus friends, both Hindus and Christians. Leo felt it was important to invite people into the community, to live this time of prayer within the community. Asha Niketan–Calcutta is in an area that is quite poor and difficult, an area which some people find inaccessible. Leo wants to show that it is quite easy to reach and that it is an oasis of peace and prayer in the midst of that wounded city. Mother Teresa gave us the land on which we built a house and workshop, next door to a house where her sisters welcome women from prisons. I was impressed by the way people listened at the retreat; they truly nourished my heart.

I saw Mother Teresa twice. In spite of her hospitalization in August, she looked radiant, full of peace and joy and even good health. I dare say she looked younger than ever! She spoke about the community they will open in October in China. What a woman! What an amazing sign of God and of the force of an irresistible faith in Jesus! She announced with such joy, "Now we are in 105 countries!" I was deeply impressed by her sisters in Dhaka as well as in Calcutta.

Right now I am at the meeting of the Spirituality Commission of L'Arche, in Trosly. It is good to share this gift of God we are called to live in our communities: God chooses the "most unlikely" people, often the rejected, in order to lead us to light.

Love,
Jean

P.S. Thanks to so many of you for your birthday greetings. It is good to be sixty-five! My first year of retirement is quite full! I rejoice in the communion that binds us together.

December 1993
Trosly

Dear Friends,

These last three days I have been in Kigali (Rwanda), sadly discovering the world of war and fear in this country, but also the world of the poor with all their beauty and simplicity. Rwanda is a beautiful country with a population of seven million people, surrounded by Uganda, Burundi, Tanzania and Zaire. It is a country of forests, volcanoes, mountains, plains and lakes, a country rich in vegetation: fruits (huge avocadoes, delicious bananas), tea, coffee, rice, potatoes. But it is a country at war!

Yesterday, with the Faith and Light leaders, I went to Goma (Zaire), a three-hour drive through the mountains. Every ten kilometres, there were checkpoints with soldiers carrying machine guns. It is something to see all these young men armed and ready to shoot. The war between ethnic groups, a painful war that began with the revolution in 1959, broke out with greater fury in October 1990, when those who were ousted from power in 1959 attacked from the north, from Uganda. Horrible massacres, terrifying cruelties took place, as in Bosnia, as in any war. Then there were the counterattacks: more massacres, more acts of violence, the spiral of hatred and fear. The consequences are that hundreds of thousands of people are now in camps of displaced persons. I visited one of the camps ten kilometres from Kigali (there are eighteen camps in Rwanda). For the last three years, thirty thousand people have been living in tents made of branches and leaves perched on the hillside. Every two weeks, the Red Cross provides two kilos of beans and one kilo of maize per person. I visited the temporary "hospital" for the dying and for women about to give birth: death and new life side by side. At one moment I met with more than a thousand children gathered together, innocent children who do not know what is happening, children who sing, laugh and manifest their joy; they play with bits and pieces or with nothing at all, since "toys" are totally unavailable; these children still believe in love. I was deeply touched by these children, many born in the camp. It's the only way of life they know. They called me the visiting "tall white man"; they knew I would go back to my country, a place of security. But I could at least look into their eyes, smile, visit the tents, shake a few hands and say in a very poor way, "I love you." But where can these people find any hope? And where do we find hope?

Soon it will be Christmas, the celebration of the weakness and vulnerability of God who becomes a tiny baby, born in poverty among the poor and who is the hope of the poor. He could have been born in one of these camps for displaced people. He himself was a refugee in Egypt. He is born today in these camps. He was born poor and vulnerable in order to invite us to live in communion and in love. Weakness and littleness can awaken hearts and draw people to compassion, or else they can disturb and frighten people who turn away and who continue with their own projects or in their own depression, anger and flight from reality. Poverty and weakness are stumbling blocks. They oblige us to choose. As our new charter says, "L'Arche is not a solution to problems but rather a sign of the value and importance of each person." Each person has a heart; each was created by God and is called to become a hidden temple of God who is love.

As you know, many African countries are living in great suffering and hardship. For many different reasons richer countries seem to be abandoning them, no longer feeling called to help them. It is truly a privilege for L'Arche and for Faith and Light to give priority to these African countries, to continue to give them our support and love; they have much to bring to our world. God is truly present in the heart of these people; they are a people of faith, in and through all their poverty, suffering and brokenness.

I would like to send each one of you my love in Jesus. It is good to be in communion one with another. As our hearts are united throughout the world, they weave a cloak of love around this earth where there is so much pain, division and inequality. Distance disappears as the mystery of communion unites us. But it is not always easy to live that union, that communion. Each one of us is so frightened and sensitive. Peace implies a constant effort to forgive, to reach out to the one who is different, to the enemy who disturbs us. Jesus, the Prince of Peace, came on this earth to give us a new energy of love in order to make us channels of peace.

Much love to you. During this new year may we become more aware of God's presence in places of suffering, in our own pain, teaching us to be gentle, kind and compassionate.

Jean

June 1994
Trosly

Dear Friends,

The events in Rwanda have been overwhelming. I have been touched particularly by the situation there for, as you know from my last letter, I was there last December. The terrible explosion of violence is more a political affair than a question of ethnic war: government leaders, particularly the military, provoking conflict between ethnic groups in order to maintain power. Amongst those who have been massacred are some Little Sisters of Jesus, a Jesuit with whom I shared a meal last December and the national chaplain of Faith and Light. We have had no news of our Faith and Light communities or of Antoinette who coordinates them. The Rwandan people are a beautiful people, like all the peoples in the African countries, but at the same time they are fragile. We know how easily we can all be manipulated, how quickly our violence comes out. I am more and more convinced that one of the most important things we have to learn in our world today is the resolution of conflict. More and more people are frustrated, discontented and no longer see any meaning to their lives. Conflict is bursting out everywhere. Fortunately there are people like Mandela and de Klerk who are showing us that the path of forgiveness and reconciliation is possible; hatred can be overcome by love. And let us pray that the peace process between the PLO and Israel will continue.

To work towards peace and the resolution of conflict is always a difficult task. The grace of God inspires and enlightens us, but we must also make efforts day after day to go beyond our own personal fears and sensitivities. I pray and hope that the communities of L'Arche and Faith and Light can become more and more places where we learn how to resolve conflict, not by force and domination but through dialogue, where each one feels understood. If our communities work in this way, they will be a source of unity for those around them, a source of peace between races and between churches, and a sign of peace and unity for our world. Let us continue to pray for Bosnia and Rwanda, and may our prayers be supported by our daily efforts to dialogue and be in contact with those with whom we have difficulty or who are frightened of us.

As usual around this time of the year, I have been in the Eastern European countries: in Moscow, Georgia, Romania and soon Slovakia. It is a joy to see the birth and deepening of Faith and Light communities in those countries. There are now 160 in Poland, 28 in Romania, 4 in Moscow and 1 beginning in Georgia. It is good to see how the cry of the poor and the weak is being heard. But that is being tarnished by all the difficulties in Eastern Europe: the mafia becoming more and more powerful in Moscow, the misery in Georgia, intercultural conflicts in Romania. And the danger for us all in richer, more comfortable countries is to be closed in on our own comfort, to ignore or not feel concerned about what is happening in other countries, to refuse to look at the poverty and the needs of the weak in our own countries.

My role in L'Arche is evolving. I have great confidence in Jo Lenon and in Émile, Alain and Robert, the international team. Little by little I feel I can leave that team, though still remaining present in the International Council. My role is more and more to announce the Good News of Jesus, in a world where there is so much bad news. Love and community are possible; the weak and the poor can find their place as a source of life; we are not condemned only to war. But I can announce this good news of love and of community life only because our L'Arche communities and Faith and Light are living it. That is what is most important. I am simply an intermediary called to announce again and again that the Gospel is not a utopia but a reality that is possible if we allow the Spirit of God to penetrate our lives.

Our path is a path of humility and littleness, a path of trust and faith. To believe that the weak and the powerless can be a source of life. To trust also that our communities in all their fragility can be a source of life, if we accept and turn to God in order to find strength. Paul, in his letter to the Corinthians, tells how he begged Jesus to free him from certain personal difficulties that he called "a thorn in the flesh." Jesus answered him, "My grace is enough. My strength is manifested in your weakness" (2 Cor. 12:9). That is where our hope lies: the strength of God is revealed in and through our weakness. I pray with each one of you for our poor world that seems to have lost its sense of direction. It does not know where it is going; each one is on the defensive. But God is there, hidden, calling us to love in the little gestures of our daily lives. Yes, it is a path of trust in his strength made manifest in our weakness.

Jean

August 1994
Orval

Dear Friends,

My four weeks in the Trappist monastery are coming to an end and I feel both wounded and blessed. (God alone can link the two together, at the same time. Is that not the meaning of each one of the Beatitudes?) Wounded because I receive news of Bosnia, Rwanda and Haiti, and I know the situation in Russia and certain countries of the former Soviet Union where there is still much suffering and where there could be an explosion of violence at any moment. Blessed because I am resting, and this rest is prayer and prayer is rest. I am deeply nourished by the silence, the liturgy, the peace and the welcome that I find here. My long walks in the forest are also a nourishment. At the same time, I know that my place is not here in the monastery but at L'Arche. In a few days I will be back into my daily life of sharing the meals at Le Val, meeting and accompanying people, and travelling to announce our spirituality. In the beginning of September I will be in Lebanon and Syria.

This year we are celebrating the thirtieth anniversary of L'Arche. My time here has been a time of confirmation: God loves and protects L'Arche because it is a privileged place of welcome for people who are weak, who have been abandoned and marginalized. God is so gentle, welcoming and loving to those who are rejected by society and to those who open their hearts to them. In the silence of prayer, I try to go deeper into the ultimate meaning of our communities of L'Arche and Faith and Light. World events confirm us in our vocation; people are crying out for places of welcome, forgiveness and prayer, for communities where we let the weaker members evangelize and transform us.

At the same time, after these thirty years of L'Arche, I want to ask forgiveness of all my brothers and sisters, especially the weakest, for my lack of compassion, attention and audacity in love, for all that has been too much my own way and not God's way. I realize that my heart has to be purified. I am working on a book that will be published in November in Paris, where I speak about the walls around our hearts which prevent communion.* As I write it, I realize all the walls around my own heart, my fear of living communion, of being vulnerable and open to others and of taking the downward path of humility. How difficult it is to bring down these walls which are our defence mechanism, our judgments and prejudices. These walls hide our fears and vulnerability and prevent us from welcoming and rejoicing in the gift of others and from letting the life of God flow freely in and through us. It is not easy to become a true follower of Jesus, poor, gentle and humble.

World events, particularly in Haiti, Bosnia and Rwanda, make me feel confused: our societies continue to live superficial values

*This book was published in English as *My Journey Home.*

as if nothing was happening, as if it were too difficult, even impossible, to look at the truth of our world.

Each one of us must continue to trust that we can do something to stop the indifference, fear and evil. Wherever we are, we can pray and keep our hearts open and loving; we can struggle against lies and hatred in us and around us. We can be close to those around us who are in pain; we can work each day to create communities that are warm and open, founded on the love of God. It would be awful if the terrible suffering of our world paralyzed and blinded us in regard to the pain of those who are close by.

There are also many many gestures of love and support given in Rwanda, people who have given their lives to save others. The heart of God rejoices in all the gestures of love, of sharing and of sacrifice in the midst of all the suffering. Each one of us is called to believe that our small acts of love and hope can help our brothers and sisters in Rwanda, Bosnia and Haiti, that each gesture has its weight in the balance of love and hate in our world. Wherever we are, we can enter more fully into the struggle and the offering of love.

September 12

I have just come back from Lebanon. This was my fifth visit but the first time I see Beirut at peace. What a relief not to be constantly threatened by soldiers with their machine guns. The country has come back to life! Many buildings remain shattered by the bombs and gunfire, but some are being rebuilt. I realize also how difficult it is to live in peace. People seem to be throwing themselves into seeking more money and more comfort. During the war, more young people were committed to Faith and Light; they had time, there was no work. Now many of them have two full-time jobs in order to earn more money. It is sad to think that only in times of danger and catastrophes is there a solidarity among people and a search for a spiritual life.

From Beirut we went by car to Syria and spent two days with the L'Arche community coming to birth in Damascus. They have bought and fixed up an old house which is not far from the home of Ananias which we read about in the Acts of the Apostles (ch. 9). It was in Damascus that Paul met Jesus and was baptized. I had the privilege of giving two talks to an audience of Christians and Muslims. It seems that some Muslim educators and parents want to invite me back to share about the vision of growth we have in L'Arche. Rima has done much to create links with many people.

I count on your prayers. Let us pray for one another, that we let the Holy Spirit purify our hearts and make us true followers of Jesus, poor, humble and gentle.

Jean Vanier

December 1994
Trosly

Dear Friends,

I am giving a retreat at the Foyer de Charité, a retreat house in Brittany (France). It is such a joy and a privilege for me to announce the message of Jesus, especially around Christmastime. Christmas is truly the feast of L'Arche, the celebration of our vulnerability which calls forth or awakens compassion, the celebration of love and communion, a celebration especially of the poor. This year I was struck more by the painful aspects of Christmas: the refusal to accept Mary and Joseph at the inn, the cold and the hunger in the cave, and especially the terrible massacre of innocent children by Herod and his soldiers. The celebration of Christmas is intimately linked to pain and suffering.

There are 230 people here on retreat. I don't know if it is because my retreats attract people in difficulty or if it is because our world produces more and more pain and brokenness, but I am touched by the number of people here living impossible situations: separation, divorce, death of a child, psychological pain, delinquency, young people wounded by conflicts with or between their parents, etc. How difficult it is for young people to make choices, life choices, in a world that is evolving so quickly. The danger for them is to become involved in sects which give security but prevent inner freedom. There are few reference points in our society other than money, success, individualism. And people can be so easily seduced by any number of new technological discoveries or forms of spirituality that have no link or commitment to the poor or to peace.

The Gospel is the light that shows me the way and gives me life. My heart needs to meet the person of Jesus, for he *is* the Good News! Through this personal meeting with Jesus I know in the depth of my heart that I am loved, protected, in security—that I am called and sent by him and with him to live and to announce the good news of love. As I grow older, I am becoming more aware of my own limits, fears and barriers, all that is wounded in me. But I also realize that I am growing in trust, the trust that Jesus truly loves me and calls me just as I am; that he lives and works in and through me. The words of Jesus to Paul have become more meaningful to me: "My grace is sufficient to you. My strength is manifested in your weakness." That is my hope. In each one of our hearts there is a cry of pain and of confusion. But Jesus is there too, in each one, waiting patiently for us to open our hearts to his presence.

The suffering and pain that exist in the world around us also exist within Christian communities, within our own communities of L'Arche and Faith and Light. Our communities are not strong. Assistants carry their questions and fragilities. It is essential to help each one live in communion with Jesus, in order to live in communion with others. If we do not have the experience of this love of God in the secret of our hearts—an experience that strengthens, liberates, affirms and is the source of our unsettled searching—we risk being seduced by an "elsewhere" and falling into confusion. This inner experience of faith permits us to remain faithful to the covenant with Jesus in weak people. The secret of L'Arche is that the weak person is an anchor that keeps us grounded. But we also need the experience of the presence of God which shows us the meaning of our lives. In a world that is becoming more and more fragmented and confused, the Gospel is a light, a reference point, a promise—a good news for the poor, for those who are visibly poor as well as for those who recognize their own inner poverty.

There can be no other source of life for L'Arche and Faith and Light than this Good News that Jesus came to announce to the poor. We need to be constantly reminded of this, because we forget it when we are pressed and stressed by things to be done or when we are frightened to announce it because others may not understand. Without the strength of the Holy Spirit, without the Good News of Jesus, our community life is impossible. We get tired and are no longer faithful.

I am convinced that we are entering into a new phase of the history of our planet. On one hand are amazing technological discoveries and experiments in genetics; on the other hand our societies produce such fatigue, stress, fragility, depression, violence and a sense of isolation. Some respond by entering into sects and strong fanatical or nationalist movements that want to put order into the world through force or fear. Yet also we see the birth of new communities, open, loving, built on the Gospel message, close to the poor, allowing themselves to be evangelized by them. They are a sign of hope. I pray that our communities may be signs of hope.

I have stayed in my own community quite a lot since I wrote to you in September. I am happy to be here, happy to accompany people, happy with all that Jesus gives us. My heart is filled with hope because God is Emmanuel, God-with-us, God hidden in the mud of the pain and littleness of each day. God answers the cry of our hearts: "Come, Lord Jesus, come. Show us your face, for your face is gentle and loving!"

May this new year be a source of life and hope for us all!

Jean

June 1995
Trosly

Dear Friends,

My heart is full even if my body is a bit weary. I have just returned from a sixteen-day visit to North America. My heart is full of thanksgiving for all that I saw and touched of L'Arche and of Faith and Light. My days too were full of meetings of all sorts.

The peak moment was my visit to Daybreak, which was celebrating its twenty-fifth anniversary and thus the twenty-fifth anniversary of L'Arche in North America. I was welcomed by all (or nearly all) of the community. We shared and laughed about the "good old days," memories of the beginnings of Daybreak filled with joy. The first people Ann and Steve welcomed talked about their memories and their journeys. What simplicity and what beauty in such gatherings! In the evening, I gave a talk at Convocation Hall in the heart of Toronto. Many, many old friends were there as well as "ambassadors" from all our North American communities. We are all truly bonded in love. Jesus has brought us together into one family, a family centred in faith in the weakest and the littlest, where each one is honoured. A family of hope where we do not have to be perfect or to excel, where we still carry a lot of pain and anguish, but where we are all on a journey of acceptance, of faith and of love.

Saturday morning was the peak of the peak moment! The Daybreak Gala, a play, a musical, in a theatre not far from Richmond Hill, was a time of immense celebration and thanksgiving. The play was written and directed by Robert Morgan and his friend Eddie, and acted out by members of the community; it tells the story, the vision and the message of Daybreak. It is filled with song, dance, times of laughter, times of witnessing and times of deep emotion. All of us in L'Arche who were in the audience cried and sang and laughed and gave thanks for the gift God has given to us. Yes, we have been given a gift which remains hidden to many people of our world who see the weak only as a cause of anguish and of pain and thus reject them. We have been put on the road to healing by them; they are leading us into the acceptance of our own weaknesses. We are allowed to be ourselves. So we can celebrate and give thanks. In the heart of God they are giving meaning to our lives.

Through it all was a sense that L'Arche and Faith and Light and the message we live together is a hope for many. Our world is such a broken world; hope is so quickly undermined. There are, of course, winners filled with their projects and their success; but there are so many more losers, who fail, who cannot make it, who have no money, no work, no hope, no vision for the future. L'Arche and Faith and Light are, of course, not the only answers in this broken world of ours. There are many wonderful people searching and living hope, so many are struggling to form new types of community where people can be themselves, welcome others and be bonded together in Jesus's love. There are also all the shadow areas of our L'Arche and Faith and Light communities; a lot of the brokenness of our world is found in our own communities. Some are in pain and in crisis.

I have written this letter just before Pentecost. May the Holy Spirit change our hearts of stone—petrified and paralyzed by fear—to hearts of flesh, open and welcoming to others.

Love,
Jean Vanier

September 19, 1995
L'Arche
Bangalore

Dear Friends,

I am in Bangalore celebrating with all our brothers and sisters of L'Arche in India the twenty-fifth anniversary of the founding of the first community in Bangalore. Asha Niketan–Bangalore was founded in 1970 when Gabrielle Einsle and Ronald Pickersgill welcomed Joseph and Gurunathan. I was with them for that first month. We worked in the garden and got to know each other. We laughed and fought, prayed and celebrated together. Today there are over 120 of us here from Asha Niketan in Bangalore, Calcutta, Madras and Nandi Bazaar. Some of the older people could not come as the journey would be too tiring. I am touched to be with so many whom I have known for a long time: Srinivasan who came to Bangalore in 1970, Kashi and Modhu who were the first to arrive in Calcutta in 1973, Ramesh and Jayakumar who came to Madras in 1974, and Ramesh and Mitran, the first to arrive in Nandi in 1977. We are meeting all together in the National Biblical, Catechetical and Liturgical Centre in Bangalore. As we gather together I realize how much we are a simple and poor people, eating, praying and celebrating in English, Malayalam, Bengali, Tamil and Kannada. Language problems! We are communicating above all by the heart, eyes, face and hands. I am deeply moved by this anniversary and by the celebrations. We are truly one family.

We met with the board chairpeople. I shared with them what I consider the five gifts of these twenty-five years:

1) The beauty, stability, holiness and maturity of our people with handicaps. It is so visible here.

2) All four communities have lived big crises and have gone through them. The crises and conflicts have been resolved by the gentle hand of God, who has saved us many times, and we have learned through our mistakes.

3) The increasing number of committed, long-term assistants and board members, wonderful people who have grown in spiritual and human maturity and who carry the vision of L'Arche in India today.

4 Our communities are now truly Indian. The local language is spoken and the local culture is part of the communities.

5) We have grown together as Hindus and Christians. We have learned to live, to celebrate, to pray and to have retreats together. We have become truly inter-religious communities.

I won't go into the points where our Asha Niketans need to grow, but as you can well imagine, they are there. There is still work to be done! But this was a time to celebrate the sacred history of our Indian communities and to give thanks.

My month of August in the Trappist monastery was so good, as you can imagine. I had been weakened by my prostate operation; the general anesthesia had tired me too. The month of rest, prayer and the regular rhythm of life each day helped me. It was hard to leave! I needed this time where I had nothing to do except to be quietly with Jesus (I drank deeply from the silence), to take walks in the forest, to write letters and a few other things.

I would like to share with you also about the Festival of Peace to which I was invited in Northern Ireland at the end of June.

Thanks be to God I was able to attend even though it was just a few weeks after my operation. It was truly a Festival of Peace, organized by Presbyterians, Methodists, Anglicans and Catholics and coordinated by Anne Gibson, the Faith and Light coordinator in Northern Ireland. There were deep moments of unity in prayer, in the group sharings, in various workshops on reconciliation and on the resolution of conflict. On the last day, in the little groups, we washed each other's feet. It was a strong moment where we all felt a real presence of God.

A ceasefire was announced in Northern Ireland about a year ago, but it remains fragile. Any day could bring an explosion provoked by those who do not want peace and which could reawaken the fire of violence. But there are many people, Christians from all denominations, who thirst for peace and are determined to work towards peace. I am deeply moved and encouraged when I hear about the number of men and women who have risked their lives over these past years in order to welcome those who are different and to seek peace. We have much to learn from Northern Ireland.

As I begin this new year, my heart is full of peace, joy and thanksgiving. I trust, for God is at work, accomplishing things little by little. Ask God to help me more and more to take the path of humility. I often speak about Jesus, gentle and humble of heart, and of his royal path of littleness, of taking the downward path in order to find Jesus in the poor. Pray with me and for me that I may live what I announce, that my heart may be poorer, closer to the poor and closer to God who is humble and poor and hidden in the poor.

May the peace of Jesus be with you,
Jean

December 31, 1995

Dear Friends,

I am travelling from Kigali to London via Addis Ababa where I change planes. It is the last day of the year 1995; tonight we begin a new year.

For more than a year I have wanted to go back to Rwanda, to meet the Faith and Light communities that were dispersed at the time of the massacres in April, May and June 1994. I knew that the communities had come to life again as we had news from the Faith and Light meeting in Nairobi in August 1995, which brought together leaders from Kenya, Uganda, Burundi, Rwanda and Zaire. I also wanted to go back as a sign of my friendship, solidarity and support for the many brothers and sisters I met in Rwanda in December 1993. The visit to Trosly of Little Sister Teya and other Little Sisters of Jesus who had remained in their country during all the events was another sign that I should set a date for my visit. And so I arrived in Kigali the day after Christmas for a short, four-day visit.

We heard so much about Rwanda through the media. But I must admit it is quite different when you meet the people who live there, when you listen to them and you visit the places where it happened. It is difficult to describe what I saw and heard. I do not think that in history there has been a tragedy as terrifying as this, except of course the Holocaust: 700,000 men, women and children (perhaps more) were killed in a premeditated and highly organized way. They were killed by bullets, by grenades, but most often by machetes. They were killed by the militia, by soldiers, but also by their own neighbours. Some people murdered in a premeditated way, others committed murder out of fear created by what false propaganda was telling them and still others killed because they were obliged to do so. All that hatred has been accumulated throughout a long, painful history, and other countries were certainly not innocent in all that!

People from the Tutsi ethnic group, who were the target of this genocide, were encouraged to seek refuge in churches, where they thought they would be safe. But they were killed in the churches, one after the other, during long hours. I visited one of these churches in the village of Mugombwa. The roof was riddled by bullets and pieces of hand grenades; hundreds of people had been martyred there. Next to the church were the open, common graves—the numerous bodies were covered over simply by sheets of thick canvas. In the church, wobbling against a wall, there was a broken monstrance, which is made to hold the sacred Host.

Two millions Hutus have fled to refugee camps in Zaire and Burundi. Some of them had participated in the genocide; many others had not but they are frightened. About sixty thousand people are waiting to be judged in prisons. These prisons, like all others, are terrible, overcrowded places of violence, pain and guilt.

How to stop this vicious circle of violence that seems to be self-perpetuating?

Such tremendous suffering! Such hatred! And all this has left the country and the people in a traumatized state of fear, pain and despair. How could such a thing happen? And as a Christian, how should one react? Through forgiveness. But how to forgive such horror, when one has lost one's whole family and when there is nobody in front of one who recognizes his or her fault? How to live grief in such circumstances?

At the same time, during all the horror, there were many thousands of signs of love and gestures of mutual aid. For the most part, these gestures of love and courage will remain hidden, unknown, but they are a sign of the strength and beauty of the human heart. I met two Tutsi priests who, paralyzed from fear, were hidden for many weeks, one in a closet in the church, the other in the space between the ceiling and the roof of the Little Sisters' house. They had been protected by a few peoples' courage and by an extraordinary Providence of God.

A few years ago in Poland, with a number of young people we organized a march through one of the concentration camps in Auschwitz. We walked through the camp in silence, each one praying in his or her heart, asking God to take away the hatred and any prejudice in regard to those who are different, asking God to help us never to hurt another person, especially the weak and the poor. In each one of our hearts there is violence and fear. I know that in myself there is still a lot of pride and hardness and that I could have hurt others who are weak if I had not been supported and protected by my community, my education and my faith. I need the Spirit of God to purify me and to continually teach me the ways of compassion and forgiveness.

It was joy for me to meet the Faith and Light communities in Butare and Kigali. In Butare, Father Augustin, a Rwandan priest, celebrated the Eucharist for about twenty mothers with their handicapped children and friends. At the Offertory, all the mothers, all quite poor, many of them widows whose husbands had been killed during the massacres, came up to the altar and offered their children to God. I almost cried. Several women spoke of all they had discovered about their own child through Faith and Light. They told me about a family with a handicapped son: when the militia came to take the family away, the son went out to meet them with outstretched arms. The militia went away.

As I leave Rwanda I am deeply moved. There is so much pain and suffering in our world, so many people locked up in fear and anguish, without hope, so many people trying to forget, who close themselves up in their own short-term projects; they refuse to open up to those who are different. Our world is at a turning point; our Christian churches are also at a turning point. I feel much poorer after this visit. Many reference points which have guided me have been shaken. But I am more and more convinced that hope for our world lies in the creation and deepening of small Christian communities centred on Jesus and on the poor and the weak, communities where we learn how to walk on the path of forgiveness and of welcoming those who are different.

At Christmas (in spite of all the strikes) I received many messages of love and affection from my brothers and sisters in L'Arche and in Faith and Light, and from many friends. I am filled with gratitude. My heart gives thanks to Jesus who is the source of this big family of hope we create together. To each one, thank you.

I pray for you in this passage into the new year. May Jesus bless us all and may he give us his strength and love so that we may be instruments of peace and hope for our divided world. May he keep us faithful to our mission. Pray for me, that I may become more humble and more compassionate as Jesus so wants.

Jean Vanier

April 1996
Trosly

Dear Friends,

We have just celebrated Holy Week, when we remember the crucifixion and resurrection of Jesus. I am more and more convinced that the communities of L'Arche are founded on this Paschal mystery. They are founded on pain and find their meaning only in relationship to pain. That is why there will always be pain in our communities and why we have to discover the joy of the resurrection and a new strength given by God in order to continue to live and love in L'Arche.

As I travel, as I listen to people and see different situations, I realize the immense suffering of our world: the pain of young people, of the unemployed, of refugees, of people who are marginalized or in impossible situations. A cry of pain rises up from our world, the cry of the poor and the weak, the cry of those who feel powerless. It is a cry born from insecurity, loneliness and anguish which sometimes is transformed into feelings of guilt. Our societies are often "bad news" for many people.

Yet Jesus came to bring a good news to the poor. What is this good news that responds to the cry of the poor? It is a simple message which is communicated not so much through words as through presence and commitment: "You are loved. You have value. You are precious. Your life has meaning. You can do something beautiful with your life."

We all need to hear this message. How quickly we become discouraged and lose confidence in ourselves. We forget that our lives have meaning and that we are can give life to others.

How can we remain open to the suffering of our world, close to people in pain? How can we remain peaceful and trusting when we touch our own inner wounds, our own depression, violence, intolerance and even psychological hatred? How can we not feel guilty when we realize that we are not what we thought we were or what we wanted to be?

The answer is that of an eleven-year-old girl with a handicap who told her mother: "Don't worry, Mummy, Jesus loves me just as I am." To discover that I am loved by God just as I am, with all my weakness and wounds. To trust that God is there, close to me, to help me to live and love more fully each day and to give me the necessary strength and force so that I will no longer be governed by fear. The answer is also in mutual support. Yesterday I received a phone call: a young mother had just discovered that the child in her womb has a handicap. She was shocked and angry. I was able to contact another mother whose child has the same kind of handicap. She has agreed to walk with the young mother. Sometimes it is only a mother who can help another mother in pain. To welcome pain, we need the presence, friendship and understanding of a compassionate friend.

I am convinced that L'Arche and Faith and Light can only exist, grow and deepen if each one of us is discovering and living the good news, and that good news is that the name of God is Emmanuel, "God-with-us." Doesn't Jesus tell us, "I am with you always to the end of time" (Matt. 28:20)? He will give us the strength to live what we have to live and to become men and women of the resurrection.

Around this Paschal time, as we prepare for the feast of Pentecost, for a new gift of the Holy Spirit, let us pray for one another, for our communities and for our world. May our hearts and minds be focused on the heart of God so that we do not run away from pain but find the strength to become men and women of compassion.

Much love to you.

Jean Vanier

August 31, 1996
Orval

Dear Friends,

My month of silence in the Trappist monastery is coming to an end. I am happy to have this time of solitude, to rest, to walk, to read a bit and just to be with Jesus. In my heart I give thanks for all that Jesus has given and continues to give to L'Arche and to Faith and Light. In spite of the pain that certain communities and people in our communities are living, we have truly been blessed by God. As time goes by and as I see the growth and maturity of L'Arche and Faith and Light, and of the people who are at the heart of our communities, the more I realize how extraordinary Père Thomas's intuition was when he invited me to come to Trosly "to do something." This "something," which has gradually become clearer, is to reveal to the world and to the Church the power of love springing from the hearts of those we have welcomed.

Jesus describes his mission by quoting from Isaiah (see Luke 4:18–19):

> The Spirit of the Lord is on me, for he has anointed me
> to bring a good news to the afflicted.
> The Lord has sent me to proclaim liberty to captives,
> sight to the blind, to let the oppressed go free,
> to proclaim a year of favour from the Lord. (Isa. 61:1)

This mission of Jesus is also ours: to bring a good news to the poor, which means to show them, not so much by our words but by our shared life with them, that they are loved, that they are important, that they have a place on this earth and, most of all, that they are loved by God, chosen by God, to accomplish a work of love. This is the role of L'Arche and of Faith and Light.

In the Gospel of Luke we see that Jesus read the first verse of Isaiah 61, but maybe he also read the rest of the text that day in the synagogue of Nazareth: "to proclaim a year of favour from the Lord and a day of vengeance for our God." What is that vengeance? Does it mean that God will punish the oppressors and evil-doers? I don't think so. God's vengeance is to raise up the weak, the humble and the afflicted. This is the folly of God.

The text of Isaiah goes on (61:2–3): "to comfort all who mourn, to give a garland instead of ashes, the oil of gladness instead of mourning, clothes of praise instead of despair." And then Isaiah speaks about how they bring life: "They will rebuild ancient ruins," which means they will renew our wounded humanity. It is true that today humanity is broken, wounded and in ruins. I recently received a letter from a L'Arche assistant on holidays: "When I look at the people around me, when I watch the news on television, I am amazed to see how difficult it is today for men and women to find their place in the world which constantly puts in front of their eyes possibilities far beyond their reach and horrible events that paralyze them."

One of these horrors was the assassination of seven Trappist monks in Algeria. It was also one of the most important religious events in recent years. These seven monks had deliberately chosen to remain in Algeria in spite of the risks. They wanted to be a sign of God's love. They were not there to convert Muslims but to be a face of God's love for each person, no matter what their political, military or religious affiliation may be. God loves each person. These monks were men of silence. Their Trappist vocation is a vocation of silence and not of proclaiming the Word.

Our people too are men and women of silence. Their gift is not the word, even though some may talk a lot! They are men and women of the heart and the heart expresses itself through gestures.

About a year before his death, Father Christian de Chergé, the prior of the monastery in Algeria, wrote his testament and left it with his family. It is a testament of love and of forgiveness. He did not want people to identify Islam with those who might kill him. His testament ends with these words to the person who might eventually kill him: "And you too, my last-minute friend, you who know not what you are doing. Yes, for you too, I want this thank you to God and this adieu which is of your planning. May we be granted to meet each other again, happy thieves, in paradise, should it please God, the Father of both of us. Amen! Insh'Allah!"

The monks' death did not provoke a cry of anger but rather gestures of love and of peace. Cardinal Lustiger went to the mosque in Paris where there was a very moving encounter with the Imam.

During the month of August, Christopher Gray, an Anglican priest who was a friend of L'Arche–Liverpool and who had spent six months in L'Arche at Ambleteuse, was assassinated in front of his church in Liverpool. He also had made a deliberate choice to live his ministry in a difficult neighbourhood, with people who were very poor. He gave his life to Jesus and for Jesus and for the afflicted. Luc Ganty, the coordinator of L'Arche in northern Europe, wrote to me: "United in prayer with Christopher and the communities of L'Arche and this cry of our world in front of which we feel so helpless; it is good to be together." The letter continues: "For me this confirms the need for a network where the Word of God takes flesh in a lived, tangible reality, shared with others." Yes, that is the vocation of L'Arche, and of other communities throughout the world: to be a sign and a promise of God's love and forgiveness.

With these thirty-two years of L'Arche, and as I approach my seventieth birthday (in two years), I would like to continue to walk along the path of littleness, to be the face of Jesus, gentle and humble. I feel happy with the structures which, all together, we have put into place in L'Arche and in Faith and Light. This means that little by little I can move out of the structures; God has called forth others to take these responsibilities. I am grateful to them and I pray with them.

I would like to walk more closely with my brothers and sisters who are weak or in pain, and with them to be a sign of God's love. I have also received the grace of sharing the Word, the Good News for the poor, the amazing vengeance of our God. This is my program for the coming year. Pray for me. Ask Jesus to teach me to love each person as he loves. Are we not all called, in spite of our fragilities and wounds, to be the face of Jesus?

In communion with you in thanksgiving and in the desire to walk humbly with the humble.

Jean

March 1997

Dear Friends,

I am in La Garriga, near Barcelona (Spain) for a meeting of the International Council of L'Arche.

We spent an evening with the two Spanish communities, El Rusc and Els Avets, and their friends. We sang, played, laughed and prayed together. Luisa and Marianna, the community leaders, shared their difficulties, particularly the lack of assistants, and looked to the council for support. The core people, some there since the beginning, were like beacons of hope. And yet these two communities have such difficulties because they are not particularly welcomed by society nor by the Church. Our world tends to reject people with disabilities; they are often seen as a catastrophe, a scandal and even in some countries as a punishment from God. No wonder few people come to live as assistants in L'Arche! L'Arche is counterculture. Assistants will stay in L'Arche only if, after perceiving the lack of respect and even the cruelty of society towards those who are weak or different, they discover their beauty and their value. Maybe then they will want to take their place in the struggle for peace and justice, to build community and live the mission of Jesus which is to bring good news to the poor.

The challenge of our communities is to attract young people who are looking for community life, who accept a simple way of life with the weak as a sign of hope and of unity for and in our societies, which are becoming more and more divided. But these assistants will also need to be loved, respected, cared for, so that they in turn can care for others and live the daily demands of community life.

The difficulties of individual communities make me realize even more the need for the International Council. We need this place of reflection in order to give hope and meaning to communities in pain; we need a place where leaders can be challenged to go further and deeper in this vision and where faith and hope can be renewed. When leaders feel the burden of pain, of chaos and of apparent failure, they need a place of sharing to find hope in order to bring hope, to deepen meaning in order to give meaning, to find love in order to love; a place where together they find the strength and wisdom to implement new ways to serve and strengthen communities.

L'Arche is evolving. Each member is rooted in his or her particular community but is also called to live in solidarity with other L'Arche communities. Each one of us is called to carry responsibility for the larger international family. A community is not just a place to give security to a few people; it is the "earth" where each person can grow in love and in wisdom, bear fruit and give life both within and outside the community. We are all called to bring good news to our world.

In February I spent a week in Haiti with L'Arche and Faith and Light. We know the distress and pain the people in this country have lived. Most of them are poor in every way. For centuries they have been crushed under dictatorships and military power. Countries and international organizations have looked down on them, regarding them as incapable. The situation has caused many to escape into violence, drink, drugs and the abuse of the weak. How to bring hope in impossible situations? Isn't hope in the heart of each person as he or she finds people who trust in him or her? Isn't it in community, in life together, that we give each other support and that we learn to forgive, to accept difference and thus little by little change the world one heart at a time?

The mission of L'Arche is to reveal the value and beauty of each person, especially of those who are weak. The first people Robert welcomed into L'Arche–Carrefour twenty years ago came from Signeau, an asylum which took in the "dregs" of society, those no one wanted. It was such a joy for me to see Yveline, Jean-Robert and Jolibois. L'Arche–Carrefour welcomes some thirty people with handicaps: eighteen in the houses, and the others come each day to the school or the workshops. It is truly a vibrant, happy, prayerful community. What a joy to see Annette, the community leader, and Damilia, Jacqueline, Augusta and all the assistants and friends of the community. The community is poor (their operational budget is four thousand dollars a month), but the houses are well built, functional and warm. You really feel "at home" there!

I could say the same of our second community in Chantal, near Les Cayes. Adrien is the new community leader of the two homes and workshop. I spent a day with the community sharing, listening, praying and giving thanks. When I welcomed Raphaël and Philippe in August 1964, I could never have imagined that one day, in a little Haitian village, this vibrant, radiant community would exist, where those who are laughed at have become a source of life!

Yes, the two L'Arche communities in Haiti are a sign of the beauty of the Gospel message. God is manifested in the hearts of the weak. L'Arche as well as Faith and Light are "folly" to the so-called wise and clever of the world, but we discover more and more that they are signs of the love of God, revealing the uniqueness and the sacredness of each human being.

During my stay in Port-au-Prince, the Episcopalian Church organized a gathering of about 150 priests, ministers and theology students from different churches. It was a moving moment to witness how a common vision of the presence of Jesus in the weak, calling us to love and to compassion, could bring together in communion disciples of Jesus from different faith backgrounds. Even if we cannot drink from the same cup at the altar, we can all drink from the cup of pain, which is also the cup of hope, as we grow in mutual love. I am so convinced that people with disabilities, in all their pain, trust and littleness, will draw us all closer to Jesus and thus to each other. The ecumenical and inter-religious aspect of L'Arche is so important as we move towards the third millennium. Let us all grow together in greater love and respect for each other, encouraging each other to be faithful to Jesus, faithful to our conscience, faithful to living close to God. Aren't all these signs of unity like new buds that are beginning to emerge in this arid land of humanity? Isn't this the message of Easter, the passage through pain to life?

Jean Vanier

August 18, 1997
Orval

Dear Friends,

My days in the monastery are coming to an end. I would like to stay in the quiet of these days for much longer. I am happy to be here. I am happy to rest, to go for walks in the surrounding woods, to read Scripture, to pray with the monks and to take time alone with Jesus. It is a time of cleansing and of replenishing, a time also when I touch what needs to be changed within me, the habits I have made that are governed by my need to be right, to prove myself or to avoid failure, conflict and rejection, all that prevents me from living more fully in truth and in love. It is a time when I offer L'Arche and Faith and Light to God, thank God for all the gifts and the protection over this last year, and say "yes" in advance to all that will be given in the coming year. It is a time when, in the silence of each day, I am in communion with each person to whom Jesus has covenanted me, all those I love and who love me, all those I am called to be with in some way or another.

I am leaving a bit earlier this year in order to participate in the Youth Festival in Paris. John Paul II will be there with some half-million young people. It will be an important time of hope for many. So even if it is hard to leave, I am happy to go and be with people at the festival and to talk about Jesus and the Good News he came to bring to the poor and the oppressed.

This last year Jesus has led me more deeply into John's Gospel. I always feel the need to be in direct contact with Scripture, the Word of God, the words of Jesus. Each day I discover more of the treasure. Sometimes I wonder how it is that I am discovering John's Gospel in a new way when I am nearly seventy! But each gift comes at the right time. Now is the time for me to enter more deeply into John's Gospel and to discover Jesus in a new way, and, dare I say, to discover more deeply the relationship between the spirituality of L'Arche and Faith and Light and the spirituality revealed by John, the beloved disciple of Jesus. John's Gospel is a real catechesis; it is a path, a gentle revelation of Jesus and of what he came to give us. It is as if John is taking me by the hand and leading me into a deeper union with Jesus in order to discover more totally his message of love. Let me explain.

After the prologue, John's Gospel begins as John the Baptist points to Jesus, calling him the "Lamb of God," not a powerful leader or a strutting general or a politician seeking acclaim and votes, but a lamb. This gentle lamb attracts two of John the Baptist's disciples, Andrew and (most probably) John, who start to follow him. Jesus turns to them and asks, "What are you looking for?" They reply, "Where do you live?" They want to be with him, to sit at his feet and learn from him. "Come and see," says Jesus.

Then Jesus attracts or calls his first followers. Over a short period of only two or three years, he forms and transforms their hearts, their inner attitudes and motivations.

Do you know where he brings them first of all? To a wedding feast in Cana! Why? Because "the kingdom of God is like a wedding feast." A wedding is a sign of love, unity, peace, fecundity, where a man and a woman become one flesh. We are not all called to be married, but we are all called to the wedding feast of the Lamb as described in the Book of Revelation. The celebration in Cana, however, is not an ordinary wedding. It is a celebration where water will be changed into wine. Our humanity is called to be transformed by God, our hearts of stone into hearts of flesh, so that the ecstasy of life, light and love becomes ours.

Then Jesus reveals to his disciples that he is the new temple where God resides; his body is now the place of love, of forgiveness, of communion, from which all life and love flow. Then Nicodemus is shown to us, and with him Jesus reveals that the ultimate gift of ecstasy, of total fulfillment for each one of us, only comes as we are born anew, from above, transformed by water and the Spirit.

After that Jesus does not lead his followers to a school of learning but to people in pain. He reveals to them the compassion in his own heart towards the poor, the broken, the oppressed, and how he comes to bring them life and hope: a good news. He takes them first to a poor woman, of another religion and ethnic group, a woman of ill repute, who is alone and lonely and who feels guilty; she has lived already with five different men. Then they meet a poor father, crushed by pain; his little boy is dying. Then they go to the local psychiatric hospital or asylum, the pool of Bethesda, where "there were crowds of sick people: blind, lame and paralysed." I myself have visited many such places in our world; they are the places where all the unwanted are dumped. I am touched that this is one of the first places Jesus brings his disciples to, so that they may meet people who are broken, rejected and in pain, and discover how he sees them, is close to them and loves them. Then the disciples begin to experience their own hearts opening up in compassion. That is how L'Arche began. In 1964, Jesus led me into places of pain where many unwanted people had been dumped, and my heart was opened up.

In chapter 6, Jesus reveals to all those who follow him what he really yearns for: not power in order to do big things, but communion with those who love and believe in him. This communion is revealed again in a striking, scandalous way later on, in chapter 13, as Jesus kneels down in front his disciples to wash their feet. He becomes smaller than they and vulnerable to them.

Yes, Jesus is truly an example for us in L'Arche and in Faith and Light.

Let us pray for each other, that we do not just catch glimpses of Jesus, but that we see him more clearly, follow him more nearly and love him more dearly day by day. L'Arche and Faith and Light are folly in the eyes of the world. To many people it is crazy to be with the people of Bethesda. But Jesus truly has chosen, and continues to choose, the foolish in order to shame the wise of this world. And he continues to invite some foolish people to share their lives with those considered foolish by the world's standards and to learn from them.

Last year was very full and the coming year will also be full. Pray that I may continue to be foolish for Jesus and for our world. This year I am entering into my seventieth year. My health is good, thanks be to God, and I feel happy. I give thanks to Jesus. Ask him to keep me faithful to our call and mission; ask that I may grow in humility, to empty myself so that I may do God's work, not my own.

Jean

November 30, 1997

Dear Friends,

I am writing to you from Trosly for once, and not from a plane or an airport. I have just come back from South Korea, filled with Asia and its fragrant odours. I was happy to visit Korea, with its ancient culture (I visited a Buddhist monastery founded in the sixth century that has been a place of prayer ever since), but which is in the process of discovering the American-style economy and Christianity. I gave a two-day retreat in Seoul. I sensed how much people there were ready to welcome the Gospel vision that we are living in L'Arche alongside people who are weak and fragile. Then I participated in the Faith and Light Zone Council for Asia, where I conducted the election process for a new zone coordinator. There were representatives of Faith and Light from Korea, Japan, Taiwan, China (Hong Kong) and the Philippines. The delegates from Taiwan and Hong Kong told us how harsh the Chinese culture is for people with handicaps. But things are changing in these countries; changes in the economy and democracy can help the situation to evolve. Parents are beginning to cry out their distress.

It was truly a privilege for me to be there, to meet parents in Faith and Light and many others who yearn for the creation of Faith and Light and L'Arche communities there. It was also a privilege to pray with some Buddhist nuns in their monastery. The mother Abbess served us food with such gentleness and tenderness! I felt so stiff and clumsy in their presence. I realized how much I have been formed in and by a culture that is often so aggressive. With the Buddhists there is compassion, gentleness, nonviolence and a deep sense of the value of every living creature in the universe.

I have travelled a great deal lately, to Egypt, Belgrade, Milan and Korea, mainly for Faith and Light. More and more I realize that people with learning disabilities are my people, whether they are my brothers and sisters in L'Arche or Faith and Light or anywhere else in the world. They are the people God has entrusted to me in a special way. They are truly amongst the most oppressed people in our world today, often voiceless. There are of course, many parents, professionals and others who are committed to them, who are their friends and who are struggling for their rights; but most of the time they are ignored and pushed aside in our societies. I sense deeply that my vocation is to be with and for them, for their liberation, so that they may find an inner peace and the joy of knowing God and discovering how much they are loved by God and that they have a gift for our world.

One of the most moving events for me these last few months was my meeting with the World Council of Churches in Geneva. Its central committee had invited me to animate its annual day on spirituality. This committee includes about 220 leaders and delegates from Christian churches all over the world. There were many Anglican, Lutheran, Methodist and Orthodox bishops, and ministers, priests and lay people from all denominations, plus two observers from the Roman Catholic Church. We began with morning prayer, then I gave a short talk after which two people spoke about what had touched them the most in my talk. Then they accepted to have the liturgy of the washing of the feet. We followed the liturgy we use in ecumenical and inter-religious Covenant Retreats, which was also used at the last retreat I gave in Belfast about two years ago.

I was so touched by the way these men and women listened to me speak about people with disabilities, who, with all their fragility and vulnerability, help us to discover the way of the heart and the communion of hearts and to come closer to Jesus, meek and gentle of heart. Then we washed each other's feet, in silence, prayer and intense emotion. Personally, I was deeply moved to see the faces of these men and women of God, so open to the message of Jesus and yearning to live in his love. And to think that I was there because of Raphaël, Philippe and other men and women who like them had been rejected and pushed aside, whom we had welcomed and who have taught me so much. Jesus truly works wonders through those who are weak and broken. God raises them up out of the dust and the persecution so that they can lead us to truth and to love.

Those who are weak have a secret power of love. If they are welcomed, they can lead Christians and men and women throughout the world towards unity. I hope that the witness of what we are living will hasten that unity. Several bishops from Africa and Asia testified that they had never realized there was such a power in people with mental handicaps and that they were so deeply loved by God. I hope my testimony can contribute in some way to the liberation of people with disabilities and can help Christian communities to welcome them.

Soon it will be Christmas. For many people Christmas is not a time of celebration but a time of suffering, as they are hungry and feel so alone. Millions of people on our earth earn less than a dollar a day! And yet Christmas is a time of hope for the poor to whom Jesus came bring the Good News. May we too bring the good news of love to the poor, by the way we live and love.

Jean

April 1998

Dear Friends,

I am writing this in the chapel of the Casa San José, our L'Arche community in Choluteca (Honduras). The community has grown since my visit two and a half years ago. It is now home to Melvin, a ten-year-old boy who used live on the streets, and in the workshop there are five more day-workers, in the school five more children, and of course new assistants. I am touched to see how this little community, which is part of a poor neighbourhood, is at the heart of the church in Choluteca. Daily life here, as everywhere else, is not easy. Pépé and Santos still have their difficulties and their anger, which is normal after such a painful, disturbed childhood. But they have found a home which is at the heart of the parish as well as the neighbourhood. Our two communities in Honduras are beautiful. They have been marked by a lot of joy as well as pain: the joy of sharing a simple day-to-day life that involves close links with the local neighbourhood; the pain of the lack of assistants and of active board members, of community conflicts and finally of the personal suffering of each person.

I came to Honduras to visit our communities but also to give a Covenant Retreat. Thirty-four people came from L'Arche in Mexico, Brazil, Haiti, Honduras and the Dominican Republic. What a joy to live this time with long-term assistants of the zone! There were also younger assistants who had come to deepen their sense of covenant in L'Arche and to prepare to announce the covenant at a future retreat. It is beautiful to see how Jesus is at work in the life of each one, moulding hearts and calling to growth in trust. I am convinced that these retreats are times of conversion and transformation, times which allow us to review our lives and to discover the deep sense of our call and of the mission of L'Arche, times which also help us to see what is preventing us from being in communion with Jesus and with all our brothers and sisters in L'Arche.

Last October I participated in a meeting of the International Covenant Commission, composed of about twelve long-term assistants from Africa, North America and Europe. We realized more fully the tension that exists between our daily workload and the deepening of our union with God and with our brothers and sisters. What can we do so that the everyday running of the community, with all the organization and administration that it implies, does not take precedence over the life of the Spirit and true self-giving? We recognized the importance of the Covenant Retreat, of announcing the covenant and of mutual support if we are to remain faithful to our vocation and our mission. We expressed the desire to see some people with handicaps announcing the covenant. Some have been living a covenant with Jesus and with their brothers and sisters in L'Arche for many years; they have grown in maturity and in their spiritual life and they have a desire to announce their commitment to Jesus in their church and in L'Arche. We still need to have some guidelines as to what preparation and what commitment such an announcement would imply. That is one of the roles of this commission, which will meet again in July to make concrete proposals to the International Council.

Having given a number of Covenant Retreats and accompanied many assistants who have announced the covenant, I am beginning to grasp that there are different aspects to it. It is first of all a call from God to share one's life with people who have a handicap. This call takes on flesh in a particular community. To announce the covenant is to announce one's desire to be part of the community and the body of the larger family of L'Arche. It means that those who announce the covenant have discovered their own hearts, touched and awoken by relationships with people with handicaps, and that they realize these covenant relationships are a path that leads to God. This aspect accentuates the notion of commitment in a body.

To announce the covenant is also to announce a desire to walk humbly with people who are weak, to take what Henri Nouwen called the "downward path." It implies walking on a road of poverty and humility. Paul describes this when he talks about Jesus "who, being in the form of God, did not count equality with God something to be grasped, but he emptied himself . . . and he was even humbler yet" (Phil. 2:6–8). Living with people who are weak we live moments of great tenderness and joy, but also times of darkness when we touch our own weaknesses, blockages, violence and poverty. Then we discover that the weak person is not only someone outside of us but within us. Thus we enter into the mystery of the first Beatitude: "Blessed are the poor, for the Kingdom of heaven is theirs." As we discover our poverty and the presence of Jesus at the heart of that poverty, we can become a source of unity in our communities.

It seems to me we cannot separate these two aspects of the covenant. If we remain simply on the level of belonging to a body, we risk wanting to have a perfect community which is better than others. If we remain only on the level of a journey to poverty, close to Jesus, weak and hidden, we risk forgetting our call and our mission as a community. Through a kind of false humility, we could forget how much our communities are loved by God just as they are and how God calls us all to risk trusting in him and in our brothers and sisters, in order to live and proclaim our mission. It is only if we try to live these two aspects together that we will be able—with the help of the Holy Spirit—to live in community without considering ourselves better than others, to accept a path of littleness and forgiveness, and to continue the struggle with and for the weak. It is a difficult struggle in all our societies. For me, to live the covenant means more and more to work humbly for unity, to accept and appreciate each person, each community, without judging them. It means accepting my gifts as well as my poverty and putting them both at the service of the Kingdom of God. My poverty makes me ask God for help and ask for the help of my brothers and sisters. To announce the covenant is to bring me close to each person God puts on my path, with all that is poor and broken within them; it is to work for unity where there is fear, conflict and division.

I am always touched by the parable Jesus tells (in Luke 14) about the man who gave a banquet. Those who were invited refused to come because they had other things to do. So the man tells his servants to go out into the streets and to invite all the poor, the lame, the blind, the people with a handicap. Isn't it the role of L'Arche and of Faith and Light to go to those who are weak and have been rejected, and to bring them to God's banquet?

Jean Vanier

August 1998

Dear Friends,

I am at the monastery of Orval for a month of rest, relaxation, prayer and time to dig more deeply into the Gospel of John. It is good for me to be here. I like to have time with nothing to do, or rather with no agenda, no telephone, no meetings, no appointments; each day is punctuated by the different times of prayer in the monastery. There are about twenty-five monks here who carry L'Arche and Faith and Light in their hearts and prayers and encourage us. They often welcome us here for individual or group retreats. I am grateful to so many monasteries throughout the world which hold us and give us support. There is a real "connivance" between our two vocations. Society often considers us both as useless and foolish . . . and it's true! Our eyes are set less on social success than on Jesus, on God and on the weak who bring a presence of God to our world.

Being here makes me feel so grateful also for a number of assistants, men and women, who have spent time in L'Arche and then felt called to follow Jesus in a religious order or as a priest or minister, and who pray for us and watch over our communities.

The past year was very full for me, particularly in the realm of ecumenism. I realize more and more our vocation, our call to work for unity—unity first of all on a social level, by helping people with a handicap to be more included in the life of society and of the churches. But also the unity between Christians belonging to different churches and with people of different religions or with no religion. When I speak about unity I am not saying "everyone becomes the same" but rather "everyone works together in the same direction." What is that direction? The recognition of the value of each person no matter what his or her limits, culture or religion may be. To work for peace by struggling against all forms of oppression; to work together so that there may be more love and compassion in our world, especially for those who are weak and marginalized, those who are in pain and living in misery; to work together so that the God of love and the love of God may be better known and welcomed in the hearts of all.

At Pentecost, John Paul II invited me and three other founders of new lay communities to speak to a gathering at which he presided, of some 350,000 people who have made a commitment within these new communities. I was asked to speak about the vision and spirituality of L'Arche and Faith and Light. Pascal Denardo, from Le Val Fleuri, was with me. During the Sunday Mass celebrated by the Pope, he brought the offerings to the Pope, who embraced him.

Then in July there was the Lambeth Conference in Canterbury for some eight hundred bishops of the Anglican Communion, more than half of whom came from Africa, Asia, Latin America and the Pacific Islands. The Archbishop of Canterbury invited me to animate an afternoon and evening of prayer for them. It began with a talk I gave on the call to holiness, which was followed by a mime prepared by the L'Arche–Kent community and a long liturgy around the washing of the feet, ending with an all-night vigil of quiet prayer.

These events were a sign for me that our churches are discovering more and more that people with a handicap have a place at the heart of the Christian community and a sign also that they are beginning to grasp the truth of Paul's words: "God has chosen the foolish and the weak in order to confound the wise and the strong" (1 Cor 1:27). When I am invited to speak at such events, I know that it is in the name of each one of us. I know that I am just a voice, a bit like John the Baptist, the voice which points to Jesus, hidden in the weak, and to the power they have to transform us if we welcome them with compassion and truth. These invitations are a recognition and a confirmation of L'Arche and of Faith and Light by our churches, who are calling us to greater faith and trust in our vocation.

Here in Orval, I have time to give thanks for these invitations, for the privilege to announce the gift of God and the treasure we have received. I give thanks to God for calling us all to work for unity between Christians. I give thanks to Jesus for giving me some of his passion for unity. I do not know if one day there will be a unity of faith and of structures between our different churches. What I do know is that today we can be in communion with one another in our desire to love and follow Jesus, to live the Gospel message, and to work together with and for the weakest, in order to build the Kingdom of God here and now.

I will soon be celebrating my seventieth birthday. I thank Jesus especially for these thirty-four years of L'Arche, the twenty-seven years of Faith and Light and the thirty years of Faith and Sharing. With you, I offer to God the coming year, the last one before the third millennium. May each one of us work this year with greater passion, wisdom and humility for unity and peace.

Jean Vanier

March 1999
Trosly

Letter to my brothers and sisters in L'Arche and in Faith and Light
Dear Friends,

INTRODUCTION
I am seventy now but I feel that Jesus still gives me a mission in L'Arche and Faith and Light, so I am writing this letter to all our communities. I realize more and more that God has entrusted us with a treasure: our shared life with people who are weak. As founder of L'Arche with Père Thomas, and of Faith and Light with Marie-Hélène Mathieu, I like to say over and over again what a

treasure we have received. In the Gospel, Jesus says that if someone found a treasure in a field, he or she would sell everything in
order to buy that field. That is what I am trying to do. I yearn to
become poorer in order to allow Jesus and each one of you to have
more place.

Two years ago in a letter to "my brothers and sisters," addressed
to assistants in L'Arche, I spoke about our vocation. In this letter
I would like to open other doors: the treasure we have received,
unity between L'Arche and Faith and Light, compassion in the
face of pain, formation and the search for truth. Do not hesitate to
send me your reflections. This letter is meant to be the beginning
of a dialogue.

I. The Treasure

For many years now I have had the privilege of giving retreats to
people with learning disabilities. Each time I marvel at their attentiveness and their openness. Last October, during a Katimavik in
Belgium, two people with severe handicaps came up to me after
one of my talks which had lasted almost an hour. Each one, in his
and her own way, said to me, "Thank you. Your words helped
me." During a recent weekend in a monastery with the people
from my own house, I shared about God, the Father of Jesus, who
is so different from many of our own fathers who can at times be
quite harsh and even violent. After one of my talks, a young man,
whom we have just welcomed and whose father can be quite violent, came up to me and said, "Your words were really helpful."
I am not sure what each one understands or remembers from my
talks, but it is clear from the way they listen and from their silence
and attentiveness that the Holy Spirit is at work in their hearts,
giving them peace, light and warmth. A few years ago, Didier from
my house said to me, "When the priest was speaking, my heart was
burning." When I asked him what the priest had said, he answered,
"I don't know." The Holy Spirit moves and works in us at a deeper

level than that of our concepts or ideas, and can use our words, the tone of our voice, to touch and awaken hearts.

People with learning disabilities seem to have less complicated defence mechanisms than we, the so-called intelligent and healthy. Their inner walls are built more around all the suffering they have lived than around pride and the need for power. Their hearts are simpler, more trusting. They respond to love with love. So it is no wonder that Paul should say in his letter to the Corinthians that God has chosen the weak and the foolish to confound the strong and the intelligent (1 Cor. 1:27)!

I love the story Marie-Hélène Mathieu tells in her book *Dieu m'aime comme je suis* (God loves me as I am).

Emmanuel was a twelve-year-old boy with disabilities. His family had just discovered that he also had leukemia. Nobody told him but he was beginning to feel his strength diminishing. One day the doctor told his family that Emmanuel did not have long to live. At Mass the following Sunday, after Communion, Emmanuel remained kneeling, his head in his hands. Concerned by this, his father asked, "Emmanuel, what are you doing?" Emmanuel replied simply, "I am praying to Jesus so that Mummy will not cry too much." One Sunday, seeing that Emmanuel was getting weaker and weaker, his father told him: "Perhaps you can watch Mass on the television today." "Papa, and the Host?" "You know that I can bring you Communion." "No, I want to go and see Jesus." "You are too tired." With great effort, Emmanuel got up, knelt down and said, "You see, Daddy, I can still do it." That Sunday, for the last time, Emmanuel went to Mass. He was hospitalized a few days later, and during his last moments his father had the courage to say to him, "Emmanuel, you will soon see Jesus." At that, Emmanuel, with one arm around his mother and the other around his father, said, "Daddy, you know that I love you. Mummy, you know that I love you." It was his way of saying good-bye to them.

The story of Emmanuel is a concrete illustration of what the Charter of L'Arche says:

> People with a mental handicap often possess qualities of welcome, wonderment, spontaneity and directness. They are able to touch hearts and to call others to unity through their simplicity and vulnerability. In this way they are a living reminder to the wider world of the essential values of the heart without which knowledge, power and action lose their meaning and purpose.
>
> Weakness and vulnerability in a person, far from being an obstacle to union with God, can foster it. It is often through weakness, recognized and accepted, that the liberating love of God is revealed. (II.3–4)

Our communities are called to be "banquets of love" prepared especially for those that society rejects and considers "useless" or a "problem." For God, each person is unique and important whatever his or her gifts, capacities and shortcomings, whatever his or her culture or religion. Each one has a heart made to love and be loved. Our goal is to treat each person with respect and love, as a unique human being, to listen to each one and to help each one become more fully him or herself in an environment of mutual friendship and trust.

So often our world is geared only to reinforcing the power of those who are strong. God wants a society where the weak and the powerless have a place. In L'Arche and in Faith and Light, assistants, parents and friends are like the servants in the parable who invite people with disabilities to the "banquet of love" and bring them to it. But once there, we are all called to celebrate together.

The "banquet of love" described in the Gospel is of course the Eucharistic meal where Jesus gives himself as nourishment; it is a spiritual event. But it is also the place where we open our hearts to one another. It is lived out in the daily life of our communities. The "banquet of love" is both profoundly human and profoundly divine. The heart is the place where heaven and earth meet, where the presence of God is revealed. In his first letter, John the Evangelist writes: "Beloved, let us love one another for love comes from God. Everyone who loves has been born of God and knows God" (1 John 4:7).

In the biblical context, to know God means to have an experience of God. If we truly love one another, we are in God. L'Arche and Faith and Light are communities where the heart of each person is called to grow, to deepen and to open up to others. We are called to drink from the Source of love, which is God, so that we ourselves become a source of love for our brothers and sisters in humanity.

People with disabilities are chosen by the God of love because they thirst for love and friendship, but we know also that they can be quite difficult, disturbed and in anguish. Some have no self-confidence; they no longer believe they are loveable. Others are full of anger and even want to die. Their deepest self is hidden behind many psychological wounds. Living with them is not always easy nor a source of peace! They can awaken our own anguish, impatience, anger and inner darkness. We are called to believe and to hope that one day their inner, hidden beauty will come to light.

Openness to others means first of all that each one becomes more aware of his or her value and discovers a new self-confidence and a trust in his or her capacity to give life. This trust develops as people discover they are loved and know others are happy they exist, and when they receive the attention, presence and psychological help they need to grow in maturity and greater inner freedom. This openness and confidence takes time. To love is to become free of our fears and prejudices; it is to welcome "strangers," those who are "different," and to enter into a covenant relationship with them.

L'Arche and Faith and Light are above all schools of love which imply a personal encounter with the God of love, who reveals to each one of us: "You are my beloved daughter, my beloved son, in whom I rejoice." L'Arche and Faith and Light are communities of faith and celebration, "banquets of love," where we learn to rejoice in the presence of each person and to give thanks to God for them.

These communities of love should not be closed in on themselves. Fear always closes people in on themselves; love opens them up to others. Love is a source of gentleness, forgiveness, openness, welcome and gift of self. That is why our communities are called to be open to our neighbours and integrated into the local churches or places of worship.

The Charter of L'Arche affirms that we are called first of all to create communities of love but also to reveal to society, and thus to our neighbours, that the value of each human being comes from their capacity to love and not from their capacity to do things. Our communities are called to witness to the importance of those who are weak. Their lives have meaning; they have a mission as a source of communion of hearts. God is present not only in the beauty and greatness of the universe, but also in weakness and in littleness, in pain and in crises which can become moments of growth and conversion. Our communities want to show that it is important to listen with love and respect to each person, especially to those who are broken and powerless. In the midst of the violence and divisions of our world we want to be witnesses to the compassion which transforms hearts.

II. AFFIRMED BY OUR CHURCHES

Three important encounters this past year confirmed this vision of L'Arche and Faith and Light: my meetings with the World Council of Churches, with the Pope and the gathering of new lay communities in Rome, and with all the bishops of the Anglican Communion.

These meetings were an encouragement for all of us to be more faithful to the "little way" that has been given to us. We need this confirmation from the different churches, just as the churches need the presence of the poor and the weak. Paul says, "It is precisely the parts of the body that seem to be the weakest that are the indispensable ones. It is the parts of the body which we consider least dignified that we surround with the greatest dignity" (1 Cor. 12:22–3). These encounters were affirmations that the weak and the needy are, in all their poverty, signs of the presence of God and that they have a mission to create unity amongst Christians.

However, our communities cannot be signs of unity for our world and our churches unless each one of us personally is seeking to live the Gospel. Our communities are founded on the charter of love which is expressed in the Beatitudes. In order to live love, we need to receive love, which implies a certain poverty and a surrender to God. It is not easy to live a long-term commitment to the Gospel and to love. We need to be nourished by rest and by the silence of prayer. Most of the time inner silence requires an external silence, places of prayer, little houses of prayer and of welcome where we can find quiet space and new strength. What a joy to see houses of prayer coming to birth in different L'Arche communities throughout the world. That was Père Thomas's intuition when he created La Ferme in Trosly.

This brings me to speak about our links with different churches. L'Arche was founded by Père Thomas and myself. Père Thomas was at the origin of my vocation, and he was at the heart of L'Arche as a priest. L'Arche and Faith and Light cannot be, and do not want to be, isolated, self-sufficient communities, closed in on themselves. Our communities form part of a larger movement of life that springs from the heart of God, calling all to love and to the gift of self. We are one of the many different communities committed to the struggle between death and life, slavery and freedom, oppression and the Good News. L'Arche and Faith and Light are places where we are called to struggle for greater respect of human rights and to show that love is stronger than hate, peace and unity stronger than war and division. We are living in solidarity with all those who believe in love, with all those who believe in the God of love. Isn't that the very meaning of the Church? That is why the Charter of L'Arche says:

> L'Arche communities are communities of faith, rooted in prayer and trust in God. They seek to be guided by God and by their weakest members, through whom God's presence is revealed. Each community member is encouraged to discover and deepen his or her spiritual life and live it according to his or her particular faith and tradition. Those who have no religious affiliation are also welcomed and respected in their freedom of conscience. (III.1.1)

Our churches are like the holy temple in the vision of Ezekiel (ch. 47) from which living waters flow that heal and give life. I give thanks for the priests, ministers and ordained men and women whom churches have sent to "walk with" us, to announce and reveal the mystery we are living and to help us be faithful to our vocation. Through them we are better integrated into our local churches. They nourish us through the Word of God, which constantly reminds us of the meaning of our life together in L'Arche and Faith and Light and invites us continually to "launch out into the deep" (Luke 5:4). We are so often taken up with busyness that we can forget the significance of our community life. We can stagnate or refuse to grow in greater love. We need those sent by our churches to bring the presence of God through their love, their words, the sacraments and particularly the sacrament of the body and blood of Jesus.

That is why I was touched by the confirmation we received in and through the events with the different churches this past year. We need this confirmation that the weak are at the heart of the churches, that they are necessary and must be "surrounded with the greatest dignity." It is good that people within our communities belong to different Christian traditions and different religions; that enables us to give witness to the love of God for our world.

III. L'ARCHE AND FAITH AND LIGHT
L'Arche and Faith and Light are two different but complementary realities, deeply bonded together through grace and through their shared history. They have something to give to and to receive from each other. We should give thanks for one another and do all we can to nourish our links and to encourage each other.

L'Arche was founded in August 1964, inspired by Père Thomas Philippe. The two of us united together, two witnesses of Jesus and of the Gospel, were at the origin of the community. We had different gifts and different temperaments. Our unity, in spite of or perhaps because of our differences, has borne much fruit. I could say the same thing for Faith and Light with Marie-Hélène Mathieu and myself.

L'Arche and Faith and Light are rooted in the same spirituality, founded on the love of God for the weakest and the poorest, and on their capacity to open up hearts to compassion and to the Gospel message. The fundamental goals of these two forms of community are the same: to welcome people with disabilities, to reveal their vocation to others and to work towards their integration into society and in Christian communities. Our journeys in ecumenism are similar. Our structures are alike. Our community life is quite different, but we celebrate in the same way. We encounter the same difficulties: fundraising and a lack of committed help (assistants in L'Arche, friends in Faith and Light). The dangers are alike too: we get caught up in questions of organization, pedagogy, leisure activities, etc., and forget the importance of community life and the spiritual value of people with disabilities, their capacity for union with God.

There are also many differences between L'Arche and Faith and Light. In many ways Faith and Light is a family movement where parents have a vital role. L'Arche welcomes people with disabilities who can no longer live with their families or who have no families. Then there are all the differences between communities where people live together and communities where people meet on a regular basis. Parents in Faith and Light are often concerned about what will happen to their son or daughter when they are no longer there; they hope that eventually he or she will be welcomed into a community of L'Arche. If that is not possible, some parents wonder if Faith and Light could help them to create a L'Arche or something similar, and of course that is not always possible.

Throughout the years, our communities have often been very close. Members of L'Arche have played an important role in the animation of Faith and Light pilgrimages. In some countries, they organized the pilgrimage in 1971. L'Arche was at the origin of Faith and Light in some places, while in others the reverse was the case. Our closeness, for we are brothers and sisters or at least first cousins, has also led to misunderstandings, jealousies and conflicts, often caused by mutual ignorance. In some countries L'Arche is quite a small reality, trying to survive as best as it can financially, while Faith and Light is quite strong, with numerous communities, good organization, formation sessions, etc. Sometimes it is just the opposite: L'Arche has the necessary funds, a good board, many assistants, formation programs and retreats, while Faith and Light feels quite fragile. Sometimes young people involved in Faith and Light become friends of a L'Arche community in their country and that can create tension, especially if L'Arche asks them for help on a day when they should be at a Faith and Light formation session! The possibilities for tension are numerous between the two organizations. A real "ecumenism" is needed between L'Arche and Faith and Light!

As I was at the origin of both L'Arche and Faith and Light and as I am on the two International Councils, I realize how each one can be so taken up with its own concerns that it forgets that the two are complementary and that the churches and society need both. L'Arche and Faith and Light have the same fundamental goals, the same spirituality, the same aspirations, the same faith, even if their immediate goals are different. Both have excellent documents which everyone could benefit from. Faith and Light puts out guidelines for monthly meetings which could be useful for L'Arche communities. Both have worked on ecumenism.

How can we organize meetings—on the local, regional, national, zone and international levels—where we can share together and keep each other informed of our growth and questions? How can we create places where we could come together to share our pain and to carry each other in prayer? How can we develop a sense of unity deeper than our differences? How can we become more aware that we are struggling and being guided by the same God of love? In my heart I yearn deeply for this unity, and I hope that at many different levels, places of dialogue and of regular meetings will be created. If we come together in a spirit of prayer and love, and in a desire for mutual support, I am sure that God will bless us and that new life will emerge. Unity that respects difference always bears much fruit.

Retreats are one of the most important places for this unity. Many individual vocations as well as new communities were born out of retreats. Much grace has been given in and through retreats, which are one of the best places for announcing our spirituality. If we want our communities to continue to grow according to God's plan and to be signs of hope, life and resurrection in a world where there are so many signs of despair and of death, if we want people with disabilities to receive the Good News of Jesus and to be able to bring it to others, these retreats are indispensable. Retreats have already been organized together in some countries. Sometimes they are organized by a separate group which includes a few people from both L'Arche and Faith and Light. Sometimes there is a loose structure, like Faith and Sharing, which began in North America after the first retreat I gave in 1968 in Marylake, and which now exists also in Ireland and in Scandinavia. In France there is the network of Katimaviks, or weekend retreats, in which both L'Arche and Faith and Light participate.

People who are weak are truly a treasure for the churches and for society. This is what Saint Lawrence witnessed to when he was martyred in the year 258. The Roman authorities wanted him to give them all the wealth of the churches in Rome. He arrived with all the poor of the city and said, "The poor are the treasure of the Church"! It is important to develop a greater unity between L'Arche and Faith and Light so that we can make this treasure more known to the churches and to the world.

IV. PAIN

L'Arche and Faith and Light are founded on pain, and in some small way they want to be a response to pain. Our communities exist in order to alleviate the pain of people with disabilities: their physical pain, their sense of failure and rejection, their difficulties of not being understood and of not understanding, the pain of not corresponding to other peoples' expectations. Our communities exist also to give support to parents who often feel guilty for having a child "like that," parents who feel alone, misunderstood and ashamed. In many countries there is little or no medical, psychological or pedagogical help available; there are no schools or workshops, only huge dismal institutions. Some parents live a kind of hell in a small apartment, alone with their disturbed child, no support, no friends. I am deeply moved by such pain.

Then there is all the pain around us and in our world. Suffering has, of course, always existed. I feel more deeply than ever the suffering that people are going through because of accident, illness, broken relationships, divorce, unemployment, rejection, death of a loved one, suicide or the feeling of being unwelcome and unable to cope alone. And there is all the suffering of war and oppression, of refugee camps, of hunger and natural disasters. What to do when we become aware of all this suffering? Run away? Try to forget? Pretend it doesn't exist? Get depressed? Feel guilty? Throw ourselves into all kinds of activities, obliged to respond to all the suffering, to be a "saviour"? But this leads to burnout. We all have to situate ourselves in front of the suffering we encounter in and around us. And this is made even more difficult because we are living in a world that seeks at all costs to pretend that suffering should not exist. People are encouraged to look for the most comfort, the greatest pleasure, the most success and to avoid all that is painful, particularly in relationships. Yet in spite of all we might try to do and all the progress in technology and all the medicine at our disposal, suffering remains.

While L'Arche and Faith and Light can bring support and relief to a few people in pain, we know full well that we cannot respond to all their pain nor to all human suffering. Parents in particular are deeply wounded by what they are living. People with disabilities will never be completely healed. In and through our communities they may begin to accept themselves, to have friends, to find a meaning to their lives and even a certain joie de vivre. Many, however, still live in pain. Assistants are often attracted to those who have attained a certain peace and maturity and who have a capacity to communicate with others. Don't we all find it difficult to remain close to people in anguish who are crying out in their pain? When we sense that we can bring some relief to someone, then we feel we are doing something useful. But when we realize that there is nothing we can do, it is more difficult.

Physical pain can be quite unbearable. Medical progress has provided ways of relieving that pain. Psychological pain—anguish, feelings of guilt, fear of others, confusion, insecurity, lack of self-confidence, the foretaste of death—is so much more difficult to bear and to treat.

Painkillers do exist and are necessary, but they have secondary effects that put people in a state of confusion. We all know that an important part of relief from pain is presence: someone who reveals to the person that he or she is not bad or all alone, a friend who is happy just to be there. Friendship communicates life to others, draws them out of depression and darkness, and gives them a new desire to live. But this friendship has to be tested. It takes time to create bonds of trust and to enable someone to believe in the fidelity of a friendship.

When people have a toothache, it is not enough to tell them that we are with them or that we love them. We should take them to a good dentist! In the same way, when people are hungry, we have to get them some food or the means to provide for their own needs with dignity. One form of compassion is to struggle against pain with all our strength, intelligence and competence. But there are circumstances when there is nothing we can do. A mother whose child has just died needs a friend who will stay with her. That is compassion in the strongest sense of the word: to "be with," to "suffer with." That is the heart of L'Arche and of Faith and Light.

But how can we remain close to a person in pain? In many ways L'Arche and Faith and Light are close to hospice care. My sister Thérèse worked as a doctor for many years at St. Christopher's Hospice in London. She introduced me to palliative care and taught me a great deal. Patients in the last stages of their lives need competent medical care; they need to feel as comfortable as possible, not cluttered with different tubes and machines; they need the presence of someone close by who can answer their questions, a friend who loves them and helps them live peacefully to the very end. We are called to live these two aspects of competence and friendship.

It is difficult to live a covenant relationship with someone in anguish, particularly if the person refuses to accept his or her weakness or is angry with life, with others and with God. To be faithful to such a covenant we need a new strength. We need a maturity of heart and of mind which means that we have come to accept our own pain and anguish and failures. That takes time and needs good accompaniment and competent help, people who can help us work on our own inner darkness and pain. Good human and spiritual formation are also necessary, as well as the proper living conditions in the community which allow us to live there on a long-term basis without too much stress or excessive fatigue. But we need most of all the strength which comes from the Holy Spirit. When we feel loved and called by God, despite all our fragility, difficulties in relationships, inner brokenness and even our sins, we can be present to other people who are living in pain and anguish.

I am not ignoring the importance of celebrations in L'Arche and Faith and Light or all the joys of communion between us, and I do not want to be pessimistic. But the experience of these thirty-four years in L'Arche have shown me that in order to be faithful on a long-term basis and to be committed to working for unity, we have to learn how to remain close to suffering, how to hold on in situations of pain. We have to discover compassion. Jesus puts compassion at the heart of the new life he came to bring: "Be compassionate as your Father is compassionate. Do not judge and you will not be judged; do not condemn and you will not be condemned; forgive and you will be forgiven" (Luke 6:36–7). To be compassionate means to walk with those in pain, to understand them, to comfort them and especially to love them and remain with them just as Mary remained with Jesus at the foot of the cross (see John 19). There was a force of love in her that allowed her to stay while the others were running away.

I feel that I am still quite far from this form of compassion. There is still a bit of fear and anguish in me which can make it difficult for me at times to remain peaceful with someone who is in pain. The covenant we live and announce in L'Arche is both gentle and painful. It is a path towards communion with God. It means that our hearts must be formed, structured and strengthened in order to live close to those who are suffering. God yearns to give us hearts of compassion, a gift of the Holy Spirit, so that we can remain close to people in pain, trusting in the resurrection.

Only when we have these hearts of compassion can we truly become instruments of peace and work for unity within and between our own communities, unity between L'Arche and Faith and Light, between Christians of different traditions and between all men and women whatever their religion may be. Unity is often broken because people are frightened of the pain provoked by difference. Compassion, like forgiveness, is a source of unity. It calls for wisdom. This brings me to the next subject.

V. FORMATION AND THE SEARCH FOR TRUTH

L'Arche and Faith and Light are schools of love and of compassion. More and more I realize that in order to be schools of love they must be schools of truth, places where we learn to discern the truth, to announce it and to be living witnesses to it. In a pluralist, global and rapidly changing world, governed and unified by communications and media, there is the danger of relativizing everything. Reality becomes merely that which gives people pleasure and money, and people even doubt that truth exists.

How to awaken or bring to birth a yearning for truth? Doesn't it take a whole lifetime for us to move beyond illusions and subjectivity to learn to love reality? So often we run away from reality because it disturbs us; it reveals our shortcomings, our deficiencies and sometimes the evil in us. We try to modify it to fit our tastes and to protect ourselves. But truth does exist. There are truths about human growth just as there is philosophical and scientific truth.

Our world is so complex and seems to be so confused. There is a tremendous need for compassion and wisdom. Our communities, and each one of us, need to discover the importance of truth. Our heads and our hearts must be unified so that we can love intelligently in order to help others grow to greater inner freedom. The heart is called to guide the intelligence and vice versa. An intelligence that is not well formed will not be a good guide—it will cut itself off from the heart—and a heart cut off from the intelligence will be governed only by subjective emotions.

If we do not develop our intelligence, we will not have the necessary certitudes to act as a basis for action or a vision of what it means to human. We risk letting ourselves be influenced only by what the mass media tell us to do. Truth gives us a structure and a vision that enable us to become more deeply, fully human. We can of course develop our minds and use our knowledge for our own glory, convinced that we are superior to others. But truth is not there to close us in on ourselves but rather to open us up to reality and to others, enabling us to listen to them, to understand them, to serve them and to welcome what they are thinking and living so that we can enter more fully into the mystery of life with hearts full of wonder. We never possess the truth, but we can humbly let truth possess us. We cannot manufacture truth ourselves, but we seek it and are called to welcome it humbly as a gift.

This search for truth is essential to our communities. I do not think that assistants can really become committed on a long-term basis if they do not have this thirst for truth. David Ford, regius professor of divinity at the University of Cambridge, told a L'Arche group: "You have a spirituality in L'Arche, but in order for that spirituality to deepen, it must be rooted in theology." Our communities will not be able to grow, to deepen and to break new ground in the years to come unless we have this thirst for truth which helps us advance on the path God is giving us.

In order to grow in this search, we need the help of philosophers, theologians, anthropologists, psychologists and sociologists from outside our communities. With them we will discern better the meaning of L'Arche and Faith and Light in our world today. If we recognize who we are in the vision of God, we will know what direction to take and will have the necessary vision and light for the journey.

We must all seek out people who can help us to grow in truth and thus to understand better the value and vision of L'Arche and Faith and Light. This vision is important for us as well as for our societies and our churches. In different countries much has already been accomplished in this area of formation, but there is still a lot to be done.

I would like to bring up four aspects in which we have to deepen our understanding.

1) *The integration between philosophy and the Word of God.* I had the privilege of meeting and learning from Père Thomas. He was not only my spiritual father, teaching me how to listen to the Holy Spirit and to discover the ways of God for me, but he was also a philosopher and theologian. It was he who advised me to do a thesis on Aristotle. It was hard work but I never regretted doing it. Aristotle taught me to distinguish between what is essential and what is secondary. Aristotle had a passion for everything human, a passion for reality. He wanted to be open to reality, to understand it and to learn from it. Aristotle opened my mind and taught me to marvel at truth. Truth is not just something that helps us to do things or to succeed in life. Truth is something we contemplate. And as we contemplate the beauty, harmony and intelligence inscribed in our own beings and in the universe, we grow in the contemplation of the Source of this universe. The Gospel helps us to discover that the Source became flesh in Jesus: "In the beginning was the Word, and the Word was towards God and the Word was God. He was in the beginning towards God. Everything was by him and without him there was nothing . . . And the Word became flesh and dwelt amongst us" (John 1).

Through revelation we discover the Word, Jesus, who became weak in order to become a friend of the weak and to bring them the Good News. We need to discover the truth about the Word who is hidden in the weak and in our own weakness. In his Gospel John says, "The Word came amongst his own and his own did not receive him, but to all those who received him he gave the power to become children of God." Isn't this the plight of those who are weak in our societies?

In L'Arche as in Faith and Light, we are called to discover the truths that come from the "earth" of our experience as well as those that come from "heaven," the Word of God. The light of life comes to us from these two sources. That is why it is important to recognize and put words on our experience, to clarify that experience with the help of professionals, but also to deepen our knowledge of the mystery of the Word who became poor so that our lives may be enriched.

2) *The importance of each human person and the call to grow in maturity.* We are living in a special day and age. There is so much chaos and oppression and at the same time a greater recognition, at least in theory, of the value and rights of each human being. More and more we are discovering that we belong to the same human race, that we share our common humanity. At the same time we recognize the fears and prejudices within us. How quickly we can close up in ourselves!

In our different cultures it is not always easy to discern what nourishes this closedness and what helps our growth towards inner freedom, maturity and a capacity to love each person.

Today there is a lot of talk about accepting each person just as he or she is. There is something beautiful in this attitude: a respect for others and a refusal to judge. This tolerance is often a reaction to an exaggerated form of moralism which used to accuse and judge. It can however, hide a refusal of truth, saying that everything is good, everything is possible. But that is not true. Everything is not good. Evil does exist. There are wars, genocides, drugs. The powerful oppress the weak. People are ready to do anything just to get money or power.

It is important to distinguish between morality and psychology. Morality is based on the intrinsic value of each person whatever his or her limits may be. In order to live that morality, we need to know what it means to be human, how at each stage of life each person is called to grow towards greater inner freedom and wholeness. We have to deepen our understanding of freedom, conscience and maturity. To become more fully human does not mean simply to act out of our emotions or willpower nor to blindly obey laws. It means to develop our conscience in order to choose maturity. For us it is a question of the maturity not only of assistants but of people with disabilities. It is no longer a question of "normalization" but of "personalization," to help each person become more fully him or herself, as free, as open and as happy as possible.

3) *The links between psychology and spirituality.* We need to discover how psychology differs from spirituality, but at the same time how our psychology, our character, our whole being make up the "earth" in which the seeds of the Holy Spirit are planted. Psychology and spirituality are not in opposition but complementary to each other.

4) *Deepening the links among philosophy, psychology and spirituality.* A vision of the human person is illuminated by the unfolding truth of the place of those who are weak in our churches and in our world. That obliges us to look at our own weakness in a new way. We are discovering how weakness opens up a new path in the search for unity and wholeness in ourselves, in our

communities, between our communities, between churches and in our societies.

CONCLUSION

Day after day I marvel at the life of our communities and of those who are at the heart of our communities. They are helping me to discover a new wisdom, the wisdom of the heart, and thus the wisdom of God who is heart. They are showing me a new anthropology, new ways of reading the Word of God (especially the Gospel of John) and new ways of perceiving the inequalities of our world, of responding to conflict and of exercising authority. I give thanks to God for leading me in 1950 to Père Thomas, who subsequently became my spiritual guide. I give thanks to God for inviting me in 1964 to welcome Raphaël and Philippe and begin the adventure first of L'Arche and then of Faith and Light. I give thanks for each one of you who will read this letter. We are called to continue this path together, to struggle for life and love in a broken world, to grow in truth and to marvel at the treasure God has entrusted to us.

Jean Vanier

May 1999
Orval

Dear Friends,

The meeting of the international family of L'Arche has just ended. Seven hundred of us met in Paray-le-Monial (France), a place of pilgrimage where, in the seventeenth century, Jesus revealed to a young sister that he was "heart" and that he yearns for us to welcome his love. Paray-le-Monial had been given to us for this meeting in a very providential way. I was touched, because L'Arche is a place of the heart, the seat of love, the place where we welcome others just as they are, the place where we give ourselves to them and the place where we live in the one we love.

Among the seven hundred participants were two hundred of our brothers and sisters with disabilities. They shaped this meeting and truly showed us how to be together and how to celebrate. They helped us to bring our heads and hearts closer together, to truly live from the depths of our hearts. They helped us to see the essence of our call to L'Arche: the covenant of love to which God calls us and the bonds of fidelity between us. Through our life together, God transforms our hearts from hearts of stone and fear into open, trusting and loving hearts. God teaches us to be motivated no longer by competition and power but by a desire to work with others, to welcome difference and to struggle for greater justice and peace.

Now I am resting in the monastery of Orval. I needed rest, to walk quietly in the forest, to have longer moments of prayer and more silence and solitude. When I think about the future, I reflect on our passage into the new millennium, the two-thousandth anniversary of the birth of Jesus. Our world is in such a state of chaos! There is conflict everywhere! We are told that there are about a million refugees from Kosovo. How many mothers are there, carrying in their arms a son or daughter with severe disabilities? A million refugees means that there are several thousand people with disabilities who are traumatized, living in anguish.

In the Book of Leviticus, you see how, every fifty years, God asked the people to live a time of renewal. According to Leviticus, the jubilee year was supposed to be a year of rest, so that people could give more time to what is essential. It was a time when they could reread their sacred story and reflect on the presence of God in their lives, a year of rest too for the earth, a time for people to reflect on the importance and meaning of God's gift of nature, a year of remittance of debts and of forgiveness, a year of liberation for slaves and those held captive.

How are we going to live this year in our communities and in our hearts? Perhaps we do not have any slaves to liberate or debts to remit! We could, however, take time to reread our story and the story of our communities and to reflect on our covenant with God. We could let God liberate us from the prisons of our fears, prejudices and needs for success and power. Perhaps we could try to learn how to exercise our authority in a new way, with more humility, compassion and truth. To live authority as Jesus did, washing the feet of his disciples. To live an authority that liberates and to deepen the meaning of forgiveness, in order to struggle for peace and unity right where we are. To gradually rediscover each day the meaning of our shared lives together. To be more concerned by people with disabilities who are lonely and do not have any community to belong to. They too are our people.

I am sure that each one of us personally and every one of our communities will find concrete ways of living this millennium year as a year of renewal. How good it would be if the transition into the millennium was not only a time for great excitement and festivals or a time of fear but also a time of renewal, so that our communities may be signs of life, hope and love for the world.

Time goes by so fast. I have not written a letter like this for a long time. And yet I have not been idle! I worked on the book *Becoming Human,* on a text on ecumenism called *Pilgrims Together* and on a long "Letter to my brothers and sisters in L'Arche and in Faith and Light." I hope that each one of you has received it.

In February, I went to Iraq with Widad, and I met so many people who have suffered so much. In Baghdad and Mosul I discovered the communities of Joy and Charity, which are quite similar to Faith and Light. To see the joy of people with disabilities there and the way that they can call others to unity in such an impossible situation was a confirmation for me of the deep intuition at the root of L'Arche and Faith and Light.

I am so grateful to God for our large family, for the covenant that bonds us together and calls us all to greater love, faithfulness and humility. Pray for me, let us pray for one another, that we may always be as Jesus wants.

Love,
Jean

August 1999
Orval

Dear Friends,

My stay in the Orval monastery is over. I am so grateful to the monks who have welcomed me each year for the last fifteen years. This time of silence, prayer, rest, walks in the forest and intellectual work with my two teachers and friends, Aristotle and John the Evangelist, is so good for me. It allows me to let go of all the things to be done, people to meet, telephone calls and travel, in order to listen more closely to God and to L'Arche and Faith and Light. I need this time away in order to see more clearly what I am called to be and live, and especially to delve more deeply into the essential message of the Gospel.

There is an immense gratitude in my heart to Jesus for L'Arche and Faith and Light. What a gift for me to know men and women with disabilities, to share my life with them and to become friends. Each year I realize more what a gift they are and how good it is to be with them. I want to spend the rest of my life with them, telling others about their gift, working with others so that they may be better accepted and recognized in our societies and churches, so that they may know more fully the joy they are destined for, and the joy of knowing that they are loved by God.

In July, I gave two retreats for young people aged eighteen to thirty, one in Quebec and one in Cleveland. They were welcomed by people from our L'Arche communities. In each of the retreats, even though a lot of work had been done with chaplaincies and parishes, there were only about sixty to eighty young people. Why do so few young people come to these gatherings organized by L'Arche and Faith and Light? And why are there so many young people from Eastern European countries in L'Arche and so few from our own countries? Is it because L'Arche is not known well enough? Certainly we have to work together to announce L'Arche more in schools and universities, etc. But isn't there a deeper reason?

I wonder if prenatal tests and the cultural and social attitudes towards people with disabilities increase the fear in parents of having a child that is "different"—and perhaps this fear is transmitted to their other children. Many young people are frightened of suffering, frightened of meeting and walking with people who have disabilities. It's true that there is something quite crazy in our vision: we affirm that befriending people who are weak liberates us, helps us to become more human and helps us to become closer to God! That can seem quite exaggerated, even impossible! It is countercultural and yet in our world there is such a need for the face of tenderness and compassion. We live in a world of competition, where importance is given to success, a good salary, efficiency, distractions, stimulations. Young people are often so taken up with all that is exciting that they have difficulty seeing how much our world needs to rediscover what is essential: committed relationships, openness and the acceptance of weakness, a life of friendship and solidarity in and through the little things we can do. It is not a question of doing extraordinary things, but rather of doing ordinary things with love. It is difficult for them to perceive the meaning of a shared life with people who are different. Our community life with its dailiness—work, cooking and housework, giving baths, meetings—does not seem to offer anything special. And yet, to eat around the same table and to serve the poor, is that not the vision of a blessed life according to the Gospel?

This month in the monastery has helped me to see how much I need conversion. It has allowed my deep thirst for the presence of God to rise up in me, to let God purify me from all that prevents his love from penetrating my whole being and passing through me to others. Each one of us individually and each community as a whole has to discover a certain wisdom in the way we live. How quickly we can become submerged by work, stress and fatigue and no longer find time for inner nourishment, quiet prayer, the Word of God, love of nature and art, and the development of our intelligence.

I am one of those people of the 1950s and '60s, motivated by the idealism and optimism of those years: no more wars! no more colonization! no more gaps between rich countries and poor countries! The reality of our world today, however, is that our societies continue to be places of suffering, oppression, violence, conflicts and inequalities. Through our intelligence and science, we have discovered many secrets of nature, of the atom, of new sources of energy, of the human body and of genetics. But we do not know how to orient our discoveries in order to create a world where there is more justice and an acceptance of each and every human being. We do not know how to liberate ourselves from the yoke of self-centredness which keeps us closed up in ourselves and our compulsions, how to grow more fully in openness and compassion, and how to work together for greater love and justice on this earth. We do not know how to awaken the energies of the heart which should guide our intelligence. That is one of the roles of those who are weak and in need, and thus of L'Arche and Faith and Light: they awaken hearts to love.

People sometimes ask me what my hope is for our communities. All I can say is: may we be faithful to our call! Growth in numbers is not so important. But may each community be a sign of the love of God and may weaker persons find life and give life. May the good news be announced to the poor, the captives, the oppressed, and not just through our communities, for God has called forth other spiritual families who have the same goals and with whom we can collaborate.

Just before leaving here this morning, my heart is full of thanksgiving for each one of you and for our two families. They are alive and well thanks to you: you who carry responsibility, you who carry the stress of daily life, you who are in pain, you who have just arrived in the community and you who support our communities through your presence, friendship, prayer and offering. It is good to be together, helping each other so that we can all be more fully alive and more faithful.

I remain close to each one of you.

Jean

January 2000
Trosly

Dear Friends,

The new millennium has come! We are in it and I hope are moving ahead towards the future with peaceful hearts, listening attentively to the message of the present moment. The passage into the new millennium was marked by storms and natural disasters. And the last decade has been marked by wars in Chechnya, East Timor, the Balkans, Rwanda, Burundi and many other countries. Then there have been all the natural catastrophes. And what will tomorrow bring? It is clear that in spite of all our technological discoveries, we human beings are not in control of everything; we are not the masters of the future or of the world.

The second millennium was a time of great divisions and wars, between churches and between religions. It was a time of the discovery of new civilizations, the development of colonialism and the horrible race for more and more sophisticated and destructive armaments. Our humanity is fragmented into multiple linguistic, religious, ethnic, cultural and social groups, more or less in conflict with one another. My prayer and my hope are that this new millennium will be a time of *reconciliation,* that individual persons and groups will open up to each other and work together for peace. That means that each one of us, wherever we are, has to learn to recognize that in spite of our differences and our difficulties in relationships, we are all part of the same family, the same common humanity. In spite of all the dangers and terrible events that are happening, in spite of all the hatred and conflicts, a new hope is coming to birth. A new maturity is being born in humanity.

Throughout the world there is a universal recognition that each and every man, woman and child is important, sacred and has rights. The Universal Declaration of Human Rights which all the countries of the world accepted in 1948 is of vital importance. The search for unity amongst Christians of different churches and the dialogue between men and women of diverse religions are tremendous steps forward. Through the mass media and the ethnic and cultural pluralism of our cities, a new sense of the human family is being born. In this pluralistic world there is, of course, the danger of chaos and of abandoning the customs and laws that were the cement of our societies. But these laws and customs can create a certain elitism by giving an image of strength and security. People are tempted to close themselves off in their own groups, ignoring or even rejecting others. I am convinced that we are all called today to strengthen our inner selves and to deepen our human and religious faith, in order to be open to those who are different, to grasp their beauty, and to respect and love them without losing our own faith or our centre. I am also convinced that in our richer societies, where so many people feel alone and cut off, it is vital to have places of belonging, communities where those who are strong and those who are weak come together and are committed to each other. Together we will find new ways of working for peace, justice and truth.

My dream for L'Arche and for Faith and Light is that our communities may be signs of love and reconciliation; signs of the beauty of each human being; signs that people who are different can live together; signs that difference can be a treasure and not a threat; signs that God is truly present at the heart of our lives, of our communities and of our societies; signs of the importance and value of those who are weak and of their secret power to open hearts and to call people to unity; in short, signs of true hope.

This can only happen under two conditions: that we put our trust in God and give ourselves to God, and that each one of us becomes more humble and loving, not seeking to be more clever than others or above them. Instead we must seek to follow the call of Paul: "Do nothing from selfishness or conceit, but in humility count others better than yourselves. Let each of you look not only to his/her own interests, but also to the interests of others . . . You should seek among yourselves to accomplish what Jesus himself did . . . who emptied himself taking the form of a servant . . . and he humbled himself even more" (Phil. 2:3–8).

If we live together in that trust and humility, our communities will be open, welcoming, a source of life for those around us and for our churches. They will be places of hope. I know quite well the weaknesses and difficulties of our communities and the pain that each person is carrying. I know the particular difficulties that arise when we live together with Christians from different churches and with people from different religious traditions. I sense that this year Jesus is going to give inner gifts to each one of us and to our communities. More people will become committed and there will be visible signs of holiness and maturity in each one. I rejoice in that. May we keep our hearts open to receive these gifts of God. Let us walk together into this new millennium without being engulfed by fear of crises, catastrophes or difficulties. Strength will be given each day. The poor and the weak at the heart of our communities will show us the way towards new horizons. Happy, holy new year. Let us remain in communion with one another.

Jean

May 8, 2000, Pentecost
Bethany (West Bank)

Dear Friends,

Today is the last day of our pilgrimage-retreat in the Holy Land. We are a group of about thirty long-term L'Arche assistants, plus Cecile and Pascale, two people welcomed in Le Caillou Blanc (a L'Arche community in Brittany), Odile's uncle, Father Ceyrac, who is eighty-six years old (sixty-three of which were spent in India), and Zenia from the Ukraine. It is a retreat where we prayed for all of L'Arche and Faith and Light. It is also a time for renewed contact with the political, economic and religious situation in this part of the world where, in the midst of much suffering and oppression, the Palestinian people continue to struggle for their survival and their identity. Israel and Palestine are places of great pain but also of great grace. Today, just as during Jesus's lifetime, the struggle goes on between those who have power and weapons, and those who are weak, crushed and unable to defend themselves.

This is the first time I have been back here since the closure of our community in Bethany during the Gulf War. This closure left a deep wound in the heart of L'Arche. For three years now Kathy Baroody has been living near Bethlehem, where she has opened a workshop for eight people. She makes regular visits to our brothers and sisters who have gone back to the Malja, an institution for people with mental and physical disabilities. Yesterday we had lunch with those who were in L'Arche–Bethany ten years ago. A reunion, full of emotion!

This land where Jesus lived and walked is beautiful and full of history. We visited the site of what I call the "asylum" of Jerusalem, where there was a pool and John (ch. 5) tells us "there were crowds of sick people, blind, lame, paralysed." Jesus healed a man who had been lying there for thirty-eight years. It is such a rich experience to pray the Gospels in this land. The message of Jesus through John's Gospel takes on new meaning when we are in the places where the events actually took place. But what is most important for me is to see the places where Jesus is present today, like in the Malja, where many sick people, blind, lame, paralyzed, are living today. Our visit to the Malja was a sign and a reminder of our vocation. Each one's face, each one's thirst for friendship and each one's tears renewed our desire to be faithful to our vocation and to our people wherever we are living.

I leave here with a deeper certitude that the Gospel and life meet each other. The message of Jesus is neither a dream nor an ideology, but a call to become more committed to the struggle for life and for justice, to share the good news that each person, whatever his or her limits, religion or culture may be, is important and loved by God. It is a call to create community with the downtrodden, those who are crushed by competition and the search for power at all costs.

A privileged moment was our meeting with a Jewish man who opened up new doors of hope for us. He told us about the visit of John Paul II to the Holy Land and how he touched the hearts of so many Jewish people. People recognized in this elderly, tired man, filled with peace and kindness, a man of God who knows how to ask for forgiveness and to find gestures of peace and reconciliation. After the Pope's visit, one of Israel's main newspapers wrote: "When are we Jewish people going to ask the Palestinians and Lebanese for forgiveness?" Our Jewish friend told us that many men and women today in Israel are beginning to question the policies of their government and the violence and distress they have caused over the last fifty years. The Pope's asking forgiveness should encourage us all to look at how each one of us, each one of our churches, each one of our religions, each one of our communities, could ask forgiveness for the way we have hurt others. In the name of God, of justice and of righteousness we have rejected and pushed others down. The history of colonization and war shows what we have done to our brothers and sisters throughout the world. Can this millennium become the millennium of reconciliation?

Our communities are called to be witnesses of the value and richness of community life in the midst of a more and more individualistic society. That is our challenge: to be places of belonging, with all the symbols, celebrations, relationships and meetings that are implied, and at the same time to be integrated into the local area and to help each person to become more mature and more free. In poorer countries, community life is nothing extraordinary; everyone is living it. What is new is that our communities are with people with disabilities as well as with people coming from different cultures, backgrounds, races and religions. This shared life with the weak can be lived only if each one of us chooses to give his or her heart to God and to let the Holy Spirit fill and guide our hearts and our lives. Happy, holy feast of Pentecost to each one!

Jean

September 2000
Trosly

Dear Friends,

I have just returned from Cuba, Mexico and Nicaragua. It was good to travel with Nadine, who has lived in L'Arche in Honduras for so many years. My heart has been rent from what I have seen. So many wonderful people in Cuba are so curtailed and constrained by a terrible lack of freedom, a lack of basic goods and of opportunity, and an incapacity to take initiative. In Nicaragua, following years of Somoza's tyrannical rule, the Sandinista period of utopia, the war and the corruption, people are in a state of despondency. Where to go? Whom to turn to? In order to survive each one has to fend for him or herself. I saw how people become attached to power and want to keep it at all costs and thus prevent the growth and freedom of others. Isn't this a question for each one of us to look at? In Mexico I was distressed by the flagrant luxury on one side—flashing lights, expensive restaurants and nightclubs—and on the other, the tremendous poverty of the vast number of people. I felt sick visiting overcrowded, death-like institutions for people with disabilities where the helpers, nurses and people in administration were so discouraged. I witnessed the overwhelming power of egotism, wealth, individualism and materialism in all its forms. And the churches seem to have lost their prophetic role and ability to speak out. They are no longer seen as the home to the "good thief," to Mary of Magdala caught up in prostitution, to the weak and the broken. No, too often the churches appear to be more a refuge for the comfortable and the morally right than for the discouraged and those in pain. Where is hope? Where is Jesus?

Time and time again my heart comes back to the Gospel of Luke (ch. 10), where Jesus responds to the question "Who is my neighbour?" and so shows us what it means to love our neighbour. He tells the story of a Jewish man attacked by bandits between

Jerusalem and Jericho, beaten and left lying on the road. Two men with important functions in Jewish society pass by, without stopping. They are frightened. Of what? Of getting their hands dirty? Of being late for an appointment? Of not knowing what to do? Of losing their status? They do not feel that this wounded man is *their* problem, but instead seem to ask the wrong question: what will happen to *me* if I stop? Then a man from Samaria passes by. The Samaritans were oppressed by the Jewish people at that time. When this Samaritan sees the man on the ground, he is moved by compassion; he stops and takes care of him. He does not say, "It is not my problem" or, "This man is my enemy, let him die!" His first concern is not where this man comes from or what is his culture or religion; he sees him foremost as *a brother in humanity*. And the "Good Samaritan" dresses the man's wounds and takes him to the local inn. He stays with him for the night, pays the innkeeper and asks him to continue to take care of the wounded man, promising to pay for any other expenses incurred.

Three things touch me in this example of the love of our neighbour:

1) The Samaritan's love is *excessive*. There are no limits. He does not calculate. He does not do just what is necessary or according to justice, but much more. He spends the night with the wounded man and commits himself to pay for his care.
2) He bridges the gap between the Jewish and the Samaritan peoples. The oppressor or enemy becomes the friend. Our neighbour is not just the members of our own community or those living and working close to us, those who are like us or with whom we feel a certain affinity. Jesus reveals here that our neighbour is the one we encounter on our path, the person in need. The man from Samaria breaks through the barriers of his own culture, religion and ethnic group, barriers that protect him and make him feel that his group is right, the best, the only one blessed

by God. He does not do this in order to convert the other to his religion, but out of love and compassion, trusting that *such love reveals the true face of God* and so calls each person to what is deepest within them.

3) By breaking out from behind his cultural barriers, the Good Samaritan dares to walk the path of insecurity. What if other Jewish people see him put this man on his donkey? They might accuse him of being the one who beat him up! What if other Samaritans see him? They might accuse him of collaborating with the enemy, of being a traitor. When we accompany broken people, no set rules and regulations protect us. We are alone in front of a person in pain. All we have is our goodwill, our love, our limited skills, ourselves. We do not know where it will lead, for to love is to risk.

Yet in this story there are two things of which I am sure:

1) By daring to act out of love and compassion, the Samaritan becomes both poorer and richer. Poorer because he senses he is alone, insecure, even maybe a bit frightened, feeling unprotected. He becomes more vulnerable. This gives him a greater awareness of his need for the help and presence of God. As soon as we enter into relationship with the poor and the weak, we feel the need for that inner strength that comes from God.

2) Both the Samaritan and the Jewish man must have been changed by this experience. Imagine the wounded man opening his eyes and discovering that be has been saved by a man belonging to the group he had despised. Perhaps with tears in his eyes he might say, "Thank you!" Never again would he despise a Samaritan. A covenant is born between these two, a covenant of understanding, love and friendship that draws both out from behind their cultural and religious barriers. Something irreversible has happened. Their prejudices have fallen. They have discovered

the presence of God in each other. Whilst they may feel isolated from and rejected by their respective groups, they become a sign of peace and unity.

I would so want to be in a world where the signs of hope are flourishing, but I am not encouraged by all the strong, closed religious groups. And I do not have a sense that everything is advancing towards a world of peace and unity. No, I receive my strength today from the men and women I encounter who, whilst being rooted in their own cultures and religious traditions, have open hearts. Men and women of compassion who can reach out to the weak and broken from many backgrounds, listening to them and learning from them, accompanying them towards the "local inn," gently, humbly washing their wounds, seeing in them a brother or sister in humanity. These gestures of love give me strength and hope. This compassion flows from the compassion of Jesus, which is nurtured in prayer.

I felt distressed when I visited the institutions, but I rejoiced in the men and women who were present to broken people, touching them with loving kindness. I felt angry when I saw the luxury and corruption in each country, but I rejoiced in the shared life of our two L'Arche communities in Mexico, which have welcomed people from the streets or from an institution. I rejoiced in the singing, dancing and dynamism of the Faith and Light communities in Mexico. I rejoiced in the commitment of the assistants, friends and board members who risk to believe in L'Arche and in Faith and Light. I rejoiced in so many others I met who want to be as the Good Samaritan and so be a sign of hope. So too the gathering of two million young people in Rome last August was a source of joy for my heart and a sign of hope for the world.

How do we grow in the love of the Good Samaritan? All I know is that I cannot do it alone. I am too weak and poor. I give thanks for my brothers and sisters in L'Arche, for all that we have witnessed and lived together during this past year. I give thanks for the time of silence and prayer in the monastery this August. I need my brothers and sisters in community to give me strength and to love, encourage and help me to grow in love. I need a community that leads me into the living waters of prayer and brings me to greater inner freedom, a community that helps me to know and love Jesus and which, through its very way of life, can be a witness of hope in our broken world. "They will know that you are my disciples," says Jesus, "by the love you have for one another" (John 13:35).

Jean Vanier

January 2001
Trosly

Dear Friends,

I remember Christmas Eve when I was a child. We used to sit around Dad, who would tell us a Christmas story, always the same one! But each year we would listen to him with just as much excitement and enthusiasm, even though we knew it by heart. It was as if he was announcing something new and wonderful, a door that was opening up into a big celebration, the celebration of love, of gifts. Christmas is the celebration of Jesus, of the family. L'Arche and Faith and Light are a family.

This year as every year, we celebrated midnight Mass (even though it wasn't quite at midnight!) with the parish. "Joyeux Noël! Merry Christmas!" could be heard all around. Then we went back to our different houses for a hot chocolate or some hot wine. The next day, Christmas dinner with turkey, the choice of Bordeaux or Coke, and Christmas pudding flambé au cognac. Just before the meal we exchanged presents. I received a book by Cardinal Martini on the Gospel of John. You know my passion for that Gospel! On Christmas night, those who could came to Le Val to relive the story of the Nativity and to reflect on what it means for us today. At one moment, we shared in little groups about our own story, the birth of the love of Jesus in our own lives, our personal Christmas. It is so important to take time to reread our story and to share it with others and thus to bear witness to Jesus in our lives.

The next day, we left on holidays . . . the celebration continued. No work for a week! I went to a retreat centre, the Foyer de Charité, to animate a retreat for some two hundred young people which had been prepared by the Foyer together with Bertrand Figarol and a few people in L'Arche. It was again a celebration: a celebration of the Word, a celebration of the Eucharist, a celebration of being together and sharing our lives as pilgrims in search of hope. These retreats have given me great joy over these last few years. So many young people are thirsting for truth, for words of life that are deeply human but which help discover the Gospel, the Word who becomes flesh and dwells amongst us.

I like to speak about the challenge of L'Arche, a challenge to "remain," to put roots down, to be faithful to relationships, to love and serve doing little things of life. This is not very acceptable language today, when many people are constantly looking for what is new, exciting, a change. To remain is to be a sign of faithfulness. That is what weaker people are yearning for: friendships that last and deepen and allow us to live and do things together. During the retreat a young man who is in L'Arche came to see me. "I am a bit bored in my L'Arche home," he said. "Life is too easy. Every day it is the same thing. It's an older community and everyone seems quite peaceful and mature." I can understand. At his age I too wanted to struggle with reality, overcome difficulties and learn new things. I wanted challenges where I could prove that I could hold my own ground. I suggested that he speak with the regional leader to see if he couldn't participate in the founding of a new community and welcome people from institutions who are in difficulty and who need someone like him with a lot of energy. Then I told him that there is also the challenge of being faithful, of putting roots down and of staying with it. Sooner or later he himself will be called to live that challenge.

This is the challenge many of our communities are living today. To live the daily life of our houses or workshops, meal after meal, day after day, year after year. To weave deep relationships. To journey in the covenant. To say yes to the bonding of our lives together. To be a sign of love and faithfulness. To do little things: housework, cooking, working in a workshop, giving baths, attending meetings, accompanying people who are growing old. All that does not seem very exciting or grandiose, but it is deeply human and it is the Gospel message.

Christmas is the celebration of the Word who becomes flesh to live with us. Emmanuel, God-with-us. To live daily life together in a world where individualism and self-sufficiency are becoming absolutes, where it seems so difficult for man and woman to live together in faithfulness, where relationships are unstable and in constant movement, where there is the tendency of each to his or her own thing, L'Arche and Faith and Light have a message to give: we are made to live and be together. It is true that within our communities there are also conflicts and difficulties in relationships. But to be human is to learn how to walk through the difficulties, accepting the wounds and the fragilities, living forgiveness and the love Paul describes: "Love is always patient and kind; love is never jealous, love is not boastful or conceited; it is never rude and never seeks its own advantage; it does not take offence or store up grievances. Love does not rejoice in wrongdoing, but finds its joy in truth. It is always ready to make allowances, to trust, to hope and to endure whatever comes" (1 Cor. 13:4–7).

To love is to let down the barriers that separate us from one another. It is to welcome others just as they are, with their differences, their gifts and their weaknesses. It is to give and receive life. It is to accept being part of a community of brothers and sisters where each one is different. It is to forgive 7 x 77 times. It is to grow in a covenant. To love is to give freely of ourselves and of our time to others because "there is no greater love than to give one's life for those we love," as Jesus says. To love, especially to love those who are most disturbing, we need a gift of God, a gift of the Holy Spirit, who transforms our hearts of stone into hearts of flesh. It is the Holy Spirit who gives us the strength to love each day and to do all the little gestures of daily life with kindness, to welcome with joy and thanksgiving each person and each event that is given to us.

Our community life with all its littleness and difficulties is a place of the presence of God. There is a contemplative aspect to our lives: to live each moment with Jesus. Isn't that the message of Christmas, of the Word that becomes flesh in Jesus so that Jesus becomes flesh in us to teach us each day how to love a little bit more? Through our love we are called to be a sign that love is stronger than hate, unity stronger than all the divisions: "Beloved, let us love one another, for Love comes from God and whoever loves is born from God and knows God" (1 John 4:7).

I am always touched to receive so many greeting cards, so many signs of communion in love. I give thanks to each one of you. In this new year may we all grow in communion and in fidelity.

Jean

June 20, 2001
Trosly

Dear Friends,

In these last six months I have had the privilege of meeting several members of our communities during retreats and visits, especially in India, the United States, western Canada, Ireland and France. I have witnessed the tenderness and gentleness in relationships between people in our communities. Tenderness could describe our life in L'Arche and in Faith and Light. They are schools of tenderness. Tenderness implies a deep desire to avoid hurting or harming a weak person. Tenderness is humble; it is an attentiveness, a listening to what people are saying and above all to what their whole bodies are expressing, for people who are weak and poor often express themselves more through their bodies: their gestures, their eyes, their cries. Tenderness or gentleness also implies touch: a way of touching another with respect and in truth, a touch that helps the person realize that she is loved and appreciated, a touch that gives support and security. It is different from a possessive touch that tends to depreciate another, preventing his growth to freedom. Tenderness is the opposite of aggressiveness in words or gestures. Tenderness implies an inner strength which allows us to love others in truth. Tenderness does not mean simply "being nice," which can be a way of hiding our fear of conflict; it means being truthful in all things. Tenderness teaches us to be true.

In Trosly in 1978, we welcomed Françoise Lebond in La Forestière. Françoise is now seventy years old. She is blind, unable to speak and has been bedridden for years, without much awareness of what is going on around her. Each time I go to La Forestière, I am amazed to see how she is accompanied in her daily needs by the assistants, their goodness, their gentleness, their care, the way they talk to her, nourish her. And what I see for Françoise I see around each person welcomed in our houses everywhere.

A few weeks ago with L'Arche–Cuise we lived the death of Thaddée Proffit. Thaddée, who had a profound handicap, was a member of the foyer La Semence; he was a real "master," a teacher of tenderness. His presence called forth tenderness in us and communicated it to us. His language—without any words—was a language of tenderness and gentleness. That doesn't mean that at times he did not have another language, the language of fear, anger, anguish and even violence, which hid his thirst for tenderness. With his brother Loïc at La Forestière, who also has a profound handicap, Thaddée was at the origin of Faith and Light. In 1965, Camille and Gerard, their parents, brought them to Lourdes, but they were not accepted in any hotel because of their children's handicap. Only one hotel said yes, as long as they had all their meals in their bedroom. Camille and Gerard shared their pain with Marie-Hélène Mathieu, who spoke to me about their rejection. So it is because of the pain and suffering of Thaddée, Loïc, Camille and Gerard that, with Marie-Hélène and a few parents, we organized an international pilgrimage to Lourdes at Easter 1971 for people with learning disabilities, their parents and friends. From that pilgrimage, Faith and Light was born.

This Easter we celebrated the thirtieth anniversary of Faith and Light with the fourth international pilgrimage to Lourdes. There were 16,500 pilgrims from seventy-three countries, including 6,000 people with disabilities. It was a tremendous gathering and celebration of "weakness," of people who have known great pain and those who wish to share their lives with them. It was a pilgrimage of tenderness which called forth the tenderness and mercy of God on us all. Thaddée and Loïc were in Lourdes together for the first time since their rejection some thirty-five years ago.

In contrast to this world of tenderness or gentleness exists the world of cruelty, where people refuse to welcome others, where there is a lack of consideration and kindness towards others. I recently read the book *Sorrow Mountain,* written by a Buddhist nun who was imprisoned by the Chinese army in Tibet for twenty-one years and liberated only after the death of Mao Zedong. She describes how she was tortured, hung by her wrists and put into a dungeon for nine months. In the complete darkness of the dungeon, the only way she knew that it was daytime was by hearing the birds sing outside. But the Chinese military were not able to crush her spirit of truth nor her love for her people and for her religious tradition. She resisted despite extreme weakness. While in the dungeon, so as not to break down or give in, she prostrated herself on the floor a hundred thousand times before the "God of Compassion." The story of this Buddhist nun, Ani Pachen, who finally escaped into Nepal and then to India to join the Dalai Lama, has given me a deep love and respect for her. She is one of these people full of faith, life and determination who do not let themselves be overwhelmed by the forces of evil and hatred and who do not give in to their desire for comfort.

I am touched by all those who resist the temptation to despair, who do not give up, just as I am moved when I meet people who exercise authority, who carry responsibilities, but who remain open and always find time to listen to those who are weak, those who come from different backgrounds. How easy it is to crush those who are weak, with few defence mechanisms, and who are different from us.

I am also touched by those who continue to believe in our life in L'Arche and Faith and Light, in spite of all the obstacles and difficulties. Our communities are so fragile because of our shortage of assistants, fragile also because of our attitudes that show so little respect, kindness and gentleness towards one another in community, especially between assistants, between younger and older assistants, or with board members, parents or neighbours. We can be so harsh with one another out of a need to "get things done"; how easily we forget the need to be kind and gentle as we welcome one another. How quickly, in the name of efficiency and productivity, we can crush those who are in a situation of weakness. I see in myself how I try to protect myself and close up in front of those who bother me, especially when I am tired. Their weakness brings up my anguish. How to remain open to the gentleness and love of God for each person and for each community? I feel my own need to be healed or "saved"; I need to receive the strength of God which was so clearly present in Ani Pachen.

Tenderness makes me gentle and open to others, not judging them but trying to help them to grow. Tenderness helps me to believe that I myself, as well as others around me, can grow and change in spite of appearances, that the child of God in each one of us can rise up. I too need to discover more each day the real tenderness and gentleness that give meaning to life. I need to trust more fully in the power of the Spirit of God in me. I call on the Holy Spirit unceasingly, asking that my heart of stone be changed into a heart of flesh. Our communities will not continue to grow and deepen unless each one of us is growing in this tenderness and gentleness that comes from God: "But you, O Lord, are a God of tenderness and mercy, slow to anger and abounding in steadfast love and faithfulness, turn to me and be gracious to me" (Psalm 85:15).

I remain close to each one of you.

Jean Vanier

PART FIVE
2001 ❦ 2007

ONE DAY IN SEPTEMBER:
AN URGENT CALL
TO NURTURE PEACE

The more L'Arche grew and the more I travelled, the more I came to see and feel not just poverty in all its forms, but also the pain of the divisions and separations among Christians and then between Christians and other religions.

L'Arche was founded in the Catholic tradition, and the Church has been the womb in which L'Arche was conceived and from which it was born. It took time for me and for L'Arche to recognize the gift of ecumenism, to take stock of what was being given and to adapt accordingly. Père Thomas, with whom I started L'Arche, was probably much more "at the roots" of the Gospel message than I was, but he also wanted L'Arche to be more traditionally Catholic. He was radical in his incredible openness to people, but he was always hoping to convert them. Little by little we discovered that to live the gift of ecumenism did not mean simply inviting Anglicans and Protestants to our Catholic Masses and celebrations but instead giving them more space to live, celebrate and nourish their own traditions—the Catholic faith at L'Arche has become just one tradition amongst others. And so it was when we moved to non-Christian countries.

There are divisions among Christians—for example, I'm deeply moved today by the way in which Archbishop Rowan Williams is struggling to maintain unity in the Anglican Communion with such wisdom and prayerfulness—but at least we are all united by a fundamental belief in Jesus, in baptism and in the cross. Finding unity with people of different religions is even more difficult: the walls between religions are greater than the walls between churches. Yet we all belong to a common humanity; we are brothers and sisters, born in the image of God, made to know and love God. And so it is obvious that when we welcome a man like Gurunathan, who had been rejected and badly treated for his disabilities, into one of our Indian communities in order to help him grow and find peace, we welcome also his icon of Ganesh, the Hindu god of beginnings, obstacles, of intellect and wisdom. With me and with L'Arche there had to be a renunciation of ideology and an embrace of practicality: what is important to Gurunathan is for him to find out who he is and for us to help him grow more fully as a human person. It's the same when we welcome Muslims and help them attend their local mosque.

Opening doors to other religions involves listening to people and being attentive to their values and their needs. And although there has been a history in the Catholic Church of closing doors, there is also a whole tradition of saints opening doors, and of great, great people—like Mother Teresa and John Paul II—making peace. And of course there are people of other faiths who strive to open doors. Mahatma Gandhi, one of the greatest prophets of the last century, was a man sent by God, a defender of the poorest and the weakest—the "untouchables"—in whom he saw the presence of God. This was a man with a vision of liberation through love, wisdom and nonviolence; a man who prayed deeply and who said he could do nothing without the strength that comes from prayer; a man who sought to bring men and women of different religions together in peace; a man who encouraged life in community and manual work; a man of God and a man of peace. And I think too of Abdul Ghaffar Khan, a Pashtun political and spiritual leader from what is now Afghanistan, who was a great ally of Gandhi's. He created an "army of peace," and the first vow his followers had to make was to respond to cruelty with forgiveness. He didn't want Afghanistan to choose sides between Hindu India and Muslim Pakistan, but to be open to all religions. For this, he was imprisoned repeatedly by the British and later by the Pakistanis. Throughout his life, he never lost faith in his nonviolent methods or in the compatibility of Islam and nonviolence.

I speak of Francis of Assisi in some of the letters, and talk of his incredible meeting with the sultan. In 1219 Francis left with a companion on a pilgrimage of nonviolence to Egypt. When he came to Damietta, not far from Cairo, he crossed the frontlines between Christian crusaders and the soldiers of Sultan Melek-el-Kamel, and was captured. He went to the sultan in poverty, in bare feet, and spent two weeks with him, sharing together, talking and listening and being attentive to each other. Francis was a peacemaker, and many in our own time have followed his path: Charles de Foucauld, who went to live among the Tuareg of North Africa; Little Sister Magdeleine; Pierre Claverie, the Bishop of Oran, whose vision of meeting with Islam was incredible but who was assassinated by extremists in 1996; Brother Roger Schutz who brought to birth the ecumenical community of reconciliation in Taizé, France; and Christian de Chergé.

Christian de Chergé was a Trappist monk in Algeria who, despite the rise of Islamic extremists in the country in the 1990s, refused to return to France. Years earlier he had become friends with an Algerian field-guard named Mohammed. One day Mohammed said to him: "It's a long time since we dug our well together," to which Christian replied, "And what do we find at the bottom of the well, Christian water or Muslim water?" Mohammed replied, "Really, after all the time we have been travelling together, you don't know? What we find is the water of God." Before Christian became a monk, a Muslim had come to his rescue during an altercation in the street. The next day this Muslim was found assassinated by his own people. He became fundamental to Christian's understanding of inter-religious dialogue, and when Christian himself was assassinated in 1996, he left behind a testament foreseeing and forgiving his own murderer.

Today we live with new wars in Afghanistan and Iraq, and post-9/11 fear and division between Western and Muslim countries, so it is particularly important to live Francis of Assisi's example. I mention in one of the later letters my time in Assisi, where we celebrated the twentieth anniversary of the first inter-religious meeting organized by John Paul II. That was and is a radical movement. It showed incredible, audacious innovation to bring together Christians, Hindus, Muslims, Jews, Native Americans, everyone. Innovation you can't even imagine—and John Paul did it at Assisi and not at Rome!

In the L'Arche charter we say that each community should identify itself as linked to a particular faith or as ecumenical or inter-religious. Each community must determine the vision in which it will ground itself. In our homes people of different faiths have discovered a place which is profoundly human, a place where all are encouraged to deepen and live their own faith and where everyone can grow to greater love. Whatever our religion we can be transformed in and through relationships with those who are weak; they bring unity and peace to our communities. It's much the same for all those at L'Arche who are secular, who come without faith, but then discover here that they believe in life, they believe in growth, they believe in people—their time in the community becomes a discovery of belief. And sometimes that spiritual belief becomes a religious belief, particularly when the religion centres on loving people, being more open, having respect for one another, and so on.

As intuition and signs of the Spirit moved L'Arche into different countries and we came to understand more and more the power of the disabled to transform our world, we had to live openness and communion more broadly. Recognizing, facilitating and welcoming other faith traditions allowed us to discover and create communities of peace and unity. It was a lesson we learned over time, as you see in the letters.

Today's L'Arche Federation of 131 communities in thirty-four countries didn't arise by avoiding painful questions of faith behind quiet, polite tolerance. It couldn't have grown behind walls of religious protectionism, and it wouldn't have flourished in a cocktail of faiths or syncretism. It could only have grown as it did: through openness, respect, trust in what is just and right, the naïveté to make mistakes, love and "touching the roots," with each of us going deeper to find the essential in his or her own faith. We in L'Arche have come a long way, but we still have a long way to go.

September 14, 2001
Trosly

Dear Friends,

We are all in a state of shock after the attack in the United States. It reveals once again the terrible vulnerability of our world and of each of our lives. Many of us are living in countries where we have felt secure. Suddenly our security and our vision of life have been shaken. Having heard from friends and many of our communities I realize how hurt we all are and how fearful we are for the future. Some of us are more deeply hurt because members of our family or friends are missing or have been killed. It seems like the world will not be the same.

I feel close to those who are in terrible pain. At the same time I sense how important it is for all of us to remain deeply centred in our love for God and in our trust in God's love for us. Yes, we are called to stand up in our hope. I give thanks for all those courageous people who came to the rescue of others in extreme difficulty, many of whom were killed in doing so.

Our world seems to be going mad. There are some winners in the realm of money, power and success. There are many more losers and even more victims of injustice throughout the world. I also think of those in many places in Africa, Asia, Latin America and the Middle East who have been living for such a long time in extreme poverty, violence, conflict, civil wars, refugee camps or oppression. We are being joined together in the insecurity of our times but also in our hope.

Yes, our hope is in God. Our hope is in our love for one another. Our hope is in our friendship with those who are weak or in need. Let us not succumb to panic, to revolt or to vengeance, but live in faith. We have all been called by God to be witnesses of love. There is a danger of an eruption of new forms of racism and divisions. Let us all hold hands with all those in pain, grief and fear throughout the world. Let us be "oned" in prayer. Let us remember that each and every gesture of kindness and tenderness, done in humility and with trust, brings unity to the world and breaks the chain of violence.

You know my love for the Gospel of John, which tells us not only about the life and message of Jesus but also reveals a spiritual, mystical way of transformation in God and in love. This is necessarily a way of compassion and proximity to the weak and the poor, for God is the God of compassion. I have just finished a television series of twenty-five half-hour talks on the Gospel of John that will be shown on Canadian television as of January 2002.* It has been an enormous privilege for me to speak of Jesus through the eyes and heart of John.

Let us remain together in our hope and our commitment to one another and to peace.

Jean Vanier

P.S. I would like to thank all those who sent me their prayers and affection for my birthday. Some have asked how old I am now . . . seventy-three! And I rejoice in getting older, a bit more vulnerable and thus called to be more open and trusting in God. I give thanks to Jesus for all he is doing in L'Arche and Faith and Light, which are called to bring a bit of light and love to our world. And I give thanks for each one of you. It is good to be bonded together in love.

---

*This documentary was called *Knowing Eternity: In Conversation with Jean Vanier* and was produced by Norflicks Productions. It is available through L'Arche–Daybreak. Another documentary, *Images of Hope*, was made ten years earlier by the same company. It was shot at Trosly.

December 2001
Trosly

Dear Friends,

> Therefore the Lord himself will give you a sign. Behold a young girl
> will conceive and bear a son and shall call him Emmanuel, God-
> with-us. He shall not eat the cream of milk and honey. He shall
> refuse what is evil and choose what is good. (Isa. 7:14–15)

Thank you for the many messages of love and communion. I
want to wish you the peace and joy of Christmas. At the same
time, never before have I been so aware of the pain and brokenness in our societies: the conflict between Israel and Palestine, the
pain of September 11, the war in Afghanistan, the dire poverty,
injustices and inequalities everywhere. Never before have I been so
conscious of my own failings, inadequacies and brokenness. And
never before have I been so grateful to Jesus for L'Arche and Faith
and Light as little signs of love in the world.

Over the past few months I have given a number of retreats and
talks. I always share about how those who are weak and fragile
can heal us of our prejudices and need for power and recognition,
leading us on the road of peace. They do not seek power but cry
out for understanding and friendship. Their cry for friendship is
like a warm paste that bonds us together. Their very weakness, the
weakness of us all, is like a call for community. People are thirsting for such a message which can give them hope and life. The
world is sick with rivalry, misunderstandings, the search for power
and elitism. Let me quote from *Expecting Adam* by Martha Beck:
"This is the story of two Harvard driven academics who found out
in midpregnancy that their unborn son would be retarded. They
decided to allow their baby to be born. What they did not realize is

that they themselves were the ones who would be 'born,' infants in a new world where Harvard professors are the slow learners and retarded babies are the master teachers."

Our communities are built on tenderness, goodness and respect for each person, especially the weakest, and are a sign of hope for the world. Yet our communities are sometimes harmed in richer countries by more and more stringent rules and regulations. Lawmakers and local authorities can be frightened of communities because they are frightened of cults, of people being brainwashed. Yet we all need community, a place of belonging, a place where we can celebrate and be committed to each other, a place where we learn to accept ourselves as we are and to forgive. Our societies, inspired by a strong sense of individualism, are fearful of commitment. That is why family life, marriage and community life are in difficulty today. Many of our communities are in difficulty, lacking funding and committed assistants. Some people living in L'Arche are even wondering whether a lifelong commitment to L'Arche is possible, whether it can be a vocation for them, whether there will be a place for them when they grow older.

Our world is going through a period of deep insecurity. It is not surprising that this insecurity penetrates also into our family and community life. Christmas reminds us that God so loved the world that God sent his beloved Son into the world, to heal us, save us and give us the security that comes from God's love and from our mutual love. Then we discover the importance of doing little things with gentleness and forgiveness and so create community. One of the great dangers of our world is division, which comes from rivalry, a need to prove that we are better than others, the refusal to see and accept the violence in our own hearts. All this turns into conflict, hate and war. We are all called to become men and women of peace and of forgiveness in order to build communities where we trust one another. Isn't there the danger also for our communities and for each of us of losing our vision because of our busyness and because of the powerful forces which want to institutionalize us, which are suspicious of any sense of belonging, which proclaim that the gift of self and love are impossible and which make us insecure?

Today more than ever before we need trust: trust in God and trust in the quiet, gentle power of the weak. In so many ways the world has lost its meaning. Many do not know where they are heading. The weak are being hurt and rejected. As I grow older, my love for those who are weak grows and deepens. I have found my harbour with them in L'Arche. My joy will be to die and be buried here where I have lived now for thirty-seven years. At Le Val, where I have been living for the past twenty years (I was in the first house of L'Arche for sixteen years, then in La Forestière for my sabbatical year), I am grateful for the way I am loved and helped by each one in the house. Even if I do not sleep in Le Val, I have most of my meals there, relax there after meals and pray there each evening. We celebrate together, and sometimes talk about serious matters together. Tonight, the Saturday before Christmas, we all went to sing Christmas carols and distribute chocolates in each of the other houses and to some neighbours and friends; it is a way of announcing the coming of Jesus, Prince of Peace, who comes to give us the strength to love.

I am happy to be here, to grow old here together with others in L'Arche. Our life is simple and human: meeting people, smiling at people, taking time with people, welcoming visitors, eating and praying together. I do not do the washing up after the meals as I used to—my house allows me to take time to sit down and read the newspaper. That is what Jesus is calling me to today. To rejoice and be together in family, in community. Even though I am still called to travel for L'Arche and Faith and Light—soon to Malaysia, Haiti and Santo Domingo—I try to keep my eyes and heart fixed on Jesus, Mary and Joseph in Nazareth. There Jesus lived for more than thirty years a simple life of love and presence to each one, revealing to neighbours, especially to those in need, that they were loved and precious.

Here in Trosly there are also all the ups and downs of life, the disappointments, misunderstandings, disagreements and even conflicts. But that is very human and natural. We come from different backgrounds, cultures and faith traditions and have different temperaments. But we are seeking to love one another and to create in this broken world of ours a tiny place that radiates love and forgiveness and a desire for unity. I believe more and more in the loving power of the Gospels. Yet we are confronted daily with the impossibility of living out the Gospel message day by day without the presence of Jesus and the wisdom God gives us. My experience is that the God of love and the love of God are hidden in those who are weak and vulnerable, in our own weakness and vulnerability; God is hidden in our communities of L'Arche and Faith and Light. I take rest and joy from that. In the darkness of our world, the light and love of Jesus shines. During this new year may our communities grow in love and in simple gestures of kindness and forgiveness.

My love to each one of you,
Jean Vanier

June 2002
Trosly

Dear Friends,

I have just come back from the General Assembly* meeting in Swanwick (UK) which has deeply touched and, I hope, changed me. There were 250 delegates from 120 L'Arche communities, coming from different countries, cultures, languages and religious traditions. We were all united around the vision of L'Arche, around the place of the weakest, and at the same time we were discovering one another; bonds of friendship were created. During that week we formed a real community. We became more aware of how much L'Arche is a body, a living body.

When I reflect on these past thirty-eight years, I see four periods in the history of L'Arche. The first period was when Sue Mosteller was international coordinator. It was a time of foundations in India, Haiti, Honduras, the Ivory Coast, Burkina Faso, Australia, Canada, the United States and different European countries. Then with Claire de Miribel there followed what I call the time of unification of the Federation, which resulted in a new charter. With Jo Lenon's mandate there was consolidation and a new constitution. Today, with Jean-Christophe Pascal, it is a time of renewal, refocusing on our identity and mission.

The world has changed since 1964 when L'Arche was founded, and L'Arche itself has changed over the years. We have reached a certain maturity. We are confronted by new challenges and new dangers. We need to name the difficulties coming from both outside and inside L'Arche. We need to name our limits, shortages and

---

*We hold General Assemblies every three years. They consist of delegates from every L'Arche community. We rotate between big and small assemblies. The international council comprises the zone coordinators, presidents of zones and executive group, or about thirty people.

doubts. Who are we today? What do we want? What is God saying to us today? What is God calling us to? These questions were at the heart of our meeting. We were not only touched, awakened, shaken, but also affirmed, for L'Arche has been entrusted to each one of us. Its future depends on all of us. It is up to us to build it as it is called to be. Challenges and fears are there because we have to set out, be converted, refind the heart, the essential. At the same time, during the meetings a great breath of hope was given. God brought L'Arche to birth. And God is with us today and will be with us always, to lead and guide us towards a deeper rooting in God and towards a new fecundity. *We are no longer strangers but pilgrims together* in a very divided world. Pilgrims of hope and of peace. Men and women of experience and wisdom, from different church backgrounds, were also there to help us reread our story and to rediscover who we are and who we are called to be in the eyes of God.

For me, at this time in my life, this meeting was very important. I will soon be leaving the International Council. I am no longer called to have a role in the structures of L'Arche but to be a witness to live and announce the mystery that we are called to live, to be there with great confidence in God, in the structures, in Jean-Christophe, Christine and the leaders God gives us. To be in communion with them and to be a source of unity. To be there to give thanks to Jesus, and be happy simply to be with and be in the family, on pilgrimage, walking humbly with our God.

I realize more and more how we are all called to be witnesses of peace and to create communities of peace. But I also realize that peace is such a fragile reality. Since September 11 there have been so many signs of war. I realize that true peace is not simply peaceful coexistence or the absence of war. The absence of armed conflict is of course a good beginning for peace. It allows people to live together without harming each other. It allows people to live more or less without fear. But isn't authentic peace something more than peaceful coexistence?

In a country I visited recently I was told that Catholics and
Orthodox live side by side in the same town but that they totally
ignore each other. Catholics meet together, go to the same church
and have the same certitudes, so too the Orthodox amongst themselves, but people from the two churches never meet together;
there is no encounter, no dialogue. Is that peace? Members of different groups, ethnic origins, races, social classes, religions can
coexist in the same country or city, respecting the laws but ignoring each other. And then if one day, through subtle manipulations,
one group begins to suspect the other of wanting to dominate or
oppress them, fear rises up. And fear quickly turns into hatred,
violence and conflict. Don't we find similar things in our own communities? Do we really meet one another?

To reach out to others, to meet, share and dialogue with them,
requires a real effort. Mutual appreciation is not something easy
to learn. People told me about an Orthodox priest in Kosovo
who, when the Serbian army was advancing during the war, hid
the Kosovars who were in danger. Later, when the Serb army
moved out and the Kosovars started to move back into their
homes and towns, he hid Serbs who were then in danger of being
killed. That priest was free to see in others, in those who were
different, a human being, a person loved by God. He was able to
reach out and go beyond the walls and limits of his own culture
and religion.

Around the year 1219, at the beginning of the fourth crusade
against the Saracens, Francis of Assisi, Il Poverello of God, went on
foot to meet the sultan in Egypt. Francis, a man of peace, a sign of
peace. The two men truly met and shared and deeply appreciated
each other. This did not stop the war, but Francis and his brothers
were a sign of hope. Francis and his brothers were convinced that
their way of working for peace in the world was by serving and
sharing the lives of the poor, the weakest, the most rejected in all

cultures. Do we believe that by sharing our lives simply day after day we too are working for peace and that our communities can also become signs of hope in our world?

But how to remain deeply rooted in one's own culture and religious tradition and at the same time be open to others, not simply coexisting? How to learn to see the light of God in others and to meet as persons? To enter into relationship with someone requires a listening heart, an openness, a vulnerability, which leads to friendship—even with those who are very different.

If we remain closed up in our own culture, there is a danger. But there is also a danger if we try to be open to others without deepening our own culture and our own faith. Very quickly the only values that bring us together are work, leisure activities and sports. The goal of every culture and religion is not to close people up but to allow each to be more open to God and to each person that God has created.

That is the objective of our L'Arche and Faith and Light communities: to be schools of relationship. Many schools exist which help people develop their intellectual capacities, and there are many places for formation which help people develop their abilities and deepen their religious faith. But there are not many "schools of the heart," "schools of compassion" or "schools of relationship" which help people open up to those who are different and to understand them.

We see so many divisions in our world, and at the same time there are many seeds of peace. Wherever I go I learn so much. Jesus, Prince of Peace, brings down the walls of hostility and brings different people together into one, through his suffering and death (see Eph. 2). Jesus calls us to be a sign of love between us and with others. I believe more and more that young people (as well as the less young!) are looking for a life commitment in this divided world and want to discover communities of peace and unity like

L'Arche and Faith and Light. And I would like to make mine the words of the late Martin Luther King, Jr.:

> I believe that unconditional truth and love will have the last word. Life, even if it appears to be defeated, is stronger than death. I also believe that one day all of humanity will recognize in God the Source of their love. I believe that one day the saving, peaceful kindness will be the law. The wolf and the lamb will be able to lie down together, each person will be able to sit under their fig tree or in their vineyard and no one will have any reason to fear.

Let us be pilgrims together who believe in peace, who work for peace and whose hearts are enfolded in peace.

My love to each one in our God of peace,
Jean Vanier

January 2003
Trosly

Dear Friends,

My heart is filled with gratitude in the beginning of this new year. God is watching over L'Arche and Faith and Light with such kindness and solicitude.

As I grow older, I love to be with the weaker members of our communities who are often so simple, loving and peaceful, accepting their reality. Maybe it is because I myself sense more my own weaknesses. Their presence gives me peace.

We are living in troubled times. So many people feel insecure and are worried for the future. Even as I write this letter people are frightened that the American government will soon trigger a new war in Iraq . . . with what consequences? . . . for oil? . . . for the whole Middle East? And in the midst of this vast world there are great numbers of very vulnerable people, with no work, no lodging, no money, no protection.

And yet we have just celebrated Christmas: "Do not be afraid. I bring you news of great joy . . . Today a Saviour has been born to you." And the angels sing: "Glory to God in the highest and peace on earth to all people of good will." War and peace. Despair and hope.

I have been reading Andrea Riccardi's book *Ils sont morts pour leur foi* (They Died for Their Faith). It tells how hundreds of thousands, even millions, of men and women were imprisoned, tortured and killed for their faith during the twentieth century. The book shows the horror, the sadism, the brutality and the hatred of so many who sought to destroy those who believed in God, in human beings, in love. At the same time this book reveals the beauty of all those men and women who dared to say yes to all that is deeply human—to freedom, to love and to God—and to say no to evil. They refused to let themselves succumb to fear or to the pressure of ideologies which awaken, maintain and sustain hatred.

Etty Hillesum, a Dutch Jewish woman who died in Auschwitz in November 1943, never condemned those who were cowards or those who tortured others; she never felt sorry for herself and her tragic fate; she never despaired of the goodness and beauty of life. "I am ready," she wrote, "to accept everything, every place on earth where it pleases God to send me, ready also to give witness in all situations, even until death, to the beauty and meaning of this life. If life has become what it is, it is not God's fault but ours. We have received all the possibilities for human fulfillment but we have not learned how to exploit these possibilities." In that desert of love, she discovered Love; she discovered hope; she discovered God. Etty and all the martyrs of our times have brought forth in me a new trust in the message of Christmas. Yes, there is truly a Good News: a Saviour has been born. Are we not all called to be witnesses (in Greek the word for "martyr" is the same as for "witness"), witnesses of peace in our societies of extreme individualism, by living simply and by the way we share our lives with the weak? I remain deeply moved by John Paul II, this elderly pope, suffering from severe disabilities, who continually cries out "Peace" and "Trust."

L'Arche is faced with a number of difficulties today: lack of assistants, lack of money, pressure from new regulations by legal authorities who want to "normalize" us. But perhaps the greatest difficulties come from our own lack of confidence in L'Arche, in God, in the Gospel message, in the value of the people we have welcomed and in the value and importance of our community life. Isn't the lack of faith in what is truly human one of the greatest dangers of our times? The wealth and comfort in our Western countries may fill our pockets with money and our lives with opportunity, but they can also fill our hearts with gloom and empty them of any desire to live in truth.

Personally I am quite well, thanks be to God. I am learning how to live my age (seventy-four), my weakness, my fatigue, my desires. I still have a lot to learn and to welcome! I am aware of the weaknesses and flaws in L'Arche and Faith and Light but I see even more their beauty and their meaning in God's plan.

I would like to thank each one who has written to me for Christmas and the New Year. I feel happy and my heart is full of trust and thanksgiving for this family God has given to us, for the deep bonds that unite us, the communion. Together may we be faithful to love, mutually supporting one another and becoming a tiny light of hope for our world.

Jean

April 2003
Trosly

Dear Friends,

Everything that is happening in our world is deeply troubling. And yet my heart is full of trust. Many governments, many groups, many hearts are hardening, closing up in themselves; they need to affirm their identity through force, to prove that they are the best. At the same time, more and more people belonging to diverse groups and religious traditions are standing up to affirm that it is possible to resolve conflict through dialogue, that universal justice does exist, that together we can live a commitment to the work of peace. They believe that we find our fulfillment in co-operation, compassion and mutual acceptance; they put their gifts and competence at the service of the weakest and the most needy. That is why my heart is so full of trust. Each one of us is called to be competent; we are all called to make real efforts to grow humanly and spiritually and to serve others. To be together to serve the good of all, not to prove that we are superior, requires humility, openness and a desire to listen to others.

Community life in L'Arche and Faith and Light is showing us how weakness can be an opportunity for sharing, personal encounters, co-operation and friendship. René Leroy from L'Arche in Compiègne said one day, "Me all alone, can't do it." To welcome our weakness is a sign of maturity: "Yes, all alone I cannot do everything. I need you." A community lives and thrives because we need one another. Peace in our world cannot come unless we discover, welcome and respect the gift of each culture.

Our human hearts are so wounded that we often find it difficult to say, "I need you." We are frightened to admit our incapacities and our limits. In order to bring down the walls we have created around us, to be disarmed, to welcome each other just as we are and become vulnerable to one other, we need a new force that comes from God. Jesus says to Paul, "My strength is manifested in weakness" (2 Cor. 12:9). But in order for us to find our strength in God, to distinguish between a weakness that opens us up to God and a weakness that is fear and depression, that can close us up in ourselves, we need to be loved and well accompanied.

Jesus shows us the way to love: "Love one another as I have loved you" (John 13:34). Love heals our hearts and enables us to love others. Love permits us to welcome and accept our weakness. When we manifest our force, we so often break, push down, destroy, frighten and awaken feelings of revenge. Love helps a person to discover *who* he or she is, his or her fundamental goodness. Only then can what is most beautiful in the individual emerge. It is true that Jesus, who loved people, was himself rejected, wounded, arrested and finally put to death. His weakness and his suffering are, however, a source of life. We need the waters flowing from his pierced heart, a sign of the Holy Spirit, so that we have the courage and the strength to take the path of disarmament, vulnerability and openness to others.

The moment of Jesus's greatest weakness and pain was followed by his resurrection. That was not a visible, spectacular event for all but a humble, small, hidden event. He did not want to humiliate those who had humiliated him. He appeared to Mary of Magdala, then to a few of his disciples; he did not judge or criticize them for their lack of trust at the time of his distress, but he gave them peace: "Peace be with you." Then, he sent them into the world so that they in turn would be a sign of peace and forgiveness. L'Arche and Faith and Light, as well as many others, want to be little signs that love, peace and community are possible.

The world's great religions all remind us that we have to be stripped of our fears and of our self-centredness in order for our deeper self to emerge, for love to spring forth from the depths of our hearts. Jesus reminds us often that in order to live and bear much fruit we have to die to ourselves. He promises to send us the

Holy Spirit so that we can be born anew, in love and in the Spirit of God. It is a long but beautiful path for all of us, so that our communities radiate peace.

And our brother Raphaël has left us! He joined Père Thomas and many other friends of L'Arche and Faith and Light. He, with Philippe, was the first person I welcomed. Raphaël has entered the Kingdom of God, the banquet of love, before us! He who would repeat so often, "Get married; get married," and who, looking at his watch, used to complain, "Too late; too late"; he who knew how to ask for forgiveness after an act of violence, sometimes in tears; he who used to look at each one with such tenderness and who often broke out in great laughter and made everyone laugh; he has entered into the eternal wedding feast. He loved his community, La Rose des Vents in Verpillières. He loved L'Arche and was deeply loved in L'Arche. He will watch over us now. God truly blessed us by sending him to L'Arche. He opened up a path of love. I give thanks for his life and for all that I personally have received from him. His weakness helped me to welcome my own weaknesses and to say, "I need you." At the time of his death, many sent messages of peace, communion and tenderness. Thank you. I sense how much we are a family created by God, where we need one another. May the God of peace be with each one of you.

Love,
Jean Vanier

August 2003
Orval

Dear Friends,

Another year has passed and a new one is beginning. And here I am once again in the monastery for a month, time to offer up to

God all that we have lived during this past year and all that will be given this year. When we look at the world events over this last year, we see the painful situations in Israel and Palestine, the war in Iraq, the fear of terrorism everywhere, the rise of religious fundamentalism, civil wars in Africa, poor countries becoming poorer. And if we look at L'Arche? In many countries there is a tension between the legislative and social requirements and the prophetic vision of our communities, a vision that is so essential to all of our lives. The shortage of assistants, of leaders, of financial resources . . . the list of difficulties in our world and in our own communities would be quite long!

At the same time, more and more people are searching for a way of life that is more deeply human, closer to the ways of God and of the Gospel; they refuse to let themselves be drowned in a sea of noise and agitation, in a sea of new technologies which develop often at the expense of personal relationships. And in the face of all the outbursts of violence and conflict, more and more people are actively working for peace—more and more people are becoming committed to the weak. In L'Arche the "identity and mission" process* has started off very well with small groups meeting to share their "sacred stories." Likewise members of Faith and Light are reflecting together on what is essential. In spite of all the shortages and needs, our communities continue to deepen, and members with disabilities are growing in maturity . . . there is such a mysterious wisdom in them. I am touched also by the growth of assistants in their love of God and in their commitment to the Gospel.

---

*The new leadership of L'Arche recognized that communities had to own their founding stories—that the mission and purpose of L'Arche had moved away from the first founding story at Trosly and had now become something much bigger, an international movement created by many acts of community, in many different places around the world. The "identity and mission" process was an extraordinary opportunity for each L'Arche community to express its part in the creation of this movement and to discover a common vision for its future.

What is this "essential" of our communities? Presence: being present to people who are fragile and being present to one another. To live fully the present moment and not to hide behind some past ideals or future utopia. Our human hearts are thirsting for presence: the presence of a friend, the presence of someone who will listen faithfully, who does not judge but who understands, appreciates and through love lowers the barriers of inner fear and anguish. This presence implies compassion and tenderness as well as competence.

Above all presence implies being present to God, listening to God. It is important not to be afraid or to feel paralyzed in front of all that is so painful in our world and in our communities. We need to discover the presence of God in the actual reality of each day. God is not to be found in the ideal but is hidden in the poverty of the present moment, in all that is broken and inadequate in our communities and in our own hearts.

In July I went to Zimbabwe and South Africa. During my visit in Zimbabwe, I went to speak in a prison. I found myself in a courtyard facing a thousand men squatting on the ground, shoulder to shoulder, squeezed together row after row. I was very moved. (I imagine that they were forced to come and listen to me!) I spoke to them about the L'Arche community in Harare, and about Moses, a boy with profound and multiple handicaps who has been welcomed into the community. I told them how important and precious Moses is because he is a human being created by God and for God, and that he needed to be accepted and loved if he was to flourish. I also reminded them that "each one of you too is precious and important. Maybe whilst you are here in prison you cannot be in touch with your families, but you can be in touch with God, with the God hidden in your hearts; and you can try to love those amongst you who are the 'most suffering.'" They listened so intensely. I was not able to visit their cells nor see what they are given to eat, but I could well imagine the depth of suffering in that prison, a sign of the unbearable suffering present throughout our world.

The secret of peacemaking is to help each person discover that he or she is unique, God's dwelling place; that in each one of us there is a deeper self, a personal conscience, a sacred place, which allows us to be free, not governed by fear, and to live in communion with God—with universal truth and justice. We know peace when we discover that, over and above all that is so terribly painful in our world, there is a God of love who is close to each one of us.

I am still reading Etty Hillesum, a young Dutch Jewish woman killed in Auschwitz in 1943. At one point she writes in her diary that she cried out to God, asking him to come and "fix" everything, to come and comfort all those who were suffering. Then she realized, "It is not me who needs God but God who needs me." God knocks on the door of each of our hearts. God waits patiently for us to open the door so that he can come and dwell within us and through us bring comfort to those in pain.

Here in the monastery I try to keep my heart open to God. It is my longing and hope that during this last period of my life I shall be able to live with my heart more and more open to God, ready to welcome with tenderness and gratitude the changes and weaknesses that will come. Can I ask you to pray for this? The best gift that you could possibly give me for my seventy-fifth birthday is to pray for me, for each one of us, that we might live in communion one with another. I love to read again and again Paul's words in his letter to the Philippians (2:2–4): "Let us be of the same mind, have the same love, be in full accord and of one mind. Let us do nothing from selfish ambition or conceit but in humility regard others as better than ourselves. Let each of us look not to our own interests but to the interests of others."

My heart is full of thanksgiving for all that Jesus has given me during these seventy-five years of my life, forty years of L'Arche and thirty-two years of Faith and Light. I have also taken time these days to reread some of Père Thomas's writings. I sense so deeply how much my union, my communion, with him in 1950 and even more since 1964 is the ground in which L'Arche and Faith and Light have grown. I have no idea what this new year will bring us, what joys and what difficulties—but I am full of confidence. I trust in God, in the folly of L'Arche and Faith and Light. I trust that God is at work in our world in and through the poor and the weak. I trust in our leaders and in each one of you. In advance I give thanks, and in particular I give thanks for the weakest and most suffering members (who are sometimes assistants) at the heart of our communities. They are a source of life.

With love,
Jean Vanier

Christmas 2003
Trosly

Dear Friends,

Christmas will soon be here with all the celebrations, special meals, visits, gifts and prayer around the crib—the prayer of the poor.

In many countries there is such a contradiction between the luxury surrounding this feast and its meaning, between the store windows abounding in expensive merchandise and the sumptuous meals and God who comes in poverty to be with the weak and the rejected. It is not easy to live this contradiction. It is good and important to rejoice and give thanks and to mark the feast with good meals and gifts. But how can we keep our hearts open? What can we do so that Christmas can be truly a celebration of love and sharing, so that those who are more fragile and alone are honoured and have a place? Christmas is truly the feast of L'Arche and Faith and Light; it is a family celebration where we celebrate our covenant with each one in the community. Christmas is the celebration of God who humbly comes into our fragility, where his presence is revealed in and through the weak and the broken. Perhaps this year you and I, all of us, can take a little more quiet time to open our inner sanctuary to receive God, who is so hidden and silent and who needs us: "I stand at the door and knock (says the Lord). If anyone hears my voice and opens the door I will come in and eat with them and they with me" (Rev. 3:20).

The contradiction we live around Christmas is lived in all places of poverty and insecurity in our world: countries at war, refugee camps, those with HIV/AIDS or the elderly, who are so often alone. We know well the litany of suffering and exclusion, but that is where Christmas is lived in a special way: God hidden in human weakness and pain. In L'Arche and Faith and Light we have the joy of being together in community, of carrying one another, carrying difficult situations together, working together for the growth and dignity of each person and for peace wherever we may be.

Sometimes I feel a bit guilty for being happy. Then I say to myself, "God created us to be happy and to spread joy around us." The source of my joy is in Jesus, Jesus who dwells with us, Jesus who dwells amongst us. It comes from my life in the foyer and in the community. Christmas is a time of hope which gives meaning to our lives, our fragility, our struggles and our pain. For God who is love became flesh in order to liberate us from fear.

Joy in my life comes also from being able to talk about the good news of God's presence and love during my retreats and talks, over these last months in Moscow, Belfast, Palermo, Montpellier, Agen, Trosly and Tressaint. Now that I am less occupied with things to do, I have more time to announce the grace and the gift of L'Arche. Perhaps I have never understood so well the importance of our communities for society and for the churches. Recently a man who has important responsibilities told me, "I love working with L'Arche because it is one of the few places which reveals love for others in a society taken up with rights for oneself."

As I grow older I am also discovering more the gift of my own poverty and weakness. When we are strong, we can often do it alone. When we feel weaker, when we live loss and anguish, we are more aware of our need for God, for others, for community. I realize more and more that the only thing that is really important is the new commandment Jesus gave us: "Love one another as I have loved you" (John 13:34). May each one of us, and each one of our communities, grow in this love.

Merry Christmas and happy New Year to you. May our hearts be at peace . . . and in that way there will be more peace in this world.

Jean Vanier

September 14, 2004
St. Thomas retreat house (Syria)

Dear Friends,

I am with the International Council of Faith and Light in this retreat house thirty kilometres outside of Damascus. We are told that the prophet Elijah stayed in a cave near here (see 1 Kings 19), where he waited for the presence of God. God came but was not in the hurricane nor in the earthquake nor in the fire. God, the God of tenderness and compassion, was present in the gentle evening breeze. It is good to be here on this little mountain and to sense the gentle presence of God in the quiet evening breeze.

I visited the main mosque in Damascus which is an amazing place of beauty and grandeur. Many people were there, sitting on rugs, talking or praying or reading the Koran; children played quietly together. It was good to pray at the tomb of that humble witness to Jesus, John the Baptist, who is venerated by Muslims in this mosque, and with so many men and women to ask God for peace: that the walls that separate cultures and religions may be lowered and that we, with all our differences, may learn how to dialogue with one another and live in communion.

The thirty-eight Faith and Light communities in Syria are full of life: many young people share the joy and pain of people with disabilities and their parents. They are a mixture of Catholics and Orthodox, encouraged and supported by their respective bishops. I gave two public talks, in Damascus and in Aleppo, which brought together about seven hundred people each time, mainly Muslim. After my talk in Aleppo, the Mufti gave a testimony on how people with disabilities are a path to God.

THE MONASTERY OF MAR MOUSSA

We have all come to Mar Moussa, in the middle of the desert. We had quite a walk through the mountains to get here. Roy helped me all along the way so that I wouldn't fall! Mar Moussa, a monastery built on ancient ruins, is a new community of men and women, monks and religious sisters, who live, work and pray together, striving to be a place of dialogue and communion between Christians and Muslims. In the midst of so much fear in our world, where so many walls are being built between cultures and religions, the Holy Spirit is bringing to birth communities of peace. They do not make much noise nor the headlines; they are like gentle breezes, signs that love and peace are stronger than hatred and war.

I think a lot about Il Poverello, Francis of Assisi, while I am here. In the midst of the crusades, in 1219, Francis, with another Franciscan brother, crossed over the line between the two enemy armies in Damietta (Egypt) to visit the sultan. Barefoot, with no money or food, like a beggar, Francis went to the sultan. The two men truly met and appreciated each other. It was a gesture of peace in a world at war. In the Franciscan Rule of life, Francis urges his brothers, in their relationship with Muslims, to be like Jesus who came humbly to serve.

RETREAT-PILGRIMAGE TO THE HOLY LAND

Last June, I had the joy of making a retreat-pilgrimage following the footsteps of Jesus in the Holy Land, which is also a land of conflict and violence—as it was in the time of Jesus. There were about forty of us, an English-speaking group coming from L'Arche in Canada, the United States, England and France. It was an important time for us, which began on the Mount of Beatitudes near Nazareth and ended at the Holy Sepulchre in Jerusalem. Kathy Baroody from L'Arche, who lives near Bethlehem, was with the group all the time. Some of us visited the workshop she opened for fifteen men and women, Christian and Muslim. We saw the new wall, eight metres high, in construction to separate Israel from Palestine: a wall of pain. We saw and heard about so many painful situations that are difficult to talk about. Our world is so full of such places of suffering. How can we live in solidarity with these people? We want our communities to be places of peace, by our welcome of those who are different, and places of hope in a world where many have lost hope.

ECUMENICAL RETREAT IN NORTHERN IRELAND

After that pilgrimage to the source of our faith, I gave a retreat in Northern Ireland, another place where two cultures have difficulty understanding one another and are in confrontation. Participants came from both cultures and from different churches. In Northern Ireland, in the midst of all the difficulties, people like Ruth Patterson work day in and day out for peace, trying to help people to know one another, to lose their fear and to begin to appreciate and forgive each other. That takes time! People have been so hurt! Forgiveness does not come easily. Hatred and vengeance seem to come more naturally to us poor human beings, who tend to close up in ourselves, behind the walls of "our group." But through the prophet Ezekiel, God promises to send a new Spirit to change our hearts of stone into hearts of flesh. We need the Holy Spirit so much today in order to see another who is different as a brother, a sister, a friend, and not as an enemy. We need the Holy Spirit in order to reach the deepest person of others, hidden behind the disability or underneath the label we stick on them. We need the Spirit of God in order to see the beauty and the light in others rather than all that is negative and wounded.

PILGRIMAGE TO LOURDES

I was invited to participate in the Pope's pilgrimage to Lourdes on August 14 and 15. I was asked to give short meditations on the luminous mysteries of the rosary: the Baptism of Jesus, the Wedding Feast in Cana, Announcing the Kingdom, the Transfiguration of Jesus on Mount Tabor and the Eucharist. During that time I walked close to John Paul II. I was moved by the seriousness of his disability, his speech difficulties due to Parkinson's disease. One person told me after the pilgrimage, "It was too hard to watch him on the television. He should retire—or die—soon!" How many times I have heard that said about people with disabilities. It is an attitude that humanly speaking is understandable! It is hard to see and be close to people in pain. Through his physical poverty, the Pope reveals a mystery; he is a living symbol of the presence of God in weakness. Even more than by his words, through his fragile body he is teaching us now the value of each human life; he is showing us a path towards holiness. I was also touched by his humility and courage, the spark of life in his eyes, the way he accepts the humiliating reality of his condition today and his extreme tenderness. In all his weakness and old age, he calls us to tenderness. He is a sign of the glory of God who is manifested in and through his poverty and vulnerability.

Our societies exalt physical strength and beauty. But is that what it means to be human? Who, in fact, inspire us to become more human? The beautiful and the powerful? Or, those who call forth what is deepest in us, the goodness and compassion in our hearts?

I feel happy, even if sometimes I have less stamina and my legs feel like cotton! I had some rest and renewal in Orval in August. My joy is to be more present in my community and in my foyer, Le Val Fleuri, but also to travel to announce Jesus and his good news, as in the retreats I gave in Prince George, BC, and Erie, Pennsylvania. I am happy that I am no longer in the decision-making bodies of L'Arche and Faith and Light, and I have great confidence in those who are called to carry responsibility today. My joy is to speak about L'Arche, Faith and Light, and the beauty of people with disabilities, who in all their vulnerability lead us to God. I am happy to continue my journey with Jesus and to pray with you with confidence for the future. Finally, I would like to thank each one for your greetings and prayers for my seventy-sixth birthday. It is good to grow older and to be in communion with each other.

Jean

Christmas 2004/New Year 2005
L'Arche–Trosly

Dear Friends,

During this Christmas season, so many people throughout the world are in grief, especially those affected by the earthquake and tidal wave in Southeast Asia. An immense tragedy! It is difficult perhaps for us to rejoice while so many others are in pain. At the same time all this has created a wonderful movement of solidarity!

But do we need such disasters in order for the world to wake up and for richer countries to share with poorer ones? This tsunami has shaken the world and reminds us of the other disaster in all our countries: the ever-widening gap between those who have and those who have not.

Christmas: the celebration of God who comes to visit us in the weakness and vulnerability of a child, God who comes to *be with* us, to share our joys and pain, so that we too can share our lives together as brothers and sisters in humanity. God comes to live a *relationship* of trust which awakens our hearts and *transforms* us into men and women of compassion. We become a *sign* of hope in the world.

The Word became flesh so that we could make the passage from being centred on ourselves to being centred on others, humbly but truthfully. It is not easy to love, to let down the barriers that close us up in ourselves and to reach out to others. As I grow older, I become more and more aware of my own fears and blockages, my difficulties in relationships. There is still a struggle in me between the desire to live simple relationships of communion with others and the need for power, to control others. And I realize that I am not going to change and acquire the inner freedom to love through my own efforts; my heart of stone needs to be transformed through the love of God into a heart of flesh, a vulnerable heart, open to others.

I sense more and more how much L'Arche and Faith and Light are a treasure that God has entrusted to us. After reading the first-year report of the "identity and mission" process, David Ford, a theologian and friend of L'Arche, told me and Christine McGrievy: "L'Arche is not only born of God and guided by God; L'Arche is the glory of God!" I like to think of each one of our communities also as the joy of God. Didn't Jesus, quivering with joy in the Holy Spirit, proclaim: "I bless You, Father, Lord of heaven and of earth, for hiding these things from the learned and the clever, and revealing them to little ones" (Luke 10:21)? God's joy is not only because we welcome those who are often marginalized in our societies but also because our communities are places where they can live and grow in a personal relationship with God.

Yes, God became flesh, revealed himself, gave himself as a friend to the weak and the poor, those who are not caught up in the desire for importance or for doing "big things." Don't we all have to become like little children in order to enter into the Kingdom of love? Life in our communities can be a source of transformation only if we let ourselves be transformed. To become little, like a child, is not a question of sentimentality, of being insipid or of pretending to be incapable of doing anything of value. It is an awareness that by ourselves we are unable to become truly free. It is the audacity to believe that if we let God live and work in us, we can do beautiful things.

I want to thank each one for your Christmas greetings and for your concern and prayers for my health. These last four weeks have been filled with doctor's appointments, a short stay in the hospital, rest and walks. I was sorry I had to cancel my trip to Honduras and miss seeing our people there. At my last appointment the doctor told me, "Continue to live and to travel! There is no danger." I still have a heart that beats too much due to my arrhythmia. I have to be careful and slow down. But the cardiologist is taking good care of me and teaching me how to live with it. Isn't that our spirituality, learning to live with our limits and weaknesses and to give thanks?

May this Christmas be truly a celebration of love and sharing for each one of us. May the new year be a time of transformation for each one and for each of our communities, and a time of consolation for those who are suffering.

Love,
Jean

June 2005
Trosly

Dear Friends,

A few weeks ago we were in Assisi for the meeting of the Family of L'Arche: 350 delegates from all the L'Arche communities throughout the world. A radiant sun warmed our hearts and spirits in this city of Il Poverello, the poor one. We felt the presence of Francis and Clare.

Francis was transformed from a rich young man into Il Poverello. His transformation took time. A decisive moment in his growth was his encounter with people with leprosy. At that time lepers were rejected and separated from the rest of society. They symbolized all that was dirty and despicable. In his *Testament,* written just before his death, Francis tells how it was the Lord himself who led him to the lepers and that after Francis had taken care of them, what had seemed bitter to him before was turned into something gentle and warm for his body and heart.

Another decisive moment was in the church of San Damiano, when he heard Jesus call to him from the cross, "Francis, go and rebuild my church that has fallen into ruins." Il Poverello took these words literally and, with a few companions, began the physical labour of rebuilding the dilapidated church of San Damiano. Later he discovered a deeper meaning to these words: he was called to rebuild and reform the Church of his time, which was ridden with scandals of power and wealth.

Two years later, he received his mission when he heard the words of Jesus in Matthew's Gospel calling his disciples to go out into the world and announce the Kingdom of God in poverty, with no money and no spare clothes. That filled his heart with a tremendous joy. He knew then what God wanted of him. Under the guidance of God, Francis rebuilt and reformed the Church of his time and helped people to rediscover the way of the Gospel, of the Beatitudes.

We also believe that L'Arche was born of God through the encounter of Père Thomas, myself, Raphaël and Philippe. Meeting with people with learning disabilities transforms us and makes our communities a sign for our society, a sign that peace and love are possible. We too have received a call to rebuild the Church and to work for unity between churches and between all people. We too have been sent forth on a mission today, with all our limits and fragilities, to announce the beauty and importance of people with disabilities, the importance of each person.

For me Saint Clare represents all those inside and outside L'Arche, sometimes hidden in monasteries or on beds of pain, who pray for us. In all our needs and shortages, we cry out to God and God hears the cry of the poor.

Much was given during this meeting in Assisi. It would be good to read the talks on the mission of L'Arche today given by Gerald Arbuckle, a Marist priest, Dr. Rowan Williams, Archbishop of Canterbury, and Cardinal Kasper, president of the Pontifical Council for the Promotion of Christian Unity. Each one was very affirming of L'Arche.

With my seventy-six years I feel more fragile and have to be careful. I am happy to use these last years of my life to announce the vision of Jesus: his love for the weak and the poor. I love spending time in my foyer, Le Val Fleuri. Before I used to carry responsibility for the foyer, taking care of each one. Now I am touched by the way each one cares for me, giving me the best chair in the room, suggesting that I get some rest or read the newspaper instead of doing the dishes, etc. I am happy to give formation sessions for L'Arche and Faith and Light and to have more time for prayer and to work on myself, so that I may grow in love, patience and truth.

The death of John Paul II affected me more than I expected. I knew and loved him personally and felt that he understood, loved and supported L'Arche and Faith and Light. Benedict XVI is, I sense, a spiritual son of John Paul II and will continue his work.

He will be a good shepherd who will nourish the flock. John Paul II was extraordinary in the way he called people of his church to be both rooted and open. We are all called to be rooted in our faith, in the Gospel, in our particular church, and at the same time open to other churches, other religious traditions, other men and women of goodwill, discovering and appreciating the gifts of each one.

Isn't that a question for each one of us and for each one of our communities? How to be rooted in our Christian faith, in our love of Jesus and in our specific church and also be open to others who do not share the same faith, to meet and listen to them and receive their gifts?

I was also deeply affected by the fire at La Vigne. Anne-Lise and Michel lost their lives in it. We do not yet know the cause. Anne-Lise and Michel were deeply loved and their death has left a great wound and great pain in us all.

L'Arche and Faith and Light are founded on pain. We are called to welcome those who suffer from rejection and disabilities. To create community together with the strong and the weak, communities of faith, and thus be a sign for our world. We will always be fragile communities. We are learning to live together with the pain, to welcome it, accept it and respond to it, to change pain into joy and to make it prayer.

In many ways we are like the poor, crying out to God. Our needs are great, especially our need for people who want to share their lives and be committed with us in order to be healed and transformed by those that society puts aside.

There is so much more I would like to share, but most of all I want to share my gratitude for L'Arche and Faith and Light, for the way they are deepening and growing, often in poverty. I would also like also to share with you my hope.

Much love,
Jean

November 2005
Trosly

Dear Friends,

It will soon be Christmas, a season that reveals a message of gentleness, of intimacy in the family, of gifts and celebrations and of the joy of little children, Christmas carols, sparkling lights in the streets, the crib and midnight services. I remember Christmas mornings when I was a child. My brother Bernard and I slept in the same room. We would rush to look under our beds where we would always find our mother's stockings filled with gifts and, at the bottom, nuts and tangerines (which at that time were Christmas fruits).

Christmas reminds us of the words of the angel, a messenger of God: "A saviour is born . . . great joy . . . a sign . . . a child . . . glory to God and peace on earth" (Luke 2:10–14). Just a few words but so meaningful. Christmas is a time of celebration of God's gift to the poor, a time for the liberation of hearts.

I love to reread St. James's letter to the Christian community, written just a few years after the death of Jesus. People were, he said, respecting the rich and the influential, giving them the best places in the assemblies and leaving out the poor: "Listen my beloved brothers and sisters: it was those who were poor according to the world that God chose to be rich in faith and to be the heirs to the kingdom which he promised to those who love him. You on the other hand have dishonoured the poor" (James 2:5–6). Christmas reminds us of the place that the weakest should hold in our lives and in our communities.

Today our world is terribly broken: peace, liberation of hearts, joy, a recognition of God seem so far from our reality. Dark clouds of violence and discouragement seem to hide the sun of peace and hope. Bad news fills our lives. Christmas itself seems to have been taken hostage by the society of consumption. Today Christmas is not so much a time of celebration for the poor but rather a time of holidays in the sun or the snow, eating and drinking a lot—too much—and so a time when the gap between the rich and the poor only widens. The weak are so easily forgotten.

At the birth of Jesus some two thousand years ago the angel's words announced a light in all the darkness. Israel was oppressed under the boots of Roman soldiers, and within Jewish society itself there were terrible divisions: those in authority seemed to be locked up in their desire to maintain and defend their power at all costs. And all the beggars, the lepers, the widows were excluded. Perhaps what we are living today is not much different. History tends to repeat itself. And today, as in the past, there are messengers of God who continue to announce hope, the liberation of hearts, joy, peace, all flowing from the heart of God. Peace is still possible if each one of us does his or her part!

Many events in past years have made people live in fear. We all risk closing up in our religious, cultural and national certitudes and securities. Walls are being built and reinforced between groups, races and religions. At the same time, however, more and more men and women are rising up against the danger of these closures. Many are taking the risk of opening their hearts to the marginalized, to those in pain and to those who are different. They are rooted in their faith and live in communion with the God of goodness, tenderness, forgiveness and compassion, a humble and vulnerable God, close to the excluded, for God himself is the most excluded one in our world today. Brother Roger Schutz of Taizé was one of these gentle, humble men. Did he have to die by shedding his blood like Jesus? His life and that of his brothers in Taizé have given so much hope to millions of young people throughout the world ever since the foundation of the community in 1940. Thank you, Brother Roger, for the gift of your life.*

---

*Brother Roger died in tragic circumstances in 2005. A mentally ill woman

This is L'Arche–Bouaké on the official opening day in 1974. Dawn is fourth from left. Louise is fifth from left, with her hands on a little girl.

L'Arche–Kampala (Uganda) was founded in 1990 and just recently opened a second home. The community already comprises a farm and a candle-making and sewing workshop.

This is Robert with Salésien, Jean-Robert and Raoul at Prés du Carrefour, Haiti, in 1976.

Nadine spent a year in Suyapa, Honduras, getting to know her neighbours and the culture before welcoming the first children into L'Arche. Here she is with Lita.

The original core members and assistants of L'Arche–Daybreak, the first L'Arche community founded in Canada. (Courtesy of L'Arche–Daybreak)
Top row: Michael, Steve Newroth holding Jean Frederick (with a gingerbread cookie) and Ann Newroth; second row: Debbie, Richard and Peter; third row: Alva, John and Ronnie; fourth row: Brian, Frank and David; bottom row: Helen, John and Bill

*Pat and Jo Lenon came
to a retreat in Edmonton
and afterwards felt called
to give up everything
to found Marymount,
a L'Arche community
outside Calgary. Here they
are in 1973 with Suzanne,
Sheila, Natacha and Dan.*

*Abby, Bob and Bill from
L'Arche–Tahoma Hope
in Tacoma, Washington.
(Courtesy of L'Arche USA)*

*John and Elsa Mae
at L'Arche–Cleveland.
(Courtesy of L'Arche USA)*

*Here is Christina weaving
at the L'Arche–Homefires
workshop in Wolfville,
Nova Scotia. (Courtesy of
L'Arche Canada)*

In 1971 we opened the New House at L'Arche–Daybreak. Here I am with Mum (seated) and Steve Newroth (at microphone). (Courtesy of L'Arche–Daybreak)

Père Thomas and I miming the beginnings of L'Arche at a federation meeting in 1978. Theatre, dancing, singing and artistry are all important to L'Arche; they give expression to the spirit within us.

Henri Nouwen knew how to talk about L'Arche in a way that made the community understood. He led people to find themselves, to find a vision. (Courtesy of Henri J. M. Nouwen Archives and Research Collection)

Robert and Jennifer from L'Arche–Harbor House in Jacksonville, Florida, go to The Arc's prom. (Courtesy of L'Arche USA)

A festive dinner at Le Val Fleuri. Meals and celebrations are important at L'Arche; they break up our routines and remind us that we are a family united.

Passover seder with Jewish members and friends at L'Arche–Daybreak. (Courtesy of L'Arche–Daybreak)

Peter and Ashoke at the Asha Niketan–Calcutta workshop, making wires for Philips in the early 1970s.

George counting eggs at the Daybreak farm. (Courtesy of L'Arche–Daybreak)

Here our people take a break from work at a workshop in 1972. (Philippe is facing the camera.) Work gives all of us a sense of dignity, independence and self-worth.

In the summer of 2002, the Spirit Movers danced at the welcome ceremony for Pope John Paul II at World Youth Day in Toronto. (Courtesy of Manfred Breuler)

Susanne and Joey at the candle-making workshop at L'Arche–Daybreak. (Courtesy of L'Arche–Daybreak)

Wayne, Jill, Barry and Juan make lunch at L'Arche–Vancouver.

Making candles in the L'Arche workshop in Liverpool, England. (Courtesy of L'Arche UK)

Thirty years after moving into the first L'Arche together, here we are reunited again: Raphaël Simi, me and Philippe Seux, celebrating at Le Val Fleuri in 1994.

Marie-Hélène Mathieu and me in 2001. (Courtesy of Faith and Light International)

Mum, Thérèse and me on Easter Sunday in Trosly. The shawl I'm putting on my mother says "Grand-mère," and was given to her by the community on her ninety-first birthday.

Barbara and Mum in the garden of Les Marronniers, my mother's house in Trosly.

I would like to give thanks also for all those who have been a light of hope for the world in recent years: John-Paul II, Mother Teresa, Oscar Romero, Jean Goss, Dorothy Day, Mahatma Gandhi, Abdul Ghaffar Khan, Etty Hillesum, Dietrich Bonhoeffer,* Cardinal von Galen (a bishop in Nazi Germany who risked his life in order to defend the life and rights of people with disabilities). The list is long of those who have worked for life. I am thinking in a special way today of Charles de Foucauld, the "universal little brother," who has just been beatified in Rome. He lived a long time in Algeria, becoming the friend of the Muslim people. It is he who inspired the Fraternities of the Little Brothers and Sisters of Jesus who live centred on Jesus in the Eucharist, close to the weak and the forgotten. Thank you, Brother Charles, for the gift of your life.

Different events I have lived during these last few months have given me much hope. In August, the World Youth Days were held in Cologne: the thirst for God in the hearts of so many young people, yearning to know the Gospel better. Then I saw all the young people in Taizé for Brother Roger's funeral: in spite of the tragic way he died, they desire to follow in his footsteps to work towards unity and reconciliation. I remain deeply touched by the Brothers of Taizé. I had the privilege of being with them for the funeral and again a few weeks later. Their way of opening the hearts of the young to God and to the weak and the poor is a light for all of us. Then there was the retreat in Slovenia organized by L'Arche and Faith and Light, and another in St. Petersburg (Russia). These

---

stabbed him during evening prayer, and he died soon afterwards. I attended his funeral in Taizé and was very moved.

*Dietrich Bonhoeffer was a German Lutheran pastor and theologian who helped found the Confessing Church. He preached against the Nazis and called for wider resistance to the regime. The Gestapo banned him from speaking publicly, but he continued to be a voice of Christian opposition to Hitler's treatment of Jews and was imprisoned for helping Jews cross into Switzerland. He was hanged in April 1945 for his involvement in a plot to assassinate Hitler.

530 OUR LIFE TOGETHER

retreats were a source of life and a real nourishment for those wanting to deepen their commitment with the weak. And I met a group that has a great desire to found a L'Arche community in Siberia . . . it will take time!

In July, I was invited to Jordan by an organization called Questscope to meet young Muslims in difficulty, some in prison or in specialized centres, and the psychologists and educators who accompany them. We worked together to find an anthropology adapted to these young people. In order to grow, to get out of their situation, they need to find someone who will accompany them as a friend; someone who can listen to them without judging and who can see the beauty in them; someone who, with others, will create a network of friendship, a community. They need also to discover their own inner space for God.

In September, the Community of Sant'Egidio organized a big inter-religious meeting in Lyon. I participated in a round-table discussion with a Muslim philosopher and a Jewish Rabbi on "an anthropology for the twenty-first century." Very interesting! The vision of the human being evolves, is transformed and deepens throughout the centuries. The closing ceremony, with the kiss of peace between rabbis, imams, Muslim theologians and leaders of Christian churches—and the whole meeting itself—was a real witness to unity and peace.

Violence and bad news are so visible on our television screens, while so much good news often remains hidden from and even ignored by the media: the commitment of many people in small communities that are signs of love; young people sharing their life with the poor, going to live in Africa, Asia or Latin America with Intercordia or other organizations, in order to discover the beauty of other cultures, to serve the poor and to become their brother, their sister; and all the people in the explosive suburbs of Paris today who are there to listen to the pain, to seek ways to relieve the suffering and to understand and repair the injustices. Change the world one heart at a time.

In our communities of L'Arche and Faith and Light we live times of struggle, grief and death, but what a joy for me to see the faithfulness, love and competence of so many committed people.

Christmas is a sign of hope, a sign that love is stronger than hatred and that peace is possible, if each one of us, wherever we are, becomes an instrument of peace. Then:

> The wolf will live with the lamb,
> the leopard lie down with the kid,
> calf and the young lion will feed together,
> with a little boy to lead them . . .
> No hurt, no harm will be done
> on all my holy mountain,
> for the country will be full
> of knowledge of Yahweh
> as the waters cover the sea. (Isa. 11:6, 9)

Peace, merry Christmas, and happy New Year!

Jean

June 2006
Trosly

Dear Friends,

From June 2 to June 4, an important conference on peace initiatives was held in Paris, organized by Christian Renoux, former president of MIR (Mouvement International de la Réconciliation). It brought together some 150 organizations involving thousands of men and women who are working for peace, men and women who are determined to move from the ways of violence and to the paths of listening, unity, dialogue and nonviolence. I had the joy of participating in a round-table discussion with Adolfo Pérez Esquivel (a recipient of the Nobel Peace Prize) and Hildegard Goss-Mayr, who for the last fifty years has been struggling for nonviolent solutions to conflict in various parts of the world. I shared about L'Arche and Faith and Light and how we want to be communities of peace. I was inspired by all the people who believe that they can do something for peace in different situations and who are also committed to humanitarian projects in areas of poverty.

We are living in the decade of the UN Millenium Declaration of peace, a decade when schools are encouraged to teach young people the ways of nonviolence. Violence breaks out in cultures of competition, where there is economic and political rivalry and the rivalry caused by civil war and international conflicts. Our education systems advocate success. To be successful in life is of course important. However, if it means only a frantic search to climb up the ladder at any cost and to show that we are better and superior to others, it is destructive; and if it means rejecting those who are weak and who do not succeed, it is also dangerous. Either we exploit other peoples' weakness and crush them as we try to reach the top or, faced with the world of rivalry in and around us, we shrug our shoulders and give up, feeling incapable of doing anything useful to change the situation, or we are discouraged and just seek compensation in things like alcohol.

A culture of peace, rather, implies an acceptance of each person with his or her gifts and weaknesses, helping each one to rediscover his or her dignity and place in the human community. In a culture of peace, people who are stronger are encouraged to recognize and accept their own weaknesses, and to serve and give support to those who are more vulnerable and to help them discover their own capacities. In a culture of peace each person is seen as unique, important and sacred.

One of the big questions for each one of us today is how to turn our backs on the culture of rivalry, individualism, conflict and depression that surrounds us, and move instead into a culture of solidarity and co-operation, peace and hope. How can this transformation come about in us?

At the end of the round-table discussion in Paris, we were asked a question: Is it possible that one day there will be paradise on earth? It seems to me that paradise on earth is not possible unless each one of us discovers the paradise within us, that little sanctuary hidden in the most intimate part of our being. Perceiving and finding this inner paradise of peace and unity implies a struggle against the culture of rivalry which is within us too. If I can catch a glimpse of this inner paradise, I will begin to see it in others. And then as several people come together who live it, we create community . . . but all that implies a real struggle.

L'Arche and Faith and Light want to be communities of peace through our way of living, the way we welcome and share with people who are weak and vulnerable. Our communities can become places of transformation through the way we welcome each other, listen to one other and resolve conflict. Welcoming the weak, recognizing their gifts and helping them discover the meaning of their life is our way of building peace.

The danger for many today is to think that history is made without us, not with us. We often shrug our shoulders and say that we can't do anything about it. We forget that if we are together and give each other mutual support, we can witness to the strength of love and to the fact that life is stronger than death.

A good institution is defined both by competence and by the capacity of people within it to work together. There are many good institutions. Community life adds something else: the desire to live faithful relationships where each person is seen as a gift, where each one gives and receives life. Community is made up of relationships. Community life is formed and revealed through the quality of personal sharing, the quality of meetings (where each person assumes his or her responsibility), the quality of celebrations (where life and unity are celebrated), and the quality of prayer life (where we affirm together our desire to live in conformity with God's ways and to let God's love and wisdom form and mould our lives so that we can radiate hope and peace).

In May, in Chicago, I received the "Blessed are the Peacemakers" Award from the Catholic Theological Union. I was happy to receive it in the name of L'Arche and Faith and Light and to realize that other people recognize that our communities are places of peace. To act for peace requires a whole new attitude, a new way of living and of encountering others, especially those who are different from us. It means trying to create a society not in the form of a pyramid but as a circle, where the weak as well as the strong have their place and find dignity and meaning to their lives, and where there is mutuality rather than rivalry.

Last February, here in Trosly, we celebrated the life and death of Jeannine Vidal, who died quietly in her sleep. She came to L'Arche more than thirty years ago with many physical as well as intellectual disabilities and much anger and violence. She gradually grew more peaceful both in her heart and body, and little by little she found her place in the community. Eventually, she discovered that she was loved, and especially loved by God. Last November, while on pilgrimage to Lourdes with the whole community to celebrate our fortieth anniversary, she confided to an assistant that she hoped to die in her sleep as she was afraid of suffering. God answered her prayer. At the end of her life she had become a gentle, peaceful woman. When I went to see her, she would often notice my tiredness and say affectionately, "Pauvre vieux" ("poor old man"). What a joy for L'Arche to be able to welcome people like Jeannine, who have known so much pain and rejection, and to become for them a place where they can grow in peace and give peace.

In March we celebrated the life and death of Lucien Meunier, a man with profound disabilities who had lived in La Forestière for the last twenty-eight years. He was truly a great teacher for me. During my sabbatical year at La Forestière, he showed me all the violence hidden deep within me, and how much I needed to be transformed in order to find greater inner peace and become a better peacemaker.

I am still profoundly touched and nourished by Etty Hillesum, the Dutch Jewish woman who was gassed in Auschwitz. She wrote in her diary during the last year of her life: "Ultimately, we have just one moral duty; to reclaim large areas of peace in ourselves, more and more peace, and to reflect it onwards to others. And the more peace there is in us, the more peace there will also be in our troubled world."*

Yes, let's begin by establishing peace first within our own hearts, and then in the hearts of others. Let's create communities and families of peace. Isn't that the responsibility of each one of us? That means that we have to work on ourselves and recognize our compulsions, self-centredness and depression. This leads us into a deeper respect for ourselves so we live our humanity more fully. Peace is not a problem just for political leaders, it is our problem. Peace comes when we live in truth and accept who we are, with our strengths and weaknesses, and when we help others with their strengths and weaknesses to do the same.

Peace also comes as we realize that we are not alone. God is with us, like a friend. God is watching over each one of us and each one of our communities; God is guiding us. And so in the midst of all our difficulties we can give thanks!

Happy holidays to those of you who are living above the equator. The word "holidays" comes from "holy days." May these holidays

---

*You can read more from this remarkable woman in *Etty Hillesum, An Interrupted Life: The Diaries, 1941–1943*, and *Letters from Westerbork*.

be a time of peace and a time to rediscover inner strength, so that we can continue on the path of love and wisdom. And happy days, also, to those who are living underneath the equator. Pray for the international meeting of Faith and Light in July, in Madrid, where we will celebrate together and name the next international leaders. Let us pray for one another, in the joy of God's presence.

Jean Vanier

November/December 2006

Dear Friends,

I am starting this letter in Bangalore (India), where I am giving a retreat to the elder members and friends of our communities of Asha Niketan in India. Yesterday I finished a first retreat for young people and for those who have been in an Asha Niketan for a short time. When I arrived in Bangalore last Tuesday I was deeply moved to be welcomed by all four communities gathered together for a day of celebration. One hundred and fifty all together! Sixty came from Kolkata—a thirty-six-hour train ride!—forty from Nandi Bazaar (Kerala), twenty from Kottivakkam (Chennai)* and thirty from Bangalore. I met many of our Indian brothers and sisters a long time ago. I felt like weeping with emotion as I was greeted by Srinivasan, Veeran, Modhu, Mitran and many of the other men and women I knew in the very early days of Asha Niketan. Some of them had been quite violent and have now become people of peace; they have been transformed to become builders of community. The joy and peace that rose up from this magnificent gathering were like the joy that must spring up in us when we discover

---

*In the last ten years India has changed the names of many of its cities. Madras became Chennai.

the Kingdom of God. In one of his poems Tagore, the Bengali poet, wrote: "Pride can never approach to where thou walkest in the clothes of the humble, among the poorest, and lowliest, and lost" (Gitanjali 10). Yes, God is truly present in the poor, the lowliest and the lost. Yet our people in Asha Niketan are no longer as poor as they were, for they are rich in love, kindness and gentleness. They are no longer lonely for they are in a place of belonging. They are no longer lost for they have been found.

Anna Politkovskaia, the Russian journalist who was recently assassinated in Moscow because she was uncovering political lies, injustices and corruption, said, "A life that is not given so that humble and insignificant people can live, is a wasted life." She went on to say that to work for justice, peace and truth is not just for superhuman people but for all of us who want to give our lives so that we may share our lives more fully.

I would have much to share with you about our communities in India and how Kunni, L'Arche coordinator for India, is leading and giving support to them, but I do not have the space in this letter. I would just like to share at least one thing: Rakki, the community leader in Kolkata, was telling me how the people in the community were being pestered and laughed at by young people in the neighbourhood. Shoes in front of the prayer room were being stolen, as well as other items. The community decided to have a public theatre in front of their home in which all the community members would take part. The theme was taken from Tagore: a story of conflict between those who were legalistic and those who were very open and liberal which ends in reconciliation and mutual understanding. Some three hundred people from the area came and were so delighted that they asked Rakki to do another in six months' time! And Rakki added that people in the area no longer laugh and make fun of us but are more and more accepting. Asha Niketan is a little sign for that area, announcing a vision of love and acceptance for everyone.

Since my last newsletter I have been involved in a number of events. Perhaps you all laughed when I said I was going to retire! In fact I am going more slowly and have more times of prayers and solitude and reading. I am cutting down on my travel and my commitments. I am so happy to be more in my community and in my home, Le Val. It is such a gift to take time together to give thanks for all that is being given and to carry in prayer what is painful and difficult.

Last September I was in Assisi for the commemoration of the first international meeting which John Paul II convened in 1996 for religious leaders from throughout the world. This celebration was organized by the Community of Sant'Egidio. We all came together to share and pray for peace and to be a sign of peace and of prayer today. There were various workshops where Muslim leaders, Jewish rabbis, bishops and other leaders met together and shared on particular topics. I was part of the workshop on "the love of God and the love of people." I shared especially about Ghadir, a young Muslim girl with severe disabilities whom we had welcomed in our L'Arche community in Bethany, and how my encounter with her had been a sign of God and a place for transformation for me.

Later that same month I was part of a two-day symposium organized by Professor John Swinton at the University of Aberdeen (Scotland) on "L'Arche: A Place of Gentleness." The other main speaker was Professor Stanley Hauerwas, a reputed theologian from Duke University (USA). I was amazed and touched by all he knows about our communities, our pedagogy, our way of life and the message of L'Arche for our world today. I was moved by the way he spoke of gentleness and of L'Arche as a place of growth and healing.

In October, I was in Krakow (Poland) for a retreat with people in L'Arche, Faith and Light and friends. It brought back to my mind many memories of the first links of L'Arche there in 1982 when it was still under the Communist regime. The first community in Sledziejowice had to remain very hidden, silent and closed up, not to attract attention from the authorities. Faith and Light had already begun a few years earlier in Wroclaw and Warsaw. So much has happened in both L'Arche and Faith and Light since then! I also gave a talk at the University of Warsaw and was able to make a little pilgrimage to the concentration camp in Auschwitz where Etty Hillesum and so many other Jewish people were exterminated. It was moving for me to pray there, and to pray for all those who are being crushed and killed today.

Etty Hillesum wrote so much about how God lives in each one of us. Tagore also reminds us that we are called to be a "shrine" of God:

Life of my life, I shall ever try to keep my body pure, knowing that thy living touch is upon all my limbs.

I shall ever try to keep all untruths out from my thoughts, knowing that thou art that truth which has kindled the light of reason in my mind.

I shall ever try to drive all evils away from my heart and keep my love in flower, knowing that thou hast thy seat in the inmost shrine of my heart.

And it shall be my endeavour to reveal thee in my actions, knowing it is thy power gives me strength to act. (Gitanjali 4)

We are all called to let God come and live in the "inmost shrine" of our hearts and to reveal God through our lives and words. May God "keep our love in flower," that is the secret: to let our hearts blossom fully and bear much fruit.

Although I am still called to travel a bit, my joy is also to give retreats at La Ferme here in·Trosly, where I can speak about the spirituality of L'Arche, how those who are weak and vulnerable can change and heal us. Last weekend was quite a special time for me and for the community. In collaboration with different associations, I gave a retreat here for fourteen "street people" from Paris, accompanied by fourteen of their friends. The first evening each one of us shared our stories. It was a gift to speak to them of the love of God for each one of us.

This letter brings my love to each of you for Christmas and the new year. May God be reborn in our hearts. May our love continue to blossom and our lives reveal the presence of God.

Jean Vanier

May 2007
Trosly

Dear Friends,

First of all I would like to tell you about what we have been living here in Trosly as Jacqueline, Barbara and Claire move into a new phase of greater fragility, and with the sudden death of Patrick Mathias.

Jacqueline was Père Thomas' secretary before L'Arche; I have known her since 1950 when I joined Père Thomas in L'Eau Vive. She has been here since the beginning, fixing up and decorating all our houses in Trosly, Cuise and Pierrefonds with competence and creativity. She has truly been a support and a source of grace for me. Today, at eighty-one, and after five years with Parkinson's disease, she is obliged to use a wheelchair and has great difficulty expressing herself. She decided to go to a home for the elderly about ten kilometres from Trosly, where she suffers sometimes from the way she is treated. But she is able to come regularly to Trosly for meals at La Ferme and to participate in the Eucharist and in retreat weekends.

Due to her cancer and a very strong chemo, Barbara is going

through a difficult moment of great fatigue and has trouble walking. Barbara arrived in Trosly in 1965 and has been my secretary, my "memory" and my support since 1967. It is beautiful to see her courage and perseverance.

Claire has had a new bout with cancer which has obliged her to begin a new treatment and to leave her role as coordinator of all the communities of L'Arche in the Oise. That has touched me and all of us deeply. She continues to be with her foyer, Massabielle, and to be full of life and hope! All of this has called forth many gestures of kindness and support and solidarity within the community and throughout the wider family of L'Arche.

I also need to write about the sudden death of Patrick Mathias, our psychiatrist for the last twenty-five years. He had a heart attack on April 24. Patrick was in fact more than a psychiatrist for us; he was a friend. Whenever one of our people was in deep pain, he brought new light. He was a man of amazing goodness, understanding what it means to be human. He had such a capacity to give life and consolation. Pierrot said that he was like Père Thomas: "After being with him you felt so much better." Patrick loved life, his family, his animals; he had deep respect for each person whatever their situation or suffering. In many ways I learned from him how to be more human, more Christian. He was a teacher of humanity. He did not share our Christian faith but was a sign and a presence of God in our community. I believe that Jesus, the Word who became flesh, came to teach us how to live more humanly, how to love in truth. Patrick taught us to be more human. He was a man of tenderness. At his funeral we read a few lines of a text he wrote:

> Tenderness is a way of life, where gentleness and kindness remind us how different it is from sentimentalism or romanticism and that it requires maturity. With tenderness there is no more protective carapace: we expose ourselves and risk being hurt at any moment . . .

How to widen the "we" in order to create a humanity where each
person is a brother, a father, a mother . . . each one like us. The "we"
both affirms the separation as well as the bonding. It is a continual
search for communication . . . Tenderness brings a sense of relaxation or well-being, a softening of our defences. It is like a hinge or a
pivot. It tempers the changes, tensions and lack of coherence in our
lives and brings together desire and love. It is a sign of complemen-
tarity. To be adult is to be tender, to be fragile, like everyone else.

I have had the opportunity to meet Stanley Hauerwas twice during these past months, once at a conference at the University of
Aberdeen and then at a meeting in Trosly. *Time* magazine named
him the most important theologian today in the United States. In
Paris, at the Institut Catholique, he also gave a talk on L'Arche as
a place of the revelation of God's tenderness. I am amazed to see
how theologians in the United States are working on questions
around the theology of people marked by disability or vulnerability—the mystery Paul reveals when he gives us Jesus's words to
him: "My strength is manifested in your weakness" (2 Cor. 12:9).
Stanley Hauerwas truly has something to tell us about the deep
meaning of L'Arche. And isn't it amazing to see how Patrick's and
Stanley's visions coincide? Shortly after Easter, I also had the joy
of making a pilgrimage to the Holy Land with thirty-five elders in
L'Arche to walk in the steps of Jesus. It was also a time of retreat,
a time for each one of us to listen to Jesus's words calling us to
rediscover and deepen the mystery of L'Arche: to be open and welcoming to the weakest and the most vulnerable at the heart of
the Church and of humanity. It was truly a time of grace. And
all this was taking place in this land of conflict and oppression,
just as during the time of Jesus. We listened to the personal testimonies of Jews and Palestinians, recognizing that today there is
a strong current in Israeli society which opposes more and more
the oppressive and brutal actions of their government. There is a

group called Women in Black who demonstrate each week against the oppression, and journalists like Amira Hass and Gideon Levy are speaking out.

I must admit I find it very hurtful personally when I am accused of being anti-Semitic because of my criticism of Israel's actions. I love the beauty of the Jewish people, and I can well understand the anger of biblical prophets who were infuriated and cried out their anger against what their leaders were doing! Obviously, the terrorist actions of Palestinians are also horrible and must be condemned. The people of Israel and of Palestine both live in fear. But the answer is not in the building of a wall and planting Jewish settlements in Palestinian territory. It is in respect for international law and a real search together for justice through dialogue and help from the international community. The situation—as in Iraq—is so fragile. Everyone is so vulnerable.

And I spoke of Barbara, Claire, Jacqueline and Patrick because their fragility is a reminder of the fragility of each one of us. The international situation is fragile. The balance of our earth is fragile. The gap between the rich and poor is widening and everywhere we find conflicts and seeds of war. Each one of us is so fragile. We were born in weakness and after a brief time of strength we move again into fragility; our hearts remain fragile and vulnerable. The communities of L'Arche and Faith and Light remain fragile. They depend on men and women who are open and vulnerable to hearing the cry of the weak and who commit themselves to live in friendship with them like brothers and sisters. Our communities are places where love and life are freely given. Governments can proclaim laws and the UN can write a charter for people marked by disability, but law can never replace authentic love and the tenderness that come from a personal commitment.

During the pilgrimage-retreat I spoke about the first Beatitude, of lack. When we are lacking something or in need, either we close up in ourselves, in our sadness or in our hardness of heart, or else we open up to a relationship in order to ask for help. We humbly turn towards others and towards Jesus. Isn't it weakness that links people together? The cry "I need you" is at the heart of community. Structures cannot create communities which are alive, open and loving (although adequate structures should help this to be so).

Community is created by people, by each person who comes freely, motivated by faith in people and by love that creates and maintains community life. The lack of assistants or lack of funds creates places where we need to ask for help. I love to say, "Come! Come and celebrate life with us and celebrate it with those who are weak and vulnerable." And especially during this time of Pentecost we cry out, "Come Holy Spirit! Fill our hearts with your love." I discover more and more the weakness and vulnerability of God. How the all-powerful one becomes powerless in front of our human freedom. God suggests, invites, offers and knocks at the doors of our hearts, but never forces the door open. God has such a deep respect for each one of us. God and the poor wait patiently for us to respond. We can deny his existence. We can turn our backs on God and turn away from others, from love. But God waits to give us a new strength, the strength of the Holy Spirit. I discover more and more the patience and vulnerability of God, and I love him more and more.

Jean Vanier

CONCLUSION ❧ LIFE FLOWS ON: GROWING INTO THE FUTURE

In many ways these letters are my own personal story, and I feel like apologizing for them because they weren't meant for the public, but for only a few friends. I would like to insist that this book is not the full story of L'Arche, which has already been written by Kathryn Spink,* it is only part of the story. Many important events concerning L'Arche or Faith and Light have not been mentioned. I hardly speak of the expansion of L'Arche in France and Belgium, and many wonderful people in our communities have not been mentioned. This is the story of some of my travels and of my growing vision of our communities in our broken world.

The letters speak often of the birth and growth of communities, of individuals, of faith, trust and hope, and of my own growth in the Spirit. When I reread these letters, I am reminded that there was something foolish, according to human standards, about the beginnings of L'Arche: the way we lived, the way we welcomed new people, the way new communities were founded. Community life seemed so easy in the utopian days of the 1960s and '70s. These letters reveal a great deal of optimism as well as perhaps a lack of understanding of the frailty and complexity of human beings and of community life. And with hindsight now, I see that

*This was published as *Jean Vanier and L'Arche: A Communion of Love.*

mistakes were made, sometimes serious ones. Some of the communities that had beautiful beginnings and flourished at the time of their creation are today in pain. But we've learned from experience: as L'Arche has become older and more established or professional, we do things with more wisdom, realizing that it takes a lot of time to found a new community.

I realize too that the letters rarely speak of endings and death; or if they do, it's mostly in the later letters, as I myself begin to age. As I've written before, L'Arche is founded on pain, and death is a reality we're very close to. Isn't weakness a sign of death? The big question at L'Arche is always how to welcome reality and not create or live in illusions, because it is reality that gives us freedom. To be free is to look reality in the face, whether it be the reality of suffering, the reality of death, the reality of people in their weaknesses or the reality of our own mistakes. In L'Arche when someone is dying the first thing we do is talk about it, and people can grieve and people can laugh. We celebrate death; we don't take it lightly, but we weep and we laugh. Who knows, maybe we're next. And when the person dies, if they die at Trosly, then the body is exposed for three or four days and we all go to visit the body. Then we have a wake and we laugh, we grieve, and we tell stories of the person who has died.

I remember way back, in 1967 or so, when François Debussy, one of the first assistants at L'Arche, had cancer and the doctors said no more could be done for him, he came to Trosly to die. When he had died and his body was laid out, two people with intellectual disabilities, Jean-Louis and Philippe, came hobbling over and asked Jacqueline, "Can we go and see François?" And she said, "Sure." Jean-Louis asked her, "Can I kiss him?" and she said, "Yes." So he kissed François and cried out, startled, "Oh shit! He's cold." And as he and Philippe were leaving the room, Jean-Louis said to Philippe, "You know Mum will be so surprised when I tell her I kissed a dead person!" Their reaction could be the same as anyone's in their first encounter with a dead body. But to understand this event more deeply, we should remember that a physical or intellectual disability indicates a presence of death. To kiss a dead body and to speak of it might have meant that Jean-Louis was accepting his own disability, that he could be and live as he was. Without acceptance, fear of death and one's own disabilities can be paralyzing.

Death is normalizing: we're all going to die, disabled or not. So when a person with a disability dies, you know that they're no longer excluded, they're no longer different—they are now "normal." After the wake and the religious service, the coffin is taken to the person's family plot or cemetery and buried there, and the person is integrated with the rest of the group. In death we all find new life together in the heart of God. No one is disabled; or rather, we are all disabled and rejoice in the love of God.

We have a L'Arche cemetery at Trosly, but there's only one person buried there, and that's Père Thomas. When he died in 1993, his funeral was attended by thirteen hundred people. Père Thomas was like a root: hidden, unseen, deep in the earth, but essential and life-giving. He was, as Marthe Robin once described him, "all heart," with something, a *charism*, that drew people to God. In many ways his life epitomized that of L'Arche itself, and for some time after his death I couldn't speak of him without weeping because the union between us had been so deep. His death, however, was not an end: life and L'Arche continue to flow with all he has given and gives.

Mother Teresa had a great gift for the dying. She was phenomenal. She understood the mystery of the body, how touching and tending a broken person could lead to a real encounter. The Missionaries of Charity Sisters, and the Brothers founded by Brother Andrew, are wonderful, beautiful people. Mother Teresa told me once that there were quite a number of Hindu women who wanted to become Sisters of Charity, but who did not want to become Catholic. And she indicated that there were Muslim women who wanted to join and remain Muslim. Just imagine Catholic Missionaries of Charity, and Hindu Missionaries of Charity and Muslim Missionaries of Charity! And then maybe Buddhists, and so on. It would have been incredible. She said she'd received permission from Rome to start a Hindu order, but it never happened, and I've never quite known why not. Did she feel in the end that it shouldn't happen? Was permission revoked or not finalized? She got so far as to ask me to preach the first retreat for these Hindu women, but alas it never took place. The project died in the bud, and new life was then not given.

Mother Teresa was an incredibly beautiful person and incredibly project-minded: every time I'd have breakfast with her or go to Mass with her, whether in India, in Rome or in the United States, she'd tell me about the community she was going to start in Russia, or in Yemen, or here or there. There was an urgency and a sort of fatigue in her face when she was working. But when she herself was sick or dying and in hospital, she was at her most beautiful: her face became translucent, there was a beauty in her skin, a freshness, a childlike quality, which I'd never seen when she was well. Her death meant a new beginning for the Missionaries of Charity: they had to assume their reality, rediscover their *charism* without the presence of their founder and forge forward in a new way while remaining a sign in the world of the compassion of God for the weak.

John Paul II was another person who came to truly understand L'Arche, but perhaps only when he became ill with Parkinson's disease. I remember the first time I had breakfast with him (in 1987, when he was still well) and I explained to him how a disabled person, like Eric, who was blind and deaf, was a healing presence in L'Arche. In his littleness Eric transformed those who lived a relationship with him. John Paul said to somebody afterwards that he hadn't understood what I meant. It's after he became sick that a deep bond arose between us, when he understood how someone "made little" by a severe handicap could transform others. In January 2004, at a meeting in Rome that focused on the disabled, John Paul said that people with disabilities can help us to discover a new world where love is stronger than aggressiveness.* After the meeting, I called his secretary to ask if I could attend the Pope's Mass; he said yes but that I would be alone with John Paul. It was a very special, moving time together—a time of prayer, communion and mutual recognition. He knew that I loved him in his weakness and I knew that he loved L'Arche and me in our weaknesses too.

I mention in the letters our time together at Lourdes in August 2004, a few months before he died. I remember I was standing in front of the Popemobile giving the meditation on the mystery of Jesus proclaiming the Kingdom of God. I was just two metres away from him, looking into his eyes. I said aloud, "Our Pope is poor. He's fragile, but he is the glory of God. God manifests himself in him." And we continued to look at one another. It was an exceptionally moving moment. Afterwards he gave me the rosary he'd been using and which I carry with me every day.

Some might say that L'Arche embodies much of the spirit of Vatican II—a prayerfulness, a presence among the poor, an ecumenical outlook—and I think that John Paul recognized that. He may have also valued L'Arche's connection to the young, as he loved young people. He had a tremendous freedom, and young people were very attracted to that, to his authenticity. He wasn't just giving out dogma or telling people what to do: he lived the Gospel message. He wasn't what other people wanted him to be; he was free from all that because he lived in the Word.

The challenge today for L'Arche is to build places of belonging, founded upon our need for one another, where people can

---

*I consider this document by John Paul II to be one of the most important writings about the affirmation of the transformative power of people with disabilities.

grow into this kind of freedom. There's a careful balance between belonging and freedom: too much freedom leads to anguish, isolation and insecurity; too much belonging, too much security, leads to stifledness and inner closedness. The other challenge is to harmonize competence and spirituality, to make sure that as society pushes towards greater and greater efficiencies and production the spiritual element, the idea of each person's preciousness in all their weakness, isn't lost.

Without that balance, the severely disabled will be seen as useless and be discarded, either before birth or after. It used to be that families or religious organizations would look after the poor, but now that is no longer possible because in most cases both parents are working. If caring for the weak and vulnerable, and funding their care, falls to the state, and one day the state has to choose between either investing in armaments to protect the country and new technologies to grow the economy or spending on the weakest members of society, it's not clear that the state will choose the poor. The situation is very complex. But it's evident that politicians cannot confront these problems alone; they require committed people. I saw a beautiful example of this in a prison for women in Guatemala: the wardens were religious women, and they ate side by side with the inmates and attended conferences with them. There was something really right and good about the arrangement. It was a wonderful example of creating a place for the poor, the lost, the rejected. In this form of community they could grow to freedom, to responsibility and to trust.

In our world of today, there's been a real shift from living with the broken, from searching for new ways to achieve peace and justice, from relying on intuition and seeing where the Spirit of God can lead, towards a growth in distrust and the need for protection and the certitudes that come from power. (And this can even happen within the churches.) The world has made extraordinary progress in terms of human rights and this is good, but I'd like to hear people talk more about human responsibility. We speak of the rights of the disabled to live on their own, to get married, to work or not work as they wish; but what about the right of that person to be different, to be loved and appreciated and find places of belonging? Technology already permits parents to choose the sex of their child or to abort a child that is likely to be disabled. But what happens when you have chosen your child to be a piano player and he doesn't become a piano player? Where do you place your anger? They have to be a good piano player because that's what was wanted and chosen. And you find the same thing happens with parents of children with Down's syndrome: parents want their children to be perfect, and so they push, push, push their children to be as "normal" as possible. But what of the children's right to be different, to be separate from their parents, to be free to be whoever they want to be? It used to be that a parent would accept the child born of them, be it a boy or a girl, able or disabled. There was a gentle acceptance of nature, of responsibility for the common good, a sense that we are responsible to each other as human beings, valuing one another as we are rather than for what we can do.

This message is now the focus of my life. My time for practical involvement in L'Arche and Faith and Light affairs has passed, and now it's the members of each community and the Federation leaders who are responsible for the groups' continuation and growth. The original founders have to know when to disappear and let go so that they don't prevent the "refounders" from accomplishing their goals. The myth of the perfect founder who does everything inspired by God is evolving in our communities into a more collective ownership of the founding story, purified of its non-essentials. Leadership at L'Arche and Faith and Light is now related to the tasks and mission of each Federation and not to the myths or charisma of the founders. This leadership transition for communities is an exciting challenge: all of the members and leaders are called into a certain littleness in and through which the Spirit of God will manifest Herself and I have such a deep trust in our leaders today and the way they are listening to the Spirit.

There was a time at Le Val Fleuri when I was seen as the leader; today they look at me and say, "Poor guy, you're looking tired, you ought to go and rest." It's a completely other form of relationship. Where they were children, now they are parents, mothering me—and these are people with disabilities! They love me and they see me weak and fragile, and their tenderness rises up from within them. I was with an old couple a few years ago, and I was holding hands with the wife when she said she didn't like growing old. And I teased, "Madame, if we were thirty years old, I couldn't be holding your hand in front of your husband!" When we're old we discover other things: we discover tenderness and fragility.

In our world today we're all confronted by the question of time: what must I do when I am no longer working, will I have enough money? When sickness and death comes we are so scared because we've rarely planned for it—though I can have an accident today and die. We must accept the reality of weakness and death without planifying it, without making it an obsession or compulsion. We have to be much more concerned with growth in love and prayerfulness than with death or with time. At my age, I have to accept my gifts but I have also a lot to learn about growing downwards, living with anguish without running away from it, acknowledging that today I'm tired and weak and I can't solve the problems of others. I am called to enter into new types of relationships and into deeper communion of love with Jesus and with all my brothers and sisters.

The poet Tagore said that "Death is not a lamp that is extinguished; it is the coming of dawn." Weakness, crises and death are never an end but are new beginnings. L'Arche and Faith and Light were founded on weakness, they will continue to grow in their mission in and through their fragility, and God will continue to be present. God works through our communities, and I am happy to see it. Life continues to flow.

INDEX

Note: Cities and L'Arche homes are identified by their location. The foyers in Trosly-Breuil are listed separately by name ("Le" and "La" are treated as part of the name). A page location such as "169n" indicates a footnote on that page.

Abidjan (Ivory Coast), 156
Aboriginal people (Australia), 209, 210, 228, 236
Adam: God's Beloved (Nouwen), 370n
Afghanistan, 247, 492–93
Africa, 202, 203, 218–19, 246–47, 407. *See also specific countries*
Afrikaners, 272, 327
Agnes, Mother (Calcutta), 94
Agré, Bernard, Bishop, 171, 185, 215, 235
Alberta, 147, 148, 308
Algeria, 428
Alleluia House (Ottawa, ON), 149, 151

Andrew, Brother (Calcutta), 90, 97–98, 249–50, 315
Anglican Church, 151, 158–59, 444, 491
Ani Pachen (Buddhist nun), 486–87
Aquino, Benigno, 282, 302
Aquino, Corazon, 282n, 301, 302
Arabs, 261–62
Arbuckle, Gerald, Father, 525
Arceo, Nonoy and Nellie, 283, 284, 303
Aristotle, 4, 462
Arns, Paulo, Cardinal, 175, 176–77, 180
Asha Niketan, 104, 249, 250–51, 404, 418–19, 536–37
    founding, 66, 71–81, 99, 418

Asha Niketan–Bangalore, 85–88, 94n, 125–27, 130, 194, 222–23, 418

Asha Niketan–Calcutta
  founding, 115, 117, 134–35, 136
  at Sealdah Station, 161, 164–68, 192–93, 241, 249
  at Tangra, 357, 418, 536, 537

Asha Niketan–Chennai (Kottivakkam), 194–95, 241–42, 250, 373, 536

Asha Niketan–Kotagiri, 88–89, 94n

Asha Niketan–Nandi Bazaar (Calicut), 221–22, 242–44, 373–74, 536

Asia, 212, 316. *See also specific countries*

Asiatic Congress on Mental Deficiency (1977), 222

Atanasios, Bishop (Egypt), 299

Auschwitz, 386, 423, 539

Australia, 208–10, 227–28, 229, 231, 280–81

Avoca House (Toronto, ON), 151

Belfast (Northern Ireland), 213–14, 232

Benedict XVI, Pope, 525–26

Beni-Abbès (Hobart, Australia), 280n

Bettelheim, Bruno, 198

Bombay (India), 69–70

Bonhoeffer, Dietrich, 529

Bosnia, 399n

Boston (MA), 308

Botton Village (England), 48

Bradburne, John, 270–71

Brazil, 174–83, 268

British Columbia, 147, 158

Brothers of St. John of God, 228

Brothers of Taizé, 190n, 528, 529

Budapest (Hungary), 351, 368

Buddhists, 437. *See also* Ani Pachen

Bundeena community (Australia), 209–10, 231

Burkina Faso (Upper Volta), 216–18, 233, 236–38, 289–91

Bangalore (India), 65–66, 70–81, 90, 222, 536. *See also* Asha Niketan–Bangalore

Bangladesh, 90n, 92–96, 99, 193, 403

Beaudry, Jacques, Father, 144, 145, 146, 172, 223

Beauvais, Bishop of, 198–99

Beck, Martha, 498–99

Bedouins, 305–6

Beirut (Lebanon), 254, 279–80, 322–24, 352, 373

Beit El Rafiq. *See* L'Arche–Bethany

Calcutta, Archbishop of, 115, 117, 119

Calcutta (Kolkata). *See also* Asha Niketan–Calcutta; Dum Dum
  in 1970s, 90–99, 114–19, 121, 130–36, 161–69, 193
  in 1980s and '90s, 249–50, 356–57, 404

Calgary (AB), 147, 148

Calicut (India), 128–29. *See also* Asha Niketan–Nandi Bazaar

Câmara, Hélder, 179–80

Camphill villages, 48, 275

Canada, 40, 378. *See also specific cities and provinces*
  L'Arche in, 33, 49, 122–25, 147–52, 308
  Native people in, 211, 308
  prisons in, 101–2, 107, 122–23, 148–49, 152–54
  retreats in, 103, 151, 158–59
  young people in, 33, 50, 152–54
Canadian Forces (Europe), 30, 67–68
Canterbury, Archbishop of, 444, 491, 525
Caritas, 90, 93, 367
Carmelites, 108
Casa San José. *See* L'Arche–Choluteca
Catholic Theological Union, 534
Catholic Worker Movement, 62
Central America, 267–69, 309, 354–56, 440. *See also specific countries*
Ceyrac, Pierre, Father, 91, 474
Chennai. *See* Madras
Chergé, Christian de, 428, 493–94
Cheshire, Group Captain, 57
Cheshire Home (Bombay), 69–70, 77
Chicago (IL), 105–6
Chile, 181
Cité Secours (Lourdes), 20, 24, 37, 53
Clare, Saint, 525
Clarke, Bill, Father, 40, 43, 110, 113–14, 208
Claudel, Paul, 403
Claverie, Pierre, Bishop, 493
Cleveland (OH), 104–5, 110–14
Cochin Hospital (Paris), 195–96, 199–201

Community and Growth (Vanier), 218–19
The Company of Strangers (Palmer), 367
Coptic Church, 299
Corpus Christi Community (Australia), 281
Corrigan, Mairead, 213
Côte d'Ivoire. *See* Ivory Coast
Crossroads (Montreal), 49–50
Cuba, 477
Czestochowa (Poland), 101, 292, 385–86

Damascus (Syria), 277, 413, 517–18
D'Antonio, Nicolas, Bishop, 187–88
Daughters of St. Mary, 299
Day, Dorothy, 62, 63, 82, 84
Deena Seva Sangha (Bangalore), 65
de Gaulle, Charles, 41n, 200
Deir Anba Bishoi monastery (Egypt), 298–99
De Roo, Remi, Bishop, 147
Desmazières, Stéphane, Bishop, 28, 35
Doherty, Catherine (Baroness de Hueck), 62–63, 83, 84
Doherty, Eddie, 63
Dominican Republic, 354, 355, 356
Doyle, Emmett, Bishop, 158
Dum Dum (India), 93–94, 193
Dutch Reformed Church, 327–28

Edmonton (AB), 147, 308
Egypt, 298–301, 372–73

El Rusc (Spain), 430
El Salvador, 257–58
Els Avets (Spain), 430
England. *See* Great Britain
Enough Room for Joy (Clarke), 208, 212
Episcopalian Church (Haiti), 432
Erie (PA), 124–25, 370n
Europe, Eastern, 359, 360, 385–86, 398–99, 409. *See also specific countries*
Expecting Adam (Beck), 498–99

Faith and Light, 142–43, 307, 316, 362, 368
  in Africa, 313, 325, 327, 408, 421, 423
  in Asia, 303, 370, 404, 437
  in Australia, 280
  in Eastern Europe, 351, 385–86, 398, 409
  in Egypt, 300–301
  founding, 486
  and L'Arche, 453–54, 455
  in Latin America, 480
  leadership, 551–52
  meetings, 401
  in Middle East, 278, 279, 324, 518
  pilgrimages, 377–78, 486
  in Poland, 292, 367, 539
Faith and Sharing, 22, 383, 400, 401, 445, 456
Fatima (Portugal), 43, 76
Festival of Peace (1995), 419–20
Flahiff, George, Bishop, 147

Focolarini Movement, 254
Ford, David, 461, 522
Foucauld, Charles de, 61, 360, 493, 529
Foyers de Charité, 63, 223, 390, 482
Franciscans, 105, 112
Francis of Assisi, Saint, 493, 504–5, 518–19, 524
Friendship House (New York), 63

Galen, Clemens von, Bishop, 529
Gandhi, Indira, 90n
Gandhi, Mohandas K., 65, 66, 75–76, 79, 492
Gemayel, Bachir, 255
Gemayel, Pierre, 255
Georgia (country), 409
Good Samaritan (parable), 477–80
Gorbachev, Mikhail, 346n, 351n, 360, 363
Goss, Jean, 174n, 359
Goss-Mayr, Hildegard, 174–76, 359, 532
Great Britain, 48, 99–100, 371–72, 393
Greek Catholic Church, 389
Guatemala, 550
Guérin, Marcel, Bishop, 187
Gulf War, 372, 374–75

Haiti, 188–89, 276–77, 354–55, 356, 398. *See also* L'Arche–Carrefour; Port-au-Prince

Halifax (NS), 123
Hauerwas, Stanley, 538, 542
The Heart Has Its Reason (film), 347
Hillesum, Etty, 507, 514, 535, 539
Hiroshima (Japan), 315
Home for the Dying (Calcutta), 93, 96–97, 116, 162
Honduras, 187–88, 189–91, 268–69, 439–40. *See also* L'Arche–Choluteca; L'Arche–Tegucigalpa
Hong Kong, 370, 437
Hueck, Baron de, 62–63
Hungary, 350–51
Hurley, Denis, Bishop, 274, 327
Hussein, Saddam, 372n
Hutin, Magdeleine, Little Sister, 61–62, 84, 360, 493

Ils sont morts pour leur foi (Riccardi), 507
Images of Hope (film), 497n
India. *See also specific cities;* Asha Niketan
  institutions in, 57, 69–70
  L'Arche in, 49–50, 56
  visits to (1970s), 69–81, 85–99, 125–36, 241–44
  visits to (1980s and '90s), 249–51, 356–58, 373–75
Institute of Philosophy (Moscow), 358–59
Intifada, 328n, 365
Iran, 247
Iran–Iraq War, 247n, 317, 322n
Iraq, 372n, 467

Ireland, 232–33. *See also* Northern Ireland
Iskandar, Georges, Bishop, 278
Israel. *See also* L'Arche–Bethany
  L'Arche in, 294–95, 304–6, 317–18
  pilgrimages to, 259–62, 474–76, 519, 542–43
Ivory Coast, 155–57, 183–85, 201–5, 214–15, 234–36, 246–47. *See also* L'Arche–Bouaké; L'Arche–Man

Jamhour (Lebanon), 323–24
Japan, 314–15, 387
Jean Vanier and L'Arche (Spink), 545
Jerusalem, 260, 261, 318, 475
Jewish people, 260, 262, 294, 543
John, Gospel of, 434–36, 497
John Paul I, Pope, 238n
John Paul II, Pope, 107n, 317, 320, 444, 494
  death, 525–26
  international role, 276, 294n, 360, 475–76
  in old age, 508, 520, 548–49
Jordan, 530
Joy and Charity (Iraq), 467

Kana-no-ie (Japan), 387
Kasper, Cardinal, 525
Katimavik retreats, 197, 446, 456
Kay Sin Josef (Haiti). *See* L'Arche–Carrefour

Khan, Abdul Ghaffar, 492–93
King, Martin Luther, Jr., 343, 506
Kingston (ON), 101–2, 122–23, 148, 152
Knowing Eternity (film), 497
Kolbe, Maximilian, 107, 386
Kolkata. *See* Calcutta
Korea, 315–16, 436–37
Kosovo, 504
Kottivakkam. *See* Asha Niketan–Chennai
Kristeva, Julia, 343
Kuwait, 317n, 322n, 372n

Lacroix, Fernand, Bishop, 103
La Forestière (Trosly), 262, 263–66, 402, 485, 535
L'Arche, 502, 512. *See also specific homes;* L'Arche assistants
  Charter, 448, 450, 452, 494
  expansion, 139–40
  founding, 5–6, 15–17, 453, 545–46
  General Assembly (2002), 502–3
  International Council, 430–31, 502n
  International Covenant Commission, 440–41
  leadership, 551–52
  as mature organization, 391, 546
  Renewal (1979), 244–45
  Spirituality Commission, 378–79
L'Arche assistants, 339–40, 341–45, 430, 457
  children of, 368
  spiritual growth of, 378–79, 393, 395, 512

L'Arche–Belgium (Le Toit), 394
L'Arche–Bethany (West Bank), 311–12, 317, 328–30, 348–49, 365, 474–75, 538
  founding, 294–95, 304–6
L'Arche–Bouaké (Ivory Coast), 155–57, 170–71, 185, 202, 204–5, 234, 289
L'Arche–Carrefour (Haiti), 188–89, 223–24, 276–77, 431–32
L'Arche–Chantal (Haiti), 432
L'Arche–Choluteca (Honduras), 309–10, 355, 439
L'Arche–Cuise (Valinhos, France), 45, 47–48, 55
L'Arche–Daybreak (Richmond Hill, ON), 56, 84, 149, 313, 370, 416, 417
L'Arche–Edmonton (Shalom), 147, 149
L'Arche–Erie (Hearth), 149, 370
L'Arche–Genesaret (Canberra, Australia), 280n
L'Arche–Kent (England), 444
L'Arche–La Merci (Courbillac, France), 39, 43, 48, 67
L'Arche–Le Caillou Blanc (Brittany, France), 474
L'Arche–Man (Ivory Coast), 215, 236
L'Arche–Mobile (Hope), 186, 370n
L'Arche–Punla (Manila, Philippines), 369
L'Arche–Sledziejowice (Poland), 398, 539
L'Arche–Stratford (Maranatha), 149, 151
L'Arche–Sydney (Australia), 280n
L'Arche–Tegucigalpa (Honduras), 206–7, 220, 225–27, 238–40, 310–11

L'Arche–Vancouver (Shiloah), 147, 158

L'Arche–Winnipeg (MB), 147–48, 149

L'Arche–Zimbabwe, 513

La Rose des Vents (Paris, France), 40–41, 45–46

La Rose des Vents (Verpillières, France), 394, 511

La Salette (France), 36, 42, 54

La Source (Trosly), 47, 53

Latin America, 207, 227, 257–58, 267–69. *See also specific countries*

La Vigne (Trosly), 526

L'Eau Vive, 4

Lebanon, 252–56, 278–80, 322–24, 351–52, 372–73, 412

Leningrad (St. Petersburg, Russia), 364–65

L'Ermitage (Trosly), 38, 41, 52–53

Les Rameaux (Trosly), 34, 35, 37, 52

Les Trois Fontaines (Ambleteuse, France), 67

L'Étable (Victoria, BC), 147, 158

Le Tremplin (Trosly), 47, 53, 55

"Let's Celebrate Jesus" (Cleveland, OH), 110–14

Le Val Fleuri (Trosly)
  as L'Arche home, 19, 22, 23
  life at, 52, 269, 289, 296, 393–95, 525
  under Père Thomas, 5, 15–16

Lisieux (France), 108n

Lithuania, 363n, 388–89

Little Brothers of Jesus (Foucauld), 181, 282, 360, 529

Little Brothers of the Gospel, 82

Little Sisters of Jesus (Foucauld), 36, 61–62, 210, 320, 360
  in Africa, 274, 421
  in Asia, 230, 282, 284, 303, 315
  in Brazil, 181, 182
  in Middle East, 254, 260, 324
  in North America, 82, 83, 106, 154

Lourdes (France)
  Faith and Light pilgrimages to, 377–78, 486
  John Paul II at, 520
  L'Arche pilgrimages to, 20, 24, 26, 37, 42, 53

Lustiger, Jean-Marie, Cardinal, 428

Madonna House (Combermere, ON), 63, 83

Madras (Chennai), 91, 194–95, 358

Magdeleine, Little Sister. *See* Hutin, Magdeleine, Little Sister

Malja (West Bank), 311, 329, 474–75

Man (Ivory Coast), 156, 171, 184–85, 201–2, 214–15, 236

Maori people, 211–12

Marcos, Ferdinand, 282, 301, 302

Mar Moussa monastery (Syria), 518

Maryfarm (nr. Ottawa, ON), 122, 149, 152

Marylake (nr. Toronto, ON), 383n

Marymount (Calgary, AB), 147

Mathias, Patrick, 363, 398, 540, 541–42

Mathieu, Marie-Hélène, 142, 368, 377, 447, 486

Matthew the Poor, 299–300

Melek-el-Kamel, 493, 504, 518

Mello, Father de (India), 75
Men, Father (Moscow), 346
Merton, Thomas, 63
Methodist Church, 274
Mexico, 355, 356, 477, 480
Middle East, 366. *See also specific countries*
Missionaries of Charity, 90n, 547–48
    in Asia, 230, 285
    in Australia, 210
    in Bangladesh, 405
    Brothers of, 97–98, 116, 165, 249–50
    in Calcutta, 93, 118, 134, 161, 241, 249, 357
    in Eastern Europe, 359
    retreats with, 162, 163
Montreal (QC), 49–50, 107, 108–9, 152–54
    prisons in, 83, 101, 152, 153
Moscow (Russia), 346–48, 358–60, 363–65, 379, 409
Mossi people (Burkina Faso), 216
Mugabe, Robert, 269–70, 325
Muslims, 238, 300
My Journey Home (Vanier), 411

New York City, 63, 82–83
New Zealand, 211–12
Nicaragua, 477
Niger, 238
Nigeria, 312–13
North America, 350, 370–71, 389–90, 416–17, 468–69. *See also specific countries*

Northern Ireland, 213–14, 232, 419–20, 519–20
Nouwen, Henri, 370
Nova Scotia, 308
Nueva Suyapa. *See* L'Arche–Tegucigalpa

Olancho (Honduras), 187–88
Orthodox Church, 299–300, 324, 364, 380, 389
Orval, Abbé d' (Belgium), 286, 297, 307, 331, 366, 390–91, 410
    group retreats at, 395
    monks at, 287, 443, 468
Ottawa (ON), 82, 83, 103, 108, 124, 151–52
Ouagadougou (Burkina Faso), 216–18, 236–38, 290
Ourscamp monastery, 21–22, 44–45
Ouvre mes bras (Vanier), 180

Pakistan, 90n, 373
Palestinians, 254, 294–95, 328–29, 365, 474, 543. *See also* L'Arche–Bethany
Palmer, Parker, 367
Papua New Guinea, 229–31
Paraguay, 181
Paramananda, Swami, 72
Paray-le-Monial (France), 465–66
Paul VI, Pope, 27–29, 68
Père Thomas. *See* Philippe, Thomas
Pérez Esquivel, Adolfo, 174–76, 268, 532

Peyriguère, Albert, 198
Philippe, Marie-Dominique, 387, 397
Philippe, Thomas, 331, 376, 380,
    387–88
  death, 396–97, 400, 402, 547
  and L'Arche, 39–40, 44, 426, 451,
    453, 491
  and Le Val Fleuri, 5, 15
  as mentor, 3–4, 200, 462
Philippines, 174n, 282–85, 301–4,
    369
Picachy, Lawrence, Cardinal, 241
Pichon, Père (Canada), 3
Poland, 292–94, 398, 409, 423,
    538–39. See also Czestochowa
Politkovskaia, Anna, 537
Popieluszko, Jerzy, 292–93
Port-au-Prince (Haiti), 144–46,
    171–74, 223–24, 276, 432
Portugal, 37, 43, 53–54
Prince Edward Island, 150–51
Proffit, Gerard and Camille, 142, 486
Proffit, Loïc, 142, 262, 263–64, 486
Proffit, Thaddée, 142, 486

Quebec (city), 123–24, 159–61
Quebec (province), 153n
  prisons in, 101, 107, 152, 153,
    154
Questscope, 530

Ramachandra, Major, 65
Ramos, Fidel, General, 301, 302n
Riccardi, Andrea, 507
Robin, Marthe, 63, 84, 390, 547

Roman Catholic Church, 318–21, 380,
    492
Romania, 367–68, 388–89
Rome (Italy), 27–28, 68
Romero, Oscar, Bishop, 257–58
Rotary Club, 39
Royal Bank of Canada, 385
Russia, 346–48, 388–89. See also
    Moscow; Soviet Union
Rwanda, 405–6, 408, 412, 421–22

Sabbah, Michel, Bishop, 349
Sainte Marie Community (Haiti),
    144–45, 146, 171–72
Saintes-Maries-de-la-Mer (France),
    36, 53
St. Macarius monastery (Egypt), 300
Sant'Egidio, Community of, 530, 538
Schutz, Roger, Brother (Taizé), 190n,
    493, 528, 529
Sealdah Station (Calcutta), 131–32,
    134, 167
Secours Catholique, 180n
Servants of Our Lord, 230
Servicio Paz y Justicia, 174n
Seux, Philippe, 5–6, 19, 22–23, 31,
    34, 394, 546
Shamir, Yitzhak, 365
Shenouda III, Pope (Coptic Church),
    299
Simi, Raphaël, 5–6, 19–20, 22–23,
    37, 43, 52, 511
Sin, Jaime, Cardinal, 301, 302n
Slovenia, 398–99
Smith, Ian, 325
Smiths Falls (ON), 102–3, 122
Social Workers' Brotherhood, 65

Solidarity, 292n, 294
Solzhenitsyn, Andrei, 155
Sorrow Mountain (Ani Pachen), 486–87
South Africa, 271–76, 326–28
South African Council of Churches, 273–74
Soviet Union, 346–48, 379–80. *See also* Moscow; Russia
Spain, 37, 42–43, 430
Spink, Kathryn, 545
Spokane (WA), Bishop of, 158
Steiner, Rudolf, 275
Storey, Peter, Reverend, 274
Suyapa. *See* L'Arche–Tegucigalpa
Synod on the Laity (1987), 317, 318–21
Syria, 253, 277–78, 413, 517–18

Tagore, Rabindranath, 537, 539, 552
Taiwan, 369–70, 437
Teresa of Calcutta, Mother, 93, 116, 120, 162–63, 193, 547–48. *See also* Missionaries of Charity
and Asha Niketan, 357, 404–5
good works, 66, 84, 96, 117–19, 135–36
influence, 105
Thérèse de Lisieux, Saint, 108n
Thomas, Père. *See* Philippe, Thomas
Tiljala (Calcutta), 163–64
Toronto (ON), 4, 33, 46, 49, 151, 416
Trappists, 287, 428, 443, 468. *See also* Orval, Abbé d'

Trosly-Breuil, 15–19, 100–101, 150, 162, 197, 262–63, 500–501, 540. *See also specific foyers*
death at, 546–47
Tutu, Desmond, 273–74

Ukraine, 398
United Church of Canada, 147, 149, 151, 158–59
United Kingdom. *See* Great Britain
United States, 84. *See also specific cities*
and Central America, 267–68
and Middle East, 317n
prisons in, 106, 186–87
Upper Volta. *See* Burkina Faso

Vancouver (BC), 147, 158
Vanier, Bernard, 527
Vanier, Georges (Benedict), 3, 152
Vanier, Georges-Philéas, 2–3, 4–5, 32–33, 481
Vanier, Pauline (née Archer), 3, 376–77, 378
Vanier, Thérèse, 99–100, 200, 458
Vatican II, 258n, 549
Verney, Stephen, Bishop, 244–45
Vietnam, 212
Village Haven (New York), 82

Walesa, Lech, 294n
Williams, Rowan, Archbishop, 491, 525
Winnipeg (MB), 147–48
Wolfensberger, Wolf, 219
Women in Black (Israel), 542–43
World Association of Adolescents in L'Arche, 368–69
World Council of Churches, 438–39

Zabluska, Ilya, 359–60
Zahlé (Lebanon), 253–54, 278–79, 323
Zaire, 405–6
Zimbabwe, 269–70, 325–26, 513–14